Second Edition

Basic Business Law

Charles F. Hemphill, Jr.
M.S., Doctor of Jurisprudence
Member, Texas State Bar

Judy A. Long
B.S., M.S., Juris Doctor
Member, California State Bar
Professor and Paralegal Coordinator,
Rio Hondo College

Regents/Prentice Hall
Englewood Cliffs, New Jersey 07632

Library of Congress Cataloging-in-Publication Data

Hemphill, Charles F.
    Basic business law / Charles F. Hemphill, Jr., Judy A. Long. —
2nd ed.
        p.   cm.
    Includes index.
    ISBN 0-13-059437-7
    1. Business law—United States.   I. Long, Judy A., (date).
II. Title.
KF889.H35   1994
346.73'07—dc20
[347.3067]   92-47120
                                                                     CIP

Acquisitions: Maureen Hall/Elizabeth Sugg
Editorial/production supervision: WordCrafters Editorial Services, Inc.
Cover design: Marianne Frasco
Prepress buyer: Ilene Levy-Sanford
Manufacturing buyer: Ed O'Dougherty
Marketing manager: Linda Bennani
Cover photo: Robert Essel, The Stock Market

© 1994, 1984 by Regents/Prentice Hall
A Division of Simon & Schuster
Englewood Cliffs, New Jersey 07632

Printed in the United States of America
10 9 8 7 6 5 4 3 2 1

ISBN 0-13-059437-7

Prentice-Hall International (UK) Limited, *London*
Prentice-Hall of Australia Pty. Limited, *Sydney*
Prentice-Hall Canada Inc., *Toronto*
Prentice-Hall Hispanoamericana, S.A., *Mexico*
Prentice-Hall of India Private Limited, *New Delhi*
Prentice-Hall of Japan, Inc., *Tokyo*
Simon & Schuster Asia Pte. Ltd., *Singapore*
Editora Prentice-Hall do Brasil, Ltda., *Rio de Janeiro*

to my grandsons: Gregory, Brian, Christopher, Matthew, Andrew, Shawn, and Nicholas

C.F.H.

to Phyllis and Michael

J.A.L.

In reading the record, one cannot avoid reflection on the . . . annoyance, money, and . . . friendship that would have been saved had the parties made timely resort to legal aid for the prevention of controversy, rather than later and compelled use of it in litigation.

JUSTICE STONE
Supreme Court of Minnesota
Field-Martin v. Fruen Milling Co., 298 N.W. 576

Contents

6 THE CONTRACT AGREEMENT: OFFER, ACCEPTANCE, COUNTEROFFER 60

7 CONSIDERATION 79

28   LEGAL AID FOR CREDITOR OR LENDER   359

29   DEBTOR'S PRIVILEGES AND PROTECTIONS; BANKRUPTCY   376

30   INSURANCE   389

Preface

All individuals should have a basic understanding of the legal principles used to make business decisions. The approach of this text is, first, to familiarize Business Law students with how basic legal principles affect the everyday procedures in business. Topics include contract law, agency, and real property law. The second aim of the text is to instruct students in the use of these legal principles in everyday life by providing them with practical knowledge of the basis for our legal system, the functions of the courts, the conduct of a lawsuit, and the laws of negligence.

With an understanding of the legal principles related to businesses, one can better protect both personal and business interests. Whether students find they need to write a contract in the office or prepare a will at home, they will gain "how-to" knowledge from this textbook.

Special Features

Although some Business Law texts include the Uniform Commercial Code and other documents in their entirety, this text summarizes the materials from those documents that the authors feel are relevant to appropriate subjects. Footnotes are provided for reference in the event students wish to research the materials. Many cases and court decisions are included, with legal citations. Pertinent excerpts from the decisions are quoted whenever necessary.

Most texts include case materials at the end of each chapter. Discussion cases in this text, however, are placed within the body of individual chapters at the point at which that particular principle is being discussed. Possible outcomes to the discussion are provided at the end of each chapter. The answers to additional case materials are included at the end of most chapters; others are provided in the Instructor's Manual.

Many Business Law texts are long, cumbersome, and difficult to read. In this text, the authors have attempted to make the study of legal principles as simple as possible so that students can concentrate on thinking and applying the principles being discussed. They are not focused on learning a new vocabulary.

New Material

Significant changes have been made in the text for this new edition. Several changes have been made throughout the text. The most notable changes are in the following chapters:

- Chapter 3—The Courts and Their Functions. The authors have expanded this chapter to include a detailed discussion of the state and federal court systems. The principles of court decisions are discussed.
- Chapter 4—How the Courts Handle Lawsuits. The authors take a case from its inception through the trial and post-trial stages. Issues of filing and service are discussed. A detailed discussion of trial procedures is included.
- Chapter 11—The Law of Torts. In this chapter, the authors explain tort law not only as it relates to business but as it relates to the individual's everyday life as well. A detailed explanation of negligence has been added, including changes in the law since the previous edition. Appropriate defenses to negligence are also included.
- Products Liability. Considerable time and media publicity have been devoted in recent years to defective products. Hence, an extensive section has been added on products liability, including strict liability, negligence, breach of warranty, and misrepresentation.
- All of the chapters have been updated to reflect changes in the law and any new laws that have been enacted since the first edition.

New Chapters

- Chapter 31—Legal Research. Any student of the law should know how to use a law library. This chapter includes statutory and case law. Primary and secondary authority are discussed. The student learns to write a case brief. Although most Business Law instructors assign case briefs to their students, textbooks rarely include instructions for their preparation. The method for preparing briefs included in this text is the method that students are taught in law school and that lawyers use in their practices. It is a simple, concise method of gathering the necessary and relevant information from a case. Laws are constantly changing, and no law text can be completely up to date. Therefore, it is advisable to utilize the methods described in Chapter 31 when undertaking current legal research on a given case or subject area of interest.
- Chapter 32—Employment Law. The working relationship between employer and employee has become more and more complex over the years.

New federal statutes have been enacted for equal employment opportunity, sexual harassment, and discrimination. Worker's compensation laws protect individuals injured in the workplace. OSHA establishes safety standards employers must follow. Both employers and employees need a broad, basic understanding of all employment laws.

• Ethics. No law text would be complete without a discussion of legal ethics. Ethical considerations are discussed in relevant portions of the text.

We wish to express our appreciation to the following reviewers of this edition: Teresa Ferguson, ITT Technical Institute; Cynthia Weishapple, Chippewa Valley Technical College; Elizabeth Fichera-Gildersleeve, Academy of Business College; Michael Posnock, Horizon Institute of Paralegal Studies; Timothy Hart, College of the Sequoias; Leslie Stomsvik, Pierce College; and Meg Cullum, North American College.

JUDY A. LONG
Seal Beach, California

Preface to First Edition

Almost everyone needs an understanding of the laws of business—not only employees, managers, and owners—but also those who deal with the business as customers or clients. This book presents the law from the viewpoints of both groups. It sets out basic legal principles and ideas, as well as their applications to individual problems. The reader who acquires this background in business law will find it helpful in decision-making processes that occur all through life.

We all know, of course, that many of our daily activities are controlled by laws or legal processes. We can choose to disregard these associations with laws, taking the attitude that we simply do not want to become involved. This would be nothing more than our right to freedom of choice. Remaining uninformed, however, will not allow us to remain unaffected by regulations or laws. By gaining a working knowledge of the law as it applies to business, we can better protect both our personal and business interests.

It is not the intent of a business law text to teach you to act as your own lawyer. Rather, its aim is to help you to study broad legal principles and to examine legal problems frequently encountered in business. Neither is this book intended to be an all-inclusive examination of our legal system. Law is a profession in which attorneys continue to learn for a lifetime.

To some extent, every study of law must include some ideas from "the musty past." A good number of these old ideas still profoundly affect the legal environment in which business operates on a day-to-day basis. In this book, insofar as feasible, recent legal cases or materials that illustrate a specific principle have been used.

Business law texts in earlier days paid little attention to environmental law. Today, legal principles of environmental protection are of increased significance. This text also focuses on consumer-customer interests and takes notice of the impact of crime and criminal law on trade and commerce. Although it is in no sense a text on criminal law or criminal procedure, it does alert the reader to many of the problems involved.

Business needs a considerable degree of stability in the law. Investors usually refuse to commit their money to business proposals where their rights are not firm. At the same time, the law must not remain inflexible; it must be able to change to accommodate the new needs and economic conditions of society. The text presents material that illuminates both needs—for stability and for responsiveness.

It is with good reason that we think of law as an involved, complicated field of study. Social processes are so interwoven with complexities that legal rules and applications cannot always be made simple. To explore completely only a single field of law could occupy a lifetime. A text of this kind can do no more than present a broad sweep of business law, highlighting aspects that are most likely to cause problems in everyday life.

Some business law texts set out student resource materials in considerable detail, including the Uniform Commercial Code (UCC), the Uniform Consumer Credit Code (UCCC), the Uniform Partnership Act, the Revised Limited Partnership Act, the Modern Business Corporation Act, and so on. These resource materials have been sumarized in the text, with appropriate footnotes so that they can be used as references.

The text contains many cases and court decisions, quoting extracts where pertinent. Legal citations have also been included, if the student desires to read the court decision in detail.

Discussion cases are included within the body of individual chapters, and solutions for these cases are given at the chapter end. This approach differs from that of most texts, which lump case materials at the end of each chapter. Spacing of these discussion cases within the text material lets the student mentally work out the legal problem before consulting the end-of-chapter answer. Some additional case materials also appear at the conclusion of most chapters.

The student's concern throughout should be with basic legal ideas and principles. No individual court decision or legislative enactment can ever tell you with complete assurance what the law will be like under changed conditions in the future. There are no absolute, final answers. In short, business law will continue to change and to expand.

CHARLES F. HEMPHILL, JR.
Long Beach, California

1

Introduction—
The Beginnings
of Business Law

COMMERCIAL ENTERPRISE AND THE NEED FOR REGULATION

Some three billion people live in the modern world, each needing and wanting food, clothing, shelter, and countless other goods and services. Taking care of these personal needs and wants through trade and commerce is the job of business. This gigantic production and supply operation needs the work, skill, and resources of a great many of the world's inhabitants. Any system that takes over the growth, production, manufacture, and distribution of trade goods on such a scale can operate best in an orderly, regulated way. Without controls, business cannot operate effectively.

What Business Law Regulates

Business law, or *commercial law* as it is sometimes called, is the body of rules that regulate and control the everyday activities of exchange. It is concerned with procurement of raw materials, manufacturing and producing, the sale of merchandise and commodities, brokerage, agency, shipping, bailment, insurance, commercial paper, and all sorts of arrangements for financing or banking business deals.

Development of Trade and Commerce

After individuals began to produce goods that might be traded, they needed facilities to make their products known. They also needed to carry the goods to the location where they could be put in trade. Eventually it was found that financing was needed when payment could not be made immediately. In addition, traders quickly learned the need for protecting goods and funds while in transit. In setting up the various procedures and controls to make trading profitable, the first rules of business law were developed.

Before money came into use, traders exchanged salt, skins, hand tools, and iron ore products, often through a series of barter transactions. After a time, gold, silver, and precious stones were accepted as having commercial value, reducing the number of barter transactions needed to obtain the specific item desired. Eventually, of course, coinage came into universal use. With more experience, enterprising business people worked out ways for extending credit and financing transactions in distant lands. Later still, paper money was substituted for bulkier coins. Negotiable instruments, such as checks, bills, notes, drafts, and warehouse receipts, came into general use to prevent the theft of money.

For thousands of years, meanwhile, difficulties in transportation remained the greatest obstacle to trade and commerce. Months or even years of slow travel were sometimes necessary. Goods and merchandise moved by human burden bearers, by camel caravans, or by trains of mules. Obviously, only certain kinds of durable goods could be shipped any distance.

As water travel developed, traders rigged boats that by standards of today were extremely slow, dangerous, and small in carrying capacity. A scattering of brave men pushed out in these tiny vessels with marketable goods. They followed along the coast of the Mediterranean, the Atlantic, the North Sea, and the Baltic. Even the most daring seldom ventured out of sight of land for long. But they continued to risk their lives, their crafts, and their merchandise in these ventures. After shipping by boat had become more common, pirates began to obtain boats of their own, crippling and looting the merchantmen.

But trading by land was hardly less hazardous than shipping by sea. Travelers usually had difficulty in communicating along the overland trade routes. Few individuals could understand languages or dialects native to the areas where they journeyed in commerce. Roads were often no more than marked trails that became a sea of mud when it rained. If a caravan became lost, the local residents could not furnish guidance, for few had ever ventured beyond the neighboring hills. Food and supplies along the route were in short supply and inns were rare.

For thousands of years these hazards continued. Exposure to the elements, cutthroat bandits, and food and water shortages all took a toll. But regardless of risks, the prospects for gain stimulated a strong desire for trade.

Then, after a time, the ancient Romans conquered most of the Mediterranean world. Hated by a great many for their military oppressions, the Romans nevertheless brought the first period of prolonged peace the world had ever known. Building the first durable roads for quick transfer of troops, the Romans allowed traders and merchants to use these roads as well. The Romans also set up a legal system that favored business and commerce. But in the end, the power of Rome declined and vast hordes of barbarians swept over the Mediterranean world. Pillaging and looting everywhere they went, these semiliterate barbarians destroyed the trade systems and controls that existed in European nations. With the Roman empire split into a number of weak feudal states, individual areas of the Western world remained isolated. People had little contact with the outside in culture, education, art, or trade. For a long time business conditions were seriously restricted.

Merchant Leagues and the "Law Merchant"

After considerable isolation, medieval merchants in logical commercial centers and coastal towns gradually began to reopen some of the old Roman trade routes. The governments of Europe were still unable to furnish much help, however, since they remained weak, small, and isolated. Intent on combining private resources, private merchants organized into trading firms and eventually into leagues of trading cities. Since they could obtain little protection from local governments, these merchant organizations hired their own guards and protective agents. Continuing to grow and cooperate in these ventures, leagues of traders functioned in areas that today make up parts of Germany, Italy, Spain, France, Belgium, Holland, and England.

As the merchant leagues became common, the local courts were often found inadequate to settle disputes among league members. The local governmental courts had no understanding of diverse business and trade customs and problems, especially those relating to trade between nations. Furthermore, there was no uniformity in court decisions or in the way laws were applied from country to country. In addition, foreign traders frequently had no standing in local courts.

Members of these international trade leagues realized that they needed speedy, inexpensive, and nontechnical ways of settling business disputes among members. The leagues already had regulations and rules that were understood among individual merchants, but local courts would not enforce rules when a member ignored them. The trade leagues, therefore, set up their own courts and code of international law for business transactions. This system included definite rules for honoring contracts, purchase and sales agreements, and enforcing shipping requirements in all commercial countries in Europe. An individual trader who ignored the league rules and resorted to the local governmental courts soon learned that it was almost impossible to do business on a large scale. Setting up their own courts, the league's judges traveled to the busier ports, major trade centers, and large country fairs. In each place the league's judges settled mercantile and shipping disputes and gradually built up a recognized code of business law. Thus, the law merchant legal system did not originate in any one country exclusively, but came to be used and accepted throughout the Western commercial world.

For several hundred years these merchants' courts continued to operate on their own with no connection whatever with the existing governmental court systems. This separation from the regular court systems continued in France, Belgium, and Latin American colonies of Spain until comparatively recent times.

In England, however, by the end of the seventeenth century, law merchant courts had ceased to exist. Their rules and decisions were gradually absorbed into the English common law and came to be recognized in English court decisions. In short, then, the principles of the law merchant became English commercial law, eventually serving as the basis for all business law in the United States. This body or rules and principles, drawn from the practical ideas of these medieval merchants, is still the source of most of our current business laws. This includes our law in the areas of contracts, agency, sales, bailments, torts, partnership, shipping, insurance, corporations, and marine law.

EFFECTS OF INDUSTRIAL TECHNOLOGY ON BUSINESS LAW _____

Law is an agent, or tool, set up by government for the benefit of the majority in controlling individuals. Present-day technology came into being through evolutionary processes in both England and the United States, complicating the existing rules of business law. It should be kept in mind that the roots of our American society go deep into the social structure of England, where we obtained most of our economic and social patterns. From this beginning, our legal system in the United States gradually adjusted itself to the changing conditions in which it now operates.

In early-day England the individual family unit almost invariably produced much of what was needed. The same individuals largely consumed what was produced and by the standards of today they had little in the way of luxuries. Since they could produce little beyond bare necessities, people had to be satisfied with what was available.

In time it became apparent that an individual could produce more by specializing in the making of one specific good or service. Some workers then quit trying to produce all the things their family needed, exchanging their production surplus for extra items created by other specialists. Of course, bartering processes were few and simple at first, and usually took place within the immediate neighborhood. But eventually specialization developed by family groups, by towns, and even by nations. With these increases in specialization, there came added pressures on society to improve technology for handling goods. Transportation and effective credit devices continued to be pressing needs.

Trade techniques in Europe and in the American colonies in the eighteenth century were in the so-called "handicraft stage." By 1800 the Industrial Revolution was well underway in England, spreading to the United States shortly after. Machinery and manufacturing procedures developed with great suddenness; small factories sprang up in many areas. But neither existing social conditions nor the legal systems were ready for these dramatic changes.

Small industrial towns quickly grew into crowded cities. Often these new areas had inadequate housing, primitive sewage systems, polluted water, food shortages, and other serious problems. There were few stores, shops, and suppliers of essentials for factory workers who had been accustomed to growing food and supplying all their own wants.

The courts also had their problems as a result of these new economic and social adjustments. Judges had little or no prior experience to draw from. Early English and American courts were accustomed to moving slowly, especially in adjusting their legal rules to new circumstances. All these factors profoundly affected the development of business law in the United States.

ROLE OF LAW IN SOCIETY

Some Origins of Law

In primitive society, people learned early to join together—for mutual protection, for hunting and fishing more effectively, and for bartering with each other. Together, individuals learned to appreciate the many benefits that flow from an organized society.

Uniting as clans and tribes, and then as governments and nations, individuals combined to set up and enforce rules for human activities. Often when people have lived together, they have found it necessary to restrict certain kinds of conduct. Individuals have never been able to exist for long without agreed-upon rules and understandings. These mutually respected customs and agreements were the beginnings of present-day government and law.

What Law Is

Law is that set of rules that control affairs and relationships within a community, as well as relationships among nations. It is the body of regulations established to make it easier for us to live with one another. Modern law is a complex interweaving of court decisions, Federal and state laws (Congressional and legislative enactments), and administrative rulings. The entire system functions within the provisions and limitations set by Federal and state constitutions.

Stated in other terms, law is the outgrowth of thousands of years of human experience, resulting in a framework of principles, regulations, and enactments. These principles, or legal rules, are applied and enforced by the courts, aided by other branches of government.

Regulation of society by the legal system helps to make individuals keep behavior within limits that will not seriously harm others. In a sense, it is regrettable that a civilized society must have rules. But because people occasionally crave an unlimited freedom of choice, there has always been a small percentage of individuals who have shown no concern for the welfare of others.

Purpose of the Law: Order, Stability, and Justice

Law is at once many things to many people. In general, the purpose of the law is to provide order, stability, and justice.

That justice which the law seeks to achieve is not always considered a universal value. It does not necessarily mean the same to all people, or to all periods of history. Social customs, home and school training, self-interest, economic pressures, news media treatment, and religion all play a part in shaping public ideas as to what is justice. Therefore, it is sometimes said that absolute justice can never be attained. But legal ends should be used to reach as high a level as possible.

The legal system first provides rules for the organization and functions of the government that supervises and enforces other laws. In addition, law regulates the manner in which business is conducted and the way we handle personal affairs that might interfere with the lives of others. Law also provides penalties for objectionable conduct that is regarded as criminal. Further, the legal system also sets up the machinery through which the rights of the individual and the general public are to be protected and enforced.

Purposes of Legal Language

Laws and legal systems frequently are difficult to understand. Legislators who draft a new law can seldom write down all that needs to be said in a few sentences, nor can they always express their intent in an uncomplicated way. This is especially so if the proposed law takes into account all the different situations that can be expected to arise in future application of the law.

Confusion can also arise when courts and lawyers use Latin phrases and archaic words. Many old legal phrases were devised hundreds of years ago to fit exact legal ideas. Each has had a narrow meaning in legal circles ever since. Some old Latin expressions have been replaced by modern English. But others have continued in use since present-day terms may not quite convey the exact legal idea or principle to the lawyers and the courts.

In recent years many individuals involved in legal aspects of business have found ways to abandon some of these old Latin terms. For example, many insurance companies have had insurance policies rewritten in words that can be understood by those who purchase insurance.

DEVELOPMENT AND CHANGES IN THE LAW _____

In every sense, law reflects society and its needs. When human activities and business relationships were not very complicated, it was not necessary to have an extensive system of law. Perhaps the earliest laws were no more than an agreement setting out the way that spoils of the hunt would be divided. In early government, legal systems had to be concerned only with such matters as keeping the peace, controlling crimes of violence, and setting up simple rules about ownership and inheritance of property.

Even today, a simple rural community may need few laws. But in a complex industrial society, relationships become more involved. Law has expanded until there are few human activities that are not regulated to some extent. This may be partly the necessary consequence of large, overpopulated cities in which the harmful results of inconsiderate behavior are greatly multiplied. In the resulting legal framework of today's world, there is a definite need for judges and lawyers. There is also a need for individuals in business to have an adequate knowledge of their legal rights and responsibilities.

Dependence of Law on Public Opinion

In a democratic nation, law is the will of the majority of the people concerning what is thought to be the greatest good for the greatest number.

A nation that wants a society built upon law must respect the laws it adopts or must change them in an orderly way when they have lost effectiveness.

Frequently, the law lags behind until popular opinion has solidified and has become known. Little will be accomplished by passing a law if the public does not have substantial agreement that it represents correct behavior. Enforcement may never be accepted if the law is almost completely opposed to public ideas about what is proper.

Long ago some states in the original American colonies passed laws prohibiting public entertainment or business transactions on Sunday. Such laws developed from the colonists' deeply held religious beliefs. Although these laws were eventually repealed in most localities, they remained on the law books for many years after they had lost public support and were often ignored by enforcement officials.

Out-of-Date Laws; Nonenforcement

To illustrate the way a law may become archaic or out of date, let us look at the statute passed by the Arizona legislature in the 1860s forbidding the hunting or shooting of camels in desert areas. Today, we can smile at such a legal prohibition. But when the law was passed, there were no highways across Arizona. Large areas of the state were hot, waterless stretches of trackless desert, dangerous to cross. United States Army Cavalry units, keeping law and order in what was then Federal territory, began importing camels to use for desert transport. These animals were very practical, but a few managed to escape and wander through the desert. Most escaped animals were eventually recaptured, but some were needlessly killed by prospectors and hunters who considered this activity a sport. The building of roads eventually eliminated the need for camels, and the wild camels in the desert did not survive. There is no need whatever for the old law, but it is still on the books in Arizona.

As another example of the need for legal change, consider one of the early-day ideas of the Massachusetts Colony. In Colonial America, the Pilgrims had a law that every male adult who attended church service must carry a gun to guard against surprise attacks from Indians. Today, we would say that the law requiring guns in church would be out of place.

With the passing years, some states have taken an opposite approach, now having laws that forbid an individual from carrying or possessing a gun in public. For better protection of the public, some cities have a law (ordinance) requiring all public vehicles parked on the street to be locked. Such a law applies to churchgoers as well as everyone else. Conditions have changed to the point where society long ago quit worrying about marauding Indians. But today there is a distinct possibility that a thief may steal the churchgoer's unlocked car, or the vehicle of anyone else.

To protect consumers, a number of years ago a large city passed a local law prohibiting any grocer from retaining meats or vegetables in stock for more than a specified period. This was before frozen and canned meats and vegetables had become common, and the law was intended to protect against the sale of spoiled edibles. Even after food processors had learned to can and freeze foods successfully, the law was still in effect. Enforcement in all instances would obviously have been an injustice.

The Need for Settled Legal Rights

While individual laws must be revised to meet changing needs of society, a basic objective of the government and law must be to provide stability for the business community. Manufacturers and suppliers must be able to buy raw materials and produce goods that can be sold for a reasonable profit. Businesses will simply refuse to risk money to bring merchandise to the community unless legal rights are settled and understood at a given time. It is good governmental policy for buyers and sellers alike to know what affairs can be conducted under the legal system. We all want to be secure in the knowledge that laws and court decisions in the future will not affect actions that are being taken today.

SOME CLASSIFICATIONS OF LAW

Substantive Law and Procedural Law

Some set classifications of law have been made by the lawyers and the courts for a number of years. Learning these classifications is worthwhile for students of business law, since these are helpful in examining problems that occur frequently.

All law is sometimes broken down into two major categories—*substantive law* and *procedural law.*

Substantive law deals with the rights and duties of persons to each other and to society in general. Put in other words, it is that area of law which sets forth, defines, and creates rights and legal relationships. It is the "substance" of the law.

Procedural law is that which furnishes the legal machinery to apply and handle substantive rights and duties—those rules and procedures by which the courts and agencies operate. Procedural law furnishes the methods and processes through which the substantive law is brought to bear on a specific problem. It includes those techniques by which a plaintiff gets a defendant into court, introduces evidence, and sets up remedies to recover damages that may be allowed as an award in a lawsuit.

For example, substantive law provides that theft from a business is a criminal offense. Procedural law sets up the ways in which charges may be filed in a criminal prosecution and in which damages may be obtained in a civil lawsuit against the offender. Substantive law shows what the law is, while procedural law tells what "procedures" must be followed to enforce or practice the law.

Public Law

Substantive law is broken down into public law and private law. *Public law* defines relationships and rights between government agencies and private individuals or private companies.

Private Law (Civil Law)

Private law is concerned with injuries and disputes between private individuals and/or private organizations. It may deal with agreements between persons (contracts), the law of torts (injuries to another), the law of property, the law of domestic relations, the law of individual obligations, and the law of damages.

Administrative Law

Administrative law is one of the major divisions or branches of public law. Administrative law adjusts differences arising from disputes between administrative officials of governmental agencies and the general public. Whether the Post Office has authority to limit the size of parcel post packages is an example of administrative law.

Municipal Ordinances

In addition to following their state laws, cities develop ordinances to regulate life in that city. For example, some cities do not allow overnight parking on certain days. In other cities, minors are required to keep a curfew, such as being off the streets after 10 P.M. These ordinances apply only to the city in which they were passed and often vary considerably from one city to the next.

Constitutional Law

Sometimes *constitutional law* is classified as an additional category of public law. It is sometimes defined as the fundamental law which sets out the powers and limitations of government as prescribed in a Federal or state constitution. Whether you have the right to have your own lawyer when under prosecution for a serious crime is a constitutional law problem.

Criminal Law

Criminal law is generally classified as another branch of public law. Criminal law defines certain activities as crimes if they are so serious as to merit strong disapproval and punishment by society.

––––––––– *DISCUSSION PROBLEMS* –––––––––––––––––––––––––––––––––––

1. Discuss the manner in which the growth of trade and commerce led to the development of business law.
2. Why is it necessary for a society to have laws?
3. Determine which laws would apply in the following situations from those listed on pages 9–10.
   A. James was caught stealing merchandise from a clothing store.
   B. Jeffrey was arrested for distributing anti-war leaflets in the neighborhood park.

C. Carol was involved in an automobile accident and wants to sue the driver of the other automobile.

D. Danielle received a parking ticket for parking in front of her house overnight.

─────── *QUESTIONS* ───────────────────────────────────

1. Are the terms *business law* and *commercial law* interchangeable?
2. Define law. How does it relate to society in general? How does it relate to business?
3. What was the *law merchant*? How did it originate? What is its significance today? Did the *law merchant* lead to uniformity in business laws between commercial nations?
4. Why does any legal system need stability and order? How does this need affect business?
5. What are the differences between *substantive law* and *procedural law*? Give examples.
6. Briefly describe *public law, private law, administrative law, constitutional law,* and *criminal law.*
7. What are municipal ordinances?

2

The Legal System
in the United States

THE BASIS FOR OUR LEGAL SYSTEM

Many of our current legal principles and background ideas of law go back to old English beginnings. In 1066 A.D., William the Conqueror brought an invading army from France, subduing England. William also brought a number of changes in the government. Before the Norman invasion, the English legal and court system was perhaps the most backward in Europe. It had been common to use trial by ordeal or to settle disputes by other crude and barbarous methods such as by individual combat.

Under the circumstances, England did not have a basic or elemental body of law to serve as a foundation for the legal system. This, of course, is at variance with our legal beginnings in the United States since our Federal Constitution was set up as the basis for government, almost from the outset. But when William took over England, that country had no constitution. The law consisted of little more than the command of the king.

Not having a large number of followers to take over the English institutions, William continued the use of local courts. These local courts settled minor legal disputes.

For the operation of his court and government, William set up an advisory council. High officials at court handled most executive and administrative functions of the government that were not handled by the king on a personal basis. Disputes occurred between some of the powerful and wealthy lords, and William settled these differences himself, not permitting such matters to reach the existing law courts.

Eventually, disputes between lords and important officials took so much of the king's time that he set up a royal court, the *curia regis* (Latin for "king's court"), to handle such matters. The judge who presided was part of the royal retinue. In time, the *curia regis* was made responsible for the supervision of the existing local courts and was made available to all common citizens, whether or not they had a connection at court. Thereafter, business before the *curia regis* increased at a rapid rate.

In time, the British Parliament evolved from the king's advisory council, and the king's court eventually came to be known as the Court of Common Pleas.

When the colonists came to America they brought with them all the laws that had been enacted in Parliament. They also set up modified replicas of the British courts. After the separation from the British crown, the colonial courts became courts of the individual states without any real changes in procedure, jurisdiction, or even in the individuals who were serving as judges.

When a case had previously been decided by a British court, the judges and lawyers in the new world continued to regard the prior British decision as controlling law for America. The treatises of English legal scholars were the texts that law students and judges continued to use in the new government of the United States.

The Common Law System

Unlike England, the United States had its own Constitution as a framework from which a legal system was set up. On this base, the Federal Congress and state legislatures passed laws that gave more meaning to the legal system. Individual case decisions by the courts served to interpret and apply the statutory (legislative) law and Constitutional law.

This idea of law from previously decided cases comes to us from the so-called *English common law*. Early-day judges in the old English Court of Common Pleas had no specific guides concerning what the law was or what it should be. But from the time of William the Conqueror, the king had instructed the judges to reach decisions that were just and right in all cases. For example, the judges had no difficulty in holding that a merchant who took the property of another trader should be required to pay for whatever was received. Justice was administered by awarding a money judgment to the merchant's victim. In a case of this kind, of course, there was not much question as to the decision that should be rendered. But in many instances the verdict that should be rendered was not so clear-cut.

Since Parliament was not even in existence, and statutory laws had not been passed as guides, these old English judges were on their own. They drew from ancient "folk law traditions" and from recognized principles acknowledged by common consent by all decent people. For example, it was undisputed that the burning down of another individual's shop or home should be punished as a crime and the culprit should be liable in damages in a civil court.

Under this so-called common law system, the judges decided a matter on its merits the first time it came before a court. This decision was then recognized as settled law. When a similar matter again came before the courts, the prior decision was considered as controlling. This, of course, is what we today call "case law."

As early as the twelfth century, English courts began the practice of citing earlier court decisions as binding when the matter came before the court in a subsequent case. As one old English judge put it, "The same decision should be reached when the facts are squarely in point with a prior case."

Beyond the restrictions or limitations set up in the Federal and state constitutions, our law in the United States is made up of two parts: (1) legislative-made law, and (2) case law from prior court holdings of the appellate courts. Today, this accumulation of prior court holdings is still commonly described by lawyers as "common law."

Legislative law is more commonly referred to as statutory law. State and federal statutes are compiled into "codes," which include all of the statutes in an alphabetical-subject reporting system.

Court decisions in this country at the appellate (higher) court level are promptly printed in law books that set out each decision made by a specific court or group of courts. These "reported cases," as they are sometimes called, comprise most of the law books that fill a law library or line the walls of a lawyer's office.

To "find the law," a lawyer must first consult the statute books to locate the legislative-made law in that particular locality. Then the lawyer must locate those court decisions handed down on the facts in that particular case. Frequently, pertinent court decisions may be scattered through many volumes of law books, requiring considerable research. There is also the possibility that the researching lawyer could fail to find a controlling decision (sometimes called an opinion).

Cases on the appellate court level, which are reported as court decisions, are known as "case law." When the appellate court hands down a decision, new rules of law are established. This case then establishes a precedent for future court decisions or interpretations of the law. When we say that a prior case establishes a "precedent," we are referring to our system of "stare decisis"; that is, a prior appellate court decision becomes a part of the case law in that particular jurisdiction. Thereafter, the judges use the law established in that case to rule on later similar cases.

There is no common law of the United States as such, but rather a separate system of common law that differs from state to state. Louisiana, for example, did not have a background of English legal history, drawing on old Roman law by way of France.

Some states in the United States have consolidated their common law legal principles into statutes. These states have usually made a declaration by statute to the effect that henceforth "the substantive . . . law of this state is entirely statutory."[1] This does not mean that there is no body of decided cases that are considered as controlling. Court decisions handed down since the passage of such statutes are sometimes termed the common law of that state.

Constitutional Sources of Law

Both legislative-made law and judicial opinions must be made within the framework of constitutional law. Any law that is contrary to the United States Constitution will be struck down on appeal. The United States (Federal) Constitution is the supreme law of the land. No law, either state or Federal, can be contrary to it. State laws must conform not only to the state constitution but to the United States Constitution as well. If a state court ruling, for example, deprived you of a right guaranteed in the United States Constitution, the ruling would be overturned by an appeal to the Federal or United States Supreme courts.

How Law Is Put into Action

It is sometimes said that law is the crystallization of the experiences of humankind concerning what is right and just between people. Law is enunciated, or made known, to the public in two ways: (1) by the action of the legislature in passing new laws or repealing old laws, and (2) by court decisions in deciding disputes referred to them for settlement.

Most legal authorities feel that the job of Congress or the state legislatures is to furnish rules for the settlement of disputes yet to arise. The job of the courts is to apply these existing legislative rules of law to actual disputes. And when a completely new situation comes up, the courts must decide whether the law applies to those facts.

THE TWO-COURT SYSTEM: LAW AND EQUITY ————————

By the time American colonists brought English law to the new world, a troublesome legal feature had come into existence. A two-court arrangement had actually developed in England, with the two systems being known as courts of law (law courts) and courts of equity (equity courts). At times the judges handling these two classes of courts were in bitter dispute.

The System of Writs

When the first king's court (*curia regis*) was set up by William the Conqueror, only the wealthy and important nobles were permitted to use the tribunal.

---

[1]California Penal Code, Secs. 6, 15.

In order to get a case heard by this court, it was necessary to have a royal writ. In substance, this was a note or writ from the king or one of his high officials directing the judges to handle the dispute.

After the passing of a generation or two, the common people were given more access to the court. But even then the judges would not accept a case for trial unless an originating royal writ could be presented. In time, a writ was no longer a personal note from the king or one of his officials. The courts had come to accept the idea that a lawsuit would be initiated if the facts were the same as those in a previously decided case. A brief written statement of facts identical to those in a prior writ was then allowed by the court as an originating writ for a later suit.

The kinds of situations presented in these writs eventually grew in number and in variety. But still only a limited number of different writs were permitted by the court. From the outset, the object of the court was to use a set of formulas that needed only the substitution of names or figures into a form to make it fit a common type of case. These frequently encountered situations came to be covered by an individual form of writ for each court-approved situation. The lawyers and the courts gave names to individual writs, such as "trover," "assumpsit," and "trespass on the case."

As cases were initiated on these writs and decided by the courts, these decisions became the basis for the English common law. The writs themselves became known as *common law writs* or *common law actions*. This writ system made it easy for judges to find what had been decided earlier in cases where a particular writ had been used. This, of course, led to uniform decisions and uniform justice. Consequently, it was usually not too difficult for a lawyer to tell a client what the law was in a particular situation where one of these writs had been used earlier.

Deficiencies in the Writ System

If your lawyer wanted to bring a lawsuit, this could be done by finding one of these writs that exactly fitted the facts of your case. But if the facts could not be pigeonholed into the requirements for one of these established writs, then the Court of Common Pleas simply refused to accept it for trial. In short, judges permitted themselves to be tied down to set procedures. There was no available legal technique for making headway against this hidebound procedural system. Actually, this deficiency in the legal system occurred at a time when England was developing from a settled, orderly rural society into an economic system of fast-changing business and trade. The courts refused to admit that changing manufacturing and industrial techniques had given rise to a great variety of new wrongs that the legal system did not acknowledge.

Eventually, there was great public clamor for more relief in the courts. To add to the problem, the Court of Common Pleas took the position that the judges were powerless to take any action against a wrongdoer until harm had actually occurred. The court persisted in this approach, even though the impending harm appeared to be great, and the likelihood that it would occur was almost a certainty. The only legal remedy was to file a lawsuit after damage had taken place. Judges declined to issue court orders (injunctions) forbidding people from committing threatened wrongs on the penalty of being thrown in jail for contempt of court.

Establishment of Equity Courts

By the middle of the fourteenth century, a number of acquaintances of King Edward III complained of injustices that were being ignored by the Court of Common Pleas. Satisfied of the legitimacy of these complaints, Edward III ordered the establishment of a supplemental court system called the *Court of Chancery* or *Court of Equity*. These courts were set up under the supervision of an official called the Lord Chancellor of England and came to be commonly known as *equity courts*.

The purpose of these new equity courts was described in an old English law dictionary:

> All the other justices [judges] in the kingdom are tied to the law courts [Court of Common Pleas], but the Chancellor hath the king's absolute power to moderate the written [common] law, govern his judgment by the law of nature and conscience. . . . He [the equity judge] is not limited by the written law [common law], but by conscience and equity, according to the circumstances of the matter.[2]

The new equity courts in England were not permitted to hear disputes in cases where there was already an adequate remedy in the common law courts (Courts of Common Pleas). But the Lord Chancellor had instructions from the king to handle any other case where substantial injustice had been done. The jurisdiction, or authority, of the equity system was therefore very great. And at times there were some very bitter disputes between the equity courts and the law courts. In the words of one early English Lord Chancellor, "One court was set up to do injustice and another to stop it." The law courts had become so narrow-minded in their procedures and policies that they would not allow a decision to be set aside because a witness gave perjured testimony. The law courts would only authorize a subsequent criminal prosecution to punish the person giving perjured testimony. Fortunately for the cause of justice, the king sided with the Lord Chancellor and the equity courts until the equity system was well established.

[2]Cowel and Jacobs' *Law Dictionary*, London, 1840.

Some Injustices Corrected by the Equity Courts

In a common law court, the usual remedy was to award money damages. Often, however, this did not effectively compensate the party that had been wronged. For example, a jeweler had a contract with a customer to make a bracelet of matched stones. The jeweler also had a contract with a jewelry supplier (wholesaler) to buy a center stone that the jeweler had selected as exactly matching the color of the other stones already in the jeweler's stock. Instead of making delivery on the sales contract, however, the jewelry supplier refused to furnish the promised stone, intending to sell it to another customer who would pay a higher price. If the jeweler sued the jewelry supplier under the common law court system, damages would be awarded. These damages would not likely compensate, however. In actuality, the jeweler could not find another matching stone anywhere on the market.

Under the procedures followed in equity, the court would issue a *writ of mandamus*. This writ would order the jewelry supplier to actually produce the desired center stone for the agreed sales price or be sent to jail for contempt of court. If this failed to cause delivery of the stone, the court might order the sheriff to seize the stone and deliver it over to the jeweler. Thus, under the equity system the jeweler could get delivery of the stone without having to make an expensive search for a substitute.

To take another case—suppose your neighbor dumped raw sewage into the stream that you legally used for kitchen water. You could sue the neighbor in a law court and you could expect to collect damages. But you might have considerable difficulty in convincing a court that you had actually sustained serious damage unless a member of your family sustained serious illness that was proved to be a result of the dumping. Then, too, the problem might linger on for a long time before the matter came up for trial. Upon hearing the facts, an equity court could issue a temporary court order (injunction), placing the neighbor in contempt of court if there were further acts of dumping. This temporary injunction would stay in effect until the matter was finally heard in a court trial when a final injunction could be issued.

But the greatest benefit from this dual court system arose from the fact that equity would award damages in any situation where there was an injustice, even in situations where one of the old common law writs would not apply.

After a time, of course, there were a number of both law courts and equity courts in England, along with inferior (lower) courts of both kinds. The two systems of courts continued to operate alongside each other in England until the passing of the Judicature Acts, beginning in 1873.

As noted earlier, we still call these two kinds of tribunals law courts and equity courts. When it was said that a dispute was being handled "in law" or "in equity," the lawyers meant that it was being decided in that particular type of court. When the colonists brought English law to the new world, they established both law courts and the supplemental courts of equity.

The New Combined Courts

Within a few years of 1848, the majority of the states in this country had adopted new codes of court procedure and codes of reformed legal pleadings. In effect, these new procedures abolished all distinctions and technical forms between lawsuits in either law courts or equity courts. The result was that the two systems combined into a single court that began to apply the legal principles of both law and equity.

Of the remaining states that did not combine law and equity into a single court, a few states adopted another system. Here, a single court was authorized to sit as a law court, or as an equity court, according to the needs of justice in a particular case. One court might sit in both capacities in a single case, depending on the issues involved.

A few states in the United States, however, have continued to the present time with separate courts of law and equity. This, of course, is a continuation of the older system. A business operating in such a state must rely on a local attorney to make certain that a legal dispute is brought before the proper court in that area.

DISCUSSION PROBLEMS

1. Discuss the manner in which our laws evolved from the English common law.
2. Determine which cases are brought in law courts and which in equity courts?
   a. Someone trespasses on your land.
   b. You want to sue for performance on a contract.
   c. You want to sue for damages on a contract.

QUESTIONS

1. Explain how the Constitution is the framework or basis of our legal system in the United States.
2. What is the difference between "case law" and "legislative-made law"? What are codes?
3. How does a lawyer use the decided cases to find out what the law is today?
4. What conditions brought about the origin of equity courts in England? What are the basic differences between law and equity courts in their approach to solving legal problems?

5. Find out whether your state has one court that applies the principles of both law and equity. Or does one court in your state alternate, sitting at times as a law court and at times as an equity court? Or does your state still have separate courts?

The Courts
and Their Functions

A court, of course, settles legal points on which individuals or groups do not agree. It defines, interprets, and applies the law.

In legal terminology, the word "court" is used in three basic ways:

1. It is the arm of government that settles legal disputes, or
2. It is the judge who presides over judicial proceedings, or
3. It refers to the time of the gathering at which disputed legal matters are heard, or the place where judges work.

Grades of Courts

A *court of first instance, court of original jurisdiction*, or *court of general jurisdiction* is the court that has the right or authority to try a matter in the first place. It is commonly called a *trial court*.

An *appellate court, appeals court*, or *court of appeals* is, of course, a higher grade of court than a court of first instance. An appellate court does not (with very rare exceptions) accept cases for trial; rather, an appellate court reviews claims that a trial court made errors in the application or interpretation of the law in the first instance. If a vital error was made, the appellate court may order a new trial, leaving out the erroneous evidence or other matter that brought about an injustice.

An appeal is allowed only if it appears to the appellate court that an error may have been instrumental in depriving one of the parties of a fair trial. In other words, the appellate court examines the law as understood and applied by the trial court. The appellate court may send the matter back to the original trial court for the clarification of some specific issue or for a complete retrial, depending on the circumstances. In some instances, too, the appellate court may completely reverse the decision of the trial court.

This appellate review or examination by the appellate court is based wholly on the study of court documents and the transcript of testimony of the court stenographer's record from the original trial. The appellate court accepts the finding of the trial court's jury as to disputed facts and usually does not raise new facts or consider matters not already in the record.

All states in the United States also have so-called *inferior courts* or *minor courts*. In a sense these are also trial courts, but the matters they handle are of lesser importance. This kind of court is usually designated as a *justice court, night court, police court, magistrate's court, traffic court, precinct court, recorder's court*, or *justice of the peace court* (abbreviated as *J.P. court*). In some instances, these bodies do not keep a stenographic record of proceedings or testimony and may not make use of a jury.

State Court Systems

There is general uniformity in the judicial systems of the state courts in the United States. At the lowest level, of course, are the inferior courts, usually handling minor criminal cases, traffic and driving violations, violations of municipal ordinances, and similar matters. These *courts of limited jurisdiction* (inferior courts) are just that—they have authority to try only a number of small matters with limits on both the subject matter and the dollar values in a lawsuit.

Most court trials that involve any substantial amount of money or a serious criminal violation are heard in the courts of original jurisdiction. Specific names for such courts of original jurisdiction vary from state to state, being called the *superior court, district court, court of common pleas, circuit court*,[1] or *county court*. New York State is an exception with original jurisdiction sometimes being in the state Supreme Court and other courts designated by the legislature. In addition, New York appellate jurisdiction is sometimes in the Supreme Court (Appellate Division).

Most state court systems have two levels, or tiers, of appellate courts with the highest being called the Supreme Court. In legal circles, this highest court in the appellate structure is called the Court of Last Resort. Texas, in effect, has two Courts of Last Resort: the Supreme Court for civil affairs and the Court of Criminal Appeals for criminal cases.

All states have some courts that are designated to try family and juvenile cases. Some courts are also set up to handle wills, probate, trust, and inheritance matters. In some states these are separate courts, and in others they are branches of the courts of general jurisdiction. These courts that specialize in specific classes of cases may be called *family courts* (divorce, annulment, separation, and so on), *probate, surrogate*, or *orphan's courts* (trusts, wills,

[1]Originally, circuit courts made use of a single judge traveling from county to county or city to city.

probate, inheritance and estate settlement, guardianship matters, and the like).

Figure 1 shows the organizational structure of the court systems in the great majority of the states in the United States.

Small Claims Court. Most states enable individuals to "have their day in court" in minor civil disputes without having to go through the expense of hiring an attorney. Small claims courts have been established for settlement of cases between private persons or consumers suing businesses. Generally, a dollar amount is set on these cases. For instance, in California the upward limit for small claims court cases is $5000. Typically, one must file a claim in the court, after which he or she receives a court date to appear and plead the case.

Some states have small claims court advisors to assist individuals in preparing their complaints, which must be filed in the court. Typical claims involve minor traffic accidents, landlord-tenant disputes, and neighborhood complaints, such as property damage and injuries. Although the judge must adhere to the laws of that state, the procedures followed are generally more informal. Those states with small claims courts require that the individual appear without an attorney.

Consumer complaints against businesses are also prevalent in small claims court. Many states utilize this system as a manner in which to protect the consumer from the unscrupulous practices of small businesses. For instance, in California the Consumer Affairs Department assists consumers with complaints against businesses. Not only do they have trained investigators on their staff to look into complaints by consumers, but they also assist

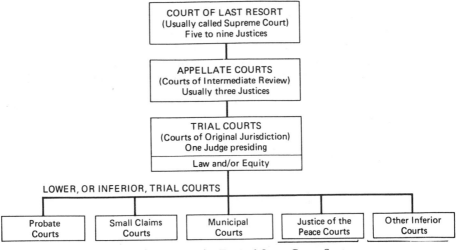

Figure 1   Structure of a Typical State Court System

individuals in completing the forms necessary to file a claim in small claims court.

The Federal Court System

The Federal government has its own system of courts, similar to the three-tiered arrangement used by most states. The Federal District Courts are, for most purposes, the basic trial courts in the Federal system. These district tribunals have original jurisdiction (authority) over the trial of Federal crimes and civil lawsuits handled in the Federal system.

Misdemeanors and minor matters can be handled by the Federal District Courts, but they are frequently handled by the *United States Commissioner* (USC), a magistrate under the supervision of the Federal District Judge. This Commissioner usually sets bail and conducts hearings in Federal criminal cases.

Appeals are usually made from the decisions of the Federal District Courts to the intermediate courts of appeal, called the *United States Courts of Appeal*. In a few types of cases, however, an appeal may be made directly from the Federal District Court to the *United States Supreme Court*. The Federal District Courts and U.S. Courts of Appeal cannot generally correct the judicial errors made by a state court. The final judgment of a state court of last resort may, however, be reviewed by the Supreme Court of the United States. In most instances, an appeal cannot be taken from the state court system to the United States Supreme Court until all appeals in the state court system have been exhausted. Before any state matter will be considered by the United States Supreme Court, it must first appear that the state decision violated the rights, immunities, or privileges of an individual granted by the United States Constitution, or that a treaty or statute is contrary to the Federal Constitution. In many instances the decision of the highest state court is not subject to Federal court review, since a Federal Constitutional question is not involved.

Additional Federal courts, sometimes known in legal circles as *constitutional courts*, process a comparatively small number of cases in specific fields:

1. The *United States Court of Claims* hears decisions in claims against the United States.
2. The *United States Tax Court* resolves disputed Federal tax matters.
3. The *United States Customs Court* and
4. The *United States Court of Customs and Patent Appeals* judge appeals directly from decisions of the *United States Patent Office*, as well as appeals from the United States Customs Court.

The organizational structure of the Federal court system is shown in Figure 2.

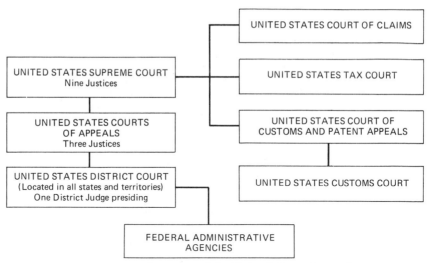

Figure 2   Structure of the Federal Court System[2]

THE PROCESSING OF LAWSUITS _____

Diversity-of-Citizenship Cases

In the great majority of cases, a lawsuit must be brought in the state courts in the locality where the plaintiff lives. In order for the case to be brought in a Federal District Court, it is necessary to show that:

1. There is a question arising under the laws or Constitution of the United States (called a Federal question), or
2. The suit must be between citizens of different states, or between a citizen and an alien, with at least $50,000 involved. As the lawyers put it, the Federal courts are not open to you unless there is a "diversity of citizenship."

These *diversity-of-citizenship* suits are permitted because the state courts may have difficulty in obtaining jurisdiction over someone living out of state. The practical result in a situation of this kind is that without such a rule someone in California might never be able to sue someone in Maine, regardless of the wrong that had been done. The Federal courts can, however, issue subpoenaes and compel people to attend Federal court no matter where they may live.

[2]Federal Administrative Agencies are shown on this chart, since their rulings can usually be appealed to the United States District Court.

Jurisdiction

Jurisdiction is the power or authority of a court to hear a legal dispute and to settle it according to the law of the land. Stated in other terms, jurisdiction is the right by which courts administer, apply, and interpret the law. It is the power of the official who has the right of judging.

A court's jurisdiction is generally conferred on it by its act of organization. The United States Constitution authorized the United States Supreme Court giving Congress the right to expand the courts to the number needed to take care of the nation's legal business. State constitutions provide somewhat similar authority to the individual states for the establishment and operation of state court systems.

The courts hold that jurisdiction has various meanings. The word jurisdiction may refer to:

1. The authority of a court to issue a decision concerning the specific legal problem or subject matter in question. Sometimes the courts refer to this as "jurisdiction over the subject matter." This means authority over that particular class of cases or disputes to which this case belongs (*Honea* v. *Graham*, 66 S.W.2d 802).
2. The authority of a court to render judgment against a specific individual or organization. The courts sometimes call this "jurisdiction in personam" or jurisdiction over the person (*Collins* v. *Powell*, 277 N.W. 477).
3. Authority to decide a dispute over the rights to property (sometimes called "jurisdiction in rem"—jurisdiction over the "thing") (*City of Phoenix* v. *Rodgers*, 34 P.2d 385, 388).

The parties to a legal dispute must be where they can answer to, or be brought under the control of, the court. It is a fundamental principle of English and American law that all "shall have their day in court." This means that everyone must be given an opportunity to present his or her version of a dispute before judgment shall be rendered. This cannot be done unless the court has jurisdiction to force an unwilling party to come into court and make a defense.

To illustrate this problem, consider the case of a Maine resident who is injured by the negligent driving of an individual who lives in Hawaii. The injured person in Maine could file a lawsuit in the Maine state courts, asking damages for the negligent injury. But in the absence of special laws, the Maine courts would have authority only over persons in Maine who could be reached by a subpoena compelling a court appearance. There would be no way to obtain jurisdiction over the Hawaiian driver unless the driver voluntarily agreed to return to Maine to face a lawsuit. In short, the Maine courts would be limited by "geographical jurisdiction" over individuals who could be reached by the court processes in that state only.

Of course, state courts seldom have any problem in obtaining jurisdiction over the plaintiff, since the plaintiff is usually eager to obtain the court's help to recover a judgment. But the defendant is usually an unwilling party to a lawsuit.

We have seen from our examination of the Federal court system that a citizen of Maine may go into the Federal courts and file a lawsuit against a citizen or resident of Hawaii under the "diversity-of-citizenship" provision in the Federal laws. But this may not be done unless the damages in the plaintiff's lawsuit total $50,000 or more. Frequently, this money limitation prevents the "diversity-of-citizenship" technique from being used.

Service of Process

The laws in practically all jurisdictions provide that a defendant in a suit in court must be given an opportunity to defend. This notice to the defendant comes about through the "service of process" by a court summons or subpoena. The basic law of process service, as used in most states, provides that:

> Service of summons [subpoena], except when otherwise exempted by statute, shall be made by leaving a copy of the summons with the defendant in person.

In most localities, of course, the service of a summons or subpoena is usually done by a professional *process server*. In some states this order for the defendant to appear in court is called not only a summons or subpoena, but a *court notice*, a *writ*, a *process*, or a *mandatory writ*.

Laws in some states require the sheriff to serve the subpoena. In other localities the plaintiff's lawyer is permitted to take this action. This summons, or writ, usually states when and where it is "returnable"—that is, when and where the defendant must appear to answer the complaint of the plaintiff. After making proper service on the defendant, the process server or whoever serves this document must return it to the office of the clerk of the court from which it was issued. An indorsement or proof of service must be made on the back by the process server, designating the way in which service was made.

After having been served, the defendant must appear and defend against the lawsuit. Otherwise, the plaintiff is entitled to judgment by default. The effect of failure to appear is that the defendant will never get an opportunity to be heard later, even though the plaintiff cannot actually prove a case in court.

A defendant, of course, may be able to avoid the service of process by simply leaving the territorial limits of the court, or by hiding. But this avoidance is seldom worth the trouble.

Today, a number of states have laws that permit alternative methods for service of process. The most common alternative is service by mail. Service is made by registered mail with return receipt by the party. However, if the person is avoiding service, then this method may also fail by his or her not accepting the document. Some states allow substituted service whereby an individual may be served through a close relative at the place of residence or by serving someone at the person's business who is in a position of authority. In those cases, some states require that a copy of the document be immediately mailed to the defendant.

If all of these methods fail and one is not able to serve the defendant, some states allow service by publication. One must generally file a document with the court stating exactly how he or she attempted to find the defendant to serve him or her. If the judge is convinced that all other avenues have been pursued with due diligence, then service may be accomplished by publication in a newspaper of general circulation. This, however, is always a last resort to get the party served.

It should be noted that service is made not only on the defendant, but on the plaintiff as well. For instance, if the plaintiff serves the defendant with a complaint, the defendant has the opportunity to serve the plaintiff with a response. Service on the plaintiff is accomplished in the same manner as on the defendant. However, since the plaintiff is initiating the suit, the defendant will usually not have a problem serving the plaintiff. If the parties have attorneys, service will generally be instituted on the attorney for the party being served.

Concurrent Jurisdiction

Concurrent jurisdiction exists when two or more court systems are each authorized to handle a legal matter at the same time. For example, in a diversity-of-citizenship lawsuit, both state and Federal courts may have concurrent jurisdiction in a lawsuit against an out-of-state business.

In similar manner, an individual who robbed a bank could be prosecuted in state court for armed robbery, while prosecutable in Federal District Court on a Federal bank robbery charge in many instances. If one authority prosecutes, the usual practice is for the other authority to "defer to the prosecutive authority of the other jurisdiction."

"Long-Arm Statutes"

When the automobile became common a number of years ago, people began to tour all over the continental United States. More and more drivers caused serious injuries and an increasing number of plaintiffs were unable to serve defendants living in distant states. After a time, transportation improvements made it easier for a defendant to go to another state to respond to a subpoena. The courts then became convinced that there was no longer any reason why an injured individual should be deprived of legal remedies in the nearby courts. Consequently, a majority of the states passed "long-arm statutes," extending court jurisdiction. These laws created a "legal fiction," stating that by making use of the roads of a state that an out-of-state driver had thereby designated a specified state official (usually the Secretary of State) to be the defendant's agent for the acceptance of process. In a lawsuit of this kind, the plaintiff causes service to be made on the designated state official, who in turn notifies the out-of-state driver by mail to the latter's last known address. The appellate courts have generally upheld process service of this kind.

Additional laws have also been passed by a number of state legislatures to extend court jurisdiction. Usually these laws grant jurisdiction to local courts in tort cases (negligence, and so on) in which the defendant owns property within the state or "does business" within the state. Usually, the maintenance of a sales office, distribution outlet, or warehouse or the handling of contracts within a state has been held sufficient to bring a breach of contract or tort lawsuit within the jurisdiction of the local courts. Therefore, it is generally held that if one does business in a state, he or she can be sued in that state.

Venue

Venue is a legal term that relates only to the place where, or the territory within which, one or both of the parties has a legal right to have a matter tried in the courts.

Venue is sometimes confused with jurisdiction. But jurisdiction means the inherent power of a court to decide a case, whereas venue designates the specific county or location in which the court with jurisdiction may hear the trial.[3]

Venue is generally set by statute. Typically, laws of this kind specify that a lawsuit must be commenced and tried in the county or district where one or more of the defendants reside, or in the county where the wrong was committed, or where the matter in dispute took place. From state to state, however, there are a number of exceptions in venue statutes.

In most states, for example, venue for a divorce suit lies in the county where one of the parties resides. Or, criminal charges must usually be filed in the county or district in which the crime took place. Business lawsuits for breach of contract often have similar limitations.

In most states the trial judge has discretion to change venue of any lawsuit, either civil or criminal, when it appears that a defendant may not get a fair trial in the locality designated for trial by venue statutes.

There is usually good logic behind venue statutes. Usually, it is less

---

[3] *Southern Sand & Gravel* v. *Massaponax Sand & Gravel*, 133 S.E. 812.

costly in both time and money for a matter to be tried close to the residences of the individuals involved. Witnesses and parties who have close access to court can keep travel costs down. Then, too, many local individuals are known by repute in the community, and this reputation is often likely to help honest citizens and reputable businesses. Of course, there could always be an objection to a venue designation, since there is more likelihood of political influence in a local trial.

PRINCIPLES OF COURT DECISIONS

Stare Decisis

In the American judicial system, an appellate judge will usually consider a number of factors in handing down a decision. The holding, of course, must be in keeping with the judge's feelings of justice in that particular case. But in addition, the court usually decides the case in light of principles evolved from earlier court holdings. This is the legal principle known as *stare decisis* (Latin: "Let the decision stand"). The idea is that once a question has been deliberately examined and decided, the holding is thereafter binding on the courts within that jurisdiction.

As early as the twelfth century, the English courts were recording and thereafter citing earlier decisions as precedent. Thus, a basic adherence to prior decisions has been regarded as necessary to the operation of the legal system in England and the United States for hundreds of years. This, of course, is the idea on which a lawyer can predict the law in a particular situation when a client wants to be advised.

Legal scholars often stress the value of the *stare decisis* principle. They assert that the job of the courts is that described by the old English legal authority, Blackstone: "Courts were not delegated to pronounce new law, but to apply old principles."

When a new situation comes up, courts must, and do, announce new rules. Thus, the judges provide for situations not covered previously, carrying out current ideas of what is just.

But courts may, and sometimes do, refuse to follow precedent. This may be because conditions have changed. A situation that was decided one way in the past may no longer reflect social or economic thinking of current times. For example, for hundreds of years the courts of almost all nations, including the United States, followed the principle laid down by ancient Rome—"Caveat emptor!" (Let the buyer beware!). For a long time this old principle had worked well. People grew or made almost everything that they used. Individuals had time to closely examine the few things that they bought. Then, too, almost everyone was competent to evaluate the worth of the few materials and items that were being offered for sale. But conditions changed. Manufacturers began to make thousands of innovative products from new ingredients and materials that buyers no longer understood. Today, a great many items that are offered for sale could possibly have hidden defects. Other products may be inherently dangerous in common usage, and this potential for harm may not be realized by the buyer. Gradually, therefore, court decisions began to place responsibility for safety and quality where it usually rests today—on the manufacturer. After all, it is the manufacturer who is in the best position to know when hidden defects may exist, or to understand whether the product has potential danger for an unwary buyer. Thus, the philosophy of the courts shifted and they no longer followed precedent. Today's principle is often described by modern courts as "Let the seller beware!"

Prior court decisions are also reversed for another basic reason. Later courts sometimes believe that the earlier decision was wrong. Judges are human and they do err. Subsequent judges, seeking to apply justice, simply may feel that they should not be held to a blunder of a prior court.

Judges as "Social Engineers"

We have noted that, in general, our courts still follow the basic idea of *stare decisis*. This adherence to precedent furnishes a system whereby a businessman or businesswoman may act in a certain way, confident that this action will have a known legal effect. At times, however, some modern judges feel that it is their duty to engage in the practice that lawyers term "social engineering"—that is, shaping the law to the judge's own individual social and economic beliefs.

When a judge tailors a decision to personal ideas about how society should operate, the holding of the court may be directly opposite to what the legislature intended by the passage of the law. Many legal observers feel that this "social engineering" by judges is an outright usurpation of the privileges and responsibilities of the legislature. Many critics feel that laws should be made by the legislative branch of government, not by the holding of a court. Business and trade interests usually favor the idea of permitting the legislature to enact the laws.

The opposite view was expressed by former Supreme Court Justice William O. Douglas:

> The alternative is to let the Constitution freeze in the pattern which one generation gave it. . . . It must never become a code which carries the overtones of one period that may be hostile to another. . . . So far as constitutional law is concerned, stare decisis must give way before the dynamic components of history. . . .[4]

[4]William O. Douglas, speaking before New York City Bar Association, June 1972.

Res Judicata

The old Latin legal phrase, *res judicata*, means a thing already decided and settled. *Res judicata* is a legal principle quite consistently followed by almost all courts. It is the rule that a final judgment or decree on the merits of a matter by a court of competent jurisdiction will be final and conclusive as to any later lawsuit on all points or matters determined in the former suit. This means that between the parties themselves the dispute is closed at the conclusion of the trial. However, this does not prevent a lower court decision from being appealed to a higher court.

This principle of *res judicata* prevents an unsuccessful litigant from taking an unfavorable decision to another trial court for a second lawsuit on the same complaint or same set of facts. *Res judicata* applies between the parties in a civil lawsuit, affecting those parties and no others.

APPEAL PROCEDURES

A harmless error made by a trial court will not result in the granting of a new trial.

The procedure followed by an appellate court is to examine all or part of the written record, or transcript, of what happened at the trial. The appellate court will then render a written *opinion*, which will affirm or strike down the trial court's verdict. The judges' (justices') reasoning behind the decision may also be included in the appellate opinion. And in the future, this opinion will serve as a precedent and become a part of our on-going case law.

In some instances the appellate court will "reverse and remand" the matter to the trial court. This means that the case will go back to the trial court for a completely new trial. In the second trial the parties will not be allowed to use evidence or material of any kind that was decided to be unfair by the appellate court. In some instances the trial judge may be required to change a ruling that he or she made, withholding evidence as inadmissible when the judge should not have done so. In some instances there simply may not be enough convincing evidence to uphold the original verdict of the trial court when the matter is tried a second time. In a civil case this means that upon a retrial the party that lost in the first trial may prevail in the second, depending upon how much believable evidence can still be admitted. If some of the evidence is struck down in the appeal in a criminal case, then the appellate court may order the acquittal (release) of the convicted individual, unless there is still enough evidence to convict on a retrial.

In most instances when an appellate court orders a retrial, the parties are put back in the same position as if no trial had ever been held. All the evidence will need to be introduced into court a second time. Occasionally, however, the appellate court may send the case back to the trial court for a clarification of only one issue on which the whole case turns.

It is also to be noted that an appellate court will never render an opinion in a theoretical case or give an advisory opinion about something likely to happen in the future. Only a dispute that is squarely before the court at the time will be decided.

In similar manner, the United States Supreme Court will not anticipate a constitutional question before it actually becomes an issue. All courts will refuse to pass on the validity of a statute on the complaint of someone who fails to show injury in the application for judicial review.

—————— DISCUSSION PROBLEMS ——————————————————————

Which courts would have jurisdiction over the following cases and why?

1. Jeff painted a house for $1,000 and has not been paid. He does not want to hire a lawyer but would like to sue.
2. Michael, a resident of California, wants to sue Carl, a resident of Nevada, for injuries sustained in an automobile accident in Nevada. His damages amount to $82,200.
3. Marie wants to have her deceased mother's will admitted to probate.
4. Jane was injured in the local Hurt Market. Her damages were $2,000.

—————— QUESTIONS ——————————————————————————————

1. Give three meanings of the word "court."
2. Define a court of first instance, court of original jurisdiction, court of general jurisdiction, trial court, and small claim court.
3. Distinguish between the workings of a trial court and an appellate court.
4. Briefly outline the organization of the state courts in most states. Is your own state court system significantly different? Explain.
5. Briefly outline the Federal court system.
6. How is an appeal made from a state court to the United States Supreme Court?
7. Explain how "diversity of citizenship" works to permit lawsuits in Federal courts.
8. Explain various meanings of jurisdiction.
9. Describe what is meant by "service of process."
10. What is concurrent jurisdiction?

11. How do "long-arm statutes" work?
12. Explain the meaning of venue.
13. What is meant by *stare decisis? Res judicata?*
14. Give a brief description of the appeals process in the court system.

How the Courts
Handle Lawsuits

TRIAL PRELIMINARIES

When an individual is held to answer for a criminal act, the matter is handled in a criminal court by state or Federal prosecutors. However, a wrong against a specific individual or business is handled as a lawsuit in a civil court. In some instances an individual who commits a wrong may be sued in civil court for damages and prosecuted as a criminal at the same time. Many wrongs or injuries are not criminal in nature and will be tried exclusively in civil court. This includes most business litigation.

In going to civil court to obtain relief for a wrong, we say that the plaintiff "brings an action" against the other party (defendant). The term *action*, or *legal action*, is used interchangeably with the legal terms *lawsuit*, *suit*, or *litigation*. To file your lawsuit, you hire a lawyer (except in some small claims court matters).

In the United States we use the words *lawyer, attorney, attorney-at-law, counsel, or counsellor* to mean any *legal advocate*.

We do not commonly use the terms *barrister* or *solicitor* in the United States. These words have special meanings in the court system in the British Isles.

Filing the Complaint

To begin a lawsuit, the lawyer who represents the party which brings the action (the plaintiff) files a written petition called a *complaint* with the clerk of the court that has jurisdiction to hear the matter. A file is then opened on the case in the office of the clerk of the court. The file is then assigned a *case number*. The person beginning the lawsuit is called the *plaintiff* and the *defendant* is the party against whom the action is brought.

If consumer Smith is the plaintiff and the lawsuit is against the ABC TV Appliance Company, the case would be known as "*Smith* v. *ABC TV Appliance Co.*" The "v." here means "versus" or "against."

Certain information must be included in the complaint, including:

1. Statement of jurisdiction (This statement tells why this court should have jurisdiction and generally includes the names and residency of the plaintiff and defendant and/or where the injury occurred.)
2. Statement of facts (In order to file a case, the plaintiff must show that there is a proper cause of action.)
3. Statement of damages (Sometimes called the "Prayer," this is the point at which the plaintiff indicates the dollar amount of the suit or other relief that might be requested, such as an injunction.)

In going into court, your attorney will likely ask for an award of money damages for the harm done to you. At the same time, if the harm is still continuing, your attorney may ask for a court order (an injunction) to have the defendant discontinue the harmful action. Either a money award or an injunction or both may be requested.

Your attorney must be sure to file your lawsuit in a court with proper jurisdiction. For example, a probate court usually has jurisdiction to handle only estate matters, wills, trusts, and probate affairs.

Serving the Defendant

When your attorney's complaint is filed with the clerk of the court, a copy is then served on the individual who allegedly caused you harm (the defendant). We have noted previously that service is usually made by personal delivery to the defendant. However, in some jurisdiction service may be accomplished by mail by sending a copy of the summons and complaint to the defendant by registered mail. Other forms of service include *substituted service*, where a copy of the summons and complaint are left with an individual at the defendant's home, and *constructive service*, where the summons and complaint are published in a legal newspaper or one with general circulation. The latter form of service is only allowed when the plaintiff has exercised "due diligence" in attempting to serve the defendant by one of the other methods described.

The summons tells the defendant that the plaintiff is suing and that the complaint must be answered in a certain number of days (usually 30). It also informs the defendant that if the complaint is not answered in the required time, the plaintiff may obtain a "judgment by default"; that is, judgment may be obtained as requested by plaintiff if no response is received by the defendant.

There are times when a defendant may actually refuse to accept service. Most states have a legal provision that merely touching the defendant's body or clothing with the service papers is sufficient, provided the papers are left with the reluctant defendant.

The Defendant's Answer

At this stage, the defendant may merely file an *entry of appearance*, reflecting that the defendant will appear in court at the proper time. Usually, however, if time permits, the defendant's attorney will file a written petition called an *answer*, which sets out a denial of some or all of the material allegations in the plaintiff's *complaint*.

On some occasions the defendant's attorney will admit the truth of the facts set out in the plaintiff's complaint. But the substance of the defendant's defense here is that, even though the things the plaintiff says are true, they still do not "spell out" the kind of legal claim that entitles the plaintiff to damages. This type of answer is legally called a *demurrer*, and it is invariably accompanied by a motion requesting that the judge dismiss the complaint.

If the defendant disputes the facts alleged in the plaintiff's complaint, then the defendant's answer may attempt to explain away the plaintiff's claim. At this stage the defendant may file a *counterclaim* or *cross-complaint*, asserting that it was actually the defendant who suffered more loss than the plaintiff as a result of dealings with the plaintiff. Legally, this may be called a *set off* or an *offset*.

It is the duty and legal responsibility of the lawyer for each party to present his or her client's case in the best possible light, never knowingly presenting untrue information to the court at any stage of the case.

Discovery Techniques

In the period before a trial, the attorneys may use a procedural technique called *discovery*. This procedure is aimed at learning more details about the opponent's case. Discovery is designed to bring all the issues and merits of the dispute into the open. Such revelations often lead to a negotiated settlement or to dropping the lawsuit altogether if discovery procedures indicate that the suit was brought out of anger or personal spite.

Discovery techniques generally make both sides aware of all statements, documents, charts, laboratory reports, physical evidence, analytical studies, or other materials that have a bearing on the case.

Depositions. Requiring sworn depositions in advance of trial (witness statements under oath) is another discovery technique. The taking of depositions is usually handled by a lawyer and a stenographic reporter. In most instances, lawyers for both sides may attend the deposition interview and ask questions. Usually a question-and-answer form is used in the deposition with all questions and replies being reduced to a stenographic transcription.

Depositions are often taken of both witnesses and the adverse party (opposing party in the lawsuit). Since both attorneys are present and the opposing attorney has the opportunity to cross-examine the witness, most courts will allow the deposition to be used at the trial as testimony if the witness is no longer available. Some courts even allow the original deposition to be videotaped. In those jurisdictions, the videotaped deposition may be introduced as testimony with the court's permission if the witness is unavailable to testify at trial.

Written Interrogatories. *Written interrogatories* are written questions sent to the opposing party in a lawsuit and may be used by either the plaintiff or the defendant. Their purpose is to elicit information about the lawsuit from the other party. Most states require that they be answered in a certain period of time, usually 30 days. Some states place limits on the number of questions that may be asked.

Requests for Admission and Document Production. Two additional discovery devices, used less frequently than depositions and written interrogatories, are Requests for Admission and Requests for Production. Requests for Admission ask a party to admit to matters at issue to avoid having to litigate those matters in court. Requests for Production ask a party to produce documents in the party's possession that are relevant to the case. In those cases where the documents to be produced are too voluminous in nature, the party may make them available at its place of business during regular office hours so that the one requesting the documents may examine and/or copy them.

The Pretrial Conference

Many state courts utilize a *pretrial conference* between the judge and the opposing lawyers. This is usually a somewhat informal meeting, often in the judge's chambers. Probable evidence and the legal issues involved are generally discussed. At this stage it may become evident to the attorney for one side that his or her client does not actually have a case and the matter may be compromised (settled) at that time.

THE TRIAL

The Adversary System

A trial in civil court has sometimes been described as "civilized warfare." The courts also describe the contest involved as the "adversary system." In this procedure there are two clearly drawn sides. The judge is an impartial arbitrator and an official who maintains order. Each side presents the facts known to it. The theory here is that the individual adversaries are in the best position to present evidence most favorable to their claims. Therefore, the truth is almost certain to come out when the searchers after truth are closing in from each side. If presentations of the facts are clearly made, the truth should always be evident to a fair-minded judge and jury.

This adversary system is somewhat different from the court system used in many other countries—the so-called *inquisitorial system*, under which the judge is not an impartial official but usually conducts inquiries and investigations.

Under the United States adversary system the judge has overall supervision of the trial. In addition, he or she rules on whether the evidence offered is relevant to the dispute at hand. After lawyers for both the plaintiff and the defendant have presented their evidence, the judge advises the jury concerning what provisions of law are applicable and instructs the jury on decisions about facts that may be in dispute.

Jury Selection and Functions

In the trial process proper, the first step is usually the selection of a jury (called *voir dire*). The judge may question prospective jurors about their backgrounds, prejudices, and possible connections with either party involved in the lawsuit. Attorneys for both sides usually have the right to question prospective jurors and to accept or reject a specified number. Any number of prospective jurors may be excused "for cause," such as the individual's bias or prejudice, or his or her acquaintance with one of the parties or attorneys. A certain number of *peremptory challenges* are allowed each attorney in order to excuse jurors without cause. The number of peremptory challenges allowed varies with the nature of the case. After these challenges to the jurors have been exhausted, the attorneys must go to trial with those jurors who remain.

The case is tried by a judge and a jury in most states if requested by either party. Otherwise, the judge handles the functions of both judge and jury.

The basic task of the jury is to decide the truth regarding facts that may be in dispute and to apply the law to those facts as the judge instructs. Actually, then, most lawsuits involve an interplay of decisions concerning what actually occurred and the law that then applies to that particular situation.

If there are no facts in dispute between the plaintiff and the defendant, the only problem before the court is to apply the law to those specific facts. The judge may decide this without the need for a formal trial. When a judge hands down a decision of this kind, it is called a *summary judgment*. Most states require that the attorney request a summary judgment by way of a motion filed with the court.

TRIAL PRESENTATION

What the Presentation Must Accomplish

At the outset of the trial, the attorney for each side usually makes a brief *opening statement*, setting out each client's version of what happened. This enables the judge and jury to subsequently evaluate the significance of isolated pieces of evidence as they are presented.

As the trial progresses, three basic questions should be answered:

1. What were the true facts of the incidents in dispute?
2. Which of the evidence that is offered is relevant and proper to prove or disprove the facts claimed to be true?
3. What is the law that can be applied when this set of facts is known to be true?

It is the jury's duty to provide the answer to the first question. The trial judge (frequently referred to as the court) provides the answer to the second. And the judge indirectly gives the answer to the third by instructing the jury concerning laws and legal principles that apply to the facts as found by the jury.

In a lawsuit, it is always the burden of the plaintiff to carry the case forward. In other words, it is up to the plaintiff to "spell out" a cause of action. Unless a case is made by the plaintiff, it is not necessary for the defendant to offer any evidence or prove anything. The defendant's lawyer can merely make a motion to dismiss in hopes that the judge will close up the whole affair at that time.

The next problem is: How much evidence must be presented? This, of course, varies from case to case. In a civil lawsuit, the plaintiff will win if able to prove his or her claims by a "preponderance of the evidence" or by the "weight of the evidence." This means, not that the plaintiff needs to produce more witnesses than the other side, but that the evidence must be more convincing or more believable than the evidence tending to disprove the plaintiff's claims.

How Evidence Is Presented

Proof of the case (evidence) is presented in open court by the oral testimony of witnesses, the introduction of documents, the presentation of physical evidence, and other techniques such as the use of laboratory reports. The bulk of evidence in most civil trials is by the oral testimony of witnesses.

In the handling of a trial, there are definite rules concerning when and how evidence may be introduced. To an outsider there are times when it appears that these rules sometimes unduly obstruct the presentation, rather than aid in the search for the truth. But these rules were devised by trial and error so that only the pertinent, relevant, and meaningful facts are brought to the attention of the jury. In this way, the jury will not be distracted by inflammatory side issues that are not really a part of the dispute.

After each party has made out its case, usually neither side can introduce new evidence unless this new evidence pertains to the facts already in issue.

Examination of Witnesses

The side that subpoenas a witness calls that person to present proof by questions and answers. This response to the attorney's questions is called *direct examination*. After the side calling the witness has completed questions, the lawyer for the other side is permitted to *cross-examine* this witness. Here, the opposing attorney may ask how the witness happens to know the facts testified to and may go over the witness' direct testimony very carefully for mistakes, inaccuracies, or possible false information. Most individuals are understandably ill at ease during cross-examination.

Then the attorney for the side that originally called the witness has the opportunity to examine the witness a second time (after cross-examination). This is so the witness can explain away or clarify matters that may not have been clear at the time of cross-examination. The legal term for this second examination of the witness is *redirect examination* or simply *redirect*. Almost always this questioning must be limited to matters covered on the cross-examination. Then the attorney for the second side may also be given a second chance to question the witness for clarification or explanation of answers; this is called *re-cross-examination*.

Jury Instructions and Findings

The judge's instructions are directed toward acquainting the jury with the law applicable to the case under trial. Attorneys for each side submit written instructions that they want the judge to pass along to the jury. These lawyers are allowed to examine and object to instructions submitted by opposing attorneys. The judge then rules on which instructions will be allowed. In some instances the judge on his or her own initiative may give other instructions to the jury.

After the jury has made findings on disputed facts, a judgment is thereafter entered by the judge.

Civil Versus Criminal Procedures

The procedures used in the trial of a civil lawsuit differ considerably from those used in a criminal prosecution. Rules of evidence are the same in some aspects of both procedures, but there are differences. A civil case is a private suit, brought by a private individual or company. A criminal prosecution is brought by a public or state prosecutor and is an action by the state against one accused of crime. Much of the scope of criminal procedure is outside the subject matter of this book.

It should be pointed out, however, that an individual's acts may be prosecutable as a crime while also being actionable in a civil lawsuit. For example, the representative of a stock brokerage firm manipulated a customer's computer records, consequently embezzling $100,000 in cash from the customer's account. The brokerage employee could be prosecuted as a criminal embezzler. In addition, the stock brokerage company and/or the defrauded customer could sue the embezzler to recover the funds that had been siphoned off from the account.

POSTTRIAL PROCEDURES

Enforcement of Money Judgment

When one side in a lawsuit wins a judgment, the money award should be paid by the loser. Because of lack of money or sheer stubbornness, this payment may not be immediately forthcoming. In that event, the winning side in the lawsuit applies for a *writ of execution*. The sheriff will then seize the loser's money and sell off the loser's property to satisfy the judgment. But it should be realized that a judgment standing alone may have little or no value. The loser of the suit may have gone into bankruptcy. Or the loser may simply have no bank account, real estate, business, car, or other property that can be reached. A person in that situation is said to be "judgment proof." Too frequently, plaintiffs press lawsuits against judgment-proof defendants, when a minimum of investigation beforehand would have disclosed that fact.

Appeal from Civil Judgment

The losing party, of course, has the right to appeal the judgment of a civil trial court to an appellate (higher) court. This is not true in a number of states, however, if the civil case was filed in small claims court. Appellate procedures are not uniform throughout the various states.

Most jurisdictions require the filing of a notice of appeal within a specified period of time after conclusion of a civil trial. In addition, the party making the appeal (the appellant) must usually file an appeal bond, guaranteeing the payment of court costs if the matter should be lost on appeal.

After these preparatory steps, the party making the appeal must then prepare and file a *legal brief* (called an *appellate brief*) for the deliberation of the appellate court. This *brief*, as it is usually called, must set out specific instances in which it is alleged the trial court made errors that supposedly deprived the appellant of a fair trial.

ARBITRATION IN DISPUTES

An Alternative to Lawsuit

Increasingly, individuals and businesses are utilizing arbitration or third-party mediation as an alternative to litigation in court. Arbitration may settle a dispute promptly, costing considerably less than a lawsuit.

At the outset, we should note that there are differences in procedures to settle consumer disputes. A *conciliator* simply brings the parties together in an atmosphere where they may be able to work out differences. A *mediator* hears the facts and then makes proposals that seem fair to a disinterested third party. The suggestions and recommendations of a mediator may carry considerable weight, but they are not binding.

An *arbitrator*, however, usually arranges a settlement that is binding on both parties. If both sides agree in writing in advance to be bound, the arbitrator's decision has the force of law. In some instances, however, it is agreed in advance that the arbitrator's ruling will be binding on the business only, not on the customer.

For example, Ford Motor Company furnishes the services of a consumer appeals board to hear grievances from individuals buying Ford autos. The board's verdict is binding on the Ford dealer who sold the car but is not binding on the complaining buyer. The agreement here is that the buyer can still go into court and sue for breach of warranty or breach of contract if unsatisfied with the board's decision.

Procedures in Arbitration

Usually arbitration hearings are conducted in an informal way with any kind of reasonable statement or evidence being admitted for consideration. Lawyers may be used in these hearings; however, they are not required.

Of course, an arbitration award can be subsequently taken into the court system by either party involved. It is extremely seldom, however, that a court will ever do anything to change the arbitration decision, unless completely new evidence is developed or unless the award was obviously contrary to the facts.

Consumers sometimes question whether they can expect a fair hearing before a board or panel sponsored by a business group. Undoubtedly, there have been some cases in which the decision seemed to favor business. On the whole, mediation and arbitration panels have seemed determined to obtain a just result and to help correct consumer injustices. Arbitration is usually faster than trial procedures.

Small Claims Court

In order to allow individuals to settle their differences without having to go through the expense of hiring an attorney, many states have instituted Small Claims Courts, where individuals plead their cases before the judge. These courts are utilized in those instances where a small amount of money is involved, usually up to $5000. The procedures are less complicated than in other civil courts, and decisions are made more quickly.

Typically, if you want to sue someone in Small Claims Court, you must fill out a Complaint form. Some courts have trained advisors to assist you. A small fee is paid; service must be made on the defendant as discussed previously. A court trial is held whereby you present your side of the case to the judge. The defendant has an opportunity to present that side. The judge will then render a decision. In some states, the plaintiff may not appeal a case from Small Claims Court. However, usually the defendant is allowed to appeal an adverse judgment.

ETHICAL CONSIDERATIONS

In the last several years, there has been a considerable amount of publicity relating to large settlements derived from lawsuits. It is not unusual to pick up a newspaper and find a million-dollar or multi-million-dollar settlement. These large settlements have given individuals an impetus to file more and more lawsuits. Hence our courts have become overcrowded, and it often takes many years to get to trial.

While most of these lawsuits are legitimate, it would appear that some might be instituted for the purpose of getting large sums of money. Usually the plaintiff's attorney receives a "contingency fee" based on a percentage of the plaintiff's award in the suit.

One should remember that it is often more economical for all concerned to settle cases out of court, avoiding the excessive expense and time of a trial. Businesses that are sued should deal with the plaintiffs fairly. Some businesses might inundate the plaintiff with an excessive amount of paperwork in discovery to attempt to have the case settled for less money and more quickly. These tactics tend to destroy the individual's confidence in big business.

Generally, the "business" side of the suit is better equipped financially to conduct its discovery. They are able to generate a large number of discovery devices on their computers. They can send many pages of written interrogatories to the plaintiff. The state of California has attempted to control this problem by the utilization of "form interrogatories." The Judicial Council of California has created several pages of typical questions asked in written interrogatories. Both sides may use these forms, but they are only able to propound 35 additional questions. In this manner, the courts have attempted to equalize the position of both parties and, at the same time, alleviate the problem of excessive paperwork.

Good business ethics require that an individual in business should deal fairly with his or her customers. While the old adage "the customer is always right" may not be true in all situations, it would appear that if both the customer and the business person dealt with each other fairly and honestly, there would be considerably fewer lawsuits.

DISCUSSION PROBLEMS

1. Discuss the methods of service.
2. Describe the different discovery devices.
3. Discuss trial procedures. If possible, attend a trial and report back to the class.

QUESTIONS

1. May the plaintiff in a lawsuit ask for both money damages and an injunction? Explain an injunction.
2. What is the defendant's answer in a lawsuit? What is a demurrer?
3. What is meant by discovery?
4. Why is a court trial sometimes described as "legalized warfare"? What is the adversary relationship?
5. Who has the burden of proof in a lawsuit? How much evidence must be presented?
6. What is meant by cross-examination? Redirect examination?
7. What is the basic function of a jury in a civil trial?
8. Briefly outline some differences between civil and criminal trials.
9. Why may arbitration sometimes be preferable to a lawsuit?
10. Describe Small Claims Court procedures.

5

Contracts—
An Introduction

Legal Definitions

Courts and legal scholars have defined a contract as:

1. A legally enforceable agreement between two or more persons, involving mutual promises to do or not to do a lawful act, or
2. An agreement that creates one or more legal obligations, and that is enforceable through legal proceedings, or
3. A bargained agreement to create, modify, or destroy a legal relationship.

Individuals have always had agreements or understandings with others. But many of these agreements do not produce any legal effect whatever. In accordance with our definitions, those agreements that create new legal relationships and responsibilities are called contracts and will be enforced by the courts. A study of contracts, then, is a study of promises.

The law does not attach enforceability to every promise. For example, the courts do not enforce an agreement that creates merely a social obligation, such as a promise to attend a basketball game. As a generalization, the kind of promise that will usually be enforced is one concerned with the production, purchasing, or selling of services or goods—something in exchange for a benefit accruing to the promising party. Frankly, the courts have never been completely clear concerning which agreements they will ignore and which they regard as contracts. As a general rule, courts will concern themselves with any agreement that involves a legitimate business relationship.

A contract requires three elements: offer, acceptance, and consideration. One party must make an offer to the other party, who must accept that offer. The mutual promises must be accompanied by consideration, which means that the person who made the offer must receive a bargained-for benefit or the person accepting the offer must receive a bargained-for detriment. For instance, if I promise to sell you my car for $200, I am receiving the benefit of $200 from you for the car; you are losing the $200 to me. However, I am also losing—my car—and you are benefiting by receiving the car. Consideration will be described more fully in Chapter 7.

DISCUSSION

CASE 1   A husband promised his wife that he would stop drinking in exchange for his wife's agreement to stop gambling. When the husband failed to keep his promise, the wife filed a lawsuit against him. Was this agreement an enforceable contract? (*Miller* v. *Miller*, 78 Iowa 177). Study the facts here and form an opinion as to whether the courts would regard this agreement as enforceable. Then compare your opinion with the answer for this case reported at the end of the chapter.

How a Contract Arises

Contracts may arise from even the most uncomplicated relationships. According to our definition, the test is whether some legal obligation results from the transaction. To illustrate, a woman filled the gas tank in a company car, using a company credit card. Driving to a nearby town, she gave a personal credit card to a hotel for overnight accommodations. Thereafter, she shopped for and purchased a birthday present, writing a personal check in exchange. The gift was then handed over to a messenger service for delivery.

These contracts with the service station, hotel, gift shop, and parcel delivery service all initiated transactions with economic consequences. There were no spoken promises to do anything, yet the employees at each firm had no doubts that the transactions would be satisfactory on both sides. Each of these four incidents would be regarded by the courts as individual contracts.

FLEXIBILITY AND VALIDITY OF CONTRACTS

Contracts are the agreements and understandings by which all businesses operate. Without the ability and freedom to make and enforce these contractual arrangements, almost all trade and industry would come to an immediate halt.

With some limitations, the parties making contract agreements can usually set their own terms and requirements. Consequently, the possibility to make different arrangements is almost endless. And in a real sense, by planning their own conditions and specifications, the contracting parties create their own rights and obligations.

Truly, business managers make use of their ability to contract as a basic planning tool. Entrepreneurs bargain for raw materials, get commitments from labor, ship raw materials and finished products, and assure themselves of a reasonable market. These are only some of the binding commitments on which definite plans can be based.

Perhaps it is because of this wide use of contracts in business that lawyers sometimes point out that trade and industry encounter more legal problems in the field of contracts than in any other area of law.

The basic rules of contract law serve as the foundation for most other areas of business law. This means that an understanding of contracts is essential to the study of agency, sales, negotiable instruments, partnerships, corporations, and security transactions.

The Freedom to Make Contracts

With our background of personal liberties under English and American law, both individuals and businesses have long had considerable freedom to make contracts. Early English common law courts placed their approval on practically all agreements of adult individuals with sound mentality. As both common law and equity courts developed, judges began to reject agreements induced by fraud or by threats of force. Meanwhile, judges in both England and the United States have consistently given court approval to the expectations of individuals who make good-faith contracts.

Requirements of Form

With certain exceptions, there has never been a legal requirement in the United States that a contract be in any specific form. In addition, the courts definitely hold that specific words are not necessary to spell out a contract.[1] Neither is it essential, in many instances, that a contract be made in writing.

Contracts of some kinds, however, will be enforced by the courts only if there is evidence of the contract in writing. In some cases this written evidence is a requirement of the so-called *statute of frauds*. Generally speaking, however, the advantage of the writing is to set down the conditions on which the minds of the two parties have met, thereby fixing the rights and duties of each.[2]

---

[1] *Arden* v. *Freydberg*, 174 N.E.2d 495; 9 N.Y.S.2d 393.
[2] *Ephraim Theater Co.* v. *Hawk*, 321 P.2d 221; 7 Utah 2d 163.

Presumed Validity

There is a distinct policy in the courts to favor the making of contracts between competent persons who are seeking to agree on any lawful purpose.[3]

There are restrictions in American law on contracts made in restraint of trade, or agreements that limit business competition. Occasionally, too, if the courts feel that there was an almost total imbalance in bargaining power between the parties involved, then the courts may strike down the contract for that reason. In addition, the courts will not honor an agreement made for the purpose of violating the law, or an agreement that works against the basic aims of society. But all these cases generally are exceptions that do not arise with any great frequency.

A contract is enforceable, however, only "if it has within itself all the essentials of a contract." The courts consistently say that "we will not write a contract for the parties." If they have not agreed on all the essential provisions, the legal process will not supply them.[4] There are times when the courts will say that the actions, rather than the words, of the contracting parties will suffice to show an agreement, even though words were not used. But the function of a court is to enforce agreements only if they are in existence at the time of trial, rather than to create them by the imposition of whatever terms the court feels could be reasonable.[5]

The fact that one of the parties is stuck with a hard bargain will not be sufficient to make the agreement invalid.[6] Only when one side is so penalized that the agreement is unconscionable will the courts consider refusing to uphold a contract. The agreement must be such that "any fair-minded person would view it with a profound sense of injustice" before a court would fail to honor it.[7] Cases of failure to uphold because of lack of basic fairness are very exceptional. Both individuals and businesses who agree to specific terms must expect to be responsible for some unforeseen consequences or harsh developments.

Interpretation or Construction by the Courts

It is the role of the courts to interpret or construe the meaning of contracts. When the wording of the agreement is obscure or ambiguous, the courts apply settled rules of construction in order to arrive at the intent of the

---

[3] *Fidelity Credit Assurance Company of California* v. *Crosby*, 265 P. 372; 90 C.A. 22.
[4] *Laseter* v. *Pet Dairy Products Co.*, 246 F.2d 747.
[5] *Brause* v. *Goldman*, 199 N.Y.S.2d 606.
[6] *Harvey Construction Co.* v. *Parmele*, 113 N.W.2d 760.
[7] *Carlson* v. *Hamilton*, 332 P.2d 989; 8 Utah 2d 272.

parties. The general rule followed by the courts here is that the wording of any contract is viewed objectively. The agreement is given a reasonable interpretation, rather than being judged subjectively. A court arrives at the meaning that terms would have to a reasonably intelligent individual acquainted with the circumstances in which the language was used. The courts say that it is immaterial what one of the parties intended, or believed was being said. The language is given effect in the way it would be interpreted by any reasonable individual standing in place of one of the parties. If one party is held to the secret intent of the other, then no one would ever be sure exactly what had been agreed to. If a contracting party does not want his or her words interpreted according to their reasonable meaning, then that party can clear up any possible future misunderstanding by being specific.

The courts hold that words are given their ordinary meaning. But technical or scientific expressions are given their technical interpretations. In a trial, the courts will allow testimony concerning accepted custom and usage in the technical field that is involved. Terms or expressions that are commonly employed in a specific trade or industry are given their trade usage. And the courts emphasize that the basic thrust of interpretation is directed toward the overall intent of the parties. In addition, the courts take into consideration the local meaning of terms that may have been used in the agreement.

If all other considerations are equal, the courts will construe an ambiguity against the party that prepared or originated the contract. This is because such party clearly had an opportunity to remove uncertain provisions at the time the agreement was drafted. The courts will also allow the showing of prior contracts between the same parties as an indication of their understanding of the current contract.

CONTRACT ESSENTIALS AND VARIETIES

Basic Elements

According to our definition, a contract is a promise or set of promises that the law will enforce. The basic requirements of any contract are:

1. The agreement must be between two or more competent parties. That is, the contract must be between parties that are *legally* competent (sane) and who have reached their majority (legal age). Contracts can be made by minors under limitations, as will be subsequently pointed out.
2. The parties must come to a common or mutual understanding, which was previously communicated from one party to the other.
3. The agreement must have been expressed in some manner, or must be inferrable from the acts of the parties.

4. The agreement must have a legal purpose, that is, it must lack criminal intent. Also, its objective must be attainable.

5. The agreement must involve the giving of consideration. Basically, consideration is the value given by one party to the other, or that which each party gives up or receives in the agreement. Usually, consideration represents a payment or benefit to the maker of the promise, or a loss, trouble, or inconvenience to, or obligation resting on, the party to whom the promise is made.

Classifications of Contracts and Terms

The lawyers and the courts frequently classify contracts and contract terms into categories as follows:

Term	Opposed in Meaning to
Formal contract, or *sealed contract* (also called *contract under seal*, or *contract of record*)	Simple contract
Oral contract	Written contract
Express contract	Implied contract
Bilateral contract	Unilateral contract

We will also examine void, voidable, and valid promises.

Formal Contract

The courts have not always upheld or recognized contracts as readily as they do today. Early law sanctioned only such promises that were written out and solemnized in a specific ceremony. This usually involved having the parties appear before a designated official who impressed a wax seal on the surface of their written agreement. The early-day English and American courts treated the formality of preparation and the use of the seal as lending the necessary legal dignity to the document. The courts reasoned that people would not go to such formality unless they really intended the agreement to be binding.

Today, such a contract under seal is sometimes called a *specialty*, or more commonly a *formal contract*. The legal system gave validity to this kind of document from its seal and formality alone.

Some states in the United States still require a seal in certain kinds of contracts—for example, for a lease of property for more than a year. In addition, a seal may be legally necessary for the giving of a bond, for a deed to property, or for a contract for the transfer of real estate.

But this legal formality of the seal has been relaxed in a number of states, where a stamp, mark, wafer, scroll, or any impression made or adopted to substitute for a seal will be sufficient. And in some localities the courts consider an agreement as a formal contract by the addition of the printed word "Seal" or the Latin abbreviation "L.S." (*Locus Sigilli*— place of the seal).

This need for a formal contract under seal varies considerably from state to state. When there is any doubt, a lawyer should be consulted, especially if the contract in any way involves the transfer of real estate or a lease for more than one year. In a large number of states the need for a seal has been done away with. If a seal should be attached, it would have no legal effect whatever. However, in those states where a seal is not used, it may still be necessary to have contracts notarized if they involve the transfer of real estate, a deed, a bond, or a long-term lease agreement.

In addition to contracts under seal, the courts say that there is a second kind of formal contract. This latter designation covers any contract that is incorporated into court records when the loser of a lawsuit agrees to pay the amount of the court judgment. This second kind of formal contract is sometimes called a *contract of record*.

Simple Contract

Simple contracts include all legal agreements that are not made under seal or that are not *contracts of record*. A simple contract may also be classified as either oral or written.

Oral Contract

An *oral contract* is an agreement reached through words spoken between the parties. The great majority of contracts are of this type. Uninformed individuals sometimes claim that a contract is not valid unless it is in writing. This, of course, is simply not so. This problem will later be considered under the statute of frauds, as certain types of contracts will not be enforced unless there is written evidence of their existence.

It is, however, usually advantageous to have written evidence of the understanding between the parties. Written terms usually leave less opportunity for dispute. Also, a court may be more easily persuaded that a written and signed version represents the true intent of the parties.

Written Contract

A *written contract* is one whose terms have been reduced to writing. Actually, the courts say that the writing is not the contract itself, but evidence of the terms of that contract. A written contract may take many forms, from a contract under seal to a letter or telegram. For example, an acquaintance may send you a telegram agreeing to buy your used car "in line with your offer to sell at $3,850."

_____ *DISCUSSION* _____

CASE 2   Two parties got together to negotiate a business deal. Part of the agreement was reduced to writing, but the writing was not finished. The parties verbally agreed to the rest of the terms. Later, one of the parties attempted to get out of the deal, stating that an agreement cannot be partly in writing and partly by word of mouth. Was this contention valid? (*Laughlin* v. *Haberfelde*, 165 P.2d 544.)

Express Contract

An *express contract* is one that is explicitly set forth in words, either spoken or written. It does not arise from actions or implications of the parties.

Implied Contract

Sometimes individuals may not actually express in specific language their intent to enter into a contract. The implied-in-fact contract is entered into based on the conduct of the parties. If you accept services from another and those services are usually paid for, you will be expected to pay the individual who performs that service. If you hire a gardener to take care of your lawn, you will be expected to pay him. An implied contract is formed and the gardener could enforce the agreement if you refused to pay. In this case, the gardener expected to be paid for his services, and you intended to pay him when you asked him to take care of your lawn.

Basically, in an implied contract, neither party will use words of promise or explicit words indicating that a contract has been formed. However, by nature of your conduct in calling the gardener and his conduct in performing the work, a valid contract will be implied. In this case, the court would look at the facts and circumstances surrounding the transaction to determine whether both parties intended to enter into an agreement.

_____ *DISCUSSION* _____

CASE 3   Plaintiff was a self-employed manufacturer's representative (salesman) who obtained a Federal government defense contract for a private builder. Plaintiff sued the private builder for a 3 percent commission on the value of the contract obtained. At the time there was a Federal law providing that no procurement or contingency fee could be paid to other than a bona fide employee of the builder, and this law relieved the builder of liability to pay a commission. The plaintiff pointed out that he had rendered services to the builder, who was benefitting at plaintiff's expense. Plaintiff also noted that the court should find an implied contract, even though there was no actual contract that could be enforced. Would the court find an implied contract here? (*Weitzel* v. *Brown-Neil Corporation.* 152 F. Supp. 540.)

Bilateral and Unilateral Contracts

A *bilateral promise* is one given in exchange for a promise from the other party. For example, when planning to go on a trip, an elderly man promised a teenager $50 to "promise to look after the security of my home while I am away." The promise of the youth would complete a bilateral contract, in which a promise was given on each side.

A *unilateral promise* is one given in exchange for an act. A man said, "I will give you $5 when you take my car to the car wash and return it." This statement required an act, rather than a promise, in order to complete the contractual agreement. In this case, the second party could expect to collect on the contract only by getting the car washed and returned. In the example immediately prior, however, the youth would have a contract upon making the promise, even before taking any action to look after the neighbor's house.

It should be emphasized that in many instances it does make a difference whether the promise required action or another promise in exchange (unilateral or bilateral). Certain legal rights become fixed (sometimes legally described as "become vested") at the instant a contract is made. If the promise made is bilateral, a contract is formed simply by giving a promise in return. But if the promise is unilateral, the contract does not come into existence until the requested act by the other party is actually done.

When the parties make their intent clear by the use of specific, precise language, the courts will honor that intention by holding that a contract was made. In cases of doubtful intent, the courts will usually say that a given promise is bilateral, rather than unilateral. So unless the language is quite specific, the courts hold that business contracts are bilateral.

In most situations where a reward is posted, the courts construe the promise to pay a reward as based on a unilateral promise, unless the opposite is completely clear. If you advertise in the newspaper: "$50 for the return of my lost dog," the courts will not hold you responsible to pay the reward unless someone actually returns the dog. On the other hand, a mere promise by a searcher to look for your dog would not constitute a contract.

Void Promises or Contracts

A *void promise* or *void contract* is one that the courts simply refuse to enforce. Frequently the reason why an agreement will not be enforced is that the promise is illegal or that the courts say it is "against public policy." For example, an agreement to sell one's self into slavery would be struck down. Slavery is both illegal and against public policy.

Neither could an individual collect on a contract to kill for a fee. Similarly, the courts would not honor an agreement to break up someone's marriage, or to be paid for deliberately committing a slander against someone. All such instances would be classified as "against public policy."

Voidable Contracts

A *voidable contract* is an agreement that may be set aside. However, the court may not necessarily take this action. It is an agreement formed under such circumstances that one party may have the privilege of escaping contract liability under it. Suppose that an individual you had never seen before offered to sell you a tennis racket in good condition. After making payment, you took home the wrapped package that this individual had given you. Then you discovered that the seller had substituted an old racket frame without strings into the wrapped parcel. Legally, you made an agreement for the purchase of another tennis racket, and you could have the transaction set aside (voided) for fraud.

There are times, however, when it may be to your advantage to ignore the voidable aspect of a contract. An antique car collector made a deal with a farmer to buy the old junked auto that had sat in the rear of the farmer's barn for over fifty years. After making the agreement, however, the dishonest farmer reasoned that the old car he had sold might have more value than he realized. Consequently, he delivered another old car that had also been stored in another area of the barn.

After discovering the substitution, the antique car buyer intended to have the courts void the contract. The buyer found that the old vehicle actually delivered was an extremely rare model, worth far more than the original vehicle that had been requested. The buyer decided to keep the car that had been delivered, profiting greatly. In a case of this kind, either party might be able to void the contract on account of error, with the farmer requesting return of the delivered vehicle. However, an error had not been made. The farmer had deliberately intended to work a substitution.

In a subsequent section, we will observe that contracts made by a minor are usually voidable when the minor becomes of age (usually 18).

The Quasi-Contract (Implied in Law)

In law we sometimes use the Latin term *"quasi"* (appearing as if), in combination with an English word, to describe something that is not quite the same as the real thing. Thus, a *quasi-contract* is a legal obligation that has a number of similarities to a contract but is not exactly the same. A quasi-contract arises not from an agreement, but from a mere relationship that comes about between individuals. It is a relationship based on actions without the reaching of an agreement. It simply means that the actions of one person have conferred a benefit on another. The law says that this latter individual should pay the reasonable value of this money benefit, if retention would work an "unjust enrichment" at the expense of the first party.

For example, a medical doctor arrived at the scene of an automobile crash and immediately treated an unconscious person who had been pulled

---

OFFER

Date: July 22, 1992

To: Joan Smith

I hereby offer to paint your house located at 240 Oak Lane, Atlanta, Georgia, if you will pay me $1200 upon completion of the painting.

Signature_____
Samuel A. Jones

ACCEPTANCE

Date: July 24, 1992

To: Samuel A. Jones

I accept your offer of July 22, 1992 regarding your painting of my house for $1200, payable upon completion.

Signature_____
Joan Smith

CONTRACT

AGREEMENT made this 28th day of July, 1992, between Joan Smith, of Atlanta, Georgia, and Samuel A. Jones, of Seal Beach, Georgia.

As consideration for the painting of the house located at 240 Oak Lane in Atlanta, Georgia, Joan Smith agrees to pay to Samuel A. Jones the sum of $1200 upon completion.

Signature_____
Joan Smith

Signature_____
Samuel A. Jones

from the wreckage. There was definitely no contract between the doctor and patient. When the injured person recovered, the doctor submitted a bill for the reasonable value of his services. There was no certainty whether the patient would have died or recovered without this treatment. The patient was unconscious and there were no movements on which an implied contract could be claimed. In instances of this kind, the courts have consistently held that there was a quasi-contract obligation to the doctor for the reasonable value of services. If the doctor was a specialist who charged more than most others, the courts would limit the recovery to reasonable value.

An automatic teller installed at the front door of a bank permitted customers to make withdrawals on the weekend. One machine of this kind malfunctioned and made $10,000 available to a customer who had used the facilities to cash a personal check for $20. The courts held that the customer had been "unjustly enriched" and must return the unrequested $10,000.

The courts frequently call the legal principle here that of "unjust enrichment." While a true contract fails to exist, the facts do not fit into any other legal category, so it is termed a quasi-contract. The courts say that a person receiving a gratuitous benefit should repay it or pay reasonable value for services, deriving from the relationship between the parties.

There are a great number of situations where the quasi-contract idea may be applied. These situations almost always involve cases in which the recipient obtains something at the plaintiff's expense, under circumstances that impose a moral duty of repayment. But the courts say that the principle of quasi-contract will not be applied in situations where the beneficiary is needlessly meddling or interfering with the defendant's affairs, trying to get the defendant obligated. In addition, the principle does not apply where a benefit is forced on the defendant or where it is clear that the defendant does not want to benefit from the circumstances. But if the defendant accepts the financial benefit, the courts sometimes say that the facts imply a fictitious promise to pay for the reasonable worth involved.

DISCUSSION

CASE 4   On his own time a dock worker invented and patented devices that would save labor costs in loading ships' cargoes. The dock worker's supervisor went to the worker's home to examine the devices and then promised the worker one-third of the savings that would result from use of the devices. The worker permitted the devices to be used, but the company did not pay. The worker (plaintiff) first filed a lawsuit seeking damages on the basis that the company supervisor had obligated the company by an express contract. The company resisted this claim on the basis that the supervisor acted beyond his authority, and that only a high company official could bind the firm. The plaintiff then amended his lawsuit, claiming that he was entitled to recovery on the quasi-contract theory of unjust enrichment. Was this claim justified? (*Matarese* v. *Moore-McCormack Lines*, 153 F.2d 631.)

CASE 5   A coal mine owner offered to mortgage the mine as security for a bank loan. The bank hesitated, but the deal was completed when the mine owner offered to include improvements, machinery, and fixtures as part of the security covered by the mortgage. The mine became unprofitable, and the bank began foreclosure. The owner contested the foreclosure by pointing out that only the mine was normally covered in an agreement of this type. To foreclose on machinery and improvements would be unduly harsh. The owner noted that the bank was already entitled to the mine, but that under the "unjust enrichment" principle the owner should be allowed to keep machinery and improvements. Was the owner's claim valid? (*Third Natl. Bank and Trust Co. of Scranton* v. *Lehigh Valley Coal Co.*, 44 A.2d 571.)

_____ QUESTIONS _____

1. Define a contract in your own terms.
2. What freedom is there to contract?
3. Describe how the courts construe the terms of a contract. Give some of the court's essential rules of construction.
4. List the essentials or requirements for every contract.
5. Describe a contract under seal (formal contract) and how it is used.
6. What are the advantages of a written contract? Why?
7. Define an express contract; an implied contract.
8. Explain the differences between a bilateral promise and a unilateral promise.
9. Give examples of a void contract. What is meant by "against public policy"?
10. Explain how a voidable contract may arise, and what can be done about it.
11. What is a quasi-contract? Give an example from real life.

_____ ANSWERS TO DISCUSSION CASES _____

CASE 1   The courts would have a never-ending task if court facilities could be used to enforce interfamily squabbles or social matters. Normally, before the courts will handle enforcement of a family agreement, there must be a financial or business angle involved. If a couple's agreement involved a property settlement in a divorce or dissolution matter, the courts would step in. Similarly, a contract involving money that was separate property of the individual spouses would likely be enforced. And, of course, if one spouse harmed the other criminally, the matter would be prosecuted in criminal (not civil) court.

CASE 2   A contract can be a combination of written and oral agreements taken together. The important thing is that there must be agreement, whether arrived at orally or in writing. It should be pointed out here that there are some instances where state law requires that contracts of certain types must be in writing. (This is under the statute of frauds.) But as a generalization, any contract may be part written and part oral.

CASE 3   The court said that where the facts show a duty of the defendant to pay, the law ordinarily imputes to the defendant an implied promise to fulfill that obligation. But the court continued that the law will never imply an obligation to do something when the law specifically prohibits an express agreement to that same effect. Stated in other terms, a court will never imply a contract obligation when the contract itself is forbidden by law. The defendant did not have to pay the commission.

CASE 4   The court agreed with the defendant that there could be no express contract binding the company unless the dock worker's supervisor had authority to bind the company. The court agreed that this authority was lacking. But the court held that even without a contract the company had enriched itself at plaintiff's expense. An award for damages was upheld on the quasi-contract theory.

CASE 5   The bank was permitted to foreclose on all the property, including fixtures, improvements, and machinery. The court said that the unjust enrichment principle . . . "is not applicable to agreements deliberately entered into by the parties, however harsh the provisions of such contracts may seem in the light of subsequent happenings."

_____ *PROBLEM CASE* _____

The operator of a threshing machine agreed to thresh all a farmer's grain at a specified price per bushel. But he found that he was not making any money and quit the job. He then endeavored to collect for the work performed, but the farmer countered with a claim for damages. Could the operator of the threshing crew collect for the work already performed on a contract basis? In the alternative, would the operator of a threshing crew be entitled to recover for work already performed on the basis of a benefit conferred on the farmer? In short, the operator of the crew was saying, "I will perform if it proves profitable, but I have no obligation to continue if it is not a money-making proposition." Who was in the right? (*Johnson* v. *Fehsefeldt*, 118 N.E. 707.)

6

The Contract Agreement: Offer, Acceptance, Counteroffer

Most contracts result from an *offer* and an *acceptance*. So our first concern is whether an offer has actually been made. In contract law, we say that an *offeror* is the person who makes the offer and an *offeree* is the person who accepts it.

A proposal to make a binding deal is an offer. Stated in other terms, an offer is a declaration of present willingness to make a contract. It is a proposal made in such a way that a reasonable individual in the position of the person receiving the offer (offeree) would believe the agreement could be concluded merely by saying, "I accept." An offer arises when someone offers to do something or pay something, or to refrain from some act, in exchange for a benefit from the other party.

The legal significance of an offer is that it creates in the offeree the power of acceptance, thereby creating a legally binding contract.

Legal Requirements for an Offer

To satisfy legal requirements, an offer must have two elements:

1. There must be a proposal, manifestation, or declaration of present contractual intent.
2. There must be certainty and definiteness of the terms that are proposed.

Expression of Intent

To constitute an offer, a proposal must go beyond an intent to talk about business, or the mere getting together for discussion. A simple invitation to negotiate or a "request to deal" is not enough. The language of any proposal must be definite. The decided cases on this point say that language like the following is not an offer to contract:

> "I'd like to get together with you on a deal."
> "I'd like to get a new. . . ."
> "Are you interested in making an agreement to. . . ."

As noted by the courts, these are just examples of talk showing a willingness to negotiate and an invitation to the addressee to make an offer.[1] There can be all kinds of discussion back and forth between the parties, but it has no real legal significance until one of them proposes a bargain with definite terms for both sides.

In a typical situation, a person may be asked whether he or she would be willing to sell a piece of property at a set price, for example, $50,000. One owner replied to this inquiry, "I wouldn't consider selling unless I received at least $60,000." In this kind of situation, the courts have usually said that the talks did not yet constitute an offer to sell at $60,000, but merely an opportunity to negotiate. The courts feel that the seller might want to set some other conditions in addition to the price, and that there has not yet been any discussion of other definite terms. In addition, it is not clear whether the price of $60,000 would be a cash price or some other kind of sale.

There are exceptions, but the courts generally hold that newspaper ads, circulars, or TV commercials are only invitations to deal, rather than offers to make a contract with the potential buyer. The court's reasoning here is that a store or another seller has directed the ad to the general public, and there is simply no way of knowing whether the seller can fill all the orders that might come in.[2]

But while ads of all kinds are normally held to be mere invitations to deal, there are times when the ad is worded in such a way that the courts will consider it an offer. For example, an ad stated:

> For sale, 40 electric blankets, double size, black, dual controls. $41.50 each, first come first served. Limit one to customer.

The courts held that this was an offer to the first forty people in line asking to buy the electric blankets.[3] If the business did not want to sell to the first forty customers in the store, the ad could have included a statement that the store retains the right to reject any and all offers.

An announcement to the general public that a reward will be paid for the return of a lost or stolen item (or the arrest, capture, and so on of a

---

[1] *Elkhorn-Hazard Coal Co.* v. *Kentucky River Corp.*, 20 F.2d 67.

[2] *Lovett* v. *Frederick Loeser and Co., Inc.*, 207 N.Y.S. 753

[3] *Lefkowitz* v. *Great Minneapolis Surplus Store, Inc.*, 86 N.W.2d 689, was another case involving the same facts. In the *Lefkowitz* case the merchandise offered for sale was a shipment of seal furs.

criminal) is normally construed by the courts as an offer for a unilateral contract. Such an offer becomes binding only when the lost or stolen item is returned.

When a merchant mails out a printed brochure listing the price of items, the courts usually regard this list as merely an offer to negotiate. It is regarded as in the class with newspaper or TV advertising. But if the brochure or communication gives the impression that it was directed to the recipient only, then the courts say that it is an offer. This is because a brochure sent to an individual recipient can only be regarded as a personal letter, and the courts generally consider it an offer.

Communication of the Offer

Normally, an individual cannot accept an offer that was directed to someone else. You may want to sell your personal coin collection to a close friend. If you make an offer by letter to this individual, it cannot be accepted by another collector who happens to see your offer on your friend's desk. If the law were otherwise, people would find that they had made contracts with individuals that they never intended to deal with. The offeror should never be forced to accept an agreement with someone he or she does not want to do business with.

So the law takes the position that an offer has not actually been made until brought directly to the attention of the offeree. Until the offer has been communicated, the offeree does not even know that an offer was even in existence and consequently cannot accept it.

Definiteness of Terms

As a matter of law, an offer must be specific enough so that a court could enforce the terms if a contract results. Consequently, the courts usually say that the terms of an offer must be definite.

When a proposal is made to sell an item that is not sufficiently identified, there can be no contract. For example, a salesperson said, "I will sell you a watch for $25." A prospective buyer accepted. But most courts would hold that a contract was not formed since there was no certainty about what was being sold.

But in another case the offeror said, "I will sell you my used car for $5,200." This was the only car that the offeror owned at the time, and the offeree knew which car was intended, having been given a trial ride in it. The courts held that the subject matter of this contract had been sufficiently identified.

In some cases it is clear that the bargaining parties want to be bound by their agreement but that the price to be paid and/or the time for performance has not been stated. The courts usually say that if the subject matter of the bargain is definite and both parties wanted to regard the agreement as binding, some deficiencies can be cured. The courts say that in such instances the parties must have intended the prevailing market price and must have intended that the contract be performed within a reasonable time. If a dispute should subsequently arise concerning price or time of performance, it would be left to a jury at the time of trial to decide what was a reasonable price and/or a reasonable time for performance.

Some other situations also are recognized by the courts as exceptions to the requirement of definiteness. For example, a supplier may agree to "furnish all the bricks that the Smith Construction Company may require for the next three years." Similarly, a supplier may agree to "furnish whatever quantity of natural gas is needed to heat the warehouse located at 210 Anderson Street, Los Angeles, California. . . ." Agreements of this type are uniformly held to be valid even though all the terms and quantities have not been determined at the time the contract is made. Agreements of this kind are sometimes called "requirement and output contracts."

Similarly, the courts uphold the legality of "cost-plus" contracts. To illustrate, a sporting goods distributor agreed to buy all of a manufacturer's output of tennis rackets, paying a figure that was the total of the manufacturer's costs plus an additional 15 percent.

Other agreements regularly upheld as contracts may specify that a professional person such as an architect or doctor supply services as needed.

The courts will almost always uphold an agreement if the price set is the "current market price at the time of delivery."

In still other cases, the court may uphold the validity of the agreement, even though no price or other specific terms were included. What happens here is that the two parties have had a history of mutual dealings in the past and they have always used a printed price list that included all necessary terms in their dealings. When it is obvious that both parties intended that the printed list supply missing details, the courts say that the offer was sufficiently definite.

―――――― *DISCUSSION* ――――――――――――――――――――

CASE 6 The parties to a business transaction settled all the important terms but one. And on this unsettled part they came to an agreement to meet at a mutually convenient time at which they would have an understanding that would be satisfactory to both. Was there a contract? (*Autry* v. *Republic Productions, Inc.*, 30 Cal.2d 144.)

CASE 7 Two parties agreed to the future sale of bulk gasoline at a figure set at 4 cents less than the market price at a specified town. Was this sufficiently definite to constitute a contract? (*Moore* v. *Shell Oil Co.*, 139 Ore. 72.)

CASE 8   The defendant, a bank, made an agreement with a corporation to supply the latter with money that would enable the corporation to carry on its business in a proper manner. This relationship was apparently not made completely definite because the company was engaged in the seasonal packing of salmon and it could not be predicted whether the salmon run would be large or small. The bank refused to stand good for some of the corporation's debts, and the corporation sued. Was a contract actually formed in which "reasonableness" would be the rule, or did the agreement fail to meet contract requirements for definiteness? (*Royal Bank of Canada* v. *Williams*, 222 N.Y.S. 425.)

CASE 9   Two parties agreed to the major, basic terms of a business arrangement, apparently intending that their understanding should be binding. However, there were still some minor points that had not been worked out. Later, one of the parties attempted to get out of the agreement, pointing out that "a contract must be good or bad at inception, and that if the terms were not settled there could be no agreement." The other party pointed out that both had intended the arrangement to be binding and that a rule of reasonableness should be followed in settling minor details. Was there a contract? (*Reich* v. *Vegex, Inc.*, 51 F.Supp. 99, affirmed in 137 F.2d 647.)

CASE 10   A firm agreed to pay an employee for the use of an invention perfected by the employee. There was no question concerning agreement to pay, but no specific amount of compensation for the employee was specified. Were the terms definite enough to form a contract on which the employee could sue for the employer's nonpayment? (*Toner* v. *Sobelman*, 86 F.Supp. 369.)

THE ACCEPTANCE

How an Acceptance Takes Place

Normally, an offer for a bilateral contract is accepted by a promise from the offeree, given in exchange for the offeror's promise.

When an offer is unilateral, the offeror will be satisfied only with completion of the act or of the forebearance requested.

But a problem arises if the offeree stops short of substantial performance. There is a difference in court decisions from state to state, but most courts hold that the offeror becomes bound when offeree begins performance and cannot withdraw so long as the offeree is making a reasonable effort to complete the required work. But the offeree has a duty to complete performance and cannot delay work unreasonably.

Form of Acceptance

Generally, the courts say an offer is deemed to invite acceptance by any communication medium that will be reasonable under the circumstances. If there is any special reason for speed, mail may not be acceptable. For example, an offer to sell in a widely fluctuating commodities market would require an almost immediate acceptance, by telephone or telegraph.

If the offeror specifies a certain type of communication, no other kind may be used. If the offeror does not state the type of communication that may be used, the courts almost uniformly hold that the acceptance may be by the same method used to send the offer.

Mental State for Acceptance

All mutual agreements arise from an offer and an acceptance by the other party. In a bilateral offer, the side receiving the offer must assent to it if a contract is to be formed. The courts say that the contract is complete at the instant when there is acceptance—"a meeting of the minds." This "objective theory" of contracts is based on the mutual assent of the parties. Confusion frequently arises here because of the misconception that the meeting of the minds is to be taken in a literal sense. This misconception is the supposition that the parties must actually and inwardly be of the same intent, in the same manner and at the same time. The courts do not expect nor require such inner agreement as necessary to the formation of a contract.

In deciding whether there has been a "meeting of the minds," the law is not concerned with what an individual actually intends in the innermost feelings. The concern is with outward or "objective manifestations," as the courts describe it. This is found in what the individual leads others reasonably to believe that he or she intends. The courts assume that no one can ever be certain of the secret thoughts of anyone. All that is necessary to the formation of a contract is a concurrence of expressed intents between the parties.

The traditional legal rule, followed by the courts, has long been that the two contracting parties are to be bound by the "plain meaning" of their words, unless the parties could show that some special meaning had arisen by custom or usage. The courts hold that any reasonable, prudent person should realize that his or her words in an agreement can only be interpreted according to the way that such words are understood by others.[4]

In recent years, however, there has been an increasing tendency for courts to permit subsequent testimony by the parties to show the real intent of the words they used in coming to agreement. The courts reason here that

---

[4] *Rowe* v. *Chesapeake Mineral Co.*, 156 F.2d 752.

language used to express thinking is not infallible, and words that seem to have "plain meaning" to a judge may have had another construction to the parties.[5] As a general proposition, however, anyone making an agreement must expect to have the offer and acceptance construed according to common understanding of the language used.

It is also to be emphasized that an acceptance must be unconditional. If the offeree expresses reservations concerning the mutuality of agreement, then there is no acceptance.

Also, the acceptance must coincide in time with the offer. Otherwise, the offer may be withdrawn before this mutual agreement can take place.

It is also essential that the acceptance be made known to the offeror. In a case of this kind, the offeree determined to accept, but did nothing whatever to indicate acceptance by word or appropriate act. The court said that a mere uncommunicated mental determination to assent (accept) cannot create any contract rights.

DISCUSSION

CASE 11   On July 18 a farmer signed a written purchase order for farm machinery specifying "immediate delivery or as soon thereafter as possible." The manufacturer's sales representative immediately telephoned the order to the factory. The farmer heard nothing from the factory, and four days later (July 22) sent a telegram stating "delivery date specified on thresher deal now past and order is hereby cancelled." The machinery had already been shipped before the farmer's telegram of cancellation had been sent. The manufacturer sued for freight costs and a specified percentage of the sale price ($1,562.50) as provided in the written purchase order. Was there a contract that gave basis to the manufacturer's lawsuit? (*Port Huron Machinery Co.* v. *Wohlers*, 221 N.W. 843.)

CASE 12   In seeking business, a company set out a choice of terms that could be used by customers desiring to make purchases. A customer accepted one such specific set of terms. Later, a dispute arose in which the company offering these alternate terms contended that there never had been a contract in the first instance. The company argued that every contract must necessarily involve a "meeting of the minds" between the parties. Continuing this argument, the company pointed out that the offeror did not know specifically what conditions the buyer (offeree) might choose; consequently there was no meeting of the minds. Was there a contract? (*Whitelaw* v. *Brady*, 121 N.E.2d 790.)

CASE 13   Defendant and plaintiff were both dealers in cattle. Defendant proposed to buy plaintiff's cattle and plaintiff accepted. Later, defendant claimed he had

[5] *Pacific Gas & Electric Co.* v. *Thomas Drayage and Rigging Co.*, 69 Cal.2d 33.

only made the offer "in a spirit of banter or fun." All the evidence indicated, however, that anyone hearing the defendant's proposal would have considered it a serious offer. What should control here, the secret intentions of the defendant, or the words that he actually uttered? (*Deitrich* v. *Sinnott*, 179 N.W. 424.)

CASE 14   The parties involved in business negotiations drew up a written contract that appeared to be lawful and proper on its face. Subsequently, however, one of the parties claimed in court that the contract should not be enforced since the other party actually had a secret, illegal motive in drawing up the contract in the first place. Will the court allow an inquiry to be made into the secret motives or intents of parties to a contract or are the courts concerned only with the obvious manifestations of the parties? Do the courts judge wholly on what the parties say and do? (*Wolcott* v. *Moser*, 262 S.W.2d 620.)

CASE 15   Plaintiff prepared two plans for construction of a building for defendant. The defendant reasonably interpreted plaintiff's written offer as referring to and incorporating the second plan rather than the first plan. Defendant expressed acceptance under the belief that he would get the second plan. Was the defendant contractually liable under the first plan? (*Field-Martin Co.* v. *Fruen Milling Co.*, 298 N.W. 574.)

Acceptance of Offers Made in Anger or Jest

An offer obviously made in jest or in anger may not be accepted by someone overhearing it to form a contract. The basic rule is that when it is apparent that there is no real intent to contract, the person making the offer may not be held to it.

For example, an automobile owner with a new battery became enraged at the vehicle when it would not start. Kicking the fender of the car viciously, the owner shouted, "I'll sell it right now for $2!" A passerby heard the purported offer and accepted on the spot. The court held that there was no contract.

Effective Time of Acceptance

When the parties are not negotiating face to face or on the telephone, it may be critical to determine when a communication from one party will legally bind the other. Subject to some exceptions, the general legal principle is that an acceptance becomes effective upon dispatch. All other communications are effective upon receipt.

For example, an offer made by mail will become a binding contract when an acceptance is placed in the mail. For many years this has been known to lawyers and courts as the "mail box rule" and has been consistently followed.[6] This principle will be discussed further when we consider termination of the offer by revocation (recall) by the offeror.

TERMINATION OF AN OFFER

Few individuals involved in business want to make an offer that could remain outstanding indefinitely. Once an offer terminates, a contract cannot be made by attempting to accept it.

Conditions That Terminate

Offers to contract may be terminated by any of the following conditions:

1. Specific rejection made by the offeree
2. Expiration of the specific terms of the offer
3. Death or insanity of either the offeror or offeree
4. Loss or termination of ownership of the specific subject matter involved
5. An intervening legal prohibition or restriction
6. Revocation (recall) by the offeror; the making of a conteroffer; or acceptance

Rejection by Offeree

A communication to the offeror to the effect that the other party does not intend to accept has the legal effect of immediately terminating the offer. Once a statement of rejection has been made to the offeror, there can be no such thing as a "revived" or "late" acceptance. The courts almost uniformly say that rejection ends the power of acceptance, even though the original offer stated that the offer would be held open until a later date. The offeree cannot, because of a change of mind, subsequently accept the offer within the deadline originally stated.[7]

When the offeree makes a statement of rejection, the offeror naturally assumes that the offeree has lost interest. Consequently, the offeror should be free to make another bargain or take other action that would not have been taken if the offeree still had the right to accept.

But the offer would continue to remain open until the stated expiration date if the original offer was an option as we will see in discussing options.

---

[6] *Adams* v. *Lindsell*, 106 Eng. Reports 250 (consistently followed by British and American courts since 1818). In some legal circles the so-called "mail box rule" is also known as the "deposited acceptance rule."

[7] *Goodwin* v. *Hidalgo County Water District*, 58 S.W.2d 1092.

Death or Insanity

The legal right to accept an offer is ended when either of the negotiating parties becomes insane or dies. Note, however, that death does not necessarily terminate a contract.

Expiration of a Specified Period

An offer to contract ends when an acceptance has not been made within the specified time period that may have been set in the offer. For example, the offeror might send a letter proposing to "sell men's hats at $18.50 each on orders mailed before October 15th." A potential buyer could not make a contract (accept) by mailing in an order after October 15th.

Where no time is stated in the offer, the courts say that the right to accept lapses after a reasonable time. Just what constitutes a reasonable time will vary with the subject matter of the offer. Factors that would be considered as to reasonableness would include the normal price fluctuations in that trade or industry, local and industry customs, and the method for communicating the acceptance (letter, telegram, or whatever). If the dispute came to a trial, the question of a reasonable time would likely be left to a jury to decide, after hearing pertinent circumstances and trade customs.

When the parties are dealing face to face or over the telephone, an offer is regarded as continuing only until the time the conversation ends. However, if it is clear that the offeror is leaving the offer open, then the offeree has a reasonable time thereafter to accept. For example, the offeror might conclude telephonic negotiations by stating, "Well, I'll give you some time to think it over. Sleep on it. I'll still be here tomorrow if you want to make a deal." In an instance of this kind, the offer would remain open at least for the next day.

Destruction or Loss of Subject Matter

Suppose you offered to sell your diamond ring but it was stolen before the potential buyer accepted. In a case of this kind the offer terminated at the time of the theft and no contract could be formed.

Intervening Legal Prohibition

Suppose a whiskey merchant made an offer to sell a truckload of whiskey, but the state legislature outlawed the sale or possession of whiskey before the offer was accepted. The courts would say that no contract had been made. The offer terminated at the time the law against sale or possession of liquor became effective in that jurisdiction.

Revocation (Recall)

A withdrawal of the offer normally terminates the offeree's power to accept. No specific style of wording is needed to constitute a revocation. Any reasonable expression that makes known the desire to terminate is sufficient. The great majority of courts interpreting contracts have said that the offeree can make a valid acceptance up to the time that notice of termination is received. A few courts hold that revocation is effective at the instant it is made by the offeror, even though the offeree may not yet be aware of the withdrawal. And a few states such as California have laws specifying that a revocation is effective at the time it is dispatched.[8]

But as pointed out, the great majority of courts hold that an offeree can still make a contract by mailing or telegraphing an acceptance without knowing that a letter or telegram of termination had already been dispatched by the offeror.

Most courts also agree that an acceptance will be governed by the law of the state where the acceptance is mailed or dispatched.[9]

───────── *DISCUSSION* ─────────────────────────────

CASE 16   An offer was made to the public at large through an advertisement in a periodical. Later, the offeror published a notice in the same periodical stating that the offer was being revoked. An individual who saw the offer was never made aware of the notice of revocation. Thereafter, the individual who had seen the publication of the offer purported to make an acceptance. Could this be done to form a contract? (*Shuey* v. *United States*, 92 U.S. 73.)

COUNTEROFFERS AND CONDITIONAL ACCEPTANCES ─────────────

Effect of a Counteroffer

A *counteroffer* by the offeree terminates the original offer in the same manner as a flat rejection of the proposal. The courts usually say that any material deviation from, or addition to, the original offer is a counteroffer. This is true, even though the original offer was silent about the matter that was added to the counteroffer. In an actual case, a homeowner made a written offer to sell a house. The offeree wrote back, "I accept your offer, but it is understood that you must install a new carved wooden door at the front entryway." Real estate brokers sometimes speak of a reply of this kind as a "qualified acceptance," or a "conditional acceptance." But legally, the courts

[8]California Civil Code, Sec. 1587.
[9]*Perry* v. *Mt. Hope Iron Co.*, 5 A. 632.

say that an answer of this kind is not an acceptance at all. It works as a termination of the original offer, replacing the offer with an entirely new offer now being made by the original offeree. The position of the parties has been reversed. In substance, the new proposal is an offer to buy the house with a newly installed wooden door at the price quoted previously by the owner (original offeror).

Sometimes the courts say that an acceptance must be a "mirror-image" of the original offer. If the acceptance varies in any way, or proposes additional conditions, it will not form a contract. The decided cases say that it is a counteroffer.[10]

_____ *DISCUSSION* _____

CASE 17   A potential buyer of real estate made an acceptance of the seller's offer, subject to court approval of the transaction. Court approval was necessary because the property being offered for sale was part of an estate being settled by an executor. Later, the real estate agreement fell through and the potential buyer sued for return of his deposit (earnest money), claiming there had never been a contract. Was there a valid contract? (*Bennett* v. *Treadway*, 134 So.2d 668.)

Acceptance That Modifies Terms

In recent years in the sale of goods or merchandise, some courts have held that a "definite and seasonable [timely] expression of acceptance" will be legally regarded as an acceptance, even though it states terms additional to or somewhat different from those in the offer. The problem is, however, that some of these courts have not clarified just what is meant by a "definite and seasonable expression of acceptance." At the same time, some of these courts state that a purported acceptance amounts to a mere counteroffer, rather than an acceptance, if it diverges from the offer on price, quality, quantity, method of payment, or delivery.

The offeror can always avoid the potential for legal disputes by clearly stating in the offer that there can be no variance from the terms of the offer.

Still another class of case is that in which the offeree expresses unconditional acceptance, followed by a wish, request, or grumbling comment. For example, the offeree in one case stated, "I accept your offer to sell me the 40 boxes of nails at $57 per box, but I do wish that you would give me a better break on the price." The court held that this was a valid acceptance. Or the offeree could make a binding contract by stating, "I accept your offer to sell me the house at the price you quoted, but I do hope that you will install a new carved wooden door before I take possession." This is nothing more

[10] *Poel* v. *Brunswick-Balke Collender Co.*, 216 N.Y. 310.

than a gratituous request for a new door and does not bind the seller to furnish one.

It is possible to make a counteroffer that does not constitute a rejection of the original offer. But in a communication of this kind, the offeree must make it clear to the offeror that the offer is still under consideration and may yet be accepted in accordance with the terms set out in the original offer.

Lost or Delayed Acceptance

As we have previously noted, most courts hold that the withdrawal of an offer (revocation) is effective only on receipt. Therefore, the offeree who is not yet aware of the revocation can make a valid acceptance, even though the revocation was made and dispatched earlier.

Most courts also hold that a lost or delayed acceptance is still a valid acceptance. The usual problem here is that it may be difficult for the offeree to prove that an acceptance was ever made if the matter is in dispute at the time of trial. The offeror can protect against a questionable acceptance by clearly stating in the offer that "we do not have a deal unless I receive an acceptance from you by ___(time)___ on ___(date)___."

Silence as Acceptance

As a generalization, the offeror can never consider silence by the offeree as an acceptance. In some cases the offeror attempts to bring about a situation of this kind by a statement in the offer to the effect that failure to reply will be construed as acceptance of the offeror's proposal. Usually, the offeree is under no obligation to reply to any business proposal. However, if the offeree requested that goods be shipped on approval, or there is a prior business arrangement or understanding between the parties, silence may be fairly construed as acceptance. These cases are exceptional, however.

A rare coin collector had an arrangement with a coin dealer to buy any old coins of a certain year and mintage that the dealer could acquire, at a predetermined price, unless advised to the contrary. When a dispute involving this arrangement was taken to court, the judge ruled that the offeree had an express duty to reject this arrangement when no longer desired. The coin collector's silence was held to be an offer to buy each coin acquired.

Avoiding Acceptance Problems

Since costs of litigating the validity of an acceptance are very expensive, many businesses are now stating terms in their offers which indicate the manner of acceptance which must be followed. For instance, one may state in the offer to contract, "The acceptance must be sent by registered mail and must be received in my office at 123 Contract Street, Los Angeles, California, by September 5, 1992, in order to validate the contract," or words to that effect. This method should avoid problems when the offeror expects to receive an acceptance in 30 days and the offeree thinks that a 60-day acceptance is reasonable. The more specific one makes the terms of the contract, the fewer problems will develop later if the validity of the contract is the subject of litigation.

――――― *DISCUSSION* ―――――――――――――――――――――

CASE 18 Defendant conducted a logging operation on a private road owned by plaintiffs (man and wife). Plaintiffs' lawyer advised defendant by letter that there was no legal agreement for use of the logging road and it would be necessary to come to an understanding if the road was to be used in the future. The letter continued: "We understand that extensive logging operations are going on at the present time and that closing this road would probably have unfortunate consequences for you . . . [P]ending a satisfactory agreement you can continue to use this road with a payment for the use thereof at the rate of twenty-five cents per thousand for all logs transported over said right of way. Until the agreement can be effected, we will expect to be provided with scale sheets by the logging company covering timber shipped over this road and a weekly settlement covering such use." The defendant received this letter but ignored it. Defendant also made no accounting or payment, but continued to make use of the road, hauling 86,289,390 board feet of timber over it. Was there a contract between the parties? (*Bakke* v. *Columbia Valley Lumber Company*, 298 P.2d 849.)

OPTION AGREEMENTS ―――――――――――――――――――――

An *option* in the law of contracts is an agreement to keep an offer open for a specified time. The courts almost uniformly hold that the offeree can always accept, up to the time of the expiration date. The courts say this is so, even though the offeree may have previously indicated a lack of interest in ever accepting.[11]

An option agreement, then, is a contract distinct from the offer to which the option relates.[12] Generally, the party that wants to keep an option open pays money or other value for this right. If it is an option to buy property, the agreement usually provides that the price paid for the option will be credited toward the purchase price of the property. If the option is not exercised, of course, the amount paid for the option cannot be recovered.

[11] *Burch* v. *Milne Truck Lines*, 199 F.Supp. 575, 578.
[12] *Warner Bros. Pictures* v. *Brodel*, 192 P.2d 949; *certiorari denied*, 335 U.S. 844, *rehearing denied*, 335 U.S. 873.

—————— *DISCUSSION* ————————————————————————

CASE 19   A party holding an option made a counteroffer during the period while the option was still outstanding. Later, after making the counteroffer, the party holding the option decided to exercise it. Was the option still in effect or had the power to accept ended when the counteroffer was made? (*Humble Oil and Refining Co.* v. *Westside Investment Corporation*, 428 S.W.2d 92.)

OFFERS AT PUBLIC AUCTIONS ————————————————————

Public auctions are governed by individual rules of contract law. Some states have special statutes that are not in accordance with auction laws in other states. Consequently, local laws should be consulted. When items are sold at auction, the courts generally construe the offer as being made by the bidder. The acceptance is made by the auctioneer through the act of dropping the hammer. Consequently, a seller can usually withdraw an article from sale at any time before the auctioneer actually recites the word "sold."

When the auction advertises that property will be for sale "without reserve," this means that the item will be sold to the highest bidder and cannot be withdrawn from sale.

Unless publicly stated prior to sale, a seller has no right to bid on his or her own property during the auction. And to have someone else bid for the owner is regarded by most courts as a form of fraud.

ETHICAL CONSIDERATIONS —————————————————————

It is important that contracts be prepared in a manner that is fair to both sides. They should be written in a language that both sides can understand.

It is important not to sign any contract that has not been completed or that leaves blank spaces. How often does one hear "just sign your name and I'll fill it out later?" Many individuals have been the victims of this unethical practice. Perhaps the individual will complete the blank spaces in a manner agreeable to both sides, but one should be able to read all terms before signing.

When individuals are involved in contract negotiations, one side may be stronger and/or more persuasive than the other. In those situations, one side may receive more favorable terms than the other. In contracts where considerable resources are at stake, one should hire an attorney to enter the negotiations and prepare the contract to avoid receiving unacceptable terms.

The situation sometimes arises where one side has knowledge not available to the other side. For instance, A may own a seemingly worthless piece of property, but B may have knowledge that that property is the site of a highway expansion. It would be unethical for B not to inform A of this fact.

However, in many cases, B may feel that it is A's responsibility to get all the information on his or her own.

As is readily apparent, there are many "gray areas" in the concept of business ethics relating to contracts. Each individual must examine his or her own conscience to determine which ethical considerations are important.

--------- *QUESTIONS* ---------

1. What are the two legal requirements for an offer?
2. Can you accept an offer that was communicated to someone else?
3. Explain what is meant by the statement that an offer must be definite.
4. What form must acceptance of a bilateral offer take? Must it be an act or a promise given in return for the promise in the offer? What form must a unilateral offer take?
5. Explain the importance of the requirement that there must be a meeting of the minds between the parties before a contract is formed.
6. What is meant by the statement that the parties to a contract are bound by their outward manifestations?
7. When an offer is made in anger or in jest, may it be accepted to form a contract? Explain your answer.
8. Explain the ways in which an offer may be brought to an end by (1) outright rejection, (2) expiration of the terms of the offer, (3) death or insanity of either offeror or offeree, (4) loss or destruction of the subject matter involved, (5) a legal prohibition or restriction, (6) and a counteroffer or an acceptance.
9. What happens when there is a lost or delayed acceptance?
10. May silence ever amount to an acceptance? Explain.
11. What is the basic difference between an option and a contract?
12. Who makes the offer and who makes the acceptance in a public auction?

--------- *ANSWERS TO DISCUSSION CASES* ---------

CASE 6   The courts say that "an agreement to agree" can never be a contract. If the basic or major requirements of the agreements are settled in advance, then the courts will almost always regard the agreement as a contract. But it is clear that the essentials, such as payment and other matters that the parties regard as vital, must be settled in advance. On the other hand, it is almost impossible to draw up an agreement that will settle every minor point that might arise in the future. But "an agreement to agree" is too nebulous, since the courts would never have any certain way of compelling the parties to come to a meeting of the minds.

CASE 7   If the material or important conditions and terms in an agreement can be fixed in relation to a definite standard, measure, or calculation, the courts almost uniformly hold that the agreement is sufficiently definite to be considered as binding. Thus, the courts said there was a contract here.

CASE 8   The court held that the agreement was "too indefinite and uncertain to make out a contract." Nor were any standards set up by which definiteness could later be determined. The court continued: "Nothing is said as to any of the essential terms of the proposed loans, namely, length of time to run, or amount of security to be given, to say nothing of the amount of the loans to be made. Who could say what funds were essential and necessary to carry out the business in a proper manner. . . ."

CASE 9   Most courts would agree that there is a contract if both parties intend to be bound and the basic terms have been worked out. Minor details that have little significance do not need to be stated in minute detail.

CASE 10 The court ruled there was a contract. Where no specific amount was given as compensation, the decided cases are to the effect that the "reasonable value" of the services was intended. The court's thought here was that "reasonable value" could be determined by a jury, based on the employer's reduced expenses, added profits, reduced number of work hours needed in production processes, and other relevant factors.

CASE 11 The parties apparently intended acceptance by an act, that of shipping the machinery. And if a promise had been wanted, it had already been given by the manufacturer's representative at the time of the signing of the order. The court noted that this was a unilateral contract and that "Words are not the only medium of expression of mutual assent. An offer may invite an acceptance to be made by merely an affirmative answer or by performing a specific act. . . . In the case of an order for goods, . . . the acceptance [is] shown by . . . the shipment of the goods."

CASE 12 The court held that there was a contract. "An offer may . . . contain a choice of terms submitted to the offeree from which he is to make a selection in his acceptance. Such an offer is necessarily indefinite but, if accepted in the way contemplated, the ultimate agreement of the parties is made definite. . . ."

CASE 13 In negotiations that precede a contract, the parties are bound by their obvious manifestations. Offers or acceptances made in jest are not considered as binding by the courts. But if an offer or acceptance appears to be serious, then the party making such a statement is bound by it.

CASE 14 The courts will almost never inquire into the secret of real intent of the parties if the contract appears to be lawful on its face. The parties are bound by their outward manifestations—by what they say and do.

CASE 15 The defendant was found to be liable under the second plan only.

CASE 16   The offeror could never expect to individually contact everyone who had read the offer in the original publication. The court said the only practical solution would be to permit revocation by publishing the notice of withdrawal in the same medium in which the offer was made. There was no contract since the offer had been revoked.

CASE 17   The court stated that there was no contract and that the buyer could back out of the agreement. The holding was that a purported acceptance, conditioned upon approval of a third party, even a court, was not an unqualified acceptance. The great majority of courts agree with this decision.

CASE 18   There was a contract, even though the defendant was silent as to acceptance. The court indicated that the defendant's acts of continuing to use the road constituted an acceptance. The court also said, "Where the offeree exercises dominion over things which are offered to him, such exercise . . . in the absence of other showing . . . is an acceptance."

CASE 19   A counteroffer normally terminates the ability to accept an offer. But an option is in a different category. An option is a contract to hold the offer open regardless, that is until the end of the option period.

_____ *PROBLEM CASES* _____

1   The following case is quite old, but this decision by the Supreme Court of the United States is still the law. Edwin M. Stanton, U.S. Secretary of War, published a newspaper reward of $25,000 for apprehension of John Surrat, an accomplice of John Wilkes Booth in the assassination of President Lincoln. After several months this same reward was declared to be canceled in the same newspapers used to make the offer. One Henry Ste. Marie subsequently furnished information to United States diplomatic officials that led to Surrat's arrest in Italy. Ste. Marie sued for the reward, pointing out that he had never been informed that the offer had been canceled. The government argued that any contract offer may be withdrawn up to the time that rights have accrued under it. Was Ste. Marie bound by a withdrawal of the offer that was never communicated to him? (*Shuey* v. *Executor*, 92 U.S. 73.)

2   A car dealer placed an ad in a newspaper, offering to sell a second-hand car for $1,795. Through error, however, the printer listed the price as $1,095. A prospective car buyer sued the dealer when the dealer refused to go through with a sale for $1,095. Did the customer have a binding contract by tendering the sum of $1,095? (*O'Keefe* v. *Calan Imports*, 202 N.E.2d 758.)

3   The owner of property signed an acceptance of an offer made by a prospective buyer. The owner furnished this acceptance to his real estate agent, but while this acceptance was still in the real estate agent's office, the owner decided to withdraw from the deal. The prospective buyer had been in-

formed of the signing of the written acceptance and he subsequently sued for breach of contract. Decide. (*Pribil* v. *Ruther*, 262 N.W.2d 460.)

4 Ryder obtained an option to buy a farm with the option to expire on September 1. In August Ryder told the owner that he was not going to exercise the option. But later in August Ryder attempted to exercise the option. Could he still do so? (*Ryder* v. *Wescoat*, 535 S.W.2d 269.)

5 An owner offered to sell her home on the installment plan or to consider a cash offer if the prospective buyer would make one. The buyer made a cash offer which was immediately rejected. The prospective buyer then advised that the installment offer was being accepted. Was this offer still valid so as to create a contract? (*Quinn* v. *Faeheny*, 233 N.W. 403.)

7

Consideration

THE NATURE OF CONSIDERATION

A basic problem in contract law is deciding what kinds of promises are legally binding. Except for an agreement under seal, a bare promise with nothing in return is usually not enforceable.

In addition to a valid offer and acceptance, the question of whether there is a binding contract frequently turns on whether there is *consideration* to the agreement. (Note: the word consideration is a technical legal expression, and not a business term.)

Legal Definitions

The courts usually define consideration as a benefit falling due to the promisor or a detriment incurred by the promisee. Consideration is the substance of what is wanted by each side to a bargain.

Other legal definitions are to the effect that consideration consists of some right, profit, interest, or benefit accruing to the one party, or a forbearance, detriment, loss, or new legal responsibility taken on or suffered by the other party. Consideration arises when the promisor gets something that he or she wants but to which he or she is not already entitled. Consideration may also spring from the promisee's agreement to perform in a way that he or she is not already bound to do.

The benefit given may also be one that falls on a third party, rather than on one of the persons making the agreement. For example, a man promised to pay $1,000 to a woman who agreed to spend two weeks as a caretaker for the man's aged mother. The man's fulfillment of his responsibility to his mother would be a sufficient benefit to constitute consideration.

As used in contract law, the terms *detriment* and *forbearance* are technical words. They mean becoming obligated to do something one is not otherwise legally required to do. Thus, an agreement to give up smoking would be a sufficient detriment or forbearance to an individual to render legally enforceable an uncle's promise to pay the smoker $3,000 on that condition. The giving up smoking for the time specified in the agreement would constitute consideration.

Consideration as the Price for a Bargain

For consideration to be recognized as valid, it must be given as the price for a bargain. Stated in other words, that which compromises consideration for a promise must be induced by that promise and given as the price for it. Consideration is the specific thing or demand that the promisor asks in return for his or her own promise or performance. However, the amount of consideration is usually not an issue.

_____ **DISCUSSION** _____

Case 20   A poultry company official signed a written employment contract in which the firm promised to hire the official for a term of five years. In this document he agreed to work for the business "when in his opinion and judgment the affairs of the aforesaid corporation require it; it is further understood and agreed that said [official] is to use his own judgment as to the time spent. . . ." After about one year the official was locked out of his office and not allowed to work. He then sued the organization for back salary on the basis that he had performed according to his best judgment. Was the corporation liable for back salary? (_Fullington_ v. _Ozark Poultry Supply Co._, 39 S.W.2d 780.)

VALIDITY OF CONSIDERATION _____

Past Consideration

Usually, the courts have held that consideration furnished prior to the time of the contract agreement is not valid consideration. The reason, of course, is that consideration is the specific price or demand that the promisor asks in return for his or her own promise of performance. How, then, can the purported consideration be the thing the promisor asks when the promisor is already in possession of that thing?

   For example, a man returned lost property to the owner without realizing that a reward had been offered. The return of the item was not motivated by the promise to reward its finder. The return was made gratuitously. Consequently, the failure of consideration will nullify a later claim by the finder that the return was consideration given to form a contract for the reward offer. Occasionally, some courts say that when benefits are conferred under circumstances that create a moral obligation, a subsequent promise to pay for the benefit may be upheld as a valid contract. These cases, however, are exceptional, and some are based on a quasi-contract theory of recovery.

Adequacy of Consideration

When an outside third party examines the terms of a contract made by others, it frequently seems that one party received far more in the bargain than the other. But it should be understood that consideration is not a guarantee of an exchange of values. The courts frequently say that they will not weigh the comparative worth of things received by each side in judging whether a contract is enforceable.[1]

Value is frequently in the eyes of the party striking a bargain. A jeweler wanting to match the size and color of a gemstone with other jewels might pay more than the going price in order to complete the set. Consequently, the courts will not, as a general rule, question the adequacy of consideration if it is found to satisfy other technical legal requirements. As one court ruled:

> Where a party contracts for a performance of an act which will afford pleasure, gratify ambition, please the fancy, or express appreciation, that party's estimate of value should be left undisturbed, unless there is evidence of fraud.[2]

DISCUSSION

Case 21   A husband and wife both signed a property division contract as part of a divorce settlement. Later, the wife went into court to contest this property division, arguing that "it was unfair . . . because of the meagerness of the allowance when contrasted with the great wealth of [the husband]." The wife's attorneys pointed out that there was an "inadequacy of consideration" because the wife was to receive only a small fraction of the husband's considerable wealth. Would the court set the agreement aside on the basis of inadequacy of consideration? (*Matthews* v. *Matthews*, 148 S.W.2d 3.)

Fraud

Although a contract where the consideration is much greater on one side than the other may be considered to be valid, an individual who suffered damages because of the deceit of the other party may have an action for fraud. In order to establish a case in fraud, one must be able to prove:

1. False statement of fact,

---

[1] *Batsakis* v. *Batsakis*, 226 S.W.2d 673.
[2] *Wolford* v. *Peters*, 85 Ind. 294.

2. Knowledge on the part of the person stating the information as "fact,"
3. Intent to deceive or to negligently mislead the "victim,"
4. Intent to have the victim rely on the misinformation and knowledge that the victim actually relied on it justifiably, and
5. Actual damages suffered by the victim.

Thus, if one is deceived into thinking that a ring is a diamond and subsequently learns that it is glass, there may be a case by the purchaser against the seller for fraud. The court will also look at the reasonableness of the reliance; that is, was the victim justified in relying on the statement of the seller? In some cases, the courts will distinguish "fact" from "puffing," where the seller exaggerates the quality of the goods to induce the purchaser to buy the merchandise but is merely stating an opinion and not a fact. For instance, an automobile salesperson states that "this car is the best car on the road." This magnification will usually be interpreted by the courts as mere "puffing" and not a factual statement which gives rise to a suit for fraud.

Illusory Promises

For a promise to constitute consideration, it must actually promise something without being illusory. For example, one party proposes: "I will sell you all the fireplace wood you may order from me at $125 per cord." The other party replies, "I agree to your offer." The courts say that an agreement of this kind is illusory. The potential buyer is not obligated to order any wood at all and has not promised to make even one purchase. In short, one party to the agreement is not bound in any way. The courts usually rule that when one party is not legally bound, neither should the other party be. Consequently, there is no contract because of an absence of consideration.

The courts hold it to be a different case, however, when the wood buyer agrees to "take all the firewood to fill my normal winter needs at $125 per cord." While the quantity is somewhat uncertain by the terms of the agreement, the courts judge that it could be readily ascertained. The buyer is therefore committed by contract to take the normal number of cords of wood he or she ordinarily uses.

An agreement to buy a certain item "if I want to" is illusory and does not form a contract of purchase. The party making such a promise has actually offered nothing, since he or she has a free way out by merely deciding not to go through with the purchase. Following similar reasoning, the courts hold that a right to terminate an agreement at will does not constitute the necessary requirement of consideration and it is not a valid contract.[3] However, a somewhat similar agreement with the right to cancel

---

[3]*Miami Coca-Cola Bottling Company* v. *Orange Crush Co.*, 296 F.2d 693.

on 90 days notice would constitute good consideration. The difference here is that neither side could get out of the agreement for at least 90 days.

An agreement between the parties to agree on something in the future is also regarded by the courts as too indefinite to make a contract. The parties might meet indefinitely without ever coming to agreement.

Recitals of Consideration

The wording in forms used for deeds and some other contracts has changed little in certain states since colonial times. For example, the introductory part of a deed form may read:

> For and in consideration of one dollar, cash in hand paid, receipt of which is hereby acknowledged, do, hereby bargain, sell, release, and forever quitclaim unto the said _____ , heirs and assigns, all _____ right, title, and interest to that certain tract or parcel of land, lying in _____ county, state of _____ , described as follows. . . .

Legally, the language of this deed form is called a "recital of consideration." Actually, it is seldom that the one dollar mentioned changes hands, regardless of the recital. The general rule of law followed by the courts is that a mere recital of consideration may be disputed by a party defending against a legal action to enforce the contract. If consideration of this kind is disputed, the contract may be set aside by the courts unless there is proof that there was more consideration than the mere recitation of the document. Of course, if one dollar was the bargained-for price of the agreement, then the contract will normally be upheld as valid.

If the consideration given is so small that it is far out of proportion to the worth of the property or performance given by the other side, then that disparity in value may be regarded as evidence of fraud. For example, a man sold a home valued at $200,000 to his daughter for $2,000 cash. If there was reason to believe that the seller was trying to put this $200,000 house beyond the reach of creditors who might sue him, then the obvious inequality of consideration could be regarded as evidence of fraud. Under circumstances of this kind, a court would likely set aside the contract of sale of the $200,000 house for $2,000.

CONSIDERATION IN REVISION OF CONTRACT _____

Promising an Already Promised Act

Sometimes an individual will refuse to complete a contract on the basis that performance is more difficult than anticipated. The promisee may then demand additional money to complete the work. At this point the other party to the agreement can sue for breach of contract or work out a new agreement to pay additional money. In one case of this kind, an excavator signed a contract with a general contractor to remove dirt for the basement of a large office building. Approximately half of the soil removal had been completed when the excavator quit work, claiming that he should have quoted the price at a figure $10,000 above the contract price. The general contractor had a pressing deadline for completion of the entire job. Unable to locate another available excavator, the contractor agreed to pay an additional $10,000 to have work continued. When the earth removal was completed, the general contractor paid the excavator only the amount due under the original agreement. The excavator sued for the additional $10,000.

When the lawsuit came to trial, the court held that there was no enforceable contract since there was no consideration to support the promise of the additional $10,000. The court said that when a party merely does that which he or she was already bound to do, additional compensation cannot be demanded. In the opinion it was also noted that the excavator had taken advantage of the general contractor's need to have the work done quickly. The promisor (general contractor) was already entitled to the performance of the promisee (excavator), and it would be against public policy to make him pay for it a second time. The court added that the law should not lend its processes to aid the wrong.

This decision represents a general principle of contract law: If the act promised is one that the promisee is already legally obligated to perform, the doing of it is not sufficient consideration to support a demand for additional money.

In a somewhat similar case, a rookie football player signed a professional contract to play three years for $80,000 per year. During the first year the player performed sensationally. His agent informed owners of the ball club that the player would "sit out" the next two years unless his salary was increased to $750,000 per year. This threat, however, turned out to be only a bluff, since a conference with an attorney convinced the player that he could not collect on a promise for additional salary. Mindful of the real worth of the player, however, the owners of the club agreed to pay an additional $200,000 per year if the player would handle four off-season speaking engagements for the club. The attorneys for both sides agreed that this additional obligation would constitute consideration for the additional payments to the player.

The courts also say that if a promised performance falls within the scope of the duties of a public official, then neither the official's promise nor performance will be regarded as consideration. For example, an individual promised to pay a policeman $500 for arresting a man wanted for murder of the promisor's brother. The policeman made the arrest and sued for the promised $500. The court ruled that the policeman was required to make the arrest in performance of his sworn duties. In effect, the court held that there was no contract because of lack consideration to support the promise of $500. Other court decisions carry this principle even farther, holding that there is a lack of consideration if the requested action is within the general scope of the official's duties, even though that particular act may not be required.

The courts also have determined that a contract may not be made to reward a private individual for performing public duties required by law. For example, every individual is required as a matter of law to testify to the truth in every court proceeding. A witness in a damage suit was somewhat reluctant to come forward and testify to what he had seen, even after being placed under subpoena. Needing the witness to make out his case, the plaintiff offered him $1,000 to testify to what had been seen and heard. The witness testified and filed a breach of contract suit when the promisor refused to pay the $1,000. The court held that every individual is already obligated to testify to the truth and the witness had therefore given the promisor nothing. The court added that there was no contract to pay $1,000 since there was no consideration.

Most courts profess to follow the general rule that a promise to complete that which the promisee is already legally obligated to do will not be sufficient for consideration. But not all courts have followed this principle. Some judges have reasoned that the surrender of a person's right to break a contract is sufficient consideration for the promise of additional payment. Other judges have noted the fallacy of this argument, in that no one has a *right* to break a contract, although everyone has the *power* to break it because of imperfections in the machinery of the legal system.

A few additional courts recognize the new agreement as a valid contract, reasoning that it is a rescission, mutual revision, or replacement of the old agreement.

As previously noted, most courts profess to follow the basic rule of law on consideration here. At the same time, however, if the courts can make out any new promise, they seem ready to regard it as a valid new contract. Any action different from that which one is already obligated to perform is generally held sufficient to constitute performance, even though the promised performance may not differ greatly from the obligation that already existed.

Then, too, the courts usually find that a second promise to perform may be sufficient for consideration if the party making the promise is already under a preexisting obligation to someone other than the promisee.

Most states make an exception of a modification of a contract for the sale of goods or merchandise, upholding the new agreement even though there is no new consideration. This holding is in keeping with long-settled practices in trade and industry that have been incorporated as an exception into the main body of contract law.[4]

---

[4]Uniform Commercial Code (UCC), Sec. 2-209(1), which is followed in most states. Under provisions of the UCC, it is immaterial whether this new agreement is oral or written.

Unanticipated Circumstances Rule

In a number of states recently the basic consideration principle has been modified somewhat under a new series of court decisions that follow the "unanticipated circumstances" rule. To illustrate, a party that was obligated to do some excavating for a building encountered hard rock strata in an unexpected location. Meeting with the other party to the contract, a general contractor, the excavator pointed out the unanticipated difficulties and the low pay figure in the excavation contract. The sympathetic general contractor agreed to pay an additional $3,000 and the excavator agreed to complete the work. Under altered circumstances, some courts hold that the second promise to perform is supported by consideration.

It should be pointed out, however, that the unexpected circumstances did not give the excavator a defense for failure to perform under the original contract. If the general contractor had held the excavator to the original terms and had not made a new promise, the excavator would have been obliged to perform or pay damages. Most courts agree that the promisee is under no obligation whatever to promise additional payment. But an increasing number of courts are following the "unanticipated circumstances" rule, holding for the promisor if more money is promised when unexpected difficulties arise.

In another case, the promisor agreed to finish a job a week earlier than scheduled on the promisee's agreement to pay an additional $5,000. The courts consistently hold that a promise of this kind is valid consideration for the promise of additional payment.

Contract Revision in Writing

Statutes in a few states provide that any existing contract may be revised or modified by a new agreement in writing, even though no new consideration is promised or given.[5]

Nonpayment of Pledged Donations

Sometimes individuals sign a pledge or agreement to pay a specified sum to a charity fund, religious subscription, or building pledge. These statements are in fact donations or gifts, and there is no consideration involved in the usual contract law concept. But the majority of courts feel that such agreements should be sustained, since they are for a public or charitable purpose. In upholding the validity of these subscription agreements, the courts sometimes say that the promise of one subscriber is supported by the promises of fellow subscribers. In effect, the courts seem to be excepting such agreements from the requirement of consideration.

[5]California Civil Code, Sec. 1697.

Failure of Consideration for a Check or Promissory Note

If a check or promissory note is given to someone who fails to give consideration in return, that fact may be used as a defense against payment of the check or note. But if the commercial paper passes into the hands of someone else in the course of a normal business transaction, the failure of consideration may not be used as a way of avoiding payment.

Discharge of Liquidated Debt or Claim

When the amount of a debt has been fixed, or can be computed, it is called a *liquidated debt* or *liquidated claim*. A contract between a debtor and a creditor to settle for a lesser amount than originally owed is regarded as invalid by courts in most states for lack of consideration. The courts say it is generally against public policy to encourage compromise or forfeiture.

Under this principle, a debtor who mails a check for less than the total amount of the debt will still be liable for the balance. This is true, even though the check carries the notation "paid in full." Disregarding this notation, the creditor may regard the check as part payment only.

But if the terms of the debt are altered by a new agreement, the courts will consider the second arrangement as a valid contract. This means that a promise to pay the debt on a date before it was originally due would constitute valid consideration for payment of a lesser amount. In similar fashion, a contract arrangement to substitute a secured promissory note for a lesser sum than the face amount of an unsecured debt would also be valid. The security for the promissory note here would generally be a mortgage or deed of trust on real estate. The courts say that this new security would give the creditor better security than that of an open account (unsecured debt).[6]

Discharge of Unliquidated Debt or Claim

An *unliquidated debt* is one that is not yet ascertained in amount. Mere computation or application of bookkeeping standards would still leave the amount unsettled.

When the amount of a claim is unliquidated or is disputed, a compromise amount agreed to by the parties is regarded by the courts as a contract to discharge the debt in full.

Sometimes a debtor will tender a check marked "paid in full" in satisfaction of the debt. A business employee should be wary of accepting such a check, since cashing it will discharge the full amount of the debt that is unliquidated. In an honest dispute over whether one party has a valid claim, payment of a lesser amount than that demanded by the debtor will also amount to a discharge in full.

[6]*Jaffrary* v. *Davis*, 124 N.Y. 164.

Composition of Creditors

A *composition* is a compromise between a debtor and several creditors in which the creditors agree to take less than the whole amount owed as payment in full. Usually, the debtor is insolvent or embarrassed and the creditors agree that each will take a pro rata lesser amount for the sake of a more prompt payment. In most instances, a composition brings together all or a considerable part of the creditors of a single debtor. An agreement of this kind is often useful in helping creditors recover a substantial part of the money that is due before a debtor's funds are dissipated.

In a typical example, a debtor owed money to parties A, B, C, D, and E. The debtor signed a contract with these creditors to turn all of his assets over to them, consisting of enough money and property to satisfy about 50 percent of what was owed. The creditors agreed to accept these assets on a proportioned basis. Each creditor individually agreed to release the debtor from his debts. But after receiving the 50 percent satisfaction, creditor A brought a lawsuit for the balance of the debt that was not paid.

The courts almost universally hold that a compromise of a claim in a *composition of creditors* is adequate consideration to uphold the compromise agreement.

FOREBEARANCE AND PROMISSORY ESTOPPEL

Forebearance to Act

As pointed out in the definition of consideration, forebearance to act will comprise that detriment or loss needed to constitute consideration. In a typical situation, one individual may feel that he or she has a legitimate claim against another. If the injured party agrees to withhold filing a lawsuit in exchange for a cash payment, the courts will recognize the agreement as a valid contract. This kind of situation is typical of a personal injury claim filed against an automobile insurance company. The party withholding the lawsuit must feel that he or she has a legitimate claim, but the supposed claim need not actually be either valid or collectable.

Promissory Estoppel

Promissory estoppel is the legal principle that someone who makes a promise and expects another to do something in reliance on that promise cannot later renege on the promise and expect that the contract will not be binding. This principle is an exception to the requirement that there be proper consideration before a promise is binding. The courts say that when a person relies on a promise to his or her own detriment, or acts on that promise, the promisor is barred from claiming the lack of consideration in order to avoid the contract. The courts say that the promise should be binding when the promisor should reasonably expect to induce, and does in fact induce, action or forebearance of a substantial nature by the other party. Simple justice requires that the agreement be regarded as a binding one.[7]

To illustrate, the owner of a business asked a consultant to fly to Mexico City to determine the suitability of a local business as an acquisition. While the consultant was en route to Mexico, the businessman decided he no longer had any interest in obtaining the property in Mexico. Under the promissory estoppel principle, the businessman would be liable for the consultant's expenses and time both to and from Mexico City.

ETHICAL CONSIDERATIONS

The area of consideration leaves a considerable amount of room for unethical practices. Perhaps one side knows something about the item unknown to the other side. One side may have better bargaining power. Sometimes, although fraud cannot be proven, the methods used for determining consideration may not be ethical.

Often the merchant or seller may have knowledge of the item being sold which is not known to the buyer. Perhaps what looks like "the best car on the road" actually has many parts that do not operate properly.

Some states have disclosure laws in certain areas to protect consumers. Some sellers offer warranties on their products. However, one should read the warranties carefully to fully understand their terms.

Some states now have "lemon laws" dealing with the purchase of new automobiles. If the same part of the automobile has been repaired a certain number of times in a given period, then the individual may be able to get a new car. However, violation of these laws is often difficult to prove and enforce.

The basic concept of ethics concerns dealing with others fairly. In determining consideration on any contract, both sides should be aware of all pertinent facts. Both sides should have equal bargaining power.

Reducing a contract to writing, even when it is not required to satisfy the Statute of Frauds, helps to alleviate problems in interpretation later. Sometimes one side understands the terms differently from the other side. In a court of law, it is often difficult to prove contractual terms which are not in writing.

QUESTIONS

1. Explain how consideration is regarded as the price for a binding bargain.
2. Do the courts usually regard prior consideration as valid? Why?

[7]*New Eureka Amusement Co.* v. *Rosinsky,* 191 A. 412.

3. When do the courts inquire into the adequacy of consideration?

4. Explain why it is said that an illusory promise does not furnish consideration for a contract.

5. When a promisee agrees to complete an act that he or she is already obligated to do, is there consideration? Expand on your answer.

6. What is meant by the unanticipated circumstances rule?

7. If a contract is revised in writing and no new consideration given, is there a lack of consideration?

8. What is meant by a liquidated debt? An unliquidated debt? Is a promise to pay less than originally owed sufficient consideration for a liquidated debt? For an unliquidated debt?

9. Explain the workings of a composition of creditors.

10. Is a forebearance to act a sufficient detriment to constitute consideration?

11. Under what circumstances may one sue for fraud?

12. Define the principle of promissory estoppel.

ANSWERS TO DISCUSSION CASES

CASE 20 The court held that the agreement lacked consideration, adding that agreements "which depend for performance on wish, will, or pleasure of one of the parties . . . cannot be enforced. [The company official (plaintiff) was] not bound to perform at all."

CASE 21 The opinion pointed out that there was no suggestion of fraud, that the agreement was voluntarily entered into, and that "courts are not at liberty to annul or change or amend a contract entered into by and between parties capable of contracting simply upon the ground that the judges may be of the opinion that a better agreement would or should have been arrived at."

PROBLEM CASES

1 An employment agency sent Seides out on a job interview after stating that the employment fee would be paid by the prospective employer. Seides took the job. His employer then refused to pay more than half of the employment fee. Seides promised the agency to pay the remainder of the fee. Seides then had a change of mind and did not pay. Could he be held to his promise? (*Arrow Employment* v. *Seides*, 311 N.Y.S.2d 182.)

2 Hayes offered Hunter a job as a flag woman on a construction project. But after having told her to quit her job at the telephone company, Hayes refused to give her the construction work. Unable to get a job for two months, Hunter sued Hayes for lost wages. Was Hayes's promise supported by consideration? (*Hunter* v. *Hayes*, 533 P.2d 952.)

3   A firm operated lunch truck routes serviced by drivers on written contracts. Cohan was hired as a route driver, signing an agreement to work for five years. He was supplied a uniform, a truck, and prepared foods. In the hiring agreement Cohan agreed not to compete with the company by soliciting business from stops in his assigned territory for 18 months after his termination of employment. After only two months Cohan quit and accepted employment with a competing firm. His first employer sought an injunction to prevent Cohan from selling or handling stops along his former route. Would such an injunction be issued? (*Cater Cart Corp.* v. *Cohan*, 231 N.Y.S.2d 192.)

4   A husband's will left property to his wife that was worth more than she was entitled to as the holder of community property. The will provided that she would receive the more valuable property, however, only if she was willing to sign a waiver of her right to the community property. Through oversight or neglect, the wife's attorney failed to have her sign and file the waiver that was requested in the will. When the will came up for probate, the court refused to allow her to receive any more than her community property share. Her attorney then signed an agreement promising to pay the widow the difference between the community property and the amount she would have received by will, if the probate court ruling was upheld on appeal. After the probate court decision was upheld, the widow's attorney refused to keep his agreement, claiming there was no consideration for his promise. Decide. (*Frasier* v. *Carter*, 437 P.2d 32.)

8

Capacity to Contract; Illegal Contracts; Mistake

LEGAL CAPACITY TO CONTRACT

The term *legal capacity* refers to the status or attributes necessary for a person to have his or her acts legally allowed and recognized. Every individual is presumed to have legal capacity to make a contract until the contrary is proved. But all states have laws that place restrictions on the capacity of persons in some classes, while still other classes may be permitted only limited capacity to perform certain legal acts. Among the classes who may not have legal capacity to contract are minors, insane persons, convicts, persons who are intoxicated or on drugs, or aliens.

Contractual Capacity of Minors

The term *minority*, sometimes used synonymously with the legal term *infancy*, denotes a person who has not yet become "of age." The legal age of *majority*, or *adulthood*, in most states is 18. However, some states still use 21 as the age of majority.

The courts frequently point out that comparatively few minors have been exposed to many worldly affairs. Out of concern for this lack of experience, the courts put up some special protections around those who have not yet become of age. The law seeks to equalize the bargaining relationship so that the normal legal consequences are not placed on the contracts of minors.

For a great many years the courts in the United States and England have consistently ruled that a minor may disaffirm a contract (refuse to accept legal responsibility), while retaining the right in most circumstances to enforce the contract against an adult. This legal disaffirmance is called *voiding* a contract. Legally, a minor's contract remains valid until disaffirmed. Normally, this disaffirmance must take place when the minor becomes of age or within a reasonable time thereafter. The courts consistently say that a minor should be responsible for his or her acts by the time majority is reached.

Therefore, if a contract is not disaffirmed by that time, it should remain in force.

In this connection, it should be pointed out that some purported contracts are void and therefore of no legal significance even from the outset. This would be the case in the event of a purported contract to kill some individual or to rob a bank. *Void* contracts are to be distinguished from *voidable* contracts, which remain valid until a disaffirmance takes place.

In choosing to disaffirm a contract made when under age, all that is usually required is for the minor to inform the adult that the contract will no longer be regarded as valid. Of course, most courts say that the minor cannot disaffirm the contract on the one hand while continuing at the same time to retain its benefits or proceeds. Usually, court decisions require the minor to return whatever was received, while at the same time obtaining a return of money or items that were paid or furnished by the minor.

In most states, a contract between two minors is voidable at the desire of either. However, a majority of the states will hold a minor liable for all contracts for "necessities," such as food, clothing, and shelter.

In most instances the minor's privilege of escaping responsibility for a contract is absolute. This means that the minor is protected, even though the minor lied about his or her age at the time the contract was made. In recent years, however, an increasing number of states have passed laws preventing a minor from voiding a contract if the minor falsely claimed to be of age.

Individuals in business should realize that there is risk in making a contract with a minor or someone who is suspected of not being a legal adult. The privilege in favor of the minor is recognized by the courts even though it can be proved that the minor is completely experienced and worldly, and has the good judgment to make business decisions.

A minor may take advantage of the privilege of voiding a contract in two ways, depending on whether the contract is *executory* (to be performed in the future) or is already *executed*. If the agreement is still executory when the minor becomes of age, the minor is not legally responsible unless he or she thereafter does something to ratify the agreement. If the contract has already been executed, it remains in force until disaffirmed at the time the minor becomes of age. As noted, most courts permit this disaffirmance to be made within a reasonable time after coming of age. A number of states have laws that place a statutory limit of two years after adulthood on disaffirmance, so that the minor can thereafter take no action to void the contract. In those states where a statutory limit on disaffirmance is not set, the courts say that a reasonable time for disaffirmance will vary from case to case, depending on all the circumstances.

A number of state courts hold that a minor cannot disaffirm unless all money or benefits received by the minor are returned to the other party. Perhaps the majority of courts, however, take a more realistic view of the minor's position at that time. All too often, the minor has lost or foolishly used up the proceeds or property obtained under the contract. Consequently, as a condition of disaffirmance, a return is required of only that property or money which is still in the minor's control or possession.

The rule followed by most courts was stated in a very old case:

> The right to rescind (disaffirm) is a legal right established for the protection of the infant, and to make it dependent upon performing an impossibility, which impossibility has resulted from acts which the law presumes him [or her] incapable of performing, would tend to impair the right and the protection.[1]

It should be pointed out, however, that as a matter of law some of the contracts that may be made by a minor are not voidable. For example, the parents of a young minor were caught in an earthquake area in Europe, leaving the minor at home without funds during their unanticipated absence. Of necessity, the minor went to a grocer and clothing store and obtained groceries and winter clothes on credit. Practically all states require that a minor's contract for necessities must be honored. If the law did not place this burden on the minor and the minor's family, businesses and adults would likely be reluctant to furnish needed items.

Most courts say that this legal obligation to pay contracts for necessities is actually a quasi-contract right. This means that the supplier can recover in a lawsuit only the reasonable value of the necessities furnished, rather than a higher contract price that may have actually been agreed upon.

Then, too, there are no hard and fast rules in the courts as to what constitutes a necessity. Usually, the decided cases hold that the term necessities does not include frills. Rather, the courts usually say that necessities include such food, clothing, and shelter as are necessary to subsistence, health, education, and well-being, considering the contracting minor's condition, age, and station in life.

In addition, most states have some other laws that restrict a minor's right to void contracts. Most jurisdictions do not permit a minor to disaffirm any contract made after marriage, regardless of the minor's age. A few states have laws that provide that all agreements of "emancipated minors" must be honored. By *emancipated*, these laws usually refer to any minor who has been permitted by the parents to make his or her way in the world and live as an adult. Emancipation generally applies to any minor who spends wages as desired, earns his or her own living, and maintains responsibility for a separate residence from the parents.

Since a minor will often not be able to obtain a college education without signing an agreement to subsequently pay tuition and other college charges, many states have laws providing that a minor's contract with a college or

---

[1]*Green* v. *Green*, 69 N.Y. 553.

university cannot be disaffirmed. Life insurance contracts entered into by minors are also binding by statute in many jurisdictions. So, too, is a contract for a military enlistment.

Capacity of Insane Persons

The courts quite consistently hold that those individuals who are "bereft of reason and understanding" are incapable of making a contract. The test usually used by the courts here is whether the party in question lacks reasonable understanding of the effect, purpose, or nature of the transaction. In practically all courts, the agreements and supposed contracts of persons known to have been judicially declared insane are held to be absolutely void at the outset, not merely voidable. In most instances, the legal guardian of an insane person will have no difficulty in having a court void a contract that was believed valid by the other party. Some courts hold an insane person's contracts to be valid if the other party was not aware of that person's real status. However, the courts that follow this decision require that the contract be examined to determine whether the terms seem to take advantage of the insane person. If it appears that the insane person did not make a reasonable bargain, then the contract will be set aside.

A contract made by an insane individual may be voided within a reasonable time after sanity has been restored. However, a contract knowingly made with an insane person is never voidable at the option of the other party.

A mere showing of emotional or psychological problems on the part of an individual making a contract is almost never regarded by the courts as sufficient to constitute insanity.

Contracts Made While Drunk or Under the Influence of Drugs

A contract is voidable by a party who was so drunk as to not understand the nature or terms of the agreement being made. The capacity of an individual to contract and the validity of the agreement are not affected if the drinking person was able to understand the specifics of the agreement. The fact that the terms of the contract showed bad judgment, or would not have been made if sober, is regarded by the courts as of no legal consequence. However, if it can be proved that one party induced the drunkenness deliberately, intending to take advantage of the drinking person, then the agreement may be disaffirmed.

Once sober, one has the legal right to rescind a binding agreement made while in a drunken state. If there is any unusual delay in taking action to disaffirm, the courts will hold that the person has been barred from claiming this right.

Similarly, a person in a drugged state is under a temporary legal incapacity to contract. The courts say that each case must be judged on the individual facts. As in intoxication, the legal test of incapacity is whether the person under the influence of drugs understood the purpose, nature, and effect of the agreement. But even if the necessary contractual capacity did not exist for the person in a drugged state, that individual is still liable in quasi-contract for reasonable benefits furnished at the request of such individual.[2]

Contracts by Convicts

So-called "civil death" statutes have been adopted in about one-fourth of the states in this country. Under these laws, a penitentiary convict is regarded as having no contractual capacity for any purpose. These civil death statutes have been held unconstitutional in some states while being upheld by the courts in others. Still some other states allow a convict to make contracts for the valid transfer of real estate or other property owned by the convict. In still other jurisdictions, no contractual limitations of any kind are imposed on convicts.[3]

Contracts by Aliens

Generally, the courts recognize that an alien has a free right to contract under most circumstances. Legally, a citizen of any country with which the United States is at war is termed an "enemy alien," even though that person may have done nothing to harm the United States. Generally, the courts or the President suspend the rights of an enemy alien to contract on the outbreak of war. Usually, too, an enemy alien is denied the right to sue on an existing contract or to make a new legal agreement.

ILLEGAL CONTRACTS

Court Enforcement Where Illegality Exists

The courts usually resolve doubts in favor of the legality of a contract. But when either the consideration or the purpose of the agreement is illegal, the courts will generally regard the contract itself as illegal. Consequently, a contract to engage in any activity specifically forbidden by law is illegal and unenforceable. This result sometimes means that one wrongdoer may benefit at the expense of another, since the courts will not extend their help to one who has committed wrong. For example, an agreement to receive money for burning down the house of another person would clearly not be enforceable.

    If a contract can be broken down into parts, the courts will usually

[2]*Backus* v. *Sessions*, 17 Cal.2d 380.
[3]*Delmore* v. *Pierce Freight Lines*, 353 F.Supp. 258.

enforce the legal part. However, such a contract will be separated only if the agreement calls for performance in different areas and consideration can be spelled out for both the legal and illegal parts.

An otherwise valid agreement is not illegal merely because its performance will indirectly bring about an illegal result, provided the illegal act is not a *serious crime* or a violation of great *moral turpitude*, by which the courts mean the kind of conduct that is involved in a felony such as murder, arson, armed robbery, assault and battery, or some other crime of considerable moral gravity. To illustrate, a student agreed to rent the car of another student intending to meet a date about 100 miles away. Both knew that the party renting the car would likely violate speeding laws, since the driver intended to arrive in little over an hour. The individual renting the car subsequently refused to pay, claiming that the object of the contract was illegal from the start. Most courts would enforce the contract without any hesitancy, pointing out that the real purpose of the agreement was to obtain transportation, a legal objective. The speeding was incidental and did not constitute a crime of great moral turpitude.

Where both parties are equally culpable in a bargain for an illegal objective, the courts will seldom come to the aid of either. In decisions on this point, the courts usually say they will not be concerned with the relative guilt of the parties. The public's stake in outlawing illegal bargains overshadows possible considerations of injustice between those who planned to break the law.

Most courts do, however, make an exception of the case where one party backs out of an illegal contract and asks return of the consideration before any real harm is done. In an instance of this kind, the party withdrawing from the illegal agreement may be able to recover the value of what was given in performance, based on a quasi-contract theory of recovery.[4]

If the contract agreement merely violates some regulation or requirement that has nothing to do with a serious crime, the agreement will generally be upheld. In some states, statutes provide that a person may work on certain jobs for no more than eight hours a day. This, of course, is a measure designed to maintain the health and well-being of workers. A woman who was regularly employed eight hours per day took a second job on a temporary basis, working two additional hours each day. After two weeks, the second employer refused to pay the worker, claiming that the contract was illegal. The courts consistently hold that such a second contract should not be set aside for illegality.[5]

Agreements Against Public Policy

At times the courts say an agreement is illegal, being "against public policy." This includes any activity that may harm public safety, health, morals, or

[4]*Wasserman* v. *Sloss*, 117 Cal. 425.
[5]*Vick* v. *Patterson*, 158 Cal. App. 2d 414.

general welfare. The term "against public policy" sometimes varies in meaning from case to case. A fire inspector stated that a citation would be issued for failing to repair a defective fire escape. On the promise of $50 from the property owner, the inspector agreed to ignore the violation. The courts consistently hold that an agreement of this kind is unenforceable because it is "against public policy."

_____ *DISCUSSION* _____

CASE 22   The plaintiff filed suit in a New York State court to recover a gambling debt won in Louisiana. Gambling was at that time legal in Louisiana and illegal in New York State. Would the New York State court enforce a contract of this nature? (*Nielsen* v. *Donnelly*, 181 N.Y.S. 509.)

CASE 23   Two parties made an agreement to produce liquor in Canada for illegal importation into the United States. Subsequently the United States law was changed and importation of liquor was no longer illegal. Did this change make the contract legal in the United States? (*Rutkin* v. *Reinfeld*, 229 F.2d 214.)

Agreements by Unlicensed Individuals

All states have licensing laws requiring registration by those who engage in certain professions, trades, and businesses—contractors, architects, barbers, doctors, stockbrokers, pawnbrokers, and so on. The legality of an agreement made by an unlicensed individual will depend on the purpose behind the licensing law. If it was set up to protect the general public against poorly trained and unqualified technicians and professional people such as contractors and doctors, then the contract is illegal.

Another class of licensing requirement is designed to bring about fiscal control and raise money. For example, many cities require every business to obtain a license in order to open its doors to the public. Such a license will be issued without any test of the applicant's competency. The contract of an individual or business that has failed to obtain such a regulatory license is still legal in doing business.

On the other hand, a contract made by a general contractor or by a doctor would be illegal if a proper professional license was not obtained. This would mean that the contractor or doctor could be sued on a contract with another party. However, either of these unlicensed individuals would be denied recovery for their services by the courts. If the lack of a license involves only a technicality, such as a late renewal that is being processed, the courts will usually not allow this failure to avoid the payment of contract obligations.

Contracts in Restraint of Trade

In general, contracts that are in restraint of trade are illegal. Most contracts of this kind are designed to eliminate competition or to fix prices. This is a complicated field of law in which the advice of a local attorney may be needed.

Contracts Not to Compete

Sometimes a firm's employee will quit and thereafter compete with the firm, thereby stealing established customers. This may make the departing employee subject to a lawsuit by the established firm, depending on state laws and various circumstances. When such circumstances arise, existing employees of the firm may be required to sign a contract agreeing not to compete in the future. Employees who are pressured to sign such an agreement frequently feel that they have no choice. Perhaps most courts hold that such an agreement not to compete is not valid, as not supported by consideration.

However, if the agreement not to compete is a precondition to employment, probably the majority of courts would rule that the offer of employment is sufficient consideration to make the agreement valid.

In general, the courts take a close look at any agreement not to compete, since a contract of this kind may deprive an individual of the right to make a living at some future time. A few states have statutes or constitutional provisions that contracts restricting employment are illegal. In jurisdictions where noncompete agreements are permitted, the courts may scrutinize a number of circumstances that surround them. For example, the nature of certain businesses is such that considerable employee secrecy is necessary. Also, some firms make use of trade secrets and they may need more protection than ordinary. Then, too, the courts usually consider whether the terms of the noncompete agreement are reasonable. If a small company has the resources and financial ability to do business only in Boston, Massachusetts, an agreement not to compete with them in the western part of the United States would probably not be upheld by the courts. The courts sometimes say that the test in this situation is whether the agreement is reasonable to both parties, depending on the circumstances of the individual case.

MISTAKE IN CONTRACTS ────────────────────────────────

Unilateral Mistake; Errors in Computation

As a general rule, when only one of the parties is under a mistake of fact on entering into a contract, the courts will not grant relief to that party.

Most courts recognize one exception to the rule that legal relief will not be granted for a unilateral mistake. If one side makes a serious error in computing a bid, then most courts hold that there was no contract if neither party knew of the error, nor should have known of the error. But if one party realizes that a mistake was obviously made, that party cannot claim the formation of a contract. As the courts say, "The principle here is that one cannot snap up an offer, knowing that it was made in mistake."

Mutual Mistake

If both parties to a contract are mistaken concerning a basic assumption of material fact on which the agreement is based, the contract is voidable by the party adversely affected. This has long been followed by the courts as a principle of contract law. For example, a stable owner sold a valuable race horse to a breeder. Unknown to the parties, the horse had died the night before. The breeder, who paid the agreed price when the contract was signed, subsequently had the contract voided.

Note, however, that this principle does not apply to a situation where the mutual mistake is one of judgment. If one party sold a carload of wheat to another, both in the belief that the market was going to make a change, the contract would not be voidable on the basis of mutual mistake.

———— *DISCUSSION* ————

CASE 24   A land owner (plaintiff) offered to sell four lots on Prospect Street in Waltham, Massachusetts. The defendant agreed to buy these. It turned out that there were actually two streets by that name in the town of Waltham. Plaintiff owned lots on one such street and the defendant had examined four lots on the other street by the same name believing he was purchasing the latter. Was this the kind of mistake that would excuse the defendant for a mutual mistake? (*Kyle* v. *Kavanaugh*, 103 Mass.356.)

The courts usually say there are two types of situations in which mutual mistake will serve to void the contract. (1) The parties have a state of mind that is simply not in accord with the facts; consequently there is no meeting of the minds. [6] (2) The subject matter of the contract was destroyed or became unusable prior to the time the parties reached agreement. An example is that of an unsuspecting individual who bought a sailboat that had been destroyed by fire a short time earlier.

In any situation where one interpretation of the facts is as reasonable as another, the parties may not have the same intent. One of the most famous old cases in English law, always followed in this situation in the United

[6] *Peerless Glass Co.* v. *Pacific Crockery & Tinware Co.*, 121 Cal. 641.

States, was *Raffles* v. *Wichelhaus*.[7] In this case the parties agreed that a load of Indian cotton would be shipped on the *Peerless* from Bombay. There were two vessels by this name in the British shipping registry, one scheduled to depart from India in September. The other vessel would not be able to bring cotton to England for several months afterward. Both vessels were capable of making the delivery, and the parties had different vessels in mind when the contract was signed. The court held that there was no meeting of the minds and consequently no enforceable contract.

―――――― QUESTIONS ――――――――――――――――――

1. Explain what is meant by legal capacity; infancy; becoming of age; minority; majority.
2. Is a minor's contract void or voidable? What are the general rules for contracts of minors?
3. Explain the mental capacity required for adults to make contracts; for convicts; for aliens.
4. Do the courts ever enforce illegal contracts?
5. Give an example of a contract that might be struck down by the courts as "against public policy."
6. Are contracts not to compete against a former employer valid? Explain.
7. What kinds of mutual mistake will justify voiding a contract?
8. May a contract be voided for a unilateral mistake? For obvious errors in computation of contract figures?

―――――― ANSWERS TO DISCUSSION CASES ――――――――――――

CASE 22   The New York State court said a contract, though valid where made, will not be treated as valid in a state where such a contract is illegal. Courts do not ordinarily lend their facilities to those who break the law.

CASE 23   No. An agreement either is a contract, or it is not, depending on the situation when it was made. Since the original purpose of the contract was illegal, it was not a contract. A change in the law could not make it such.

CASE 24   The court ruled that there was no contract. The parties had different lots in mind in their agreement to buy and sell. Consequently, there was no meeting of the minds.

―――――― PROBLEM CASES ――――――――――――――――――

1   Both parties to a contract were minors. One such minor elected to claim the right to rescind, but the other minor wanted to stand by the contract. It was

[7]59 Eng. Rep. 375.

held by the trial court that either party could elect to rescind upon becoming of age. Would this be upheld on appeal? (*Hurwitz* v. *Barr*, 193 A.2d 360.)

2   Plaintiff, a minor, bought a motorcycle from an agency that sold these vehicles commercially. The sale price was $325 with down payment of $125 and monthly payments of $25. After a month the buyer returned the motorcycle stating that he wanted to disaffirm the contract and to obtain a refund of the down payment. The seller refused to return the down payment, pointing out that the motorcycle had been damaged to the extent of $156.65. Should a juvenile be allowed to disaffirm without paying for the damage caused? (*Petit* v. *Liston*, 191 P. 660.)

3   A minor claimed to be an adult at the time a contract was signed. Subsequently the minor asked to disaffirm the agreement on the basis that he had been a minor when the contract was signed. Should disaffirmance be allowed? In one case the adult involved in a situation of this kind claimed that the minor was liable in damages for the tort of deceit. The adult maintained this tort of deceit was a separate legal matter from the contract right of a minor to disaffirm. Would this claim of a tort injury be upheld? (*Byers* v. *LeMay Bank and Trust*, 282 S.W.2d 512.)

5   Plaintiff, a building contractor, gave the state of New Hampshire a bid of $102,171.98 for construction of an addition to a state college dormitory. Estimates by the state for this project were approximately $158,000. Other contractors submitted bids of from $159,000 upward. It was subsequently found that the adding machine used by the plaintiff to add up the costs was defective. Evidence showed plaintiff had used considerable care in verifying cost figures and other projections. Upon discovering the adding machine errors the plaintiff asked to withdraw, but the state refused this request. The plaintiff then sued for return of the performance bond that had been posted and for cancellation of the contract. It was undisputed that there was no negligence and that the mistake was honest. Plaintiff admitted that there was no mutual mistake, but maintained it would be unconscionable to enforce the contract. Decide. (*Curran Inc.* v. *State*, 215 A.2d 702.)

9

The Statute of Frauds; Parol Evidence Rule; Fraud; Assignment of Contracts

THE STATUTE OF FRAUDS

The original *statute of frauds* was a law passed by the English Parliament in 1677. It was brought to the United States and adopted in some form in every state. In essence, the law provides that the courts will not enforce certain types of contracts unless there is some written evidence of the contract. Parliament passed the English version of the law to prevent fraud and perjuries that grew out of trials that were held to prove oral contracts. Before the law was enacted, English judges frequently said that "an oral contract is the refuge of scoundrels."

Unfortunately, attention given to the statute of frauds created the popular and stubborn misconception that no contract is valid unless it is in writing. Actually, the law applies only to certain kinds of contracts. To be technical, the statute of frauds does not state that any contracts are illegal, but only that certain kinds will not be enforced by the courts unless the agreement or a memorandum of it is in writing and signed by the person sought to be charged or by that person's agent.

CONTRACTS THAT MUST BE WRITTEN

The five types of contracts required to be in writing by the statute of frauds in most states are:

1. Contracts for the sale of real estate or any interest in real property. The courts have usually included a lease of land, growing timber, and the like. Statutes in most states provide that the lease must be in writing if the term runs for more than a year.

2. Contracts for the sale of specific goods. State statutes usually make the writing requirement applicable if the goods are valued at $500 or more.[1]

3. Contracts that are incapable of being performed within one year.

4. Guarantee contracts—agreements to stand good for the payment of the debts of another.

5. Contracts in consideration of marriage—prenuptial agreements.

The courts agree that perennial plants, bushes, trees, and items that grow without new planting each year are part of the realty, and the sale of these items must be in writing. However, if the owner severs trees or like items from the soil, the property becomes personal property and not real estate. When this severance occurs, there is no longer any need for a written contract, according to the usual interpretation of the statute of frauds. Growing crops that require annual planting and cultivation are not regarded as part of the realty. Accordingly, wheat, corn, tomatoes, and similar items can be sold without a written contract.

Section 2-201 of the Uniform Commercial Code requires a written contract if the agreement for agricultural sales is to be enforced. Not all states, however, follow this $500 minimum for contracts involving the sale of goods. In some states this minimum figure is set at $30, $50, or $100. The term "goods" is usually held to apply to products, wares, or merchandise of whatever kind.

If a contract can reasonably be performed within one year after it is made, the courts usually hold that it need not be in writing even though it may not actually have been performed within the year.

Guarantee contracts are usually those in which a person agrees to stand good for the debts of another. Promises of an executor, executrix, administrator or administratrix to pay the debts owed by a deceased person out of his or her own private funds must be in writing to be enforceable.

Mutual promises between a man and a woman to marry are binding in some states, even though made orally. A pledge made by the prospective husband or wife, or by members of their family, to settle money or property on one of the marital partners is a promise made in consideration of marriage. This is different from a promise to marry. A promise made in consideration of marriage must therefore be in writing to be enforceable.

The Kind of Writing Required

The courts are in general agreement that any kind of writing will suffice, whether a letter, telegram, or formal contract. The writing will satisfy the statute of frauds if it includes:

---

[1]Section 2-201 of the Uniform Commercial Code is to the same effect and is followed in most jurisdictions.

1. The identity of the parties making the agreement.
2. A listing or description of the subject matter involved in the contract.
3. The conditions and terms of the agreement.
4. The signature of the individual sought to be charged with financial responsibility.
5. Some states require a statement of the consideration for the agreement.

There is no requirement that the party seeking to enforce the contract must sign the writing. The signature of the party sought to be held must appear, however. Practically all courts say that this signature can appear anywhere in the writing. And almost all courts permit initials, a printed name, a typed name, or a mark, so long as it was intended as a signature.

The courts are also very liberal in interpreting almost any document as a writing. The requirement may be satisfied by combining several documents, provided each incorporates or refers to the others in some way. If the documents are stapled together or physically attached, this will usually be sufficient for integration of documents that might not suffice if standing alone.

The Uniform Commercial Code, Secs. 549-550 and 2-201, provides that there need only be "some writing sufficient to indicate that a contract for sale has been made."

In most states failure to comply with the statute of frauds makes the contract unenforceable against a party who did not sign the required written memorandum. In a few states the courts take the view that failure to comply with the statute makes the contract void from the outset. In those states that follow the majority view, a third party cannot plead the statute of frauds even if it is unenforceable against the contracting parties. This means that a subtenant cannot use the statute to get out of paying rent, although an oral lease could not be enforced against the tenant.

The signature of an agent can bind a principal under the requirements of the statute of frauds.

A business that leases property for more than one year should seek legal advice in the preparation of a lease since statutes in most states require the lease to be in writing if it extends for more than a year.

Some modern decisions hold that a court has power to stop either of the contracting parties from claiming the statute of frauds as a defense whenever "one party has received an unjust enrichment" or the other party has been subjected to unconscionable injury if the contract is not upheld.[2]

THE PAROL EVIDENCE RULE

The courts have long followed the principle that business affairs need definiteness and certainty of terms, otherwise "commerce degenerates into chica-

[2]*Monarcho v. LoGreco*, 35 Cal.2d 621; *Goldstein v. McNeil*, 122 Cal. App. 2d 608.

nery, and trade becomes another name for trickery."[3] Therefore, the courts have favored written contracts, as eliminating much of the dispute that could arise from oral agreements. Further, the courts have also followed the basic principle that the written agreement almost invariably represents the parties' understanding more adequately than the oral.

Long ago these basic ideas led to the adoption in the English and American courts of the so-called *parol evidence* rule. The idea is that when parties put their agreement in writing, all their prior oral agreements merge into written form. The basic rule of law is that a written contract cannot be modified or changed by oral (parol) evidence outside the written agreement. In further explanation here, it is to be noted that unwritten evidence, tending to contradict the terms of the writing, is called parol evidence.

Nothing in the parol evidence rule, however, prevents the proof of a new verbal contract, altering the terms of the earlier writing. Nor does the rule prevent the parties from showing in court that a clerical or typographical error was made in reducing the agreement to writing.

In addition, most courts hold that a written agreement does not lose its force as a written contract because parol evidence is necessary to explain some of the words or terms that the parties included in the written provisions.[4]

The courts also consistently hold that parol evidence will be admitted to show mistake, fraud, or duress that is claimed as a defense to enforcement of a written agreement. Parol evidence will also be allowed in a court action to reform or rescind a written agreement induced by fraud or duress.

FRAUD OR DURESS

If one side to a contract has been defrauded or tricked into executing the agreement, then it is apparent there was no mutual consent at the time the contract was made. The injured party need not sit by and wait for the other to seek enforcement of the contract. A rescission may be obtained and the injured party is usually justified in seeking return of the consideration or anything of worth that was given up in the deal. Rescission is discussed in more detail in Chapter 10.

The courts are also in complete agreement that neither party should be allowed to force the other party to come to an agreement. Physical force, threatened or real, is sufficient cause to obtain a rescission or to void a contract. In addition, most courts hold that a contract induced by threats of extortion, blackmail, or exposure of a character trait is voidable.

Modern courts also tend to regard economic duress as justification to

---

[3]*Moffitt* v. *Maness*, 102 N.C. 457.
[4]*National Bank of Commerce* v. *Moody*, 90 S.W.2d 279.

void a contract. This is especially so if the person exerting pressure for a contract has been in some way responsible for the economic plight of the other party.

_____ *DISCUSSION* _____

CASE 25   A Federal taxpayer hired a tax counsel to resist a large tax deficiency that had been assessed against the taxpayer by the U.S. Internal Revenue Service. The counsel delayed until just before the deadline for filing a reply with Internal Revenue. Then the counsel forced the taxpayer to sign a contingency fee arrangement, stating that unless the fee arrangement was signed the counsel would not file the necessary papers. Failure to file, of course, would make the taxpayer liable for the full assessment. Was this contract voidable on account of economic duress? (*Thompson Crane & Trucking* v. *Eyman Co.*, 123 Cal. App. 2d 904.)

CASE 26   Plaintiff sued for a rescission of her contract with defendant, claiming it was signed after defendant's fraudulent inducements. Experienced in business and logging practices, plaintiff apparently wanted to get out of the contract when the price of timber went up and defendant proved to be slow and inexperienced in logging operations. Plaintiff claimed that she was misled and defrauded because: (1) defendant claimed to be a "practical logger," when in fact he was nothing more than a "woodsman"; (2) defendant said that he had the means and the ability to harvest the trees; (3) defendant stated he had a partner who was the "owner of a logging outfit ready to use in logging the timber." It was not clear whether this so-called partner was actually a technical, legal partner or merely an acquaintance or close friend. The evidence suggests there was no claim that this individual was a legal partner. It was agreed in the contract that the defendant could assign the contract or have someone else perform the actual work. Were the claims by the defendant sufficiently misleading to justify rescission of the contract? (*Axtell* v. *MacRae*, 233 P. 934.)

ASSIGNMENT OF CONTRACTS _____

How an Assignment Operates

A contract is, of course, a form of property. An important question concerning any form of property is: To what extent may it be transferred or sold? In legal circles a shifting of contract rights or duties is called an *assignment of contract rights,* or simply an *assignment.* At times it is also referred to as a *delegation.* Generally one "assigns" benefits or rights and "delegates" duties.

   In a third-party beneficiary contract, the original agreement contemplates that performance should be made to one not a party to the contract (to the third-party beneficiary). But in an assignment, or delegation, the contract does not contemplate performance to a third party. By assignment, one of the parties wants to achieve this same result by acts subsequent to the formation of the contract. Legally, an assignment operates to extinguish the rights of an assignor and transfer such rights to the assignee. This gives the assignee a direct right against the obligor under the contract.

Normally, an assignment is made by the assignor without consulting the other party to the contract (the obligor). If a third party (the assignee) does assume contractual responsibilities and obligations with the consent of the obligor, the transaction is no longer an assignment. It has become a *novation*. Legally, a novation is the substitution of a new contract for the old one, terminating all rights under the old agreement.

In considering the legality of assignments, we must first distinguish between contract rights and contract duties. A promisor, who had undertaken contract responsibilities, cannot, in many instances, delegate the performance of those duties to another individual unless the second party will agree. The reason is that the second party has bargained for the performance of the promisor and should not be required to accept the conduct of another. However, if the undertaking can be done by one person just as well as by another, the courts usually take the view that the promisor may delegate the performance. For example, if the contract calls for the delivery of fireplace wood by the promisor, it makes no difference who cuts the wood and delivers it. But if the contract obligation involves personal skill, judgment, taste, or other qualities that are individual to the promisor, the duties may not be delegated.

The fact that a contract duty has been delegated by the promisor does not, however, relieve that party of responsibility for nonperformance. This delegation of duty means nothing more than that the promisor has hired someone to do the act. Default of the representative (the assignee) is still default of the principal (the assignor).

In general, the assignability of rights under a contract will depend on the type of agreement and the nature of the contract obligation assumed, rather than a supposed intent of the parties. The courts will, however, generally uphold a prohibition against the assignment of contract rights if the parties so specify in the agreement.

The right to receive money is not intimately related to the obligation of the promisor to perform. So long as you receive money that you are entitled to, it makes little difference whether it is paid by the promisor or by the promisor's delegate. Accordingly, the courts almost always permit assignment of the right to receive money.

Nonassignable Matters

The general rule of the courts is to favor the free flow of commerce and the assignment of business or industrial obligations. In some types of situations, assignment could work hardships that were never bargained for. The courts usually follow the principle that a right may not be assigned where it would:

> materially change the duty of the obligor, or materially increase the burden or risk imposed on him [or her] by his [or her] contract, or materially impair his [or her] chance of obtaining return performance or materially reduce its value to him or her.[5]

Personal service contracts are generally held not to be assignable. Agreements for the services of a physician, architect, tutor, artist, lawyer, musician, actor, and so on are regarded by the courts as personal service contracts. The law presumes that a contract with a professional person is based on the desire to maintain a personal relationship. For example, an actor and an advertising agency had a contract to handle the actor's public relations. The actor could not assign this contract to another actor. The advertising agency might feel that the second actor was too temperamental to deal with or might object for some other reason.

Contracts that may materially increase the risk assumed by the obligor are also not subject to assignment. For example, a student had an automobile collision policy with an insurance company. In selling his car, the student attempted to assign this policy to the new buyer. The courts quite uniformly hold that this cannot be done.

A contract that involves the credit of a firm or an individual may not be assigned to a new buyer. The obligor should not be required to accept the credit of one company or one person in place of the credit of another, even though the latter may have a good credit rating. The parties bargained for the credit of the buyer in a sales transaction. Purchase money mortgages fall under this same principle. Most courts hold that the new buyer of a mortgaged home may not be substituted for the prior buyer without the approval of the lender. The purchase contract and mortgage may not be assigned unless the mortgagee (lender) agrees. This is because the new buyer's credit is not the security that the lender bargained for in the original mortgage loan. This is true, even though the same real estate is to serve as security for the mortgage debt. A mortgage has the creditworthiness of the borrower behind it, as well as the pledge of the real estate.

The "Holder-in-Due-Course Trap"

The party to whom an assignment is made (the assignee) succeeds to whatever rights the assignor had against the obligor. This means that if the obligor entered into the contract because of the fraudulent inducement of the assignor, the obligor can raise the defense of fraud against an assignee who is trying to enforce the contract as well as against the assignor.

[5]RESTATEMENT OF CONTRACTS (2d), 149(2), and Uniform Commercial Code (UCC), Sec. 2-210(2), which applies to assignments of contracts for the sale of goods or merchandise.

As noted earlier, the courts tend to favor assignability of contracts to encourage the free flow of trade. In some situations, however, this has posed serious hardships in consumer purchasing. If a housewife buys a washing machine on time payments, the courts have long recognized the buyer's right to claim faulty performance in a lawsuit for not meeting the time payments. But historically, retail stores have often needed financing in order to replace goods that are sold. In the typical situation, the washing machine buyer signed a promissory note and a contract for installment payments. This note was assigned to a bank in exchange for cash to the retail store. The bank then began collection on the installment contract, knowing nothing of the nonperformance of the washing machine. In this situation, the courts said that the bank is a *holder in due course*. As defined by the courts, a holder in due course is an innocent purchaser or assignee of a negotiable instrument such as a promissory note, having no knowledge of any fraud or claim associated with the instrument. And in order to encourage the free flow of commercial paper, the courts habitually have allowed a holder in due course to demand payment without regard to a claim of fraud against the retail store (the assignor).

In this situation, of course, the housewife could eventually go back against the retail store in a lawsuit. This would take time and money, which the consumer-housewife might not have. In the meantime, she would be required to continue to make installment payments to the bank for a non-working appliance.

This does not mean that there is little merit to the old holder-in-due-course doctrine. In major commercial transactions there is still considerable justification for continuing to follow the rule. The harm caused to small consumers in recent years resulted in the passage of consumer legislation in a number of states. In general, these laws provide that faulty product performance or fraud can be asserted against a finance company, bank, or any other holder in due course that is seeking to enforce a buyer's promissory note in the purchase of an appliance or household item.[6]

In addition to these state statutes to help consumers, the Federal Trade Commission (FTC) rules now also have the force of law, protecting consumers against the "holder in due course trap." The FTC rule requires any seller of consumer goods or services on credit to include a warning that an assignee (finance company, bank, or whatever) takes subject to all defenses that the buyer-debtor may assert against the original seller (assignor). This rule shifts the burden of loss resulting from seller misconduct in the consumer field back to the assignee-creditor who finances the retail store. Most legal observers believe that this is as it should be, since the assignee is in a better position than the consumer to regulate the seller.

[6]California Civ. Code, 1804.2 and 2983.5.

Wording and Form of an Assignment

No special form of wording is needed for an assignment. Even an oral statement is sufficient if the matter is not in conflict with the statute of frauds. Almost all states now have statutes requiring assignments to be written. As a practical matter, they are almost always made in writing. Unlike a deed, there is no legal requirement that an assignment must be delivered to the assignee or anyone else.

Normally, an assignment may be revoked unless the assignor received consideration.

Filing Notice of an Assignment

An otherwise valid assignment takes effect at the time it is made. There is no legal requirement that either the assignee or the assignor give notice of the assignment to the obligor, but it is almost always advisable to do so. In the first place, any money due under the contract may be paid by the obligor to the assignor. If this happens because the obligor is ignorant of the assignment, there is no way that the obligor can be made to pay a second time.

While there is no right to do so, a dishonest obligor could assign the contract rights a second time. An obligee with notice of only the second assignment could pay to the second assignee.

There is also the likelihood that the obligor may have some kind of a claim or offset (sometimes called setoff) arising out of the contract. If notice of the assignment is promptly given to the obligor, the latter cannot thereafter assert a claim or offset arising after such notice with respect to a matter that is not a part of the assigned claim.

Assignment of Future Wages

A number of states have statutory limitations on the assignment of future wages. Most of these laws require such an assignment to be in writing, accompanied by written approval of the worker's spouse. In similar fashion, a parent must give written approval of an assignment of wages of a minor. In addition, such wage assignments are usually only permitted for "necessities" furnished by the assignee.

_____ *DISCUSSION* _____

Case 27   Eastern Brick Company sold bricks that were delivered to Hudson Supply Co. The bricks were not paid for and Eastern Brick assigned the accounts receivable to Home Factors Corporation (the assignee). Thereafter, Home Factors Corporation (the plaintiff) sued Hudson Supply for the value of the accounts receivable ($1,034.25) At the trial Hudson Supply offered evidence to show that it had claims against Eastern of over $2,000, growing out of brick purchases. The trial court held for the plaintiff, ruling that Home Factors Corporation was entitled to a judgment. Did this decision represent a valid statement of the law that would hold up on appeal? (*Hudson Supply & Equipment Co.* v. *Home Factors Corp.*, 210 A.2d 837.)

_____ QUESTIONS _____

1. What is the basic purpose of the statute of frauds?
2. In what situations does the statute of frauds apply?
3. Describe the requirements for the kind of writing that will satisfy the statute of frauds.
4. Explain the parol evidence rule.
5. Tell how fraud in the inducement may be used by the injured party to void a contract.
6. What is the basic rule in the assignment of contracts?
7. What is a holder in due course?
8. Should notice of an assignment be promptly given? Why?

_____ ANSWERS TO DISCUSSION CASES _____

CASE 25   The court said that economic duress would be a defense in this situation. To a large extent, the tax counsel had forced the other party "against the wall."

CASE 26   The court said that almost everyone going into a contract believes that they have the "means and ability" to carry out the agreement. The court also pointed out that the timber owner (plaintiff) was not an inexperienced businesswoman, that she was represented by an attorney, and that she was in position to judge what qualities were needed to handle a logging operation. Representations and inducements, if not completely accurate, were not so gross or fraudulent as to furnish a basis for rescission.

CASE 27   The appellate (higher) court said the trial court "misconceived the law relating to assignments," pointing out the general rule that the assignee, "takes subject to all defenses, including set-offs existing at the time of the assignment." The lower court was reversed.

_____ PROBLEM CASES _____

1   Gibson bought a TV set on credit at an agreed price of $189 plus carrying charges. He signed a printed conditional sales contract that was blank in part. On arriving home Gibson found that the sale price had been filled in

as $289 plus charges. When the store opened for business, Gibson promptly returned the set, pointing out that the price was $100 more than he had agreed to. Store personnel refused to accept the television, but Gibson left it there. When Gibson paid nothing on the account, the store sued, contending that Gibson had signed and must pay. Decide. (*Hollywood Credit Clothing Co.* v. *Gibson*, 188 A.2d 348.)

2   A developer sold lots to a builder knowing that the salt content of the soil was so high that the land was unsuitable for homes. Nevertheless, builders erected homes and sold them. A house buyer brought suit against the developer on the basis that the developer should have disclosed the defect. Evidence showed that the land defect was not readily discoverable by a buyer. Since there was no direct contractual relationship between the buyer and the developer, was the concealment actionable? (*Griffith* v. *Byers Construction Co.*, 510 P.2d 198.)

3   The statute of frauds requires certain types of contracts to be in writing or in a memorandum. Plaintiff tried to establish the existence of a contract from separate writings "connected with one another expressly or by internal evidence of subject matter and occasion." Will the courts look to the totality of individual writings or must the agreement be spelled out in one single document? If accepted as a contract, must each individual document be signed by the party who is to be charged with contract responsibility? (*Marks* v. *Cowdin*, 123 N.E. 139.)

4   An orthopedic surgeon was called to a hospital to treat a fracture suffered by the defendant's friend. The defendant said, "Don't worry about the bill, Doc, I'll take care of everything." The surgeon then made a number of treatments but was never paid. The surgeon sued defendant. Except for the expression set out previously, specific statements made by the parties could not be remembered at the time of trial. Was the defendant's oral promise an original undertaking on his part to pay for treatment, or was it a promise to pay the debt of another and void as not signed as required by the statute of frauds? What are the differences here? (*Dr. F. Marshall* v. *Bellin*, 133 N.W.2d 751.)

10

Discharge (Completion) of Contracts; The Consequences of Breach

BREACH AND ITS REMEDIES

When all provisions of a contract have been complied with, the contract is said to have been *discharged*. In effect, the contract no longer exists. Sometimes, however, the contract may never reach this stage, since one party may simply refuse to perform or may handle the agreement in an unsatisfactory manner. On occasion, this failure to perform may arise from changed conditions that make performance impossible, but at other times there may be no real justification.

A *breach of contract* is the failure, without legal excuse, to perform any promise that comprises the whole or part of a contract.

Major and Minor Breach

The courts say that whether the breach of a contract is major or relatively minor makes a significant legal difference. But the courts do not lay down hard and fast rules for deciding whether the breach is major or minor. In general, a minor breach involves a somewhat insignificant deviation in quantity or quality—something that may be corrected or offset without serious harm. A minor breach may involve a small delay of an hour or two in performance when the time of completion is not really critical.

This does not mean that the party bargaining for a specified product or service can be cheated out of the contract specifications. The aggrieved party is entitled to damages to make up for the difference. But if the breach is minor, the damages or other remedies are limited to those caused by the breach, and the contract is said to be "substantially performed."

On the other hand, a major breach is something that goes to the very substance of the agreement. In a situation of this kind, the injured party is immediately excused from the counterperformance owing under the terms of the agreement.

114

Options of Injured Party

When a major breach of contract occurs, the injured party to the agreement will usually have several options:

1. Filing suit for monetary damages.
2. Asking the court for specific performance by the other party.
3. Instituting rescission (cancellation) and restitution.
4. Seeking money damages in a lawsuit not based on contract law, but rather based on tort or quasi-contract (unjust enrichment) principles.

Of these possible remedies, a request for specific performance seeks to enforce the contract, whereas the remedy of rescission requests a cancellation of the contract.

Monetary Damages for Breach

The underlying principle of United States law is that a legally wronged party should be compensated for the harm that was done. This award is through a court grant of monetary damages.

At the conclusion of a civil suit, the courts try to place the wronged party, as nearly as possible, in the situation that would have existed had the harm not occurred. This means that in contract cases the award should be designed to allow the plaintiff those advantages that would have accrued had the contract been performed. In tort cases (principally products liability, personal injury, or negligence matters), the damages are supposed to return the injured party to approximately the same situation as before the wrong occurred, and can be much greater than in a contract action since the courts may award "punishment" (punitive) damages as well.

Compensatory Damages

The basic kinds of damages allowed by the courts in contract actions are called compensatory damages, that is, money that will compensate for the loss. The measure of damages will be the difference in value between the contract for performance and the actual performance delivered. Although "punishment" damages are allowed in tort actions, in most contract cases only compensatory and consequential damages may be awarded.

Consequential Damages. As pointed out, the courts allow compensatory damages for breach of contract. These may sometimes include the kind of award called *consequential damages*, referring to those injuries or damages that were within the contemplation of the parties at the time the contract was made—those losses that "reasonably flow from the act or are in consequence of it," as the courts say.

Nominal (Minimal) Damages. In all states even the most minimal breach of contract entitles the aggrieved party to sue. However, it is left to the discretion of the trial judge in most states whether to award court costs and minimal damages where no actual harm or loss has been proved.

Nominal damages involve the award to the plaintiff of trivial amounts such as 5 cents or 1 dollar. The courts usually allow awards of this kind when a legal wrong has been done, but the matter was at most a technical breach of a legal duty. The courts like to discourage suits of this kind, of course, but no one can be excluded from using the court system. For example, a mentally troubled newspaper subscriber sued the newspaper for breach of contract in failing to make delivery of one daily paper. Unquestionably the newspaper was at fault, so the jury awarded court-approved nominal damages of 1 cent to the plaintiff.

Setting the Measure of Damages

The injured party must be able to show a reasonable computation of loss in seeking damages for breach of contract. The plaintiff will not be allowed by the court to pull speculative figures out of the air, so to speak.

Most courts follow the Uniform Commercial Code (UCC) in setting the amount of damages, or *measure of damages*, as it is called in legal terms for contracts for the sale of goods. On the seller's breach of a contract for the sale of goods, the buyer is normally entitled to the difference between the contract price and the market price at the time of the breach. Upon notification of a breach, the buyer has the right to go out in the open market and buy from another seller, eventually recovering the difference from the party breaching the contract.

If the buyer refuses to take goods on a contract, the seller is entitled to sell them in any reasonable commercial transaction, recovering the sale costs and differential between the contract price and what was obtained in the sale. However, if the items are made especially for that buyer, such as printed business cards, the seller may recover the full contract price if the goods cannot be sold within a reasonable period of time to another buyer.

The measure of damages allowed in a contract for the sale of goods is a specialized rule of law set by the Uniform Commercial Code. Many courts apply this same measure of damages in a contract for the sale of real estate.

When a builder fails to finish a house or any other structure on a construction contract, the courts generally allow the buyer to recover the cost of completion plus reasonable damages for delay. In late performance on a building contract, the owner can recover damages for loss of use of the property. Most courts also allow consequential damages for breach or delay in a building contract.

Mitigation of Damages

The injured party in any lawsuit is generally under a duty to use reasonable effort to *mitigate*, or lighten, the damages that may be sustained. For example, a builder made a contract with an individual to construct a home. The residence was near completion when the buyer made an inspection of the premises after workers had departed for the day. A faucet had been left on by a cement finisher and was flooding the basement. It was only common sense, of course, that motivated the buyer to cut off the flooding faucet. In any event, the buyer could demand damages for the water in the basement. And it was not the buyer's responsibility to make certain that the basement was not flooded. However, had the buyer deliberately ignored the situation, the court would not have allowed damages caused by further flooding, since these damages could have been reasonably avoided. The injured party is required to mitigate damages or the courts will not allow recovery of damages that could have been avoided through reasonable action.

It is also to be noted that the injured party can collect reasonable expenses incurred in mitigating damages.

Contracts Between Employers and Employees

If an employee has a contract to be employed for a certain firm for a specified period of time, and the employer breaches the contract by dismissing the employee, damages recoverable would generally be the unpaid salary at the time of dismissal. Some courts allow the employee to collect wages up to the period of time at which a new job is found, as long as the employee "mitigates damages" by actively seeking employment. On the other hand, if the employee walks out without cause, then the employer may recover the cost of replacing the employee. This would include any additional salary that must be paid to the new employee which is greater than the previous employee's salary.

Exculpatory Provisions

One party to an agreement may insist on including a provision that the other party will be liable for damages or injury caused by certain happenings. Or the agreement may state that one party will not be held liable in the event of specific occurrences. In general, few courts uphold provisions of this kind. The courts have often ruled there should be close scrutiny of an understanding that seeks to excuse one party from that side's own fault or negligence. Consequently, recent court decisions have increasingly disallowed exculpatory provisions where it appeared that there was unequal bargaining power that in some way seemed oppressive or unconscionable. In general, exculpatory clauses are not allowed in contracts for the sale of consumer goods when personal injuries result.

Stipulated Damages

Some contracts are written with a provision that a specific monetary penalty will be imposed if performance is not completed within a designated time. For example, a contract might state that a penalty of $10,000 will be paid if a builder's project is not finished by April 1. Usually, the courts will not allow such an award if it appears to be an attempt to impose a penalty, rather than a repayment for actual injury. The courts call an award of this kind *stipulated damages* or *liquidated damages*. To be valid and collectable, it must appear to the court that the parties made a good-faith effort to estimate the actual damages that would result from a breach when they specified the amount of such damages in the contract. Consequently, the parties to a contract should not include a penalty provision that sets out flat sums unrelated to the nature of the default.

In order to be enforceable by the courts, the contract provision for stipulated damages must be a reasonable forecast of injury. If the court finds that the designated figure meets this test, then this figure stipulated as damages will be the sole measure of recovery, regardless of what actual damages can be proved. No larger or smaller sum of money can be awarded if the stipulation clause in the contract is recognized as valid.[1]

Specific Performance

As pointed out, the party injured by a breach of contract may file a lawsuit asking for money damages. Or the injured party can ask for specific performance. That is, the injured party may ask the court to compel the defaulting (breaching) party to actually carry out what should have been done under the terms of the agreement. Normally, all courts recognize that the aggrieved party can demand compensatory damages, but specific performance is up to the fairness and judgment of the court. Of course, the plaintiff cannot expect to receive both an award of damages and an order for specific performance. Such a judgment would constitute "double enrichment," as the courts term it.

Judges consistently say that no one has an absolute right to specific performance, since such relief is within the court's discretion. In many situations, however, the measure of damages that can be awarded will not be an adequate remedy.

Almost invariably a court will order specific performance of an agreement to sell a home or land, or to lease real estate of any kind. But specific performance will seldom be ordered for the sale of personal property (chattels) unless the subject matter of the sale is unique or almost impossible to obtain elsewhere. Usually, personal goods can be bought on the open market and an award of monetary damages will be considered adequate.

---

[1] *Stone Sand & Gravel Co. v. United States*, 234 U.S. 270.

For example, a coin collector spent years in locating an owner who was willing to sell a specific mintage of rare penny. The collector made a contract to purchase this coin, but the owner refused to deliver after the agreement had been made. A court would likely order specific performance (delivery of the coin upon payment of the price). This is because the coin would not be available in comparable condition from other coin dealers.

The courts will usually order specific performance of a contract for personal services for an actor, artist, singer, portrait painter, or someone with unique talents. At the same time, specific performance would not likely be ordered for a contract to paint a house. The party injured by the default could likely obtain another house painter, suing the first for damages.

In some other cases, specific performance will not be ordered because the court feels this requirement could work an undue hardship on the defaulting party. At other times the court may simply not have sufficient technical background to supervise specific performance of some matters. Thus, a judge might order specific performance of a contract to sell an office building but would not order specific performance of a contract to build an office building.

Rescission and Restitution

Rescission is the procedure for annulling a contract—for treating the contract as though it had never existed. Thus, when a substantial breach occurs, the injured party may rescind the contract, refusing to perform or to be bound any longer.

In some situations it is more advantageous for the injured party to rescind, rather than to sue for damages or to ask for specific performance. In rescinding, the party taking such action may recover any money already paid or may recover for any work already performed in furtherance of the contract. This recovery, however, is based on a quasi-contract right which the law implies to force a wrongdoer to pay for what was received and to prevent a wrongdoer from profiteering. In the rescission process, as a general rule the injured party must restore both parties to their original position, in so far as circumstances will permit.

If the party claiming a rescission is mistaken about the facts and there was no major breach, then that party has committed a breach of contract and is liable for damages in a lawsuit.

It is also worth noting that there can be no partial rescission of a contract. The entire agreement must be treated as at an end.

In addition to rescinding the contract, the injured party has a right to restitution of benefits given to the defendant.

Liability in Tort

If one can show that there was a tort action involved in the breach of the contract, then it is possible to sue under a tort theory. In that case, one may obtain not only compensatory and consequential damages, but punitive damages as well.

Punitive Damages. The award of punitive damages is rather common in tort suits. It is usually up to the discretion of the court as to whether such damages may be added to compensatory damages. Practically all courts rule that exemplary damages cannot be granted in breach of contract suits; however, an exception will be made if the defendant is a public service company, such as the telephone company, power and light company, or the like.

Any deliberate assault or malicious injury to an individual (a tort) will usually result in the award of both compensatory and exemplary damages. The courts are in agreement that unusual negligence, deliberate discrimination, or aggravated wrong may give rise to such an award, even though the plaintiff may not be able to show much actual harm.

This is typical in a products liability action, where the plaintiff is injured because of a defective product purchased from the defendant, if it can be shown that the defendant manufacturer placed the defective product on the market with reckless disregard for the safety of consumers.

Quasi-Contract

If the agreement involves services performed by one of the parties and the other refuses to pay therefor, the injured party may sue under a quasi-contract theory. In that case, the court would allow recovery for the reasonable value of the services performed. For instance, if you hire someone to paint your house and then refuse to pay the amount due, the painter could sue under a theory of quasi-contract for the reasonable value of services performed. Usually the court requires the individual to provide evidence of what is reasonable for the particular services performed. It should be noted that the quasi-contract provides an equitable remedy to the individual providing the service.

CONTRACT CONDITIONS AND COVENANTS

In analyzing the wording of contracts, the courts say that some words used by the parties are mere promises (covenants) while others are conditions. Although the courts hold that all promises in a contract should be honored, a failure to live up to some promises may not be fatal to the entire contract. Damages will be awarded for any failure to meet a promise, but a substantial breach of a condition will justify the remedy of rescission, along with an award of damages. In general, the courts prefer to construe the language of an agreement as a promise, rather than a condition. This is because rescission may work a considerable hardship on a party that is in partial compliance.

A *condition* is a fact or event, the occurrence or nonoccurrence of which creates or extinguishes a duty on the part of the promisor. Stated in other words, a condition is a future and uncertain event, upon the happening of which is made to depend the existence of an obligation. A condition, then, is a responsibility-triggering event—a promise that is not absolute at the time made. Some conditions can be under the control of the promisor. On the other hand, a condition may be a happening that cannot be controlled by anyone. And it should also be realized that a condition may never come to pass.

Conditions Precedent, Concurrent, and Subsequent

Conditions are classified as conditions precedent, conditions concurrent, and conditions subsequent. Contracts, of course, frequently provide that one party must perform before performance can be demanded of the other. If a parent agrees to transfer the family farm to a child upon the child's marriage, the wedding would be a *condition precedent* to the parent's legal obligation to transfer the property.

Concurrent conditions are those that must take place at the same time. For example, the buyer of a house may promise to pay the purchase price while the seller promises to sign and deliver the deed to the property.

A *condition subsequent* is a happening, the occurrence of which takes away rights that would otherwise exist. For example, unless a policyholder files a claim of loss within 60 days following a fire, the policy may provide that no claim will be paid.

As a general rule of law, some conditions precedent are not regarded by the courts as important enough to justify rescission. What happens here is that the injured party merely deducts the value of damages caused by the breach and both parties go ahead with their respective performance. Admittedly, this is a very indefinite area of the law. If the injury caused by the breach can be readily measured in money terms, or if the justifiable expectations of the contracting parties have not been substantially harmed, most courts usually allow only damages, rather than a rescission.

Both unimportant and very substantial breaches of conditions precedent were pointed out by the court and analyzed in the case of *Whiteley* v. *O'Dell*.[2]

> Plaintiffs contend the trial court erred in finding defendant had not breached the contract . . . there were variances from the contract specifications in at least three respects. First, the bathroom fixtures were not the color specified in the contract. . . . It is not every breach which gives rise to the right to rescind a contract. In order to warrant rescission of a contract, the breach must be material and the failure

[2]*Whiteley* v. *O'Dell*, 548 P.2d 798.

to perform so substantial as to defeat the object of the parties in making the agreement. Obviously, the variance in the appearance of the bathroom fixtures is not so substantial that it would constitute a material breach of contract.

The variances in the shingles and the brick veneer are entirely different matters. While the sealdown shingles used by the builder differed only in appearance from those specified, the contract disclosed that the plaintiffs specifically ordered T-lock shingles. From the testimony it is apparent to this court that the defendant had no intention of curing this defect. . . .

An even more serious variance of the contract specifications was discovered . . . brick veneer was added only to the front of the house. The contract specified the house was to be all brick. The normal method of adding brick veneer to a house is to extend the foundation so a ledge is formed to support the brick veneer. O'Dell testified his employees had omitted the [supporting] ledge on three sides of the house by mistake. . . . It was neither the normal nor the desired method for construction of a brick veneer. . . . [The court pointed out that this was definitely a major breach.] If it is clear that one party to a contract is going to be unable to perform it, the other party need not wait for the date when performance is due. He is entitled to treat the contract at an end and pursue his remedies. . . .

In this case the appellate court held that the breach concerning the wrong color of bathroom fixtures could be compensated for in damages. But installing a cheaper shingle for the more lasting T-lock type was a major breach. In addition, the failure to provide a proper foundation for the brick veneer, and leaving the veneer off entirely on three sides, was inexcusable. The appellate court allowed a rescission, as well as a judgment for money damages in favor of the home buyers (plaintiff).

Express Conditions

The parties making a contract can specify that certain terms in the agreement are to be construed as conditions precedent. Failure to perform exactly as specified in the contract will provide grounds for rescission unless it is clear that the clause was intended as a penalty provision; penalty provisions will normally be held as unenforceable.

If one of the parties feels it is very important to have the work done within a certain time frame, the contract may provide that "time is of the essence." Such a provision is ordinarily construed as a condition precedent to the requirement that the other party perform. A prudent buyer of a home that is being built on a contract may also specify that approval by a designated architect is a condition precedent to payment to the builder. In a situation of this kind, the architect cannot withhold approval for a capricious reason or for no reason at all.

Delayed Performance

Delayed performance will always justify a claim of damage where it can be shown that loss was occasioned by the delay. Most courts hold, however, that delayed performance will not be a material breach justifying rescission unless performance by a certain date is a condition precedent in the contract. If the late performer has any reasonable excuse for delay, the courts may allow damages but will seldom agree to a rescission.

In agreements for the sale of marketable merchandise, however, a contract calling for shipment or other performance within a designated time is generally held to be a condition precedent. The difference between merchandise contracts and other contracts is in the position of the injured parties. A delay of a week in obtaining possession of a new home would not likely be crucial to the average home buyer. But a merchant's success depends on the prompt delivery of goods to customers. Often advertising and sales programs are scheduled around specific delivery dates. Consequently, a delay in the shipment of merchandise is usually held to be a material breach.

Delay cannot be tolerated indefinitely in any kind of contract, however. After the passage of a reasonable time without performance the courts will permit rescission in almost any kind of contract. What is a reasonable time will vary with the type of agreement and all the surrounding circumstances. If no date is specified in the agreement, the courts interpret this to mean that performance must be done within a reasonable time. When time is of great importance, the contract should always be drafted to read that "time is definitely of the essence in the performance of this contract."

In a bilateral contract, the injured party cannot regard the other party as being in default until the injured party has offered to perform. In legal circles, this offer by the injured party is called a *tender*. Depending on the terms of the contract, the tender must be either an offer to pay or an offer to perform a service.

ANTICIPATORY REPUDIATION

When one party to a contract announces in advance that the contract will not be performed, an *anticipatory repudiation* results. The injured party may do one of three things after receiving this notice of anticipatory breach:

1. Treat the declaration as an immediate breach and rescind the contract;
2. Ignore the declaration and continue to insist on performance, seeking legal relief when the time for performance is past; or
3. Treat the declaration as an immediate breach and sue for damages.

When one party, by his or her actions, makes it impossible to perform on a contract, the other party may treat this action as an anticipatory breach. For example, an owner contracted to sell his farm to a specific buyer within three weeks. Instead of taking this action, however, the owner transferred (conveyed) the farm by deed to a third party. The party holding the original contract to purchase would be entitled to treat this transfer as an anticipatory breach.

Usually, the courts will allow withdrawal of a declaration of intent to breach if the other party to the contract has not yet suffered damage or changed position in reliance on the declaration of breach.

After an anticipatory breach, an injured merchant may "cover" the possibility of loss by purchasing other goods on the open market. The damages that may then be recovered in a lawsuit will consist of the difference between the cost of cover merchandise and the contract price, along with any consequential damages or necessary expenses of purchasing the cover goods. But if the merchant does not obtain cover merchandise, damages may still be obtained for nondelivery. The measure of such damages would be the amount of loss that would have been incurred by obtaining cover merchandise. (Uniform Commercial Code, Sec. 2-712, covers this problem in most states.)

WAIVER OF BREACH

Effect of Waiver

An injured party is not always obliged to file a lawsuit for damages or to declare a rescission in case of a major breach. The injured party may find it advantageous to ignore or waive the breach. A waiver (voluntary relinquishment) of some rights under a contract does not mean that other rights under the agreement have been surrendered. For example, a builder agreed to construct a summer home in the mountains before September 1. Construction was delayed, and the lot owner could have sued for breach of contract at that time. The owner instructed the builder to continue, however, and to complete the construction as soon as possible. This constituted a waiver of the lot owner's right to object to delay to that point. But the waiver would not excuse the builder from installing a fireplace that was defective. Neither would this waiver excuse a builder who thereafter failed to pursue the job diligently, instead emphasizing a potentially more lucrative building contract on the side.

Waiver as Modification of Contract

If a binding agreement between the parties calls for a continuing performance, the courts usually construe a waiver at one stage as applying to future parts of the continuing performance. For example, a landlord may waive a tenant's breach of contract in paying the rent 10 days late. Many courts hold that this waiver applies to future rent payments and that the landlord has waived the right to demand the next payment until it is 10 days late. Many courts hold that the landlord may cure this waiver by insisting in advance that future payments be made on time and by taking legal action after the next payment is late.

CONTRACT LIABILITY TO THIRD PARTIES

Contracts are frequently made for the benefit of an outsider who is not a party to the agreement. A life insurance policy is a common example of this kind of contract. The face amount of the policy is payable to a so-called *third-party beneficiary* upon the death of the insured. The general rule of law is that the third-party beneficiary, while not a party to the agreement, can nevertheless sue for enforcement when the contract is for his or her benefit.

If the outsider is not able to sue as a third-party beneficiary, the courts may nevertheless allow this third party to sue on a tort basis for negligence or for willful injury.

If one party owes an obligation to the general public or to another, then the obligation may be shifted to still another party by contract. For example, the owner of an office building contracted with a commercial fire protection firm to keep the building's fire escapes in good repair. A passerby was injured after the fire protection company had negligently failed to make needed repairs. In a failure to perform a contract of this kind, the injured passerby could, in many courts, recover damages from the office building owner as primarily responsible. In the alternative, the injured passerby could recover damages from the fire protection firm on a tort basis. The courts state in this situation that the injury is a tort arising out of contract.

Some courts differ, however, on whether a contractor is legally responsible to an injured third party if the contractor is negligent or makes an improper installation. Most older decisions refused to hold a contractor liable to a third party, while permitting the other party to the contract to recover. But the modern trend of the courts seems to impose tort liability on the third party, reasoning that the third party would eventually recover from the contractor in an indirect way by suing the building owner.

ETHICAL CONSIDERATIONS

The deliberate breach of a contract is not only unethical but, in most cases, illegal. Although minor breaches may usually be corrected without serious harm, the injured party may be entitled to damages.

In the case of an employment contract, discussed previously, it would be unethical to dismiss an employee who has a definite contract without good cause. Certain discriminatory practices are not allowed, such as discrimination based on race, age, sex, or ethnic background. Some employers might dismiss an employee based on age, but state that the person was not performing well. Unless these charges can be proven, the individual will be re-employed and, in addition, receive damages.

QUESTIONS

1. What difference does it make whether a breach of contract is major or minor?
2. What may the injured party do when a major breach occurs?
3. Define: compensatory damages, punitive damages, consequential damages, and nominal damages.
4. What do we mean by the measure of damages?
5. How does one mitigate damages?
6. What is the general rule when a penalty provision for breach is included in a contract?
7. Describe how specific performance works. When may it be granted?
8. What is the remedy of rescission?
9. When will the courts permit rescission?
10. Explain the meaning of a condition subsequent.
11. How does a condition affect the relations between the contracting parties?
12. What is an anticipatory breach?
13. How does a waiver of breach of contract work?
14. Do the courts seem to be favoring the right of an injured third party to sue in a contract situation? Explain.

PROBLEM CASES

1   Drews contracted to haul all the pulp wood that could be cut from a tract of land at a set price per cord of wood. About 30 percent of the pay was to be withheld until the wood was all removed. Drews hauled 8,345 cords. The tract owner continued to withhold the 30 percent compensation and Drews sued. The defendants found 7½ cords of wood that had been covered by snow. Had Drews performed on the contract? (*Drews* v. *Davis*, 52 A. 971.)

2   A chemical named cryolite was almost unobtainable when the plaintiff and defendant made a contract whereby defendant was to deliver this product. Plaintiff asked the court for specific performance when the defendant did not deliver the promised cryolite. Was this a case for specific performance

or only for an award of damages? (*Kaiser* v. *Associated Metals*, 321 F.Supp. 923.)

3   A home owner gave a contractor a check in payment for plumbing modifications. When the parties disagreed as to the amount that was due, the home owner wrote "payment of account in full" on the face of the check. The contractor crossed through these words and wrote "paid on account" on the face of the check. The contractor then deposited the check in his account. Could the home owner regard the matter as paid in full? (*Burgamy* v. *Davis*, 313 S.W.2d 365.)

4   In a contract dispute the facts disclosed that an actual time for performance had not been specified. One of the parties contended that obviously a "reasonable time" had been intended and that reasonableness depends on custom or usage in the trade, in the community, or according to prior dealings between the parties. Is such a test satisfactory to the courts? (*Automatic Sprinkler Co.* v. *Sherman*, 294 F. 533.)

11

The Law of Torts

TORTS AS INVASIONS OF RIGHTS

Every government throughout history has placed limits on certain kinds of individual activity. Society always wants as much freedom as possible for the individual. But out of regard for the common welfare, governments must impose penalties on activities that harm others.

The United States legal system considers certain interests worth protecting for every individual. We all want to be secure in the privacy of our personal lives, to enjoy personal rights and liberties, and to hold property free from molestation or intrusion. Any invasion of, or interference with, these rights is legally called a *tort*.

One who commits a tort is called a *tortfeasor* (sometimes written as tortfeasor or tort feasor). Damages may be sought in the courts for any tort. There is an old saying in legal circles that "*tortious* conduct is liability-imposing conduct."

Definitions of Torts

In writings on the subject, judges and legal scholars often state that they cannot define a tort. Nevertheless, the courts say that a tort is any legal wrong committed against a person or against a person's property except for those wrongs that arise from breach of contract. A tort is a violation of that responsibility which the law requires every person to maintain toward others for the purpose of protecting the personal and economic interests of everyone. Defined in another way, a tort is any wrong causing physical or emotional damage to someone else's protected interest. As the courts usually put it:

One must so conduct one's self, manage one's own affairs, and use one's own property so as not to infringe on the rights of others.[1]

It is no defense to a lawsuit for damages that the tortfeasor was performing some duty required by contract or that the tortfeasor was acting under the orders of another person. Proof that wrongful conduct was undertaken at the direction of someone else may impose tort liability on the part of the person giving directions, but such proof will not excuse the wrongdoer.

Conduct which is lawful at the time begun may be unlawful if continued, depending on whether the rights of another are subsequently violated.

One's remedy in a tort action is a lawsuit in civil court for money damages. The courts have generally held that when an individual causes harm to another, he or she must make compensation to the victim for any damages that result.

Individual Responsibility

Adults, juveniles, insane persons, and individuals of all classes, sexes, and ages are responsible in damages for their own torts. In some instances both parents and children are legally responsible for the children's torts. Under the law in a number of states, parental responsibility is imposed if the parents themselves are in some way at fault or if the child is acting as an agent for the parent, as in running an errand. But responsibility of the parent for the child's tort varies from state to state and from tort to tort.

Some states follow the so-called "family-purpose doctrine" of liability. When an automobile is owned and operated by a parent for the convenience of the family, all drivers in the family are presumed to be agents of the parent in the operation of the car. Consequently, any tort by an underage driver is the financial responsibility of the parent. In some states that follow the family-purpose principle, however, the parent is allowed to avoid personal responsibility by showing that there was actually no agency relationship between the driver and the parent.

To make owners responsible, some states have passed laws providing that anyone operating a motor vehicle with the permission of the owner is the owner's agent. This, of course, fixes responsibility on the owner. Statutes of this kind usually cause car owners to obtain adequate insurance and to exercise care in lending their vehicles. Many states have extended the owner's responsibility further by passing laws requiring liability insurance for all owners and operators of motor vehicles.

In general, private business firms, corporations, and partnerships are all responsible for the torts of their workers committed during the course of

---

[1]*Chadwick* v. *Bush*, 163 So. 823; *Ford* v. *Grand Union Co.*, 270 N.Y.S. 162; *Spartan Drilling Co.* v. *Bull*, 252 S.W.2d 408.

their employment. This employer responsibility, also known as vicarious liability, is in addition to the responsibility of the tortious employee.

CONDITIONS FOR TORT LIABILITY

Basic Types of Torts

All torts fall into three general classifications:

1. Intentional torts
2. Injury through negligence
3. Absolute (strict) liability torts

Tort Versus Contract Liability

Contract liability arises from a breach of a duty that the parties voluntarily assumed. A tort is a breach of that kind of conduct which one individual owes to every other person based on what the law regards as wrong. Tort liability exists for everyone, whether individuals want to assume it or not.

Impossibility of Listing All Torts

There are as many kinds of torts as there are wrongs that can be committed against property, against an individual's person, or against an individual's reputation and feelings. As pointed out by the court in *Miller* v. *Monsen*,[2] "the law is simply silent when it comes to listing all the potential injuries that may be classified as torts." Early-day English and American courts designated certain injuries as "common law torts." As industry and commerce developed, many other kinds of injuries began to come before the civil courts. As noted by one of the judges in the *Miller* case, the American courts have the right to recognize new injuries as additional types of torts. The judge continued that this is a principle "susceptible of adoption to new conditions, interests, relations, and usages as the progress of society may require."

In short, there is no such thing as an all-inclusive list of torts. Undoubtedly future courts will continue to recognize new torts, based on society's need for justice.

Extent of Tortfeasor's Responsibility

Once a wrongdoer sets in motion an act that causes injury, most courts hold the tortfeasor responsible for all damage that subsequently happens to the injured person. For example, a drunk driver lost control of his vehicle and

[2]*Miller* v. *Monsen*, 37 N.W.2d 543.

seriously hurt a blameless pedestrian. More than likely the victim would have survived had a blood transfusion been available. An ambulance rushed the victim to the nearest hospital, but the blood supply had just been depleted and an ambulance bringing more blood had been struck by a second drunk driver. The victim died before more blood could arrive. When sued in tort, the first drunk driver contended he should be responsible only for damages for the wrongful injury and that the victim's eventual death was caused by an unfortunate intervening accident. If the court accepted the defendant's contention, the difference in damages could be considerable. The victim had had a good job and a long life expectancy; the victim's heirs could expect heavy compensatory damages for the wrongful death. In practically all cases of this kind the courts hold the original tortfeasor responsible for all ensuing damage.

If an injured person dies because of mistreatment or malpractice by an attending physician, the victim will usually be able to recover against both the original tortfeasor and the physician. But this does not change the fact that the original wrongdoer is responsible for all the injury suffered as a result of the tort originally committed.

DISCUSSION

CASE 28   Injured in a mine accident, the plaintiff agreed to a monetary settlement from the mine owner. Thereafter, the plaintiff sued the hospital and doctor who treated him for the injury. The plaintiff asked for damages from the doctor and hospital for alleged negligence and unskillful treatment of the injury that caused additional harm beyond the mine accident. Could the plaintiff recover against either the doctor or the hospital on this basis? (*Makarenko* v. *Scott*, 55 S.E.2d 88.)

CASE 29   A young girl who worked for a businessman was raped. The man responsible for this attack was apprehended and subsequently convicted in criminal court. The victim's parents were apparently no longer living, so a civil court allowed a friend to come into court and sue for tort damages for the victim. (Generally, a parent, guardian, administrator, or other adult must pursue a civil lawsuit in behalf of a minor. An adult who undertakes this responsibility in place of a parent is legally termed a guardian *ad litem*.) When the criminal conviction was returned, could the defendant in the tort suit defend on the basis that he had already "paid his debt to society"? (*Shaw* v. *Fletcher*, 188 So. 135.)

INTENTIONAL TORTS

When one deliberately commits an act that results in injury to another, an intentional tort results. In order for a victim (plaintiff) to prevail in a lawsuit, it must be proven that the defendant intended to commit the tortious act, which caused harm to the plaintiff. The most common intentional torts are assault, battery, false imprisonment, trespass, conversion, and intentional infliction of emotional distress.

Many of these torts are also crimes. Thus, one may be prosecuted by the state in criminal court and sued by an individual in civil court for the commission of the same act. For instance, if A beats B severely, a criminal complaint may be filed against A. A might be tried and convicted. Subsequently, B might sue A in civil court for money damages for injuries that result.

Intent

In order to prevail in a civil suit based on an intentional tort, the plaintiff must prove the defendant *intended* to commit the act in question. In addition to the commission of a deliberate act, the plaintiff may prove intent by showing that the defendant knew the consequences of the act would produce harm or that the defendant's conduct was so extreme that it showed the defendant acted with reckless disregard for the likelihood of harm. For example, if the defendant were discharging a pistol on a crowded street and the plaintiff was hit, it might be proven that the defendant's actions were so reckless that an intentional tort resulted.

Categories of Intentional Torts

Intentional torts have been classified into two general categories: intentional torts to the person and intentional torts to property. Intentional torts to the person include:

1. Assault
2. Battery
3. False imprisonment
4. Intentional infliction of emotional distress

Assault is the intentional placing of another in reasonable apprehension of an imminent harmful or offensive touching. Courts have held that one must not necessarily be in fear that a battery will occur but must look forward to the event with a feeling of unpleasantness. The defendant must intend to place the plaintiff in apprehension. Plaintiff must likewise be aware of the defendant's actions at the time of their occurrence to satisfy the "apprehension" requirement.

The apprehension must be immediate. Therefore, if the defendant telephones plaintiff and says, "The next time I see you, I'm going to shoot you," there would be no assault. However, if the defendant approaches the plaintiff with a gun and says, "I'm going to shoot you," the element of immediacy would be present.

Battery is the harmful or offensive touching of another without consent. Even if the defendant does not harm the plaintiff, such as with an unwelcome kiss, there would still be a battery if the plaintiff did not wish to be kissed by the defendant. Any physical contact with plaintiff or anything attached to the body, such as a purse, chair, plate, hat, or dog's leash would be sufficient to constitute a battery if a reasonable person would be offended by the touching. The plaintiff may seek damages for any physical or emotional injuries.

In order to establish the defendant's intent to commit a battery, it must be proven that the defendant knew or was substantially certain that a battery (or harmful physical contact) would occur.

False imprisonment has been defined as the intentional physical or psychological confinement of another without reasonable means of egress. Plaintiff must prove that the defendant intended to confine, that confinement resulted, and that the plaintiff was aware of the confinement or injured by it. If plaintiff has a reasonable means of escape of which he or she is aware, no false imprisonment results.

The requisite confinement may be accomplished by physical force, threat of immediate physical force, threat of immediate physical force, or actual physical barriers. The barriers do not have to enclose plaintiff, but may be such that there is no reasonable means of escape. Thus, when plaintiff voluntarily goes aboard defendant's boat and defendant subsequently refuses to allow the plaintiff to get off, the court held that this constituted false imprisonment since swimming to shore was not a reasonable means of escape.[3]

A major problem in today's business world is shoplifting. However, businesses must take care to act reasonably in their detention of suspected shoplifters. Most states recognize that if an individual is reasonably believed to have stolen merchandise from a store, he or she may be detained for a reasonable period of time, even if the individual has not stolen the merchandise. Although some states may require that the suspect is in the store when detained, others enable the individual to be stopped within a short distance from the store, such as in the parking lot. The court will examine whether the belief that the individual stole merchandise and the detention were both reasonable under the facts of the case.[4]

Intentional infliction of emotional distress is extreme and outrageous conduct which is likely to cause and which actually causes severe emotional distress. Liability is generally found where the conduct is so outrageous that it goes beyond the bounds of decency and is not tolerated in a civilized society. However, one may not recover for mere annoyance or if the mental injury was exaggerated.

For example, in the *Siliznoff*[5] case, the plaintiff, who was a rubbish

---

[3]*Whittaker v. Sanford*, 85 A. 399.
[4]*Collyer v. Kress*, 54 P2d 20.
[5]*State Rubbish Col. Assn. v. Siliznoff*, 38 Cal2d 330.

collector, became ill from fright when the defendants threatened to severely injure him and burn his truck unless he paid them money for collecting rubbish in a territory which they had assigned to someone else. In this case, the plaintiff was able to recover damages for his mental distress. Some states require that the mental distress be accompanied by actual physical manifestations of the injury, which assists the court in assessing damages.

Generally, those in business who are dealing with their own customers owe a special duty and are held to a higher standard of conduct. Thus, if a flight attendant on defendant's plane uses abusive language on plaintiff, a paying passenger, there would be liability on the part of the airline if the plaintiff suffered great emotional distress. However, if the plaintiff met the same flight attendant on a public street and the same language was used, the airline would not be liable.

Intentional Torts to Property

Included in this category are the following:

1. Trespass to land
2. Trespass to chattel (personal property)
3. Conversion

Trespass to land includes any act of intrusion by the defendant on the land of a plaintiff who has the right to possession of the land. Thus, if the defendant merely walks on the land of the plaintiff, he or she can be held liable for trespass. The right protected in this case is the plaintiff's interest in the exclusive use of the property. Even if the defendant accidentally enters the land, he or she can be held liable for nominal damages. If the defendant causes an object to enter the plaintiff's land, liability for trespass would still lie. For example, defendant may dump dirt on plaintiff's land or have a tree branch hanging over his or her next-door neighbor's property. However, if the defendant has the plaintiff's consent to enter onto the property, no trespass exists. If the defendant is playing ball and the ball accidentally goes onto the plaintiff's property, the defendant may retrieve it but is liable for any damages which result.

Trespass to chattel and *conversion* are very similar torts but with different damages. Therefore, they will be treated together. Each involves an act by the defendant to exercise control over the property of the plaintiff. In other words, the defendant commits an act which interferes with the plaintiff's possession of his or her personal property. Whether or not one would sue for trespass to chattel or conversion usually depends on the amount of damage done to the property. In an action for trespass, the defendant would be required to pay the cost of any repairs required on the plaintiff's property as a result of his or her actions. However, in an action for conversion, the damages amount to a forced sale. That is, the defendant would be required to pay the fair market value of the property at the time of the conversion.

Defamation

Defamation may be defined as the injuring of another's character by making malicious statements about him or her. If the statement is made orally, it is called *slander*. A written statement is called *libel*. If the defendant can prove, however, that the statement made about the plaintiff was true, there will be no case. In order to prevail, the plaintiff must prove that the defendant made a defamatory statement about the plaintiff to a third person and that as a result the plaintiff suffered certain damages (called special damages.) In most states, the statement must adversely affect the plaintiff's reputation or lower his or her esteem in the minds of others.

Whether or not one must prove special damages varies among the states. However, most states hold that in the case of slander, it is not necessary to prove special damages if the statement related to the plaintiff's trade or business, accused plaintiff of a serious crime, or implied that plaintiff had a loathsome disease. In these cases, the courts have held that damages are implied from the nature of the statement. If one must prove special damages, then it must be shown in court that actual monetary losses occurred as a result of the defamatory statement.

In libel cases, however, since the statement is of permanent form, most courts have dispensed with the requirement for proving special damages as long as the statement needs no other information to understand it is about the plaintiff. Thus, if the statement is made that "A is a thief," no additional information is required to understand that the statement is made to defame A.

It should be noted, however, that the statement made by the defendant must be stated as fact and not opinion. If defendant states, "I think A is a thief" or "In my opinion, I think A is a thief," this may not be considered defamatory.

A landmark case in the area of defamation occurred in 1964. The court in *New York Times* v. *Sullivan* [6] made defamation a First Amendment issue. In that case, an advertisement was published in the *Times* which criticized the activities of the police during a recent civil rights demonstration. The police sued the *Times* for libel. The court held that the right of free speech was so great that one who is a public official and in the public eye cannot collect damages for defamation unless it can be proven that the newspaper acted with "actual malice," which was defined as the publication of a statement known to be false or with reckless disregard for the truth. Courts have generally required that newspapers at least check their sources for the accuracy of the statements. This rule has been further extended to include

[6] *N. Y. Times* v. *Sullivan*, 376 U.S. 254.

public figures. The rationale of the courts in extending the rule has been that public officials and public figures have chosen to be in the public eye and therefore are open to public scrutiny.

The subject of defamation is necessarily very complex and could constitute a separate course in law. Therefore, it should be noted that the description here is necessarily very brief and generalized. If the reader requires a more in-depth understanding of the subject, a text on that subject should be consulted.

NEGLIGENCE

As previously noted, in many situations the law imposes tort liability for failure to act that constitutes negligence. Basically, this comes about in situations where the law imposes a duty to act.

Definitions of Negligence

Negligence is defined as a failure to exercise a reasonable or ordinary amount of care in a situation that causes harm to either a person or to property. Negligence may involve either doing something carelessly or completely failing to do something that should be done.

Other courts have defined negligence as:

An improper disregard for the safety of the person or property of another. The failure to exercise the care of an ordinary person.

There is no tort liability for a pure accident as such, unless the actor was negligent. But negligence is present in the great majority of situations involving an accident. For tort liability to arise, the wrongful act or negligence must coincide with the invasion of the protected right of someone else.

Standards of conduct that are demanded of an individual who would avoid tort liability are variable. What was reasonable by yesterday's standards may constitute negligence under today's law. In a tort suit, the plaintiff always has the burden of proving negligence, if such is claimed. Frequently, negligence is a question to be decided by the jury, acting under instructions from the trial judge. A typical charge that the judge gives to the jury in this regard is as follows:

Negligence is the lack of care that an ordinary prudent person would use under similar circumstances. This does not mean that the defendant must have used such a high degree of care as would have prevented harm, nor yet the amount or degree of care that "everybody else uses." It is whatever care should be expected by a reasonably prudent person.

This reasonable-person test for the jury applies the standards of an imaginary person. It is not the conduct of the average of the jurors, since they may be more or less careful than the ordinarily prudent person. In like fashion, it is not a measure of standards of that particular community, which may be above or below those of an ordinarily prudent person.

The Elements of Negligence

Although individual state laws may differ in a number of aspects, certain basic requirements are common to all negligence cases:

1. A legal duty was owed to the victim.
2. There was an infringement or breach of duty to the victim.
3. Injury (or damages) resulted.
4. The damage was the proximate result of what the defendant did or failed to do when legally required.

The Wrongful Act. Generally, a tort arises out of the defendant's wrongful act. In negligence situations there may be an affirmative duty to do something that never came about. In most cases, however, a tort lawsuit cannot be sustained on the defendant's failure to act, unless there was negligence. The courts have never seen fit to require you to rescue someone from drowning, unless the victim's peril was the direct result of your own actions. Similarly, the law does not require you to pull someone from in front of a speeding train or to save someone in a burning building. There may well be a moral duty in cases of this kind, but there is no legal duty unless the defendant was somehow responsible for the victim's plight. The law simply refuses to say, for example, that one swimmer must rescue another, since the danger may be great for even a strong swimmer.

So in most tort situations the courts rule that it is the defendant's *wrongful* act that makes for tort liability.

Proximate Cause. The mere fact that plaintiff suffered damage is not sufficient to place the loss on the defendant unless it can be proved that defendant caused the injury. In the language of the courts, the defendant's negligent act must be the *proximate cause* of the plaintiff's loss. But frequently the courts have had difficulty in explaining exactly what is meant by proximate cause, which has been defined as:

That which, in a natural and continuous sequence, unbroken by intervening cause, produces or causes an injury.

That which is nearest in responsible order of causation.

The proximate cause is not necessarily the immediate cause, which may be nearer in point of time or space. Where two or more causes combine to produce an injury, the last intervening cause is generally referred to as the *immediate cause*. Some other agency, more remote in time or space, may, in causal relation, be the nearer to the result and thus be the proximate cause.

Under the proximate cause principle, the courts hold a wrongdoer to those injuries that are "in the train of physical causation, and not entirely outside the range of expectation or probability, as viewed by ordinary men [or women]."[7]

For example, a tortfeasor who stabbed another person would be responsible for the immediate injuries of the victim, as well as for the death of a victim who subsequently died in a hospital because of infection to the stab wounds. But if the stabbing victim recovered somewhat and was later killed by a speeding car while en route to the doctor for further treatment, the stabber would be legally responsible for the knife injuries, but not for the automobile-caused death.

It is not necessary for the wrongdoer to reasonably foresee all the consequences that actually result from his or her misconduct. For example, a driver may race around a blind corner without realizing that another car may be met head-on or that there may be road repairs that the driver did not anticipate.

For recovery, the act complained of must be the wrongful act of the defendant. A plaintiff cannot recover damages for an alleged injury, the sole proximate cause of which was the plaintiff's own independent action.[8]

Proof of Negligence

Negligence as a Matter of Law (Negligence per se). Some conduct is held to be negligence as a matter of law and is not passed on to the jury for a finding. Violation of any statutory provision in the law is normally regarded by the courts as automatically holding the violator to be negligent. For example, if the state speed limit is set at 55 miles per hour, anyone driving at a greater rate of speed is automatically negligent. Most traffic regulations fall in this category. Failure to stop at a posted stop sign, failure to properly yield right of way, driving through a red light, and driving while intoxicated are all regulated by state laws. A violation of any such requirement may impose both criminal and tort liability on the basis of negligence.

Res Ipsa Loquitur. Sometimes an instrumentality, machine, device, or process that caused injury is within the exclusive control of the defendant. Since the plaintiff cannot get at this injury-causing instrumentality, it may be highly unlikely that the plaintiff will ever be able to prove how the injury was caused. Under the legal theory of *res ipsa loquitur*, the courts shift the burden of proof onto the defendant. Negligence is presumed, subject to disproof by

---

[7]*In Re: The Mars*, 9 F.2d 183.
[8]*Overmoe v. J. C. Penney Co.*, 202 N.W. 648.

the defendant. Sometimes the courts say that this doctrine applies if the accident is the kind that would not happen in the absence of negligence, and if the instrumentality was under the defendant's control. It is then up to the defendant to prove that negligence did not in fact occur.

Damages

Money damages in tort actions are of three types: compensatory, punitive, and nominal.

Compensatory damages are those which are awarded to return the victim to his or her former status or to make him or her whole again. Included are medical bills, lost wages, repair or replacement of damaged property, and any other actual costs incurred by the plaintiff because of the defendant's actions.

Punitive damages are awarded to punish the defendant for an act committed with the intent to harm the plaintiff. It must generally be shown that the defendant acted deliberately and willfully, with malice. Some states allow punitive damages in cases of gross negligence, which will be discussed below.

Nominal damages (usually $1) are awarded in cases where the plaintiff wants to show that a right was violated and a tort committed, but no actual money damages resulted. For instance, if the defendant has trespassed on plaintiff's property, a lawsuit would establish the plaintiff's right to exclusive possession of the property.

Defenses to Negligence

Contributory and Comparative Negligence. Negligent conduct on the part of one who was harmed by another's negligence is called *contributory negligence*. Under the law in some states, a plaintiff cannot recover damages for the negligence of another party if the plaintiff's own negligence contributed to the injury. To bar recovery, however, the plaintiff's contributory negligence must be such that it contributed to, or played a part in bringing about, the injury.

A majority of states, however, have relaxed this harsh rule in favor of one which allows a negligent plaintiff to recover for a portion of his or her injuries under a theory of *comparative negligence*. In these states, a plaintiff may recover the proportion of the damages which can be apportioned to the defendant. Thus, if the court rules that the defendant was 80% negligent and the plaintiff 20% negligent, and the plaintiff's damages amount to $50,000, then the plaintiff would recover $40,000 from the defendant (or 80% of $50,000). Some states apply this principle only in cases where the plaintiff was less than 50% negligent.

Assumption of the Risk. If an individual knowingly engages in a dangerous act, knows the risks involved, and voluntarily assumes the risk, then he or she will not be allowed to recover in a subsequent tort action. Therefore, an individual who knowingly takes part in a boxing match is assuming the risk of injury and cannot later recover in a suit for battery. A race car driver may not recover for injuries sustained during the race if his or her injuries are a direct result of the race itself. In order to use this defense, one must prove that the plaintiff knew the risk involved in the commission of the act and voluntarily committed the act, thus assuming the risk involved.

Attractive Nuisance Principle

In some states the courts follow the so-called *attractive nuisance* theory of tort liability. This places a special burden on every business or individual property owner or operator to make certain protection is afforded to every dangerous condition, machine, agency, or instrumentality that may be attractive to young children. The courts say that children of tender age do not have the experience or background to appreciate the danger of such attractions. If a child is injured by an attractive nuisance, the owner or operator of the property will be liable unless it can be proved that extreme protective measures were being used. It is no defense to the operator of an attractive nuisance that an injured child was a trespasser.

Concurring Causes

The courts note that the proximate cause need not be the only cause of an injury. If several causes all contribute to the harm, and without the operation of each the injury would not have occurred, then every individual cause is regarded as the proximate cause. This usually means, of course, that more than one wrongdoer may be legally responsible for a single tort injury. As a practical matter, the injured person may sue any tortfeasor whose act was the proximate cause of the harm.

———— *DISCUSSION* ————

CASE 30   Evidence in a lawsuit showed that a heavy truck was proceeding down a highway at excessive speed. A second vehicle, operated by a mailman making deliveries in a rural area, illegally crossed a double white center line to reach a mailbox on the wrong side of the road. Evidence showed the mailman did not signal before making the illegal crossing, nor did the mailman first ascertain that the road was clear. Still driving at excessive speed, the heavy truck hit the mail vehicle, causing it to strike the plaintiff's home, knocking the structure from the foundation. In a tort suit by the homeowner, the mailman defended on the ground that the action of the speeding truck was the proximate cause of the injury. The mailman pointed out that his actions, in and of themselves, would never have resulted in the damage, except for the negligence of the speeding truck driver. Was the mailman responsible? (*Schools* v. *Walker*, 47 S.E.2d 418.)

NO-FAULT INSURANCE

Much of present-day tort law is concerned with automobile accidents. Under the prevailing "fault system" followed by the courts in most states, one party is responsible and is required to pay damages. Students of this system have frequently criticized the fault concept in auto accident cases because of uneven, unrealistic verdicts that frequently result. In this connection it should be pointed out that tort awards frequently are much higher than those granted in breach of contract cases. This may be due largely to the fact that the courts permit both compensatory damages and punitive damages to be awarded in tort cases. Ordinarily only compensatory damages are awarded in breach of contract cases. Sympathetic juries sometimes let passions control their awards.

In a tort case, usually all the vital action took place in a matter of a few seconds. Often there are no witnesses except the parties involved. Those other witnesses who can be found are often unreliable since it is almost impossible to judge the speed of a car that may be observed casually for only a fraction of a second. Honest witnesses are often at odds concerning whether a traffic signal was red or green at the exact instant a crash occurred. Then, too, juries often favor an individual plaintiff against an impersonal insurance company. Dramatizations of pain and suffering may lead to very heavy awards which may or may not be deserved. Realistic legal scholars point out that in some instances large awards tend to encourage litigation.

Because of uneven results in actual court cases, in recent years some states have adopted a so-called *no-fault system*, sometimes known as a "system of first-party insurance." There are a number of varieties of no-fault insurance laws from state to state. Basically, a person who has been injured in a car accident collects from his or her own insurance company in the manner that one would collect on a health insurance policy if involved in surgery. Usually, the insured person is entitled to collect hospital and medical bills, lost wages or salary, and out-of-pocket expenses up to a specified amount. The insured collects this money regardless of fault. Under no-fault laws in some states, the insured can still file a tort suit under certain conditions. No-fault insurance has been both praised and condemned. Proponents say that costs of insurance have been lowered appreciably in states where the no-fault system has been used.

ABSOLUTE TORT LIABILITY

As noted previously, the law does not usually impose tort liability unless the defendant has committed a wrongful act or has been negligent. In some instances the defendant is held to liability without being at fault or being negligent. This is called the legal principle of *absolute fault* (or the rule of *liability without fault*). The idea here is that the defendant has undertaken an activity that presents considerable hazard and must therefore assume any risk connected with it. For example, an individual kept a pet tiger in a backyard cage. The owner was convinced the animal was tame; nevertheless, it was always kept securely caged. When an earthquake occurred, the tiger escaped through a broken cage door and thereafter mauled a passerby. The court held that there was absolute tort liability, notwithstanding that the owner had used the utmost care.

Absolute tort liability arises both from court decisions and from legislative enactments that have extended the principle. The courts almost uniformly hold that a landowner acts at his or her own peril in bringing unnatural conditions into play if these conditions have the likelihood for causing damage or injury to the person or property of neighbors. For example, impounding flood waters behind a dam may make the owner of the dam liable to persons or property that is flooded. Absolute liability also applies when one stores dynamite or other explosives, appreciable quantities of dangerous chemicals, or volatile gasses.

Pure food statutes in some states impose absolute liability on the manufacturer, canner, or processor if adulterants are found in canned or packaged foods. Additional consumer protection statues are being considered with regularity by the legislatures in some states.

In somewhat similar fashion, worker's compensation laws impose absolute liability on the employer of an injured worker. Before the enactment of such laws, an injured employee could recover damages only if it could be proved that the employer or one of the employer's agents (another worker) was negligent. Often this negligence was difficult or impossible to prove, also involving prolonged and costly litigation. Under worker's compensation laws, the question of blame is not in issue, and the employee is compensated for the injury if it arises out of and in the course of employment. All states now have some form of worker's compensation. Generally, the employer cannot escape liability in these cases unless the employee's injury was self-inflicted or took place while the employee was intoxicated.

RESPONDEAT SUPERIOR

American courts have long followed the old English legal principle called *respondeat superior*, which can be traced back to ancient Roman law. A translation of this term would be: "Let the master answer." The idea is that a business must be responsible in tort for the wrongful acts of its agents or employees. This will be discussed in more detail in Chapter 13.

The respondeat principle was worked out by the courts for the protection of innocent third persons who may be harmed by uncontrolled or unsupervised employees. As summarized by the judge in one case:

> . . . the act of the employee becomes the act of the employer, the individuality of the employee being identified with that of the employer. The latter is deemed to be constructively present; the act of the employee is his [or her] act; and [the employer] becomes accountable for his [or her] own proper act or omission. . . . If the employer engages improper or untrustworthy agents, it is [the employer's] fault, . . . An employer may be held accountable for the wrongful act of his [or her] employee although he [or she] had no knowledge thereof, or disapproved it, or even had expressly forbidden it. And so the employer may be made liable for acts done in violation of . . . instructions.[9]

Note, however, that an employer will not usually be held responsible for the torts of employees, unless it can be proved that the tortious acts were done within the scope of the employment or in furtherance of the employer's interests. This problem will be discussed in more detail in the material on agency (Chapter 12 and 13).

BUSINESS TORTS

Torts committed by one business to injure another business or individual will be treated as "business torts." The business committing the wrongful act may be held liable to pay damages and/or to cease its injurious activity.

Interference with Contract Rights and Business Relations

In order to enable individuals to contract fairly, the law does not allow third parties to deliberately interfere with either the making of a contract or the performance thereon. In order to sue under this theory, the plaintiff must show that the third party's interference was done with a malicious intent— that is, deliberately and intentionally to injure the plaintiff. Basically, this tort would include the third party's deliberate inducement not to enter into the contract for the purpose of injuring or taking business away from the plaintiff.

It should be noted that this tort will not be found if the defendant was merely engaging in competition. For instance, if Company Y asks contractors

[9]*Ford* v. *Grand Union Co.*, 270 N.Y.S. 163.

to bid on a construction project and Business A puts in a lower bid than Business B, B could not sue A for interference with contract rights. This would be considered justified competition.

Similar Package/Products (Unfair Competition)

It is unlawful for a business to copy another business's product or packaging to induce the public into thinking it is the same product. For instance, there are inexpensive copies on the market of expensive watches, such as Rolex and Gucci. In many cases, the original names are also included. The manufacturer of these products is engaging in an unlawful practice and is subject to prosecution and may be held liable for damages.

Similarly, if an individual were to open a hamburger stand called "McDonald's," it would be an unfair copy of the McDonald name.

Many states require that a corporation seeking a name file the name with the Secretary of State. If the name is already being used by another corporation, the state will not allow the new business to use that name. Any attempt by the defendant to deceive the public into believing that its product is actually a different brand would be considered actionable.

PRODUCTS LIABILITY

Over the years, individuals have demanded stricter laws to protect them from faulty products. Consumer protection statutes have been enacted in most states. Manufacturers, wholesalers, and retailers are generally responsible to the user of a product if he or she is harmed by it. Three theories of liability have been established:

1. Absolute or strict liability
2. Negligence
3. Breach of warranty (express or implied) and misrepresentation

Absolute or Strict Liability

Many states have adopted the principle of strict liability for defective products. Generally, if one sells a defective product which is unreasonably dangerous to a user, he or she becomes responsible for any physical harm caused to one who uses the product if his or her business is the sale of such products and the product is not altered subsequent to its sale. (§402A, Restatement 2d of Torts.)

Let us examine this rule more carefully. If you go to your local hardware store to purchase a power lawn mower and are subsequently injured because the mower was not made properly, you would be able to obtain damages for your injuries from the manufacturer and retailer who sold you the lawn mower. You would not have to prove that either was knowledgeable about the defect, but merely that there was a defect in the mower which created an unreasonable risk of harm to you. You would also have to show that the use to which you put the mower was foreseeable; that is, you were mowing your lawn.

Negligence

Manufacturers and sellers may also be held liable on a negligence theory. One must be able to prove the elements of negligence described above. Manufacturers may also be held liable if there are latent defects in the product, and no warning is given. For instance, if the cleaner used on your windows contains a chemical which could be harmful if it comes in contact with your eyes, the manufacturer could be liable for damages if no warning was placed on the bottle.

Breach of Warranty (Express or Implied); Misrepresentation

The Uniform Commercial Code has imposed liability on manufacturers and sellers based on express or implied warranty. However, this theory of recovery is generally based on contract and not tort. Liability is imposed for any warranties made expressly by the manufacturer or seller. An implied warranty of fitness applies to products; they must be "merchantable" or fit for the purpose for which they were made. This is sometimes referred to as the "implied warranty of merchantability."

A similar theory in tort is based on *misrepresentation*. If the seller of the product misrepresents a material fact about the nature or the quality of the product, and by nature of this misrepresentation the plaintiff is injured, then the plaintiff may recover under a tort theory. However, this theory is so similar to breach of warranty that they will be covered together.

If the statement made by the seller relates to the general value of the product, or the seller is obviously rendering an opinion on the quality of the merchandise, this may be considered "puffing" and is not actionable.

To illustrate the difference, suppose you go to a car dealer and the salesperson tells you, "This is the best car on the road." In that case, you would probably not be reasonable if you believe the salesperson is telling you a fact. It would merely be an exaggeration regarding the car to induce you to purchase it. However, if the salesperson represents to you that the car will need its oil changed only every 5,000 miles, and that he is an expert on oil changes because he was formerly the service technician who did this service, you may have a cause of action against the dealer if there are damages (injuries) resulting from changing the oil after 5,000 miles.

Notice the similarity between these theories—breach of express warranty and misrepresentation. Contrast the misrepresentation described previously to the defendant having expressly warranted to you, the buyer, that the car had to have its oil changed only every 5,000 miles. If you go to court under the misrepresentation theory, you must be able to prove that your reliance on the defendant's statement was reasonable. In addition, this theory is only applicable if the defendant is in the business of selling this type of item. If you buy a car from your neighbor, you would not be able to sue for misrepresentation if the above results.

When the courts review whether a statement was "puffing," they consider if the statement was general in nature and whether you reasonably relied on the statement. If the seller can prove that you misused the car (product), you will probably not prevail in the lawsuit.

Using a contract theory of breach of express warranty, you must be able to prove that the salesperson made an express statement to you and, because of that statement, you bought the product. In the case described previously, you would have to prove that a major reason you purchased the car was that the oil had to be changed only every 5,000 miles. Under this theory, you may sue an individual who is not a commercial seller of the product (such as your neighbor who sold you a car). Most states allow recovery for personal injuries to the buyer, members of the household, or guests in the home.

FRAUDULENT MISREPRESENTATION (DECEIT) ⎯⎯⎯⎯⎯⎯⎯⎯⎯

Different jurisdictions call this tort fraud, misrepresentation, or deceit. The basic elements of the tort follow:

1. False statement of a material fact.
2. Defendant knows the statement is false and intends to deceive the plaintiff.
3. As a result of relying on the defendant's false statement, the plaintiff is damaged.

One key element of this tort is that the defendant must, in fact, intend to deceive the plaintiff. If he or she makes a false statement in error and with no fraudulent intent, then all elements of the tort are not met. However, the plaintiff's reliance on the defendant's statement must be reasonable.

Suppose you purchase a refrigerator which is on sale, and the salesperson tells you it is a new refrigerator. Upon taking delivery, you find that it has been used. There are scratches on the door, and the inside shows signs of use. In this case, you purchased the refrigerator at the sale price assuming it was new. The salesperson told you it was a new refrigerator. You may have an action for misrepresentation if the salesperson knew the refrigerator was used but sold it to you at the price for a new refrigerator. You could sue the store where you purchased the refrigerator.

_____ *QUESTIONS* _____

1. Define in your own words a tort; a tortfeasor.
2. Generally, under what circumstances is a parent responsible for a child's tort?
3. What are the three basic classifications or types of torts?
4. How many different torts are there? Is there an all-inclusive list of these wrongs that is recognized by the courts?
5. What must be the intent of the tortfeasor before there is civil liability?
6. Is the tortfeasor responsible for all the consequences of the tortious act or only such harm as can be reasonably foreseen or predicted?
7. May an individual be subjected to tort liability after sustaining a criminal conviction for the same wrong?
8. What is the difference between assault and battery?
9. What is defamation?
10. What is your understanding of the term proximate cause?
11. Is it correct to say that the wrongful act must be the proximate cause of the injury before tort liability exists?
12. If two separate causes combine to result in tortious injury, are the first, the last, or both acts regarded as the sole proximate cause?
13. What is negligence? Explain.
14. What is the idea of *res ipsa loquitur*?
15. In most states can one who is contributorily negligent recover in damages against the person who caused most of the harm? When both parties are negligent, do some courts permit a recovery by one party measured on the comparative responsibility of the two parties?
16. Explain the way that liability may result from an attractive nuisance.
17. Explain how no-fault insurance works. Does it have benefits?
18. What is absolute tort liability?
19. What are the three theories utilized in products liability actions. Explain each.
20. What is the theory used in products liability in a tort action which is similar to a contracts theory? Explain the similarities and differences.
21. What is deceit? Given an example.

_____ *ANSWERS TO DISCUSSION CASES* _____

CASE 28   Most courts hold that there is no basis for recovery against the doctor or hospital here. The court pointed out: "It is a general rule . . . that the law regards an injury resulting from mistakes of the physician or his want of skill, or a failure of the means employed to effect a cure, as a part of the immediate and direct damages which naturally flow from the original injury. . . . a recovery may be had against the person causing the injury. . . . the injured person, in settling with the wrongdoer receives full compensation for all injuries. . . . Another well established rule is that when a plaintiff has accepted satisfaction in full for an injury done to him, the law will not permit him to recover again for the same damages. . . ."

CASE 29   Liability in damages for every tort stands on its own, regardless of the fact that the same incident may comprise a criminal violation. The tort is separate from the crime, and a judgment or conviction for one has no bearing on the other. A criminal wrongdoer owes one responsibility to the state and another (tort) responsibility to the injured person. Criminal prosecution results from the one responsibility, while the tort is redressed by a private civil suit. As a practical matter, there are comparatively few tort suits against convicted criminals for the simple reason that individuals in jail seldom have any assets that can be reached if a judgment is granted in a tort suit.

CASE 30   The court held: "It is not essential, therefore, for a plaintiff to show that an act, claimed to have been the proximate cause of a certain result, was the only cause. It is sufficient if it be established that the defendant's act produced or set in motion other agencies, which in turn produced or contributed to the final result. . . . If two defendants are negligent, one of them cannot be exonerated by urging and showing the negligence of the other. Where the concurring negligence of the two produces a single injury and each is its proximate cause, they are both liable."

_____ *PROBLEM CASES* _____

1   During construction a building contractor left a mortar box containing sand and lime in an open area near where children played. A five-year-old child who frequented the area suffered loss of sight when a companion threw some of the mixture into her eyes. Was the builder liable for tort? (*Johnson* v. *Wood*, 21 So.2d 353.)

2   A fire started by sparks from a railroad locomotive joined with another fire having no known origin. The railroad fire began from improperly controlled engine sparks. The united blaze set fire to the plaintiff's logs and timber, causing extensive loss. The railroad denied responsibility, pointing out that the same loss would have occurred from the fire of unknown origin. Should the railroad be held responsible? (*Kingston* v. *Chicago* N.W.Ry., 211 N.W. 913.)

3   A party leasing office space was injured in falling on ice on a parking lot controlled and maintained by the landlord. In the absence of a written agreement, would the landlord be liable for the negligent maintenance of common areas and passageways? (*Kopke* v. *AAA Corp.*, 494 P.2d 1307.)

4   A homeowner and a movie theater sued a manufacturer whose plant emitted foul, noxious odors. This condition made the home very undesirable as a place of entertainment and caused the movie theater's business to drop off to almost zero. Was this a nuisance and therefore actionable as a tort? (*Schatz* v. *Abbott Laboratories*, 281 N.E.2d 323.)

5   Chemical Corporation of America used a number of ads that were markedly similar in background and settings to those already being used by Budweiser Beer. In addition, Budweiser had previously spent substantial sums utilizing a slogan: "Where there's life—there's Bud!" Chemical Corporation of America began marketing an insecticide product using an advertising theme: "Where there's life—there's bugs!" Budweiser went to court seeking an injunction forbidding Chemical Corporation from using materials similar to those of Budweiser. The lawsuit was defended on the basis that the two firms were not in competition with each other and that no direct harm resulted from pirating of business. Decide. (*Chemical Corp. of America* v. *Anheuser-Busch*, 306 F.2d 433, cert. denied [result upheld on appeal], 372 U.S. 965.)

12

Agency

NATURE OF THE AGENCY RELATIONSHIP

Agency is a legal relationship in which one person acts for or represents another by the latter's authority. The agency relationship is always a voluntary one.

Agency concerns the liability of one person (the *principal* or *master*) for the acts of another (known as the *agent* or *servant*) done on behalf of the principal or master. The principal may be either a private person or a business. Most of the legal problems here center around the principal's liability for commitments made or acts done by the agent. Rights and liabilities between the principal and agent may also be involved.

Agency is used as an operational technique by almost any business, large or small.

Properly speaking, agency relates only to commercial or business transactions. The basic idea traces back to old Roman law, described in the Latin maxim: *Qui facit per alium facit per se* ("He who acts through another acts himself"). In most instances agency is founded on either an express or an implied contract. The law of agency, then, is essentially a continuation of both the law of contracts and the law of torts.

The Old Master–Servant Relationship

Early colonists brought indentured servants and the apprentice system to the new world from England. Principles of this old master–servant relationship became so deeply imbedded in business and legal systems that even today courts often speak of any employer–employee relationship as that of master–servant.

Today, there are distinct legal relationships between someone who engages people to work (the employer or master) and those who work under the employer's direction. Differing rights exist between these parties as to third persons in the following situations:

1. The employer (master)–employee (servant) relationship
2. The employer–agent relationship
3. The employer–independent contractor relationship

Servant Status of Employees

The master always had the right to control the physical activities of the servant in the employment process. A servant was regarded as having no discretion, always acting under orders from the master. Today the United States courts still follow this idea to include all employees of whatever rank or position. And as will be noted subsequently, the employer is almost always responsible for work-related torts of the employee, as long as the employee is acting within the scope of his or her employment.

The Agent as Having Discretion

An agent acts in place of and for the principal in creating or changing legal relationships with third persons. A servant (an employee) has no such authority. There may be occasions when a hired individual may function as both employee and agent or as employee and independent contractor in a continuing course of action. For example, a manufacturer hired an individual to sell and distribute the manufacturer's goods, physically unloading the merchandise after its arrival on the customer's dock. The person hired was an independent contractor according to the distribution agreement and an employee of the manufacturer while unloading the goods.

In a somewhat similar manner, a store clerk may be the company's agent in ordering new merchandise but will be regarded as an employee in placing empty merchandise boxes in the trash container after they have been unloaded.

The Independent Contractor

The basic characteristic distinguishing an independent contractor and an employee is that the employer has no right of control over how the work of the contractor is to be performed. An independent contractor is hired to accomplish a given result, rendering services according to a contract that specifies only the job to be accomplished.

A principal is generally not legally responsible for the torts of an independent contractor, even though such torts may cause great harm to a third party. In addition, the distinction between an independent contractor and an agent will usually fix responsibility as to whether the employer must pay worker benefits under worker's compensation laws and unemployment insurance liability. The independent contractor is almost always responsible for these costs, whereas an employer is liable for such costs in the servant (employee) and agency relationships.

In most instances an employer pays an independent contractor by installments as the required work progresses or in a lump sum at the completion of the contract. As long as the worker has independent control over the project and can hire and fire assistants, a court would usually hold that the worker is an independent contractor.

SCOPE OF THE AGENCY RELATIONSHIP

Usually, there are no limits on the scope of the agency relationship so long as the purpose of the agreement is not illegal. The terms *general agent* and *special agent* often are used in business. There is no basic legal distinction between these two kinds of agents. Usually, a general agent has authority to represent the principal in the transaction of any kind of business, while the special agent may have authority in only a specific situation or for only a special, restricted function. In any case, the authority of the agent rests on whatever authority the principal has granted in the agency contract.

What Acts Can Be Delegated

There are some acts of such a personal nature that the courts will not permit them to be carried out through an agent. For example, a person cannot designate an agent to vote for the principal in a public election. While a *proxy* may stand in for someone who is getting married in absentia, another person cannot be authorized to actually enter into the marriage relationship itself.

As we noted in discussing contract law, a third person cannot be delegated as an agent to fulfill a personal services contract. For example, a portrait painter with a contract to draw a likeness cannot delegate this duty to an assistant, even by showing that the assistant has more talent than the portrait painter.

But as a general proposition, an individual can do anything through an agent that can be done personally. Of course, the principal cannot give authority that will excuse the agent in committing a fraud, in assaulting someone, in slandering a business rival, or in committing any other illegal act. The principal will be held criminally responsible for ordering a criminal act, and the agent will be held to criminal accountability whether or not authority was ostensibly given by the principal.

Authority of the Agent

The courts usually say that an agent cannot do that which the principal cannot do for himself or herself. Any person who has legal capacity to contract can act through a representative (an agent). A few courts allow a minor to appoint an agent, but there is no uniformity among court decisions. Some of an agent's contracts made for a minor may be held void, while others may be held voidable. In those states where a minor is permitted to utilize an agent, the latter's authority may be restricted to contracting only for the minor's necessities of life. Generally, the courts do not uphold the authority of incompetents to appoint agents.

While a principal must have the necessary capacity to contract, this is not always true for the agent. The courts reason that if a principal is willing to trust business matters to an idiot, the principal cannot complain if the agent does an idiotic thing. And a third party who may be harmed by the agent's acts is not really in a position to complain about the agent's ability or capacity, since the third party got into the deal with the agent voluntarily. But while the third party cannot complain of the agent's capacity, there is nothing to keep the third party from suing if the agent acts improperly or commits a tort.

Nevertheless, most courts hold that aliens, minors, and those who are not legally competent may act as agents.

CREATION OF THE AGENCY RELATIONSHIP

Express and Implied Contract

In most instances, an agency is created by an express contract between the parties. The agreement need not be in writing so long as the contract is consistent with the statute of frauds. Nor is there a requirement that consideration be paid to create the relationship; it may be voluntary with one side receiving nothing for serving as agent. And the courts usually agree that there is no absolute requirement for an explicit agreement; at times the relationship may be implied from all the circumstances. As stated in an old landmark case:

> It is axiomatic in the law of agency that no one can become the agent of another except by the will of the principal, either express or implied from certain circumstances; that an agent cannot create in himself [or herself] authority to do a particular act by its own performance; and that the authority of an agent cannot be proved by his [or her] own statement that he [or she] is such.[1]

DISCUSSION

CASE 31   A walnut farmer habitually left his unshelled crop with a produce broker who sold the nuts at the prevailing price year after year. One fall the farmer left his crop as usual, saying nothing to the broker about authority to sell.

[1]*Graves* v. *Horton*, 38 Minn. 66.

After receiving a check for the nuts, the farmer pointed out that the walnuts in question were of somewhat better quality than usual and that the broker should have shopped around more before completing a sale at the standard price. Was the farmer justified in asking for more money from the broker?

Agency by Subsequent Ratification

There are times when an individual purports to be the agent of someone without actually having such authority. Of course, there are also instances when an agent will exceed the authority that has been given by the principal. In either instance, the unauthorized act of the agent does not ordinarily bind the principal. However, proper agency relationship may result if subsequently the principal accepts the benefits of the agent's unauthorized act or expressly affirms the agency relationship.

Most courts hold, however, that a subsequent ratification is valid only if the principal ratifies the entire conduct of the agent and not an isolated act. In addition, the agent must have purported to act for the principal at the time the unauthorized act occurred. The courts also say that for subsequent ratification to be recognized, the principal must have had the capacity to authorize the act in question, both at the time when committed and when ratified. Should the third party withdraw before the ratification takes place, then there was nothing that the principal could ever ratify.

Ostensible Agency; Agency by Estoppel

While there may be no authorization for an agent's acts, the courts hold that a principal should not be allowed to mislead a third party into believing that there is actual authority. This is the legal principal called *ostensible agency, agency by appearances, acquiescence by the principal*, or *agency by estoppel*. The courts point out that actually there is no agency at all in this situation. Nevertheless, the principal permitted the belief of agency to arise, so the principal should be "estopped to deny that it exists."

—————— *DISCUSSION* ——————

CASE 32   The owner of a manufacturing company allowed persons to send mail to company officials at only one address, a plant office. The owner also represented to the world that one Landauer, the "Works Manager," was the top management official to receive mail. Landauer was permitted to purchase, sign payroll checks, negotiate for supplies, and handle other day-to-day business matters. The owner also allowed Landauer to announce that he had full competence to deal with outside contractors. In the course of business the owner had Landauer sign bids for a number of unsuccessful governmental contracts. Later, a government bid was received signed by Landauer as

"Works Manager." When this bid was accepted by the government, the owner had decided that the bid should not have been submitted. The owner then advised that Landauer was not actually the official in charge of the plant and that he had no authority to act as the owner's agent. Could the owner avoid the contract by this claim that Landauer had never been given agency authority? (*American Anchor and Chain Corp.* v. *United States*, 331 F.2d 860.)

Proof of Agency

The rule of procedural law is that the party claiming a benefit from an alleged agency has the burden of proving the relationship in court. For example, the party seeking to enforce a contract made with an agent must present evidence to convince the court that the agent had either authority or apparent (ostensible) authority and that an agreement was in fact made with that agent. This proof may be offered by written documents, by any kind of circumstantial evidence, or by oral testimony of witnesses to the transaction.

RIGHTS AND RESPONSIBILITIES BETWEEN PRINCIPAL AND AGENT AND THIRD PARTIES

Duty to Perform in a Responsible Way

The courts consistently hold that there is an implied duty for every principal and agent to perform in a responsible manner toward each other. Similarly, every employee or agent must perform reasonably in any job or hiring arrangement. An employee, for example, must use reasonable care, skill, and diligence in duties assigned by the employer. If an agent causes loss to the principal by performing duties in a careless or improper manner, the agent may be liable to the principal for breach of the employment contract as well as for negligence (tort).

If an individual agrees to perform an agent's duties without compensation, the agent is still held by the courts to a standard of reasonable care and skill. However, a gratuitous agent is responsible only in tort, since there was no consideration for the formation of a contract.[2]

DISCUSSION

CASE 33   A business placed an order for some insurance. However, the insurance company handling the matter carelessly placed an order for the wrong kind of insurance coverage (protection). As a result, the business firm sustained a loss that was not covered by insurance. Can the business recover from the

[2]*McPhetridge* v. *Smith*, 101 Cal. App. 122.

company that was asked to write the proper insurance? (*Colpe Inv. Co.* v. *Seeley & Co.*, 132 Cal. App. 16.)

Agent's Fiduciary Responsibility

The courts consistently follow the idea that every agent owes the principal "the obligation of faithful service" in all aspects of the agency. The principal's trade secrets, customer lists, formulas, sales projections, and any other confidential company or industry information fall in this protected category. The agent's responsibility to protect such information continues even after the agency relationship has terminated. Typically, the agent in a situation of this kind may be an outside salesperson. The fact that a former agent may become a business competitor will make no difference in this fiduciary relationship.

The fiduciary obligation to the principal requires the agent to avoid taking any position contrary to the interests of the employer unless the employer (the principal) consents. In some industries it is rather common for a manufacturer's representative to handle sales for two or more competing lines of merchandise. The courts have long acknowledged the existence of this practice, holding that it is proper if the custom in that particular business is to permit this exception.

A real estate broker or salesperson authorized to sell property by the owner (principal) cannot purchase the property on his or her own account unless the owner consents. Experience shows that such consent should be in writing. The courts reason here that the real estate broker or salesperson would likely obtain a better price by selling to an outsider. In addition, the courts reason that the necessary fiduciary relationship with the property owner could wrongly be avoided if the broker or salesperson is allowed to purchase the property indirectly through a sham or dummy transaction.

Any violation of the agent's fiduciary duty to the principal makes the agency contract immediately voidable by the principal. In addition, the agent may be liable on the basis of both tort and breach of contract and will be forced by the courts to give up any secret profits that were made in the transaction. If bad faith on the part of the agent can be proved, punitive damages may be added to the compensatory damages allowed by the court.

Payments by Debtor to an Authorized Agent

A payment by a debtor to an authorized agent is deemed in law to be a payment to the principal, provided the payment is made in good faith and without reason to believe the agent would embezzle the payment. But a debtor's payment to one who is not actually the agent of the principal will not discharge the debt.

Hiring Subagents

If by its nature the agent's business is so large that the agent cannot handle all of it in person, the courts say the authority to hire subagents is implied. Similarly, subagents may be hired if the business is one where this is customarily done. The agreement of the principal to hire subagents may always be implied from the circumstances or express permission may be obtained from the principal.

In general, the subagent owes the same duties and responsibilities to the principal as does the agent. In turn, the agent is responsible to the principal for the subagent's misconduct or torts, even though the agent used reasonable care in hiring the subagent.

If the subagent was hired without authority from the principal, either express or implied, then there is no agency relationship between the principal and the subagent. Consequently, the principal is not liable in damages to an outside party for the wrongful acts of the subagent. In this situation, the agent would continue to be liable to the principal for loss sustained by the principal as an outgrowth of the subagent's wrongful acts.

Principal's Responsibilities to the Agent

The principal has a basic responsibility to cooperate with the agent and assist in the completion of the agent's duties. The principal is not permitted to obstruct or hinder the agent's performance.

Practically all states have laws that regulate hours and working conditions of employees. These statutes also generally specify the time, manner, and place for the payment of wages to employees. These laws, of course, take precedence over principles of agency law, but generally these laws correspond with agency principles.

The agent always has the right to payment of wages, commissions, or other compensation that is due from the principal. Whenever a remedy is due to the agent, it may be enforced by a lawsuit based on the agency contract. The agent also has the right to hold the principal to an exclusive sales territory agreement, allowing the agent to recover from the distributor or manufacturer (the principal) whatever profits would have been made on total sales in the territory. Other courts have sometimes held, however, that while a company cannot appoint other agents to compete in an exclusive territory, the principal itself will be allowed to use salaried employees to compete in the territory.

In general, an agent cannot claim compensation for acts that were unauthorized or forbidden by the principal or were against the principal's known interests. Nor does the agent have a right to receive pay for illegal acts or in instances where the principal suffered due to the agent's negligence or misconduct. If the agent's work was handled by an unauthorized sub-agent, the latter cannot look to the principal for pay.

In most states the agent has a lien right, permitting the agent to hold the principal's property for wages or commissions due so long as the property was already lawfully in the agent's possession. Items that may be held include such things as sales manuals, sample products, and accounting records.

QUESTIONS

1. Define agency.
2. What distinguishes the principal–agent relationship from the principal–independent contractor relationship?
3. What types of matters may not be delegated to an agent for handling?
4. Can anyone enter into an agency contract as a principal? As an agent, what limits are there, if any?
5. Is an agent's own statement of authority sufficient proof of agency?
6. What are the requirements for agency by ratification?
7. Describe ostensible agency. Why is this principle necessary in agency law?
8. Describe the fiduciary relationship between an agent and the principal.
9. Is a principal bound by a debtor's payments to the principal's agent?
10. Will most courts uphold an agent's exclusive right to be the company's only sales representative in that territory? Explain.

ANSWERS TO DISCUSSION CASES

CASE 31   When the walnut crop was left without any discussion, an agency by implication arose. The farmer had no basis for claiming compensation above the prevailing market price.

CASE 32   The facts here constituted an ostensible agency. The court said: "Through carelessness or design, this principal pushed its agent (Landauer) to the very forefront of its sole operation and kept well hidden all the strings it had tied to him. It cannot complain if . . . he broke the strings and grasped the substance of the role it allowed him to appear to have."

CASE 33   The court held that the company that was requested to place the insurance did not live up to the implied duty to perform responsibly and should pay damages on a breach of agency contract.

_____ *PROBLEM CASES* _____

1   An individual agreed to sell coal for a commission. He then found that coal could be sold for a higher price than the coal supplier was aware. Must the seller account for this excess over the profit expected by the supplier (the principal)? (*Smokeless Fuel Co.* v. *Western United Corp.,* 19 F.2d 834.)

2   Thad Sparkman sent his brother John to fetch Dr. McCowen, M.D., to make a house call for Thad Sparkman's wife. Not being able to find Dr. McCowen, John Sparkman requested Dr. Bartlett to proceed to Thad Sparkman's residence. When Dr. Bartlett arrived, Thad Sparkman came out and informed the doctor that his services were no longer needed, since the emergency was over. Could Dr. Bartlett charge for this call on an agency-contract basis? (*Bartlett v. Sparkman,* 8 S.W. 406. [This is an old horse-and-buggy age case that is still the law.])

3   Selling liquor to a minor is a criminal offense in all states. Undisputed evidence showed that the liquor store owner gave liquor to a nine-year-old minor for the account of an adult. The liquor was given to the adult, as requested. Was the minor merely an agent for the adult? Was the minor guilty of a crime? (*Harley* v. *State,* 56 S.E. 452.)

4   A meat supplier furnished meat to a restaurant managed by Sullivan. Subsequently, Sullivan told the supplier that he was opening a new restaurant named "The Shah." After a considerable bill for meat had been run up at "The Shah," Sullivan informed the supplier that "The Shah" was actually owned and operated by Protective Services Inc. Sullivan disclaimed responsibility for payment of meat delivered to "The Shah." Was he liable? (*McClusky Commissary* v. *Sullivan,* 524 P.2d 1063.)

5   Oddo bought baked goods for his grocery store from Interstate Bakeries. Cooley made deliveries for Interstate in the area when he falsely increased the records of deliveries, causing Oddo to pay for more baked goods than actually received. This went on for nearly six years, amounting to about $79,000 in overcharges. Interstate had not known of the fraud and had not profited directly from this activity. Oddo sued Interstate for the overcharges on the basis that Cooley was Interstate's agent and that Interstate had placed Cooley in a position where this fraud could be perpetrated. Was this claim proper? (*Oddo* v. *Interstate Bakeries,* 271 F.2d 417.)

13

Responsibility on Agency Contracts; Respondeat Superior

PRINCIPAL'S LIABILITY

Agent's Authorized or Unauthorized Acts; Misconduct

When an agent acts within the authority granted by a known principal, any contract that the agent negotiates becomes one between the principal and the third party. The only recourse of the third party is against the principal. The courts also consistently agree that at this time the agent has no rights in the contract against the third person. In effect, the agent has stepped out of the picture regarding liability for breach of contract.

But if the agent acted without authority, or in fact exceeded the authority granted by the principal, the agent alone is liable to the third party on the contract. The principal cannot be held by the third party unless the principal subsequently ratifies the acts of the agent or unless there was an ostensible agency. If the agent did not in fact have authority, the agent can be held liable by the third party even though the agent had a good-faith belief that he or she was so authorized.

An agent is always responsible to third persons for injury resulting from the agent's negligent, malicious, or fraudulent acts. The agent cannot escape legal responsibility for misconduct by pointing out that he or she was acting for a principal or that the injured person can obtain adequate recourse against the principal. If harm is done by the agent on orders of the principal, the injured third party may proceed against the principal alone, against the agent alone, or against the two jointly.

If the agent indicates to a third party that there is some doubt about the agent's authority, the agent will not subsequently be personally liable on a purported contract that failed because the principal had not granted authority. The agent alone may enforce a contract against a third party if it turns out that the agent did not actually receive authority from the principal. If the agent's acts exceeded authority and the third party renders all or part

160

performance on the contract, the third party may be able to recover the value or the performance in a quasi-contract action.

Undisclosed Agency

Sometimes an agent declines to advise others of the fact that he or she is actually an agent for someone else. In legal circles this is called *undisclosed agency*. If the agent signs a contract with a third party with his or her own name, the agent becomes personally liable on the contract. This, of course, is consistent with contract law principles since the other party is entitled to rely on the undisclosed agent's outward manifestations.

An agent also becomes personally liable on a contract when the agent reveals the agency relationship but refuses to furnish the name of the principal.

If an agent sells goods furnished by the principal without disclosing the principal's identity, the agent must be responsible to the buyer on the principal's implied warranty of ownership (title). The agent is then liable to the buyer if the goods turned out to be stolen and were confiscated by the police from an innocent third-party buyer.

An agent may sue a third party for breach of contract in an undisclosed-agency situation. As a general rule the undisclosed principal may also sue the third party for a breach of contract. But when a contract is under seal, the undisclosed principal may not bring a lawsuit to enforce a contract, since the principal was not a party to the sealed instrument and has no standing to sue on it.

A third person cannot sue an undisclosed principal if the third individual has already elected to hold the agent, rather than the principal. Then, too, the third person cannot sue the principal if the principal has already made a good-faith settlement with the agent regarding the contract.

TERMINATION OF AGENCY _____

Notice to Agent and Third Parties

It is important that termination of an agency relationship be made known to third parties who are still in position to deal with the agent. If these third parties are not advised, the agent may still have the power to bind the principal to an unwanted contract. The reason, of course, is that the third party is entitled to act on appearances, deceived by an ostensible agency. Therefore, both the agent and those likely to deal with the agent should be notified immediately upon termination.

If the agency agreement is withdrawn by the principal, the withdrawal does not become effective until received by the agent. Thereafter, if the agent should attempt to make a contract with a third party, the agent would be liable to the principal. As a practical matter, however, holding the agent responsible may not be a sufficient legal remedy, especially if the agent has little financial worth. As to the agent, termination takes effect whether or not notice is given to third persons.

Methods of Termination

The agency relationship may be ended by the following methods:

1. Termination by expiration of the specified period in which the agent was to act. The courts say that the agency was for a "reasonable" time if no specific duration was stated in the agency agreement. The meaning of the term "reasonable time" is construed by the courts on a case-by-case basis, depending on the nature of the agency, the difficulty of accomplishment, and other controlling factors.

2. Termination by specific agreement to do so between the principal and the agent.

3. Termination by death or legal incapacity (insanity and so on) of either the principal or the agent. Most courts also hold that bankruptcy of either the principal or the agent terminates the relationship. However, the agent may still dispose of the principal's property that is being held at the time of the bankruptcy.

4. Termination through revocation by the principal. The agency contract is one that the principal is allowed to end at any time without giving any reason. Of course, if the agent has been hired as a salesperson for a specified period, the terms of the contract will prevail over the general principles of agency law. But a mere statement of displeasure with some of the work of the agent does not constitute revocation. If the agency is based on an agreement to hire the agent for a specified period, the principal is liable to the agent in damages for a wrongful discharge. But many courts hold that even though the principal is liable for damages for wrongful discharge, the agency may still be terminated. According to these holdings, the principal always has the right to bring the agency to an end, but must expect to pay for a wrongful termination.

5. Termination by withdrawal of the agent. This may be done at any time in an *agency at will*. If the agent is operating under a contract for a specified time of service or until a certain event is accomplished, the agent will be liable for damages to a principal who was not at fault in bringing about the termination.

6. Termination by loss or destruction of the subject matter or by change of circumstances. The agent's authority is lost if the subject matter is seri-

ously disabled, lost, or destroyed. For example, a real estate agent had authority to sell a lot; however, ownership of the lot was taken by the state in a condemnation proceeding. The courts also generally hold that the outbreak of war between the country of the principal and that of the agent brings the relationship to an end. In addition, a physical impossibility terminates the relationship.

7. Termination by rescission. The general rules of law concerning rescission apply to an agency contract.

RESPONDEAT SUPERIOR ("LET THE MASTER RESPOND") _____

A fundamental idea of tort and agency law is that both the employer and the employee are responsible for the employee's torts committed within the scope of the employment. As noted earlier, the employer's responsibility is based on the old Roman legal maxim: *Respondeat superior* ("Let the master respond"). Of course, an employee is no longer regarded as "property," as was a servant in colonial America. But the basic idea has continued in modern law that an employer should have enough control over the employee to be responsible for the employee's acts. Modern courts still speak of this master–servant relationship in referring to the employer–employee relationship where the worker's physical activities are supervised by management.

Legal Justification for Employer Liability
Under Respondeat Superior

It is basically the owner who decides how a business project will be set up and implemented. The courts feel that by giving direction and control to a project by which someone may be injured, the owner should be responsible for resulting injuries. Having initiated the risk, management should be prepared to assume it.

The courts reason that as between the employer and the employee, "it is almost always the employer who has the deeper pocket," as some legal writers put it. In short, the employer has more assets from which losses may be paid.

In addition, the employer is usually equipped to protect against business injury risks by providing insurance, and spreading the cost of the insurance over the entire operation. Individual workers can seldom afford such insurance.

The courts also reason that if employers are forced to pay for tort losses, they will maintain the kind of working standards that avoid the likelihood of costly lawsuits. In addition, employers will hire more carefully, reducing injuries both to workers and to outsiders.

When Respondeat Superior Will Apply

In deciding whether the doctrine of *respondeat superior* will apply, the courts say that two basic requirements must be established:

1. That there was a master–servant or employer–employee relationship between the individual who caused the injury and the employer who is sought to be held liable for it.
2. That the servant's or employee's wrongful act (tort) was committed within the course and scope of the employment.

When a Tort Falls Within the Scope of the Employment

If the employer–employee relationship can be proved, tort liability of the employer turns on whether the employee was acting within the scope of the employment at the time the tort was committed. In essence, this means that the employee perpetrated the tort within working hours and generally while engaged in the kind of work that the employee was assigned to do. The courts usually weigh some or all of the following considerations in arriving at a decision[1]:

1. Whether the act was authorized (or incidental to any act authorized) by the master [employer];
2. The time, place, and purpose of the act;
3. Whether the act was one commonly performed by employees on behalf of their employers;
4. The extent to which the employer's interests were advanced by the act;
5. The extent to which the private interests of the employee were involved therein;
6. Whether the employer furnished the means or instrumentality (truck, machine, or whatever) by which the injury was inflicted;
7. Whether the employer had reason to know that the employee would do the act in question, and whether the employee had ever done it before; and
8. Whether the act involved the commission of a serious crime.

---

[1]From the RESTATEMENT OF TORTS (2d), Sec. 229, which is followed by a majority of courts.

Right to Control Employee's Physical Acts as Test of Employer's Liability

In many situations the courts consistently hold that the employer's right to control physical activities of the worker is the dominant factor in deciding the employer's liability to an outsider injured by the worker. This, of course, has continued the master–servant principle.[2]

The courts also hold that the *respondeat superior* principle does not apply to the principal–agency relationship unless the agency contract specifies that the principal's control extends to the activities of the agent's physical responsibilities. Agency contracts that include this specification are not very common; therefore the *respondeat superior* doctrine does not usually apply to an agency relationship. In some instances one person may function both as a servant and as an agent for the employer. Liability rests with the employer if a tort is committed while a part-time servant–agent is functioning as a worker under the control of the employer.

In an employer–independent contractor situation, the employer is never held responsible for the contractor's torts unless the employer has neglected some duty to the injured person. With very rare exceptions, the control over worker activities that the employer has surrendered to an independent contractor is sufficient to excuse the employer for the worker's torts to outsiders.

Limitation of Victim to Single Recovery

Of course, the victim of an injury caused by an employee is entitled to only one recovery. An award of damages against either the employee or the employer will bar a recovery against the other.

In most instances if the employee is exonerated from liability by a court, such action usually excuses the employer as well. In isolated instances liability may be imposed on an employer after the employee was exonerated, based on the breach of some existing legal duty that the employer owed to the injured third party.

Torts by Agent or Independent Contractor

As a general proposition, both an agent and an independent contractor are responsible for their own torts or those of their employees. Lacking physical control over either the agent or the independent contractor, the employer cannot be held for their torts. Neither the agent nor the independent contrac-

---

[2]*Gifford-Hill Co.* v. *Moore,* 479 S.W.2d 711.

tor can escape tort liability by pointing out that the work was being done for someone else.

Torts of a Subagent

As previously noted, an agent may hire a subagent. The principal is liable for the subagent's tort when the subagent is working under the direct control of the principal.

Ostensible Employment

The employer–employee relationship is always based on a mutual agreement between the parties. Neither may enter into the hiring arrangement without the consent of the other. Therefore, the courts hold that one who negligently or intentionally gives the appearance of having another as an employee may be estopped from denying an employment relationship to a third party. It is necessary here that the third party rely on this appearance for the purported employer to be held responsible under the master–servant theory of ostensible employment.

"Borrowed Servant" Principle

At times an employer may loan workers to another, either for pay or as a favor. This commonly occurs when one contractor or employer loans a piece of heavy equipment or a specialized machine and sends along a skilled operator. Liability here, as in most situations, depends on which employer or contractor has the right to control the physical activities of the borrowed worker. This may be a question for a jury to decide from all the facts brought out during the course of a trial.

An employer utilizing the services of a borrowed employee will be liable in any event if this employer orders the borrowed worker to perform a specific act from which tortious injury results.

Usually a firm that makes a business of renting out heavy machinery is presumed to retain control over the loaned employee who often goes along with the equipment. This presumption may be rebutted, however, if the rental company can establish that the agreement called for the customer (lessee) who rented the equipment to take over control of the operator.

Distinguishing Between Employee and Independent Contractor

In practice there is often doubt about whether an individual is functioning on the job as an employee or as an independent contractor. The courts frequently apply the following tests in making this determination:

1. Whether the individual performing the work is in an occupation or specialization that is generally different from that of the employer;
2. Whether work of this kind is usually given over to the worker's discretion or followed step by step by the employer's supervisor;
3. The way in which payment is made to the worker;
4. Whether the tools are those of the worker and whether they are of a specialized kind;
5. Whether unusual skills are needed to perform the job; and
6. The length of time for which the worker is employed, whether continuously for several years or for this specific task.

Absolute Tort Liability of Independent Contractor

In some isolated instances an employer may be held responsible for injurious acts committed by an independent contractor working on a project for the employer. The courts say that an employer cannot evade responsibility for tort by contracting with someone else to handle a dangerous project where the only purpose is to evade liability. The courts frequently extend this idea to such activities as storing or handling dynamite, explosives, poisonous gases, dangerous acids, or volatile chemicals. On both agency and tort principles, the courts, as a matter of policy, impose absolute liability on the party wanting to use, store, or transport extra-hazardous substances.

In some instances an employer may specifically order an employee not to do a specific tortious act under any circumstances. Nevertheless, if the employee thereafter does the forbidden act with a resulting third-party injury, the employer is responsible. The employer's order forbidding the tort is never an excuse. Otherwise, an employer could forever be freed from employees' torts by reciting an all-inclusive list of forbidden activities at the time every employee first went to work.

Employee's Misuse of Employer's Equipment

Liability does not automatically fall on the employer when a worker misuses a company delivery vehicle or piece of equipment. The employer is liable only when the firm's equipment is being used in furtherance of the employer's business interests. A slight deviation en route by a delivery employee, or a stop along the way to say hello to a friend, would likely result in liability for the employer. Clearly there is liability on the employer if the employee negligently strikes another vehicle along the assigned delivery route. But if a company van was taken by an employee without permission and for the purpose of driving to a fishing spot, practically all courts would agree that these circumstances were not within the scope of employment. Many cases fall somewhere between the two extremes with the results varying from case to case and from state to state.

Torts During Employee's Nonbusiness Travel

Perhaps the majority of courts consider employee travel to or from lunch in a company car, or travel to and from the employee's home, as outside the scope of employment. Consequently, a tort occurring during the course of such travel is the sole responsibility of the employee. If, however, an employee was asked to take a deposit to the bank during the course of travel to lunch, most courts would construe this driving as within the scope of employment.

Automobile "Permissive Use" Laws

A number of states have so-called permissive use laws imposing limited liability on the owner of a motor vehicle involved in an injury to a third party when the car is under loan. Usually, it is immaterial whether the permission given was express or implied. Liability under these statutes falls on the owner automatically, whether or not the car was being used by an employee of the owner within the course of employment.

———— QUESTIONS ————————————————————————————

1. Is the agent personally liable when a valid contract has been made by the agent with a third party? Explain.
2. Explain the nature of undisclosed agency.
3. What are the third party's rights in an undisclosed agency? The rights of the principal? The rights of the agent?
4. What is it important to give notice to third persons of the termination of an agency?
5. May the principal withdraw from an agency relationship at any time? Explain.
6. What results if a principal attempts to wrongfully withdraw from an agency agreement where the agent had received a contract to handle sales for the principal for a specified period of time that had not yet expired?
7. List the ways in which an agency relationship may be terminated.
8. Why is it usually more desirable for an employee's torts to be paid for by the employer?

9. List the two basic requirements for holding the employer responsible for a worker's torts to a third party.

10. List some of the considerations that the courts weigh in deciding whether a tort falls within the scope of the worker's employment.

11. How does the right to control the worker's physical activities place the responsibility for the worker's torts on the employer?

12. Is the employer responsible for the torts of an agent? Of an independent contractor?

13. Explain the idea that ostensible employment shifts tort responsibility.

14. When a subagent performs acts under the direct control of the principal, who is responsible for the subagent's torts that injure a third party?

15. What is the "borrowed servant" doctrine?

16. How do the courts decide whether an individual is a servant or an independent contractor?

17. May an employer evade tort liability by hiring an independent contractor solely to assume the employer's potential tort liability for dangerous acts?

18. What general considerations are used by the courts in deciding whether a company delivery vehicle is being operated within the scope of the driver's employment?

_____ *PROBLEM CASES* _____

1   Floyd was a car salesperson for Morristown European Motors, operating on a verbal contract. Floyd was paid a commission of 25 percent of net profit to Morristown European Motors with a draw of $100 per week. The parties did not specify when commissions would become earned. Floyd accepted 10 percent of the expected purchase price of three new models in January and February, although the new car price had not been set. These customers were given to understand that their deposits were refundable. When Floyd was on a leave of absence in March, the three cars arrived and the customers took delivery. Floyd asked for a commission of about $721 on these sales but the motor company refused to pay. Floyd sued and the firm defended on the basis that the deposits made by the customers were refundable and that the deals were not actually made until March when Floyd was not an active employee. Was the motor company liable? (*Floyd* v. *Morristown European Motors, Inc.*, 351 A.2d 791.)

2   A full-time employee of a veneer mill performed part-time cleaning for a small bank. The bank furnished her a key as well as cleaning supplies. She was given no supervision by the bank and was never given instruction or

orders. At times, any member of this woman's family substituted for her and she performed as she saw fit. She also set her own hours. No social security or other benefits were furnished. Was this woman an independent contractor or an employee of the bank? (*Farmers & Merchants Bank* v. *Vocelle*, 106 So.2d 92.)

3   A railroad engineer ran a train across an automobile crossing at a high rate of speed, without giving the crossing warnings required by law. Is the engineer personally liable for a tort if negligent operation of the train caused injury to an automobile passenger at the crossing? Under agency principles and the idea of *respondeat superior*, is the railroad also liable for negligent injury? If a judgment is collected against the railroad, can the engineer also be sued? (*Southern Railway* v. *Grizzle*, 53 S.E. 244.)

4   Anderson owned a diner known as "Jack's Lunch." A customer named Covert entered the diner during early morning hours and was disorderly. The night employee who ran the diner then evicted Covert, beating him severely, kicking him, and knocking out several teeth. Covert sued Anderson, owner of the diner. Was Anderson liable? (*Anderson* v. *Covert*, 245 S.W.2d 770.)

5   At the close of business an employee was instructed to take a company car to a garage. The employee gave a fellow worker a ride home but was returning to the garage when an accident occurred. Since the employee driving the car had not deviated greatly from the route and had not taken the car for any extended time, was the accident one that occurred during the course of employment? Were both employer and employee liable? (*Rooks* v. *Swift and Company*, 98 So. 16.)

6   A third party was injured during the course of dealings with an individual who claimed to be an agent in the sale of real estate. Actually, it turned out that the supposed agent did not have authority. Unable to establish the agency relationship, the injured person sued the supposed agent. The basis for this lawsuit was an implied warranty of authority as well as claim of an action for deceit (a tort). In an instance of this kind would the supposed agent be liable in damages? (*Oliver* v. *Morawetz*, 72 N.W. 877.)

14

Property Rights;
Personal Property

NATURE OF PROPERTY AND OWNERSHIP

Property is a creation of the law. Property consists of all those things that are held or owned under the protection of the government. Legal writers sometimes point out that the seas and oceans and the atmosphere around the earth are so vast that they are for the use of all peoples. They can become the exclusive possession of no one individual, therefore they are not designable as property.

Reduction to Physical Possession

The courts frequently say that property is anything that can be reduced to the physical possession of one individual, the owner. For example, an individual becomes the owner of a wild deer by catching the animal and keeping it in a pen, so long as this does not violate wild game laws. Atmosphere can be reduced to possession by pumping it into an automobile tire, but ownership is lost if the air leaks out.

A thing may be subject to ownership, however, without actually being in the complete physical possession of the owner. You may own a car or a tract of land, yet everyone recognizes that the property cannot be stuffed into a pocket.

The courts also emphasize that dominion or control over a thing is one of the characteristics that denotes ownership. One can exercise dominion over property without actually ever being in complete possession of it. It is this right to enjoy through exercising dominion, to do with it as one pleases—even to the point of destroying it completely—that makes for ownership.

The courts also say that transferability is a distinguishing feature of property. This idea implies not only that something is capable of being transferred, but that this change does take place. Ownership therefore involves a relationship between the individual and the thing in question, as well as between the individual and other persons: Who may be excluded from the use of the property? Who will be permitted to possess it, profit from it, enjoy the use of it, and so on?

A person's good name is not transferable; a reputation cannot be sold to another. In addition, one's children are not property. However, the good will created by a business firm is transferable and may be bartered or sold.

Ownership as a Bundle of Rights

Usually we visualize property as the substance, the thing itself. Legally, however, we think of ownership of property as that bundle of rights associated with the physical object, rather than the object itself. These rights, of course, are created and enforced by law and the court system.

Bare possession of property, with nothing more, would hardly be satisfactory to most owners. Each right in this ownership bundle carries some specific additional privileges and remedies that the owner can use to obtain enjoyment and benefit from the property. Some remedies include the right to sue for damages for misuse or abuse of the property or the right to obtain an injunction forbidding an outsider from interfering with the property. As part of this bundle of rights, the owner can hold the property indefinitely, can profit from it, use it, give it away, sell it, or dispose of it in any way not forbidden by law.

Limitations on Ownership

All this does not mean that there are no limits on this bundle of rights held by an owner. As far as we can tell, every government yet established has had restrictions on the uses and privileges of property. Everyone owns, subject to the limitations imposed by the legal system itself. For example, there are usually laws that prohibit the usage of property in a way that pollutes the water supply of other people.

But in defining ownership, the courts hold that it consists of a totality of all those rights, privileges, powers, and immunities that are legally permitted with respect to the property in question.

The terms *ownership, property right*, and *title* are frequently used interchangeably in legal terminology.

KINDS OF PROPERTY _____

Personal and Real Property

Under United States law, all property is usually classified as either personal property or real property,[1] and a number of legal rights depend on which

[1]Once the crops are severed from the land, however, they become personal property.

class of property is involved. For example, a contract for the sale of a house and lot works a transfer of ownership of all real property located on that land. If a living room bookcase inside a house is personal property, then ownership of the bookcase does not pass to a buyer of the house. Whether a house trailer is classified as personal property (a vehicle) or as real property (a residence) may determine whether the property is to be taxed at substantially different rates. An insurance policy may be written to cover all real property on a tract of land. If the house trailer is real property, then insurance coverage would extend to the house trailer in case of destruction by fire.

In legal terminology, the words *personalty, chattels,* and *personal property* are often used interchangeably. Chattel derives from an old French word for cattle, an early symbol of wealth. But today the word chattel pertains to any kind of personal property.

Trees, vines, shrubs, and crops that are produced by nature alone are generally regarded as part of the realty to which they are attached by roots. Such things continue to be real property until severed. Legally called *fructus naturales*, these may be sold separately from the land. For example, standing timber may be sold to a lumber mill. Planted crops, such as grain growing in a field, may be either personal property or real property, depending on state laws. Generally, growing crops that have not been severed pass to the buyer of the land, unless reserved in writing. Once the crops are severed from the land, however, they become personal property.

The Movability Test

As a generalization, the courts classify all movable items as personal property. All other kinds of property are realty. Movable items include all sorts of things that are not affixed to the land—cars, clothes, jewelry, money, stocks and bonds, cattle, and unattached furniture. Immovables, such as farming tracts, city lots, houses, offices, apartment buildings, bridges, power plants, and other things secured to the land are all classified as real property.

It is worth noting that all property does not carry a permanent, unchanging classification as either personal or real. For example, a tree growing on a tree farm in the state of Washington is affixed to the land and is therefore real property. Sawed down in a logging operation, the tree becomes personal property. Used as lumber to build a cabin, it once again becomes real property. If the cabin should be torn down for salvage, the lumber would again revert to the personal property category.

Personal Property: Tangible or Intangible Property

Personal property may be divided into two classes: (1) physical or corporeal personal property, including tangible and most movable things, and (2) incorporeal personal property, including stocks, bonds, copyrights, patents, some leases, annuities, and the right to sue (called a *chose in action*). Cattle, clothing, and merchandise are examples of physical, tangible personal property. It is usually said that an intangible has no intrinsic or marketable value in itself; it is merely the representative of value. Real property is always tangible, a thing of physical substance.

ACQUIRING TITLE TO PERSONAL PROPERTY

Title to personal property may be gained in a variety of ways. In general, personal property created through mental or physical endeavors belongs to the person who expended the effort to produce it. If the creator is under a contract to produce for someone else, then the courts will usually honor the contract. Some of the ways of obtaining title to personal property are outlined below.

Title by Subjecting Wild Products or Animals to Dominion

Unless game laws or other regulations are to the contrary, ownership of wildlife can be gained by obtaining possession and dominion. A butterfly may be owned by catching it in a net.

Title by Natural Increase; by Making from Raw Materials

When an item is fabricated or manufactured from raw materials, the finished product is normally owned by the person who had title to the raw materials.

Title by Purchase

In many instances, of course, the ownership of personal property is obtained by purchase. Buyers customarily accept store merchandise without asking whether the store actually has title to the things offered for sale. Usually no proof of ownership is needed when an individual sells a personal item that has been possessed for an appreciable period. However, prudent buyers usually retain proof of ownership for a reasonable time for any purchase that involves great expenditure.

A deed is almost always needed to transfer ownership of real property, but a bill of sale will usually suffice for personal property. No particular wording or formality is needed for preparing a bill of sale. Usually a written statement that the article is being sold is sufficient if the writing describes the item, gives the name of the buyer, and is signed and dated by the seller. A serial number should be included if available.

Most states have laws, however, that require automobiles to be transferred according to a specified procedure. Usually a special form called a "pink slip" or a registration is required by state authorities. Sales that involve guns, explosives, and some other dangerous items are also frequently regulated by state statutes.

The basic rules of law in selling personal property usually work to the advantage of the owner. A seller can never convey better title to the buyer than the seller possesses. Therefore, a seller of stolen property gives no ownership interest to the buyer, regardless of the buyer's good faith.

Title by Inheritance, by Will, or by Gift

The owner of real or personal property may transfer good title by leaving the item to someone in a will or by passing it on to heirs by the state laws of succession when there is no valid will.

Title to personal property may be transferred by either of two types of gifts: (1) a *gift inter vivos*, or (2) a *gift causa mortis*. The first type is a gift from a normal, living person, while the second is one made by an individual who is on the threshold of death. The two kinds of gifts have differing legal requirements but all legally valid gifts have three basic requirements:

1. There must be an intent by the owner to pass title to the property as a gift;
2. There must be a delivery of the property; and
3. There must be an acceptance of the gift by the beneficiary (the *donee*).

Usually, the courts are not troubled in finding that the giver intended to make a gift. However, it must be clear that the intent is to pass ownership immediately, rather than at some future date. At times the *donor* (the giver) may hold onto property after stating that it has been given as a gift. Usually the courts say that if the donor has not given up control, the alleged gift failed for lack of delivery. However, the courts habitually recognize a symbolic act as a substitute for delivery. A gift of a bank account would be considered valid from the standpoint of delivery if the passbook was handed to the donee. If, however, the donor died before actually making delivery or even a symbolic transfer, the courts would rule that title was not transferred. The deceased's executor or executrix does not have the legal power to make this transfer after the donor's death.

The courts say that a gift inter vivos transfers ownership immediately when the donor states that a gift is being made and a delivery takes place. Actually, most courts hold that the title is in suspense for a short time here since the donee has a right to refuse the gift if this refusal takes place promptly after learning of the transfer.

————— *DISCUSSION* —————————————————

CASE 34   A young man advised his girl friend that he was making her the gift of a new car. Actually, he never got around to bringing the car over to her. Later, the pair broke up, and the former girl friend sued for specific performance, claiming the car. Justify whether or not a court would award the car to her.

In a gift causa mortis, the donor must be under the belief that death is impending and imminent. The donor must then actually deliver the property in question. The courts say that title to the property passes to the new owner upon the death of the donor. However, the courts regard a gift causa mortis as being different from a regular gift. The donor in a causa mortis transaction has the right to revoke the gift at any moment until the time when death actually occurs. The courts also hold that a transfer of title does not take place here unless death actually results soon after the gift is made. In addition, title does not change hands if the recipient dies before the donor.

The transfer of gifts or property is subject to Federal gift tax under certain conditions. In most instances a donor can make gifts up to the value of $10,000 to any number of individuals in one year, repeating the gift year after year, without being subject to tax. The services of an attorney may be advisable if a gift of more than $10,000 is given to any one party in a year.

DISCUSSION

CASE 35   The owner of a famous race horse advised that he wanted to give one of the horse's colts to his grandson. A number of family members were notified of this intent. The owner delivered the colt's registry papers to the grandson but died before he actually got around to handing over the animal. The owner's heirs contended the colt was part of the owner's (grandfather's) estate because of "failure of delivery." Who actually owned the colt?

Title by Confusion

Confusion is the legal term for blending or intermixing personal property with other personal property from which it cannot be distinguished. Crude oil, corn, wheat, and products of this kind are often intentionally mixed in storage. Deliberate confusion by a wrongdoer has the legal effect of passing a rebuttable title of the whole mass to an innocent party whose property was intermingled. The wrongdoer may regain title to part of the mass, but only by showing a court convincing proof of the wrongdoer's contribution. The courts almost always insist that the burden of proof must be on the wrongdoer.

Title by Accession

Accession is the deliberate or natural addition of something new to an item of personal property. To take an actual case, a student's car was stolen and sold by a thief. The buyer ripped out the old seat covers and replaced them. In addition, the thief had installed a radio where there had been none. Police subsequently recovered the stolen car. As the buyer had no better title than the thief had to sell, the police returned the car to the student-owner. The general principle of law under accession is that the owner of the major part of the goods gains title to that which was added. However, an addition by an innocent party can be removed if this can be done without serious damage to the original goods. Accordingly, most courts would not permit removal of the new seat covers that had been added by the buyer who obtained the car from the thief. The old seat covers had been discarded and obviously could not be put back on. Had the radio been installed by the new buyer, it could be removed if this could be accomplished without serious damage to the vehicle. Since the radio had been added by the thief, title to the radio went to the original owner through accession.

DISCUSSION

CASE 36   An individual bought an automobile on a contract which provided that the seller could repossess the vehicle if monthly payments were not met. When payments were not made, the seller took the automobile back. The buyer then pointed out that he had just replaced the worn-out tires with new ones. He contended that the new tires belonged to him under the accession principle as they could be easily removed without doing damage to the automobile proper. Could the buyer get the tires returned? (*Valley Chevrolet Co. v. O. S. Stapley Co.*, 72 P.2d 945.)

Title to Lost and Abandoned Property

Property is *abandoned* when it is given up with no intention to ever reclaim it. No one has title when the relinquishment or disclaimer takes place. The first person who takes possession and control gains title to the abandoned article. While everyone has the right to abandon property, the state also has an interest in protecting the environment. Some jurisdictions have laws that make it a criminal offense to leave an abandoned car on a public street or alley.

Lost or mislaid property is in a different legal category from abandoned property. Title to mislaid or lost property continues in the true owner. The finder gains only possession and must give up the property when the owner gives proof of ownership. But the finder has a better claim than other non-owners. The rule consistently followed by the courts is: "The finder has the right to possession against all the world, except the true owner."

There is, however, one special exception to the finder's right to retain lost property. If misplaced or lost property is found in a public place where the owner would logically return to look for it, then the property must be turned over to the custody of the manager or proprietor of such public place.

A number of states have laws permitting the finder of a lost article to sell it after advertising in a newspaper and after the passage of a specified time for the owner to reply.

JOINT OWNERSHIP OF PROPERTY

Methods for Joint Ownership

Property may be owned individually (sole ownership) or title may be held jointly by the following methods:

1. *Tenancy in common;*
2. *Joint tenancy,* sometimes called *joint tenancy with the right of survivorship;*
3. *Tenancy by the entirety;* or
4. *Community property* ownership.

All states in the United States may be classified as having either common law systems of property ownership or community property ownership. The majority of the states operate their legal systems under the older common law ideas. A growing minority of states follow community property principles, as does Puerto Rico.

Tenancy in Common

A *tenancy in common* is the holding or ownership of property by two or more different persons. Either personal property or real estate may be owned in this manner. Cotenants own undivided interests, but these interests need not be equal in either size or duration. The cotenants have no right of survivorship to the property of a cotenant who dies, the title passing to the decedent's heirs.

If the property in question is, say, an 80-acre farm owned by four tenants in common, with shares of equal size, it is not that each tenant owns a specific 20 acres. Rather, each owns an undivided one-fourth in the entire 80-acre tract and each has the right of occupancy and possession. The interest of each tenant can be devised (transferred by will) or it can be sold by that tenant without the permission of any other owner.

Joint Tenancy (with Right of Survivorship)

Joint tenancy is a form of a co-ownership of property by any two or more persons. Legally, it is regarded as a single estate (single ownership) held by two or more persons jointly. Joint tenants hold as though they collectively constituted but one person, a fictitious entity. The main characteristic of joint tenancy is the right of survivorship. When a joint tenant dies, that individual's interest in the property is terminated and the ownership continues in the survivor or survivors. When there is but one survivor, as in most instances, the estate automatically becomes an *estate in severalty* (sole ownership).

Both personal property, such as a joint bank account, and real property may be owned in joint tenancy.

Frequently a married couple chooses to own real property in joint tenancy because such ownership passes property to the survivor. This eliminates the need for a will and the expense and bother of having a will probated. Such an arrangement, however, sometimes causes serious tax problems and legal entanglements that may be far more complicated than those of probating a will. In some situations joint tenancy has definite advantages, but it is usually best to consult an attorney before using this method of ownership.

Tenancy by the Entirety (Sometimes Called Tenancy by the Entireties)

Tenancy by the entirety (or entireties) is a variation of the joint tenancy arrangement. Where used in a few common law states, this form of ownership can be held only by a husband and wife.

If a deed to real estate is made out in the names of both husband and wife, in these common law states the property is owned as tenants by the entirety. Neither the husband nor wife can sell the property without the other's consent. This means that the buyer must insist on receiving the signatures of both spouses on a deed of purchase or on a sales contract. In addition, property owned by this arrangement cannot be left to anyone by will since the deceased's interest passes to the surviving spouse.

Community Property

Community property is the joint ownership system used by a husband and wife in many states, as well as Puerto Rico. The basic idea is that the efforts of both spouses contribute to the couple's financial picture; therefore, all property acquired during marriage is jointly owned under the rule of community property. Usually, the only holdings not considered community property in those states consist of property the husband or wife already owned separately before marriage, property inherited individually (other than from the spouse) after marriage, or individual gifts received during marriage.

All community property states have some differences. In most of these states each marriage partner is the owner of an undivided half interest in the common property. Each spouse has the right to dispose of one-half of this community property by will, as well as the right to dispose of individually owned (separate) property. In most instances it is immaterial which spouse's name is put on a deed or on a bank account since it is community property if acquired after marriage. In most of these states neither husband nor wife has the individual right to sell community property or to borrow on it without permission of the other mate.

_____ *QUESTIONS* _____

1. Describe how each of the following relates to, or is a characteristic of, property ownership: A) reduction to possession; B) dominion or control over the thing in question; and C) transferability.

2. Explain the "bundle of rights" concept that goes along with property ownership.

3. Why is it important to be able to distinguish between personal property and real property? What has movability to do with this problem in most instances?

4. Explain how personal property is acquired by: A) dominion over the property; B) title by natural increase; C) title by making from raw materials; D) title by purchase; E) title by inheritance, by will, or by gift; F) title by confusion; and G) title by accession.

5. Is the finder of lost property entitled to hold it against the demands of nonowners? Explain.

6. Describe ownership by tenancy in common.

7. Give the basic features of joint tenancy with the right of survivorship; tenancy in the entirety.

8. Outline the basic features of joint ownership in a common law state.

_____ *ANSWERS TO DISCUSSION CASES* _____

Case 34   The female friend could not sue for breach of contract; there was no contract, since there was no consideration for the promise to deliver the car. Title would have passed to the female friend, however, on the basis of a gift inter vivos, had there been an actual delivery. If the value of the gift was in excess of $10,000, the giver would probably be liable for Federal gift tax.

Case 35   The grandfather (the owner) made a *constructive delivery* in handing over the colt's registry papers. The grandson accepted and thereby acquired title to the colt as a gift.

Case 36   Under the accession principle of law, the owner of the car was entitled to have it returned in the condition in which it was sold. Since the original tires could not be produced, the seller was entitled to the new ones. The new tires could not be removed without seriously harming the car's value. In another sense, too, nothing new had been added to the car; the tires had merely been replaced.

_____ *PROBLEM CASES* _____

1   A hotel maid found $800 under a closet shelf lining in a guest room at the hotel. The maid turned the money over to hotel management. The manage-

ment tried to locate the owner of the money by corresponding with every guest who had registered in the room for the last three months. No claims for the money were filed. The maid then sued the hotel, claiming that she was entitled to the $800. Would a court award her the money? (*Jackson* v. *Steinberg*, 200 P.2d 37.)

2   A World War II refugee fled Europe just ahead of Hitler's Nazi troops. The refugee's art works were seized by the Germans. After the war, one of these paintings was found in an art gallery. The refugee sued to recover the painting. The defendant art gallery argued that the refugee had lost title by abandonment. Decide. (*Menzel* v. *List*, 267 N.Y.S.2d 807.)

3   A railroad company owned a tract of land but needed only enough space above the surface of the ground to provide clearance for trains (about 24 feet). The state built a toll road in the airspace over this real estate without using any of the railroad's ground property. Should the state pay for this invasion of the airspace? (*Indiana Toll Road Commn.* v. *Jankovich*, 193 N.E.2d 237.)

4   The Fountainebleu resort hotel built a 14-story addition to an existing hotel. This addition blocked sunlight from the solar collector of the adjoining Eden Roc Hotel which was located solely on the Eden Roc property. The Eden Roc sued the Fountainebleau, on the basis that the addition destroyed the Eden Roc's right to unobstructed sunlight. Who would win this lawsuit? (*Fountaine-bleu Hotel Corp.* v. *Forty-five Twenty-five Inc.*, 114 So.2d 357.) Would it make a difference if the 14 stories had been added as a spite measure?

5   A chandelier was attached to the ceiling of a room with screws. When the house was sold, the seller removed this item. The buyer sued for the value of the chandelier. The seller advised the court that when the chandelier had been installed it had been his intent to regard this item as personal property. He argued that his intent at the time of installation controlled. Decide. (*Strain* v. *Green*, 172 P.2d 216.)

6   A complete kitchen unit, made up of a range, cabinet, and refrigerator, was installed in each unit of an efficiency apartment building. The living area in each suite was converted into a bedroom by the use of a fold-down bed swung on pivots that were screwed to the wall. The mortgage lender fore-closed when the owner was unable to meet payments. The builder then attempted to remove the kitchen units and folding beds. Could the builder do so? (*Mortgage Bond Co.* v. *Stephens*, 74 P.2d 361.)

15

Real Property

As previously noted, all property is classified as either personal property or real property. The terms *land, real property, real estate,* and *realty* are all used interchangeably in legal circles. In general, all basic principles of contract law, tort law, and agency law apply to real property transfers, disputes, and problems.

What Real Property Includes

Real property includes not only the bare ground, but any building, office, apartment, house, or other construction of any kind that is permanently affixed to the ground. Any fixtures or improvements attached to the structures are also realty. In addition, real property includes all those things above and below the ground level—rocks, minerals, growing timber, grass rooted to the soil, and other shrubs and vegetation.

Ownership of real property extends downward to the center of the earth and is usually considered as extending upward indefinitely. With differing court interpretations from state to state, the ownership of land includes the airspace above the property. This ownership is generally subject to an airplane's right to flight that does not interfere with reasonable use of the surface and that is not harmful or dangerous to individuals or property lawfully on the land. The courts often say that the airspace is a public highway, available to anyone. Nevertheless, the property owner has exclusive right to as much of the airspace above the surface as he or she can occupy and use in connection with the land.

Some state laws and court decisions of recent years have modified the idea that ownership of the surface extends upward indefinitely. In a multistory condominium, the owner of a condominium unit located above the ground level is usually regarded as owning only the airspace and the structure of that individual unit. (Actually, the condominium owner may jointly own some other parts of the structure, such as the lobby or recreation room.) The question as to who owns the airspace above the top level of a multistory condominium has not been completely settled in the courts. Under the law in most states the property owner has a right to obtain sunlight from directly above the property but not from across adjoining property. This may be of increasing significance as sunlight is increasingly used as a source for generating energy.

Real estate includes anything that is imbedded in or attached to the earth. This includes gravel beds, mineral deposits in or on the soil, a meteorite that strikes the surface, or the buried skeleton of a fossilized saber-toothed tiger. Oil and gas are viewed in a number of states as part of the real estate. In some other jurisdictions, however, early-day judges believed oil and gas deposits were not permanently embedded, wandering from place to place. Under this theory, which is still followed in some states, oil and gas deposits are not absolutely owned by the surface owner as minerals in place. This so-called "capture theory" of ownership gives the surface owner the right to drill for these minerals but does not give title until the oil or gas is permanently reduced to possession.

A sale of land normally includes whatever minerals may be found inside the earth. And the surface owner has the right to sell the land and the mineral rights separately. This reservation of mineral rights is rather common where it is suspected that oil, gas, uranium, or other valuable deposits may be found. In addition, the surface owner may sell off the mineral rights while retaining the surface interest in the land. When this happens, the owner of the minerals has a right to sink wells or mine shafts, or to pump out mineral deposits such as sulfur, paying the surface owner for destroyed crops or for other surface damage.

The following installations and structures have been held by the courts to be part of the real estate: electric light poles, culverts, toll bridges, piers, concrete driveways, railroad tracks, sluices and canals, elevated street railway facilities, and many other installations affixed to the land.

There is little uniformity in court decisions concerning the right to water in or under land. In general, the owner of land bordering on a waterway or stream does not have ownership of the water. The majority of the courts say that the surface owner has a *riparian* water right along with all the other owners bordering on the stream. This riparian water right permits the holder to make reasonable use of the water but not to deprive downstream owners of a fair share. Lawsuits have frequently contested what is reasonable use. Most courts place underground waters in a different category from water in flowing streams, giving the owner of the land absolute ownership and control over underground waters. Here again, however, some courts permit only reasonable use by an individual landowner.

Since anything affixed to the land becomes part of the realty, it is important for a builder to be absolutely certain that a structure is being erected within the owner's property lines. Most courts hold that building construction is at the owner's risk, awarding the ownership of a structure on the wrong lot to whoever owns the land where the structure is located. In a few states, however, the courts have allowed some compensation to the contractor who builds on the wrong lot, while at the same time giving ownership of the structure to the lot owner.

DISCUSSION

CASE 37   A new county airport was located near the realty of a chicken farmer in a semirural area. Thereafter, the farmer's hens consistently refused to lay eggs and other birds could not be properly fattened for market. The farmer filed a lawsuit, alleging that his chickens were greatly disturbed by the airplanes that came over his property at very low levels. The farmer contended that these flights were a trespass on his airspace for which he was entitled to damages. Was he correct in this claim? (*Griggs* v. *County of Allegheny*, 369 U.S. 84.)

Fixtures

A *fixture* is an article or piece of property that was originally a chattel (personalty) and was affixed later to land or a building with the intention that it was to become part of the realty.

When realty is bought or sold, it is important to know whether valuable items that can possibly be removed from the property are personalty or fixtures, thereby remaining with the real estate. The general rule is that a fixture cannot be removed upon the sale of real estate, except with the permission of the owner. There are, however, some variations of this rule in almost all states.

Wall-to-wall carpeting, permanently affixed to the floor in a home, is almost always regarded by the courts as a fixture. But a Persian rug, thrown loosely on the floor, is not a fixture, even though it may have cost far more than a sizable installation of wall-to-wall carpeting. Usually, a movable electrical appliance such as a refrigerator remains an item of personal property, since it is portable and can be detached by merely pulling an electrical plug. But a built-in bookcase or an *attached* microwave oven or a dishwasher that was bolted to a kitchen counter is usually held to be part of the realty (a fixture).

So-called "trade fixtures" are an exception to the general legal rule, not being regarded as part of the realty. Tradesmen and shop owners would frequently be unable to continue their businesses if deprived of their equipment. Therefore, the courts generally allow such items to be removed when the building is sold, even though a butcher's display case, a shoemaker's bench, or a barber's chair may all be permanently affixed to the floor of the building.

Tests for Fixtures

Excepting trade fixtures, the courts generally use five tests in determining whether something is a fixture:

1. The understanding between the parties involved.
2. The intent of the party affixing.
3. The nature of the item and its suitability for continued use at another location.
4. The manner in which the article is affixed—loosely attached or securely welded to a steel wall girder.
5. The nature of the relationship between the parties. For example, the sale of a shoe factory to another shoe manufacturer with fixtures consisting of machinery designed to carry on the shoemaking process would likely result in a holding that the machinery was intended to pass as part of the realty. A court might hold otherwise if the building was being converted to a skating rink where shoemaking items might be worthless except for salvage.

TYPES OF ESTATES OR OWNERSHIP INTERESTS IN REAL PROPERTY

There are a number of kinds of ownership or property interests that may be held in realty. One of these interests is spoken of in legal circles as a *tenancy*, an *estate*, an *estate in realty*, or simply as *real estate*.

The term *tenant* is commonly used throughout the United States to describe one who has been granted the right to use property by the owner, usually for a month, a week, or any short period. A tenant of this type is often called a *renter*. Legally speaking, however, a tenant is one who holds any interest in real estate, varying from absolute ownership to temporary occupancy.

The term *estate* usually designates the length of time that the tenant's interest will continue or the degree of control that the holder of the interest will have over the property.

Ownership in Fee Simple

The term *ownership in fee simple* is used interchangeably with *tenancy in fee simple*, *estate in fee*, *fee simple estate*, or *fee simple absolute*. The owner in fee simple is said to be the owner of the entire tenancy or entire estate. This is absolute ownership as it is commonly understood. It is the most complete interest in property that one may hold.

A fee simple interest can be sold or transferred at any time. It may be left by will if the owner so chooses, subject only to inheritance limitations provided by state laws. The owner may make any use of the property that is desired so long as the use is not illegal, contrary to zoning or other regulations, or of a tortious nature toward others.

Life Estate (Life Tenancy)

A *life estate* or *life tenancy* gives the holder the occupancy and complete use of property during the lifetime of an individual specified in the document that creates this kind of estate. Usually the duration of this tenancy is for the lifetime of the holder but occasionally it is for the lifetime of another named individual. In most instances a life estate is created by deed or is set up as one of the terms of the will of the property owner.

In some instances a life estate is created for two people. Usually the courts interpret such a tenancy as continuing so long as any holder of the tenancy is still alive.

A spouse sometimes leaves a provision in a will, creating an estate in a valuable piece of real estate for the surviving spouse, whose interest may specify that a life estate terminates in the event remarriage. On remarriage, the property would pass to the couple's children.

Unless there are restrictions in the document that created the life estate, the tenancy may be mortgaged or sold. The buyer, of course, would receive the balance of the life estate, rather than a fee simple interest.

The holder of a life estate has the rights to all income from the property but may not destroy the substance or permanent value of the estate. Ordinarily, the life tenant cannot remove mineral deposits or oil and gas but may grow and sell livestock, crops, produce, fruit and nuts, hay, and so on (but not sell growing timber). There are, however, differences from state to state as to what may be sold from the produce or increase from the property. The owner of such an estate must pay taxes, keep the property in reasonable repair, and (usually) meet mortgage interest payments, although in most instances the courts hold that the life tenant need not pay off the principal of a mortgage. This tenant has no responsibility to make permanent improvements and can subject the property to normal wear and tear.

The destruction, dissipation, or abuse of the property by the life tenant is legally called *waste*. Such wrongful misuse is a tort, subjecting the life tenant to damages. In addition, the holder of the balance of the estate can go into court and obtain an injunction that forbids the life tenant from committing further waste.

Reversions and Remainders

When a life estate is created, there is always another estate left over, legally called a *remainder*. The owner of such an estate is called *remainderman* (even though the owner may be a woman). The remainder is, in effect, the estate that remains after the expiration of a life estate. Legally, a remainder is a present, *vested* interest in real estate, although it does not accrue to the holder's benefit immediately. Normally, the remainderman takes a fee simple interest in the property on the death of the individual whose life measures the length of the life estate. In instances where a life estate is granted to revert back to the original owner, it is called a *reversion*. If the original owner (grantor) has died by the time the reversion takes place, then the fee simple estate reverts to the heirs of the original owner (grantor).

Either a remainder or a reversionary interest may be mortgaged, sold, or transferred in the same manner as a fee simple interest.

Leases; Tenancies

A *lease* or *leasehold interest* is simply a rental for a specified period of time. Typically, the rent is paid on a monthly or yearly basis and the lease extends for a year or more. However, a lease may be for any period. Most states require that a lease for a year or longer must be in writing. Leases are discussed further in Chapter 16.

A *periodic tenancy* is an occupancy for a specified period, usually from month to month or week to week. A *tenancy at will* involves an occupancy of the property that can be terminated at the wish of either party. A *tenancy at sufferance* occurs when a tenant's right to occupy the premises expires and the tenant "holds over" without the landlord's permission.

Easement

An *easement* is a property right that allows its holder to use the property of another in a specific way or for a specific purpose. It is an interest in land that falls short of a tenancy but permits a limited use. For example, a typical easement involves the right to cross over the land of another. In many instances an easement originates by grant in a deed given by the owner.

The owner of a tract of land usually conveys an easement for passage over the owner's land when selling an inner, landlocked tract. This enables the owner of the landlocked parcel to have access without trespassing. Since an easement is an interest in land, most courts hold that the granting of an easement must be in writing in order to comply with the statute of frauds.

Sometimes the courts hold that a landowner holds an easement by implication or an *easement by necessity*. This is usually granted by the courts when it is obvious that the grantor selling a tract of land forgot to provide a passageway for that tract. The courts reason here that some kind of access must have been intended.

Individuals may also acquire an easement right that is called an *easement by prescription*. This happens when someone openly subjects the land of another to a regular use for a period of years specified (prescribed) by state law. For example, an outsider may wear a path across a landowner's vacant lot on a daily basis. Actually the person making use of this path is a trespasser and may be sued as such. But if this regular use continues for 5, 10, 15, or 20 years, or whatever is provided by state law, the continued use "ripens" into an easement, giving the user the right to continue such use indefinitely. Some state laws provide for the placement of no-trespassing signs that serve to interrupt the legal effect of this continued use, stopping an easement from coming into being. Usually, it is to the property owner's best interest to interrupt the trespasser's continuing use short of the statutory period by fencing off access. After an easement has arisen, the easement interest may be erased by having its holder sign a written release form or a quitclaim deed. This, of course, may necessitate a monetary payment to the holder.

Conditions and Covenants

Sometimes the person selling land may place limitations on its future use by including restrictions in the deed. Restrictions of this kind may also be included in a master deed for a subdivision, applying to all individual lots in the plat. By such a technique, a developer may limit individual lot usage to residential housing of a specified size and cost. Restrictions of this kind are usually called *covenants*. In legal effect they are promises on the part of the buyer (grantee) and they apply equally to subsequent purchasers in the chain of title. Often, such a covenant is legally called "a covenant running with the land."

These covenants usually are inserted in the deed for the protection of surrounding landowners and may be enforced in court by such owners. The courts, though they will normally honor covenants of this kind, tend to favor the free and open use of land, sometimes construing covenants against the party seeking enforcement.

Covenants that attempt to prohibit resale of property to individuals of a specified race or religion were rather common at one time in the United States. Any restriction on the transfer or use of real estate on account of color, race, religion, or national origin has been prohibited by the Supreme Court of the United States. A covenant that seeks to enforce such a restriction is ignored by the courts.

ACQUIRING AND DISPOSING OF REAL PROPERTY _____

Real property may be acquired and disposed of in a variety of ways. Originally, title to much of the land in the western two-thirds of this country was acquired from the Federal government by purchase or by homesteading on vacant lands. The document by which the government gave title to these lands was a *patent*. Today, ownership to real property is usually based on deeds derived from these patents. Real property may also be acquired by inheritance or by will and less frequently by accretion or adverse possession.

The Use of a Deed

A *deed* is a written instrument executed by the grantor (typically a seller) and delivered to the grantee. In some eastern and northern states a deed must be a sealed instrument. But there are some formal requirements for a deed in all jurisdictions, usually requiring notarization and/or a seal.

There is no legal requirement that a deed must contain specific wording, but the instrument must utilize apt words of transfer, such as "convey," "grant," or "transfer." Most courts require the deed to specify the name of the grantor and the grantee, along with sufficient legal description of the property for unmistakable identification. Some states have statutory deed forms which are mandatory.

A deed may contain a recitation of outstanding liens, mortgages, or other claims and encumbrances against the property. In addition, the deed should be dated, acknowledged by the grantor, and witnessed where this is required in some states. A deed from a corporation should carry the signature of the appropriate official of the corporation.

In many instances the grantee does not obtain clear title unless the spouse of the grantor also joins in signing the deed. Whether or not both spouses must sign depends on state laws and the type of ownership. A deed is not legally effective until a delivery of the deed has been made. *Delivery* is the process by which the grantor's intent to transfer is manifested. While delivery does not necessarily require a physical transfer of the deed to the grantee, it must be indicated from the facts that the grantor has passed on control of the deed to another party.

Warranty Deed

Several types of deed may transfer title and they may have different legal effects. The majority of the states use a *warranty deed*, sometimes known as a *general warranty deed* or a *full covenant deed*. From the buyer's viewpoint, a warranty deed offers more protection than any other. In it the grantor makes a series of legal promises or guarantees that a clear, valid, unencumbered title is being transferred, except as stated in the deed. These assurances or warranties are called *covenants of title*. The significance of these guarantees is that the grantor will be held liable in court if the title is not completely as represented. If the grantee should ever experience future loss on account of misrepresentations, the grantor will still be held responsible.

A buyer obtains maximum protection by inspecting the property, by insisting on a warranty deed, and by having a title insurance policy, which guarantees title to the property. The insurance may be valuable, since no deed will ever give the buyer absolute assurance of good title. While it is unusual, a warranty deed could turn out to be worthless if the grantor actually had no title to sell. Swindlers sometimes claim to own property, disappearing with the buyer's money after giving a warranty deed. In an instance of this kind the defrauded buyer could, of course, sue for the breach of the warranties, but a judgment would likely be of no value if the seller had disappeared.

Special Warranty Deed

A *special warranty deed* is used in some states. In a deed of this kind the grantor promises or covenants only to defend the property title against lawful claims of all persons claiming by, under, or through the grantor. If it subsequently happened that an outsider came into court with a better title than the grantor on the special warranty deed, then the buyer (the grantee) could not hold the grantor responsible. Obviously, this kind of deed does not afford as much buyer protection as a warranty deed.

Grant Deed; Bargain and Sale Deed

Some other states commonly utilize a so-called *grant deed* or a variation thereof called a *bargain and sale deed*. A grant deed does not include a warranty that the grantor is the owner of the property or that the property is not encumbered. The grantor here merely warrants that he or she has not previously conveyed or encumbered (placed debts against) the property in question.

In a bargain and sale deed the grantor makes a binding promise that he or she has done nothing to cause a defect in title; the grantor will not be responsible for any defect that he or she knows nothing about.

Quitclaim Deed

In addition to a warranty deed or one of the other types, practically all states use a *quitclaim deed*. Such a deed is unique in that it contains no warranties or promises whatever. The quitclaim form merely conveys whatever ownership or title the grantor possesses at the time of the alleged transfer. In the great majority of cases there is no objection to a quitclaim deed; the buyer should be on guard to the fact that the grantor is merely conveying whatever title or interest he or she has.

If for some reason the grantor has no actual title to the property, none will be acquired by the grantee. If this should be the case, the buyer has no cause of action on the deed itself. Of course, the buyer may have a lawsuit of doubtful worth if misrepresentations or false inducements were made.

Sometimes an heir to land will purport to sell it before actually receiving title. Legally, this is called an *after-acquired* title situation. If the heir attempted this sale by a warranty deed, a special warranty deed, a grant deed, or a bargain and sale deed, practically all courts will award the title to the buyer when ownership passes into the heir's hands. However, if the heir gave a quitclaim deed, the courts consistently say that the heir had nothing to convey to the buyer.

Gift Deed

A *gift deed* is not a type or form of deed instrument such as a warranty deed, grant deed, or quitclaim deed. The term merely signifies that there was no payment or compensation for the transfer of the real estate in question. A gift deed is proper, standing alone. If it should turn out that the gift transfer was made for the purpose of putting a debtor's property beyond the reach of creditors, a court may set it aside on an appropriate request by a creditor.

Acquisition of Real Property by Devise and Descent; by Inheritance

Title to real property may be acquired by *devise and descent* when the ownership is left by a valid will. Title passes to the person named in the owner's will, the transfer taking place when the estate is settled in the probate process.

Real property may also be acquired by inheritance. This occurs when the owner dies without a valid will and title is transferred to the heirs by operation of state law. The percentage of ownership that passes to specific heirs is regulated by state statutes and varies considerably from state to state.

Acquisition by Judicial Sale

Judicial foreclosures, tax sales, and sheriff's sales result in the transfer of real estate ownership from a defaulting debtor. A number of judicial procedures may be involved here. The trustee of a deed of trust may sell the property under some circumstances when the debtor cannot pay, or a levy of execution by a court may follow the issuance of a court judgment for failure to pay.

In isolated instances, ownership of property may revert to the state if a private owner dies without a will and without heirs. This legal procedure is called *escheat*. Bank accounts that are dormant for a considerable period may also be subject to escheat, although the owner is still alive.

Accretion

Existing land is sometimes increased in size by new soil washed up by a stream or ocean. Where the addition is made gradually, title is considered to be with the new owner. This is called title by *accretion*. If a river suddenly cuts new banks, drastically changing property lines, the courts generally allow the previous owner to reclaim the land that was lost.

Adverse Possession

Adverse possession is a means of acquiring title to real estate after a lapse of time; this is based on continued possession. Normally, the legal system works to protect real estate owners. At the same time, the courts have long indicated that land should be put to productive use rather than lie unproductive and fallow for years. The principle of adverse possession is usually applied when there are two claimants to the title, one of whom aggressively pursues the possession and use of the property. Adverse possession is usually more than a mere "squatting" on land. For example, the adverse claimant may have received a quitclaim deed from someone who actually had no title to the property, but who gave the claimant the impression of ownership.

In most cases five essentials must be satisfied before title can be gained by adverse possession:

1. There must be an actual occupation of the land by the claimant, such occupation being open and notorious.
2. Possession must be opposed to the true owner's title or ownership.
3. This possession must be under some claim of right, such as a defective or a duplicate deed.
4. The possession must be continuous and unbroken for whatever term of years is set by state statutes.
5. The claimant must have paid all property taxes levied during the statutory period.

These requirements vary somewhat from state to state.

Condemnation

Condemnation is the proceeding by which private property is taken for public use without the consent of the owner and upon the payment of just compensation (to be established by a court). Usually the property is taken for governmental use, but it may also be taken for public utilities and other facilities that operate for the general public. Undoubtedly there are instances when the compensation paid is not adequate for the loss suffered by the property owner. But under the law in most states the owner has the right to have the award set by a jury under court supervision.

––––––– *QUESTIONS* –––––––

1. In transferring real property, what rights does the owner have to minerals? Surface water? Flowing water in streams? Oil and gas?
2. What is a fixture? Who owns fixtures when the property is sold?
3. What are some tests for court determination of a fixture?
4. What is the "trade fixture" exception?
5. Define an estate in fee simple.
6. What are the rights of the parties in a life estate?
7. Explain the meaning of a remainder.
8. What is an easement? How are easements generally brought into being?
9. When a deed covenant or restriction "runs with the land," is a new buyer bound by the restriction?
10. What are the advantages of a warranty deed for the buyer?
11. Why is a warranty deed usually more desirable than a grant deed? Special warranty deed? Bargain and sale deed?
12. Explain why a real estate buyer should be wary of a quitclaim deed.
13. Is adverse possession a mere squatting on land with the expectation of someday gaining ownership? Explain.

––––––– *ANSWER TO DISCUSSION CASE* –––––––

CASE 37   The Supreme Court of the United States held that consistently low flights into the airspace constituted an unauthorized "taking" of the property of another for which damages should be paid.

––––––– *PROBLEM CASES* –––––––

1   A sold B a tract of land that was completely landlocked inside a larger tract owned by A. For a considerable time B drove across A's land to obtain entry. Eventually, however, A placed a barbed wire fence around all of his property, cutting off B's access. B sued to prevent continuance of this obstruction. Who would prevail? (*Hansen* v. *Smikahl*, 113 N.W.2d 210.)

2   One of the parties in a land sale transaction claimed that the deed was inoperative, since there had been no delivery and acceptance of the deed. Is such a claim valid? (*Blankenship* v. *Meyers*, 544 P.2d 314.)

3   A restriction in the deed prevented any use of a lot other than residential. A restaurant owner across the street acquired the lot, intending to use it for off-street parking for customers. The restaurant owner maintained that this use would be proper since the restaurant would be wholly across the street

and the lot would not be used as a business. Is this proper? (*Bennett v. Consolidated Realty*, 11 S.W.2d 910.)

4   The owner of agricultural land moved onto the property and began to farm it in 1924. He rebuilt fences, enclosing his own property along with 4.7 acres of the adjoining property that admittedly belonged to Burton at the time. Over a period of 50 years the farmer treated the 4.7 acres as his own, cultivating part and using another part as pasture. The farmer worked this property continuously, cutting timber and keeping fences in repair. Eventually the Burton interests discovered that the property had been occupied by the farmer and filed suit to recover the 4.7 acres. State statutes provided that possession of real property for 30 years under circumstances that are continuous, uninterrupted, public, and unequivocal gives title to the possessor. Did the farmer own the 4.7 acres by adverse possession? (*Burton Industries v. Cook*, 322 So.2d 880.)

16

Leases and Real Estate Transfers

LEASES (INCLUDING RENTALS)

Nature of a Lease

A *lease* is a contract for the use of land or buildings but not for their purchase. Payment for leased property is called *rent*. The *landlord* in the lease arrangement is legally called the *lessor* and the *tenant* is the *lessee*. Sometimes a lease is called a *leasehold* or a *leasehold estate*.

A lease is a conveyance or grant of the landlord's interest in an estate for a term less than the landlord's tenancy. By the very nature of the arrangement the landlord must still have a reversionary interest in the property. But in addition to being a conveyance or grant of an interest in land, a lease is also a contract between the parties. It is thus subject to the usual provisions of contract law. If one party to the contract breaches a covenant in the lease, the injured party has the contract rights that apply to a breach of contract.

Rights in Every Lease

Every lease includes two sets of rights and obligations, arising from (1) the legal relationship of the landlord and the tenant, sometimes termed the *privity of estate*, and (2) the express provisions of the contract.

Lawyers are sometimes at a loss to explain why, but the tenant's (lessee's) right in a lease for a definite period is usually considered to be real property. A lease for an indefinite period is usually classified by the courts as personal property.

Various types of tenancies may be arranged by someone wanting to use the landlord's property, including a *periodic tenancy*, a *tenancy for a fixed term*, a *tenancy at will*, or a *tenancy at sufferance*.

Periodic Tenancy (Renting)

A *periodic tenancy* is created to continue for successive periods of the same length unless it is terminated earlier by notice. This kind of tenancy does not end by the lapse of a set measure of time. It is legally considered to be renewed at the end of each of the successive periods for which rent is paid. Usually, the term of a periodic tenancy runs for one month. Commonly called a rental rather than a lease, this has been the most frequently used leasing arrangement throughout the United States until recent years. Today, increasing numbers of tenants are insisting on a tenancy for a fixed term.

State law varies somewhat, but usually in a periodic tenancy either the landlord or the tenant can terminate by giving a thirty-day notice in writing. This right is commonly set by state law. Rent is due and payable at the end of the successive periods, usually monthly or weekly as agreed by the parties.

Tenancy for a Fixed Term (Estate for Years)

Tenancy for a fixed term (also called an *estate for years*) gives the tenant the right to exclusive possession and use for a fixed period, usually for one or more years. This is the arrangement generally used for commercial purposes. The lease term can run for any specified period, not necessarily for a year or multiples thereof. Statutes in most states specify that a lease for one year or more must be in writing. Some states require a written lease only if the tenancy extends for three years or more. Of course, it is only common sense for a business to obtain a written lease whenever considerable money is to be spent for improvements on the property.

Written leases must be prepared with precise formality in some jurisdictions with lease preparation having the same requirements as those for a deed. A seal must be used on a deed in some areas with notarization and witnesses to signatures in others. Experience shows that the services of an attorney are advisable in preparing a business or industrial lease. In addition to handling technicalities required by local law, the lawyer can be expected to include provisions that protect the client's interests.

Tenancy at Will

A *tenancy at will* may be terminated at the wish of either party at any time. Today, this type of lease is seldom used, but sometimes a tenant merely needs occupancy pending negotiations for a written lease of another type. After granting occupancy to a tenant at will, the landlord may create a periodic tenancy by accepting a rent payment for a specified period.

Tenancy at Sufferance

A *tenancy at sufferance* is not a trespasser but nevertheless enjoys little legal protection. A tenant at sufferance is one who obtains possession of the premises in a proper way but becomes a *holdover tenant* after the lease has expired or without the landlord's permission. Sometimes the courts say that a tenant at sufferance is not a tenant at all but a mere occupier of the property. The landlord has the right to eject a tenant at sufferance, usually without notice. Even if ejected, the tenant at sufferance is legally liable for the value of the reasonable use of the premises. If the landlord does agree to accept rent or otherwise to regard the holdover tenant as a regular tenant, then the occupancy becomes a periodic tenancy for the time covered for the rent paid.

Liens for Nonpayment of Rent

Usually a landlord does not have a lien on the tenant's property unless such a provision was included in the terms of the lease arrangement. Practically all states do, however, give a lien to the operators of hotels, motels, inns, and boardinghouses, permitting retention of baggage or other property of the tenant for nonpayment of rent. A number of states have broadened lien statutes to give such protection to operators of apartments, cottages, and bungalow courts. Liens may be enforced in some jurisdictions by sale of the tenant's property after a statutory waiting period, during which it may be redeemed by the tenant.

Landlord–Tenant Relationship

The *landlord–tenant relationship* arises whenever there is a hiring of real property. The tenant has the right to undisturbed possession and occupancy. Unless the lease has restrictive agreements, the tenant is entitled to use the property for any purpose for which it is ordinarily used. Of course, the tenant cannot operate the premises in a way that is forbidden by law or contrary to zoning ordinances. Frequently a written lease specifies the use to which the tenant may put the property. If the lease is silent on usage, the tenant is still legally under a duty to use the premises in a proper way.

The tenant has a basic responsibility to keep the property in the same condition as when occupancy began. Undoubtedly there will be some deterioration from normal wear and tear. The tenant has no right, however, to make unauthorized alterations that change the physical layout or to install new doors or walls even though some alterations may actually increase the value of the property. When windows or doors are broken, they must be repaired by the tenant who deliberately or carelessly broke them, and inoperative facilities must be restored before the property is turned back to the landlord. Gas, electricity, plumbing, and other installations must be used as intended.

The tenant also has the responsibility to pay rent when due. Failure to do this does not ordinarily justify a forfeiture of the agreement. State laws vary considerably on this point, but generally a demand for payment must first be made and it is the beginning of the eviction procedure. If the landlord elects, a lawsuit can be filed for unpaid rent, even though the tenant has already been evicted. It is usually advisable for the landlord to use a local attorney for eviction procedures.

Most lease forms contain a provision that the lessee's interest cannot be assigned to a subtenant (cannot be subleased) without written permission of the landlord. Subleasing is proper in most states, however, if it is not prohibited by the leasing agreement.

If the landlord sells the property, the lease arrangement continues with the new owner unless otherwise provided in the leasing agreement. If there should be an assignment of the lease, the subtenant can take no more rights than those held by the tenant.

Termination of Lease

A lease may come to an end by expiration of the promised term. If the tenant abandons the lease, the landlord may sue the tenant for the remaining rent, thus considering the lease agreement to still be in effect; or the landlord may consider the lease at an end and physically take over the property. In addition, the landlord has another option: to sublet the premises and hold the original tenant legally responsible for any difference in the rent. However, the landlord has a duty to mitigate damages and must make a reasonable attempt to lease the premises to another tenant.

If the tenant violates conditions in the lease, often these conditions are construed by the courts as a condition precedent to the occupancy and use of the property. In an instance of this kind, the landlord may declare a forfeiture and evict the tenant. An attorney is almost always needed for this procedure.

A tenant may sue a landlord who insists on disturbing the tenant's right to peaceful occupancy and use of the leased premises. Interference with the tenant's right to full enjoyment and use is legally termed *constructive eviction*.

Delivery and Recording of Lease

Legally, a written lease is not considered operative until it is executed and delivered by the landlord to the tenant in the same manner that a deed must be delivered. Most lawyers also advise that every written lease agreement should be recorded. Recording may be especially important for leases involving oil and gas interests or any other business transaction.

State antidiscrimination statutes in most jurisdictions prohibit any kind of housing discrimination in renting, leasing, or selling of residential units. Federal laws also prohibit such practices involving discrimination on account of race, color, religion, or national origin.

RESPONSIBILITY UNDER LEASES

Injuries on the Premises

Under early English and American law, the courts regarded the landlord as having no responsibility to keep rented or leased properties in repair. If a building turned out to be dangerous or unfit for use, the tenant could not turn back the premises to the landlord. The tenant had to continue to make rent payments for the balance of the lease.

At one time the courts tended to excuse the landlord for injuries that occurred on rented or leased premises. For a number of years court decisions have tended to shift responsibility to the landlord, especially if the landlord has been warned of an existing hazard or safety violation. Some modern leases contain provisions holding the tenant responsible to guest or visitors who injure themselves in the lobby or on the stairway of an apartment building. More and more, however, rental and leasing agreements are requiring the landlord to make repairs. This means that the landlord is generally held liable for an injury in any part of the building.

The landlord cannot be held responsible for a dangerous condition that developed after the lease began and that has not been brought to the landlord's attention. The landlord cannot know about some hazards since he or she has no right to come on the leased or rented premises except in emergencies or other unusual situations. Accordingly, the tenant has the responsibility to advise the landlord of a newly developed condition that needs repairs. The landlord is thereafter held responsible by most courts if corrective action is not taken and an injury results from this dangerous condition.

Tenant–landlord responsibility for injuries on rented or leased property is still unsettled in various situations. In most states, responsibility for injuries rests on the party that has control over that part of the premises where the injury occurred. This means that the landlord is usually held responsible for the safety and security of common areas of a building such as the lobby, elevator, washroom, or stairs. The tenant is responsible for conditions inside the tenant's apartment, unless the landlord has retained responsibility to make repairs and has been advised of unsafe or dangerous conditions.

The owner or occupant of a residence or business also has a responsibility toward individuals coming into the yard or passing down the sidewalk, even though they may be trespassers. Some courts rule that the occupant is under no duty to keep streets or sidewalks in safe condition. Many courts, however, hold the occupant responsible to keep sidewalks safe for pedestrians. If ice forms on the sidewalk during the night when the owner is unaware, most courts relieve the occupant or owner of responsibility. In the majority of instances liability would not be imposed if the occupant had shoveled off the walk and sprinkled it with sand or followed other precautions usually taken by prudent occupants. State statutes differ in this area, however.

Responsibility Toward People Coming on Business Property

United States courts hold that the occupier of a business property may be liable to some classes of persons coming on the premises without being considered negligent toward other classes. In short, the courts usually impose different degrees of responsibility toward: (1) *trespassers*, (2) *licensees*, or (3) *invitees* (sometimes called *guests*).

A *trespasser* is one who comes on a property without permission or authority. Ordinarily the occupier of property has only a duty to refrain from causing deliberate injury once the presence of a trespasser is known. A few courts hold that if it is established that the trespasser regularly intrudes on certain property, the occupier has a duty to warn of any newly developed dangers or hidden conditions that might injure the trespasser. The majority of courts rule, however, that there is no duty toward a trespasser unless that trespasser is a child. The attractive nuisance theory of liability was discussed in detail in the material on torts. It should be emphasized again, however, that the occupier always has a special duty to protect children against any dangerous condition on the premises.

A *licensee* is a person who has a legal right to be on property, such as a meter reader, a letter carrier, or a building inspector. The licensee, while uninvited, is nevertheless not a trespasser. Today, most courts hold that the owner or occupier of property has no positive duty to search out the premises to warn of the presence of dangers. Most courts have decided that the occupant must maintain premises in a reasonably safe condition for a licensee. At the minimum, however, almost all courts say that there is a legal duty to notify the licensee of any recent changes in conditions that could lead to injury.

A customer who comes into a store or commercial establishment is an *invitee* in legal terminology. Children or those who accompany a customer are also in this class. Anyone entering the premises for the purpose of engaging in business is usually regarded as an invitee or (in the terminology of some courts) a guest. In most cases the courts have decided that the occupier of the premises is not the "absolute insurer of the safety of the invitee." Nevertheless, the occupier must take all reasonable precautions to prevent injury to every invitee. Failing to take such steps, the occupier of the commercial premises (the merchant, banker, or whoever) will be liable in tort for the negligent injury of invitees.

In recent years the courts in a number of states have begun a trend of determining that property occupiers or owners are liable for negligence in the maintenance of property, whether the injured party was a trespasser, licensee, or invitee. The effect of these decisions is that in the future the occupier or owner may be responsible for dangerous conditions under all circumstances. This means that every business should maintain the premises in a safe condition at all times.

Habitability

Rented Residential Property. Most courts today hold that a landlord has the responsibility to provide a renter with a residence or apartment unit that conforms to all health and safety standards. This is the so-called warranty of *habitability*. The premises should be vermin free; sewer and septic tank connections should function properly. There should be adequate plumbing as well as hot and cold running water. Trash and sanitation disposal facilities should be adequate. Heating and air conditioning (if provided) should function properly. Locks, doors, windows, fire escapes, and stairs should be in good operating condition. There must be no leaking gas or dangerous electrical connections. In short, the property must be suitable for human occupancy.

The warranty of habitability is a comparatively recent development in United States law; however, it is being enforced by more and more courts. Most states have statutes that address this issue.

Today many courts will permit the tenant to break a lease or move out of a rental if the premises are not habitable. Various courts now seem to favor a number of remedies to force the landlord to keep the premises in sanitary, safe condition. Some courts will allow the tenant to withhold rent until the warranty of habitability is complied with; some others will allow the tenant to sue for damages.

In the past a landlord could, without giving reason, evict a tenant who complained about the habitability of a residential unit. Today most courts will not allow eviction when the landlord's only reason is to get even with a complaining tenant. A situation of this kind is called *retaliatory eviction*, and in most courts such action gives the tenant cause for damages against the landlord. Modern courts reason that if the law were otherwise, tenants would be reluctant to report even the most serious conditions.

The courts have seldom applied habitability standards to industrial or business properties. Instead, they have usually paid more attention to conditions that relate to employee health and safety in the work environment.

Habitability of New Home Construction. The Courts are increasingly keeping builders and contractors to a warranty of habitability for new home construction. This means that the builder must stand good for a roof that leaks, a basement that stays under water, or any basic structural defect. Usually the courts do not hold a seller to such a warranty unless the seller is the builder or is involved in the business of selling housing. Contract law rules concerning rescission apply to the situation where the builder tries to foist off serious defects on the home buyer. Some states, however, require sellers to report to buyers any known defects on the property.

Security Deposits

Friction between landlords and tenants frequently results from the landlord's failure to return a security deposit posted at the beginning of the rental occupancy. The landlord, of course, is entitled to apply the security deposit to repair costs of damages caused by the renter. But the landlord cannot withhold return of the deposit to pay for ordinary wear and tear on the property. Increasingly, renters have been going to small claims court to obtain the return of their funds. In some states additional damages are allowed against the landlord if the renter's money is withheld capriciously.

REAL ESTATE TRANSFERS

The purchase of a home or a business is normally the largest individual transaction of a lifetime. The importance of such a transaction should not be underemphasized.

Three interests in real property may be sold: surface rights, mineral rights, and air rights. Unless the deed transferring the property specifically makes exceptions, all three of these property interests are included in the transfer.

Real Estate Contracts

Most transfers of real property occur through a contract to purchase. Typically, the offer to buy comes about when a potential buyer makes an offer to the real estate broker handling the transaction for the owner. The usual rules of contract law apply here. In many instances the acceptance of the original offer brings about the only contract that comes into existence. In most states this is usually recognized as enforceable. It is usually desirable, however, for the buyer to have an attorney draw up a formal written contract that incorporates all aspects of the transaction. It is also advisable for the buyer to emphasize to the seller that this is the only contract on which the parties will be bound, rather than by the preliminary understanding. In most jurisdictions this contract is prepared by an attorney, although a real estate broker had handled the preliminary negotiations. For the broker to prepare the contract would, in some states, constitute the illegal practice of law.

It is also advisable for the seller to utilize an attorney to review the contract for the exchange of title. The seller may want to make certain that escrow provisions in the contract are in accordance with his or her own interests. A forfeiture clause may also be a wise addition to the sales contract to cover the possibility of nonpayment by the buyer.

Real estate sales–purchase contracts do not vary greatly from state to state. Usually the buyer and seller specify how real estate taxes for the current year will be split and what escrow firm will be utilized. In many instances the contract will specify the type of deed that must be furnished by the seller: warranty deed, grant deed, quitclaim deed, or whatever. An insurance provision is usually included, specifying which party will stand the loss in the event the property is destroyed by fire, earthquake, or the like while the transaction is still in escrow. It is also usual in many states for the contract to specify that the earnest money deposit will be forfeited to the seller as liquidated damages in the event of default by the buyer.

Experience shows that escrow is usually a desirable procedure, since a deed is not effective unless it is delivered while the grantor (seller) is living. Through accident or otherwise, the grantor sometimes dies before the transaction can be completed. If the deed has been delivered to the escrow agent, the transaction will go through regardless of the seller's death.

While the escrow is in progress, the buyer's lawyer will determine whether the seller actually has marketable title to the property. There are occasions when the purported seller has no ownership or an imperfect title at best and is trying to commit a fraud. In other instances the seller believes that he or she has good title, but there may be some kind of a "cloud on the title" that should be cleared up so there is no question as to the buyer's ownership.

The attorney for the buyer usually examines the chain of title to the property or obtains a report from an abstract or title company. The attorney's report to the buyer on the validity of title is almost always reliable, but it is only the attorney's opinion as to ownership. Even the most careful attorney could make a mistake, so the safest approach is to obtain the attorney's opinion along with a title insurance policy.

In view of the large amount of money that often is involved, the buyer may want to be as safe as possible. Therefore the buyer might insist that the seller prepare a sworn affidavit, stating whether there are mechanics' or suppliers' liens or other encumbrances on the property in favor of a subcontractor, laborer, or supplier of materials.

The buyer should also obtain a statement in advance as to abstract costs, taxes, sewer and improvement loans and assessments, and any other charges that may be outstanding. It is almost always preferable to know of such costs in advance of the purchase.

Conditional Sales Agreements

Another method for the transfer of real property is called a *conditional sales contract* or a *contract for a deed*. Sometimes this is known as an *installment land contract*. Typically this is used when the buyer cannot raise enough down payment to make a conventional purchase. Basically it is an agreement that title will pass at a future time. Usually the seller places the deed in escrow with a provision that delivery of the deed will be made when the last payment on the property has been received. A contract of this type usually specifies that the buyer must pay taxes and bear the risk of loss to buildings by fire, earthquake, and so on during the escrow. In some sales of this kind the deed is not placed in escrow but remains in the hands of the seller until the payments have all been made. This is a very undesirable arrangement from the buyer's standpoint, since the seller could actually dispose of the property to a second buyer who would be unaware of the existing sales contract. Of course, a duplicate sale would constitute a criminal fraud in most states but the possibility always exists that it could take place unless the deed is recorded and placed in escrow.

Conditional sales contracts often include a provision placing the buyer in default if even one installment payment is missed. The contract usually calls for forfeiture of all payments made previously in that situation. Of course, if the buyer has paid off a substantial part of the contract, a forfeiture would work a severe hardship. Consequently, the courts in most states will permit a forced sale, paying off the seller's unpaid balance and giving the buyer some return for the payments made.

ETHICAL CONSIDERATIONS

Many ethical problems are inherent in landlord and tenant relationships. It is not only unethical, but also unlawful, to refuse to rent to individuals because of race, color, ethnic background, sex, or age. One may not refuse to rent to families with children. An exception is made for senior citizen housing.

DISCUSSION

CASE 38   A tenant leased premises that were used as a drug store. Subsequently, store merchandise was moved to another location while the tenant continued to pay rent. Without permission, the landlord entered the premises and made extensive alterations to suit two doctors who wanted to use the building for offices. The tenant, a druggist, notified the landlord that the unauthorized entry and alterations constituted grounds for cancellation of the lease. The landlord countered by suing the druggist for the difference between the rent that the tenant was paying and the rent the doctors were being charged for the remainder of the lease term. Was the tenant legally responsible for this difference in rent? (*Saputa* v. *Cantanese*, 182 So.2d 826.)

_____ *QUESTIONS* _____

1. Define a lease. What is the basic relationship between the landlord and tenant in such an arrangement?
2. Explain the workings of a periodic tenancy.
3. When must a lease be in writing? What formalities are usually required in the preparation of a lease for a year or more?
4. Describe whether the landlord is responsible for injuries that occur on leased or rented residential property.
5. When is a store owner responsible for injuries sustained by a trespasser? By a licensee? By an invitee?
6. How is a warranty of habitability applied to residential property? Describe a builder's warranty of habitability on a new house.
7. What is usually included in a real estate contract? What protective steps can be taken by the buyer to prevent loss in a contract of this kind? By the seller?
8. Describe a conditional sales agreement. From the buyer's standpoint may this arrangement be less desirable than a conventional sales arrangement? Explain.

_____ *ANSWER TO DISCUSSION CASE* _____

CASE 38   The tenant was not liable for the remaining rent. The landlord's unauthorized entry and alterations constituted a constructive eviction, which made the landlord liable in damages for depriving the tenant of uninterrupted possession of the premises.

_____ *PROBLEM CASES* _____

1   A deed for the transfer of property was written in a foreign language. Would it be valid between the two parties (buyer and seller)? If it were recorded, would it serve as notice to third parties of the buyer's interest in the property? (*Moroz* v *Ransom*, 285 N.Y.S. 846.)

2   In the sale of property the seller specified that the buyer could resell the property only to a person of the Caucasian race. If someone in the chain of

title eventually sold to a non-Anglo, would the courts enforce the original restriction in the deed? (A number of cases may be of interest here including: *Shelly* v. *Kramer*, 334 U.S. 1; *Barrows* v. *Jackson*, 346 U.S. 249; *Mayers* v. *Ridley*, 465 F.2d 630.)

3   The grantor of a deed signed the original. An unsigned carbon copy was duly recorded with the county recorder. Would this recording have any legal effect? (*Herzer* v. *Dembosz*, 167 N.E.2d 210.)

4   A rancher contracted to sell "the Evergreen Ranch in Coles County, Colorado, containing 640 acres, more or less, at a price of $500,000." A survey by the buyer showed the property consisted of only 620 acres. Would this be construed as a sale of the ranch, regardless of size, or as a sale of 640 acres of land? What if the parties agreed to swap a "certain quarter section of land for a certain quarter section of land" and it turned out that one tract was somewhat smaller in size? (*Maxwell* v. *Redd*, 496 P.2d 1320.)

5   The holder of a lease with an option to renew was required to give notice within six months prior to the expiration if the lease was to be extended. The notice was written, signed, stamped, addressed, and deposited in the mail. The property owner, however, claimed this notice was never received. Was the renewal valid? (*Palo Alto Town & Country* v. *BBTC Co.*, 110 Cal. Reporter 93.)

17

Bailments

NATURE OF A BAILMENT

Personal property may not always remain under the owner's care and control. A variety of legal rights and claims may come into play when personal property is loaned, sent for repairs, stored, or otherwise placed in the custody of someone other than the owner—a type of transaction known as a *bailment*.

Bailment Defined

A bailment is a delivery of possession of goods or personal property to another for temporary custody, care, repair, or use by the recipient. The subject of a bailment transaction is always personal property. The person turning over the property is called the *bailor*, and the person taking custody of the property is known as the *bailee*. Under appropriate circumstances the concept of bailment may include many types of transactions, among them the deposit, storage, rental, loan, checking, pledge, or repair of property or the holding of lost property. Bailments are sometimes divided into several classes by the courts, according to who is to benefit. These courts impose a greater degree of care on those who benefit most.

The bailor of property is usually the owner, but not necessarily. A thief who checks a stolen briefcase at a parcel checkroom is a bailor, even though the thief does not have title. A friend who borrows a set of golf clubs becomes a bailor when the clubs are left at a repair shop.

A bailee is never one who has title to the property or who is expected to gain title. If the intent of the parties is for the receiver to gain title, then the transaction is a sale or barter (a variation of a sale) rather than a bailment. Title is to remain with the owner in every bailment.

As one of the requirements of a bailment, it is expected that the identical goods will be returned to the bailor. The courts say that "bailment is characterized by a transfer of possession, as distinguished from a change in ownership." It is often part of the bailment arrangement, however, that the property will be returned in altered form. For example, a broken watch may be returned in working condition; soiled laundry may be returned as clean; milk may be returned as cheese; or wheat may be ground and returned as flour.

A bailment is usually regarded by the courts as a contract arrangement.

Basic Requirements for a Bailment

The courts sometimes list three requirements for a bailment:

1. Title to personal property is not transferred.
2. Temporary possession and control is given to and accepted by the bailee.
3. Possession eventually reverts back to the bailor or to someone designated by the bailor.

How Bailment Differs from Sale

When the transaction between the parties is a sale rather than a bailment, loss or destruction of the property will normally be paid for by the party receiving the property. But if the transaction is a bailment, the party receiving the property (bailee) will not be liable for nonnegligent loss or damage. For example, if a famous race horse was struck by lightning after being transferred into the pasture of a buyer, the loss of the horse would fall on the buyer. But if the animal was transferred into the field for a stud fee (bailment), the loss would remain with the party that placed the horse for the fee (the owner). It is obvious, then, that the difference between a sale and a bailment may sometimes cost many thousands of dollars.

The test used by the courts to determine a bailment is whether the identical thing is to be returned,[1] even though in an altered form.[2] If the receiver is entitled to return something that is not identical, the deal involves barter, which is a form of sale.[3] The question here is in determining the intent of the parties, both from the contract itself and from the construction put on it by the parties.[4] In case the matter comes to trial, the intent of the parties is a question of fact to be decided by the jury, under proper instructions from the judge.[5]

---

[1]*Dryden* v. *Michigan State Industries*, 66 F.2d 950; *Norris* v. *Boston Music Co.*, 151 N.W. 971.
[2]*In re Eichengren*, 18 F.2d 101.
[3]*Keystone Pipe & Supply* v. *Herbert Oil Corp.*, 62 S.W.2d 606.
[4]*Samson Tire and Rubber Co.* v. *Eggleston*, 45 F.2d 502.
[5]*Charles M. Stieff Inc.* v. *City of San Antonio*, 111 S.W.2d 1086.

Storage of Fungible Goods

Some types of property, called *fungible goods*, cannot be distinguished from other units or quantities of the same kind. For example, one bushel of wheat may be exactly like every other bushel of wheat in a grain elevator; a barrel of jellybeans may be like every other container of jellybeans; a gallon of oil may be like every other gallon in the tank. In the case of fungible goods, the law makes an exception to the bailment requirement that identical goods be returned. The courts consider the transaction as a bailment when there is a legal obligation to return only an equal quantity of fungible goods of the same grade or class as the goods originally delivered. Consequently an agreement to store and return 10,000 gallons of the same grade of gasoline as delivered would be construed as a bailment.

Business or individuals contracting for storage should make certain that the contract clearly specifies whether the transaction is to be construed by the parties as a sale or as a bailment.

Contracts to Manufacture Raw Goods into Finished Products

The owner of raw materials frequently delivers them to someone who is to make them into finished products. Sometimes raw materials are so altered in the manufacturing process that they are not recognizable as the goods that were originally furnished. A contract of this kind may be either a bailment or a sale, depending on the intentions of the parties to the contract.[6]

Constructive Bailments

Although it should be mentioned that most bailments are founded on a contractual relationship, many courts also note that "some bailments arise by operation of law." These latter instances are sometimes called *constructive* bailments. For example, a mislaid briefcase left in a hotel lobby was turned over to the hotel manager. The courts regard the hotel manager as the bailee of the briefcase, although there was no direct authority from the owner to leave it with the hotel official.

—————— *DISCUSSION* ——————————————————————————

CASE 39   A supplier of acetylene gas for welding sold the gas in tanks by a contract that expressly reserved title to the tanks. The sales agreement provided that the supplier would keep filled tanks in reserve and exchange them for empty

[6]*Smith v. Brandenburg Instruments Co.*, 50 N.Y.S.2d 264.

tanks that would be returned without charge, except for their gaseous contents. A customer contended that the tanks were obviously included in the acetylene purchase and that there was no legal responsibility to return the tanks to the supplier. Was the customer's contention right? (*Auto Acetylene Co. v. Prest-O-Lite Co.*, 276 F.537.)

RIGHTS AND RESPONSIBILITIES IN BAILMENTS

Principle of "Ordinary Care"

Early United States courts frequently divided bailments into three classes: (1) bailments for the sole benefit of the bailor, (2) bailments for the sole benefit of the bailee, and (3) bailments that worked for the benefit of both parties. These same courts usually held that a bailee, for his or her own sole benefit, must exercise a great degree of care in protecting the property involved; for the bailor's sole benefit, only slight care; and for their mutual benefit, reasonable care.

After a number of years, however, many American courts began to realize that these differing standards of care were often very confusing to jurors, who often could not apply them with any real consistency. Consequently, most courts began to determine that every bailee should always be held to exercise "ordinary care"—such care as a "reasonably prudent person would use in handling this kind of property under the same or similar circumstances." The courts pointed out that this "ordinary care" was a varying standard, requiring more care in the protection of a diamond ring than in that of a bag of potatoes. This principle of "ordinary care" is followed by most courts today, although the courts in a few states still classify bailments as to which party will benefit, thereafter applying different degrees of care.

DISCUSSION

CASE 40   A dry cleaning establishment returned a man's suit to the wrong customer. When the misdelivered item could not be retrieved, the owner of the suit claimed that the dry cleaner was obligated to pay for it. Was this contention correct, or was the possibility that someone could have stolen the suit off the delivery truck sufficient to relieve the dry cleaner of the responsibility? (*Potomac Insurance Co. v. Nickerson*, 231 P. 445.)

Bailee's Right to a Lien

As a general rule of law, a bailee is entitled to be paid for work performed on or rendered in connection with bailed property unless the transaction is a gratuitous bailment. In most states the bailee has a lien entitling the bailee to hold the property until labor charges are paid.

If the bailed property is damaged or destroyed through negligence or mishandling by the bailee, then the bailee must make good the loss. But if the bailed property is destroyed or harmed without the bailee's fault, then the bailee is still entitled to be paid for the work performed.[7]

Although the bailee has the right to a lien, a number of courts do not permit the bailee to do more than hold the property. In those states it cannot be sold to enforce the lien. Laws concerning the right to sell the bailed property where the bailee's work has not been paid for vary from state to state.

Exculpatory Clauses

Claim checks issued by automobile parking lots and similar businesses frequently seek to avoid legal responsibility for property entrusted to those companies. The printed statement on the tickets disclaiming or limiting responsibility is called an *exculpatory clause*. If the business receiving the property (the bailee) is a public or quasi-public institution, an exculpatory clause is little defense against negligence. For example, a claim check issued by a city stadium could not effectively avoid responsibility according to most courts.

The exculpatory clause on some claim checks attempts to place a ceiling on the amount of liability, rather to avoid liability altogether. Disclaimers of this kind are usually treated more kindly by the courts. Some courts examine the relationship between the parties, striking down the exculpatory clause completely if the customer appears to have little choice but to accept the claim check or be denied service; they reason that the bargaining powers between the parties are obviously unequal. Some other courts strike down the exculpatory clause on the basis that it is printed in very fine type and may be difficult to read in the few seconds that a customer has to decide whether to accept or go elsewhere. Court decisions vary widely in this matter.

Parking Lot Bailments

The question of liability for damage or theft on a public automobile parking lot often hinges on whether the transaction was a bailment or a mere renting of space. If the facts are construed as a bailment, the parking lot is liable for loss occasioned by negligence. Most courts examine the facts and allow one factor to determine whether the parking lot is liable. Control over the parked

[7]*Shoreland Freezers* v. *Textile Ice and Fuel Co.*, 129 S.E.2d 424.

vehicle seems to be the test—whether the auto was parked and the keys retained by the parking lot attendant. The courts frequently rule that when the driver comes on the lot, parks in a convenient space, and keeps the key, the arrangement is a *license* rather than a bailment.

─────── *DISCUSSION* ───────────────────────────────

CASE 41   A doctor and his wife went to a concert in separate automobiles, since the doctor expected to go to a hospital afterwards. The doctor parked in a stall that he had already rented by the month. The doctor's wife gave her keys to the lot attendant and her automobile was placed in the adjacent slot. During the concert both cars were damaged in an incident for which the parking lot attendants denied responsibility, alleging that they did not see or hear any other driver strike the damaged cars. Since the doctor owned both autos, he sued for the harm to each. What would be the outcome? (*McFarland* v. *C. A. R. Corp.*, 156 A.2d 58; *Johnson* v. *Hanna*, 101 N.W.2d 830, is similar.)

Although the motor vehicle may not be devalued in a parking lot bailment, it is quite common for property inside it to be stolen. Most courts hold that responsibility of the bailee in this situation depends on whether the bailee was put on notice before the loss takes place that the property was in the car. The courts generally hold that this notice to the bailee need not be actual or express; constructive notice may suffice. In *Hallman* v. *Federal Parking Services*[8] the court said:

> Clearly the hotel [defendant] was put on notice that plaintiff was a traveler and the apparel hanging from the racks was in plain view. Upon [the bellboy's entering] the car, the luggage on the floor and rear seats could easily be seen, and common knowledge and experience could anticipate that the car might contain in its interior other articles normally carried by travelers. . . . [Judgment against the hotel-defendant-bailee].

Coats and Hats Hanging in a Restaurant

Clearly a bailment exists when a coat or another item is deposited at a hotel or restaurant cloakroom with an attendant who gives a claim check in return. But a coat left on a hook in a restaurant is in a somewhat different category. Usually the courts conclude that the property in question was not actually turned over to the possession and control of a restaurant employee, even though the waiter may have assisted in removing the coat and placing it on the hook. Most decisions state that acts of this kind are mere courtesies;

[8]*Hallman* v. *Federal Parking Services*, 134 A.2d 382.

here, handing over an item of clothing is not such a delivery as to constitute a bailment. As pointed out in *Apfel* v. *Whyte's Inc.*[9]:

> The customer, had he at any time so desired, was at perfect liberty to take down his coat for any purpose, or to take out anything there may have been in the pocket of the coat. . . . How can it be said that the restaurant had been given control of something that the owner may freely take at any moment without asking leave to do so?

SPECIAL BAILMENTS

The law gives special treatment to certain bailments—those of hotelkeepers, common carriers, warehousemen, and factors.

Hotelkeeper (Innkeeper) Bailments

Practically all courts in the United States have long decided that an innkeeper has absolute responsibility for protecting the luggage and property of a guest. An innkeeper who does not live up to this responsibility is liable to the guest for damages. This liability may not extend to someone who merely comes into the hotel for a conference or another affair without registering. This responsibility as a bailee was placed on innkeepers because they have traditionally retained control over all room keys. This basic bailment principle has been extended by practically all courts to hotels, motels, and other facilities that offer living accommodations to travelers. Most states have statutes that limit the liability of the hotel for stolen valuables unless these articles are placed in a lock box located in the hotel office.

To give hotelkeepers some protection, the law gives them a lien right on a guest's baggage or other private property. Most states have statutes that regulate how the hotelkeeper can enforce this lien by sale of the guest's property. Under the law in many states the guest must be given an opportunity to redeem this property before the sale can take place.

Common Carriers

A *common carrier* is one engaged in the business of transporting goods or persons for hire. A common carrier who is licensed to carry freight cannot refuse to accept shipments unless the goods are inherently dangerous. Shipping by common carrier constitutes a bailment for mutual benefit. Unlike most other bailees, however, a common carrier is liable for the safe delivery of items to their destination. This liability is absolute unless the carrier can show that damage or loss was occasioned by one of the following:

[9]*Apfel* v. *Whyte's Inc.*, 180 N.Y.S. 712.

1. An uncontrollable disaster called "an act of God," such as a hurricane sweeping a railroad boxcar off the track;
2. Interference by the shipper or the shipper's employee. For example, the owner of a cattle ranch sent an employee in a railroad boxcar with a shipment of prize cattle. The rancher's attendant negligently set the straw in the boxcar afire, killing the cattle;
3. The inherent makeup of the goods, such as a shipment of eggs that spoiled where refrigeration was not requested of the carrier;
4. An act of an enemy in time of war; or
5. Delay ordered by police, military, or governmental authorities.

Goods are frequently transferred from one common carrier to another, especially on a long shipment. Damages may be recovered by the shipper from the original carrier or by the consignee from the carrier who actually made the eventual delivery. In order to recover, the shipper is required to prove that the shipment was in good condition at the time it was turned over to the carrier. This proof creates a *prima facie* case of liability on the part of the carrier.

Liability begins as soon as the shipment is delivered to the carrier. A shipment by railroad boxcar is considered as delivered when the boxcar is "spotted" on the consignee's spur track alongside the dock, even though this car may be left during the middle of the night. In other delivery situations, however, the courts differ widely as to when the carrier's liability comes to an end. Some courts hold that "delivery" has not been made until the consignee has been notified and given a reasonable time in which to pick up the shipment from the warehouse of destination. Other courts hold that the shipper's liability comes to an end when the shipment is unloaded from the truck or boxcar and placed in a freight house or terminal at the destination. A third group of courts find that the shipper's liability continues until the consignee has had a reasonable time to inspect the shipment after picking it up at the place of destination.

Public Warehouses

Public warehouses store goods for the general public without discrimination. Most states have special statutes that apply to the operation of public warehouses. In most situations the obligations and duties of a public warehouseman are those of a bailee for mutual benefit. Usually state statutes require a public warehouse to be operated according to safe and suitable standards for the public's benefit. In practically all states a public warehouseman can be sued for improper storage of goods, at the same time having a lien against the stored merchandise for reasonable charges.

A *warehouse receipt* is a certification that specified goods have been received for storage from a named depositor. It also sets out the terms of the storage contract. Warehouse receipts are evidence of title to goods and are of two types, negotiable and nonnegotiable. A *negotiable warehouse receipt* is a fully negotiable instrument which provides that the goods will be delivered to the named depositor or to the bearer. The warehouse must deliver the goods upon the presentation of such a receipt, at which time a cancellation of the document is made. A *nonnegotiable warehouse receipt* will permit delivery only to the depositor or to a person specified by the depositor.

The Factor as Bailee

A *factor* is a commercial agent hired by a principal to sell merchandise consigned to the factor, usually in the factor's own name. The factor is basically a commission salesperson who acts as bailee of the owner's goods. A sale by the factor will normally pass title of the factor's principal (consignor) to the purchaser. The factor, of course, is liable to the principal in case of embezzlement of the principal's merchandise.

QUESTIONS

1. What are the three basic requirements of a bailment?
2. Distinguish between a bailment and a sale.
3. What are fungible goods? What exception does the law of bailments make with respect to fungible goods?
4. What kind of care does the law require of the owner's property by a bailee? Are different degrees of care required for different classes of bailments? What is the basic law in this regard in most states today?
5. Does an exculpatory clause on a claim check excuse a bailee from responsibility over an owner's property? Explain.
6. When a car is parked on a public parking lot, what test is used by the courts to determine whether the transaction was a bailment or a rental of space?
7. Who is responsible for the property inside an automobile in a bailment on a public parking lot?
8. Is a restaurant owner usually liable for the theft of a customer's hat from the restaurant?
9. What responsibility has a hotelkeeper as bailee of a guest's property? Discuss the hotelkeeper's lien rights.
10. Outline the responsibilities and duties of a common carrier handling shipments.
11. What is a negotiable warehouse receipt? Could it be used by a thief to obtain stored property?

ANSWERS TO DISCUSSION CASES

CASE 39 The contract specified that there was no sale of the tanks. There was a sale of the acetylene but a bailment of the tanks. The tanks must be returned by the customer, as they are still the property of the supplier.

CASE 40 The dry cleaner was obligated to pay for the suit. The transaction was a bailment and obviously the dry cleaner did not take proper care of the bailor's property.

CASE 41 The transaction as to the doctor's car was a mere rental of space. But the parking lot was responsible for the damage to the wife's car since that transaction was a bailment and the bailee was responsible for obvious negligence.

PROBLEM CASES

1 An upholstery firm did not follow instructions in rebuilding a sofa. As a result, the sofa no longer had value to the customer. The repair firm sued for the contract price. The customer countersued, denying liability and asking to be repaid for the value of the sofa. What should be the outcome? (*Baena Bros.* v. *Welge*, 207 A.2d 749.)

2 A salesman left trunks of display samples with a potential customer who was a guest in a hotel. when the hotel resident did not pay his bill, the hotel seized his baggage along with the display trunks. Could the owner of the display trunks demand that his samples be released? (*Torrey* v. *McClellan*, 45 S.W. 64.)

3 Plaintiff went to a men's store in Philadelphia to buy a suit of clothes. On the salesman's instructions the plaintiff put his watch in a drawer while the plaintiff went to adjust and measure the clothes being fitted. The watch was missing when the plaintiff returned. When the store declined to pay for the watch, plaintiff sued. Should damages be awarded? (*Woodruff* v. *Painter*, 24 A. 621.)

4 The owner of a valuable diamond ring left it with a jewelry store to be sold on commission. Thereafter, armed robbers entered the store and took the ring with other loot in a holdup. The owner of the ring sued for loss of the item. The store owner defended on the basis that he was not liable for the misconduct of others. Evidence showed that there was no lock on the display door. Nor was there a guard or display grating on the display window. The store owner had taken no special precautions and the store had been robbed twice in recent months. Should the store owner be liable in this bailment? (*Morse* v. *Homer's Inc.*, 4 N.E.2d 625.)

5 A bank rented a safe deposit box to a customer. Entry could be made only when the bank's master key and the customer's individual key were in the

lock at the same time. A loss was discovered through no fault of the customer. The bank was unable to pin down the reason for the loss. The customer sued on the basis that a bailment existed and that the bank should have exercised better care over the customer's property. The bank defended on the basis that the institution never did have exclusive possession of the customer's valuables. Decide. (*National Safe Deposit Co. v. Stead*, 95 N.E. 973.)

18

Wills and Trusts

What a Will Accomplishes

A *will* is a revocable legal document by which an individual disposes of property. It takes effect upon the maker's death. The person making a disposition of property by will is called the *testator* if male or the *testatrix* if female. Someone who leaves no valid will is said to die *intestate*; one who has a will dies *testate*.

If there is no valid will, the laws of the state where death occurs specify which heirs of the deceased will inherit property and in what amounts. These laws of *descent and distribution*, as they are called, vary considerably from state to state. Recent surveys show that approximately 75 percent of adults in a number of states could not correctly identify the proportion of property that would pass to specific relatives if the respondents died without a will. Many people are under the impression that the surviving wife or husband will automatically receive all or most of the property that is left. In a number of states this is simply not true. For example, in some states the share of the surviving wife or husband is the same as that for each minor child. If there are no children, in some states half or more of the deceased wife's or husband's estate may go to the deceased's parents. Obviously the terms of descent and distribution laws often come as an unpleasant surprise.

Probate courts supervise the settlement of estates and usually handle guardianship and adoption cases as well. The actual work of estate settlement is performed by an executor (male) or an executrix (female) if the deceased left a will. If there is no will, the court will appoint an administrator or an administratrix. In some states a probate court is known as a *surrogate court*, or *court of ordinary* or an *orphan's court*. In legal circles all such courts may be referred to as probate courts.

Children may inherit money or property, of course, but a minor child is not permitted to spend that inheritance or sell inherited property without prior approval of the probate court. In most instances the surviving wife or husband will be able to qualify as guardian of the minor children with court-supervised authority to distribute their funds. In most states, however, the guardian would need a court order to spend the children's money for anything but bare necessities and would be required to account for all expenditures in minute detail. This involvement in probate matters often results in a loss of time for the surviving parent. In addition, related court fees and other costs may eat heavily into funds intended for family support.

Costs for bonding a guardian and for court supervision may be considerable when children inherit from an intestate parent. Expenditure of inherited money to send a deserving child to college usually requires a court order and there is always a possibility that the supervising judge may not agree with this expenditure. This guardianship difficulty may be avoided if money is left to the child in an outright bequest by will, provided the will specifies the executor may use independent judgment.

It should also be pointed out that the distribution of property usually takes longer when no will is left. Any delay experienced by the heirs in receiving money usually comes at a time when family members may be in real need.

The executor or executrix who is to handle an estate settlement is named by the maker of the will. If there is no will, the probate judge appoints an administrator or administratrix. Often the administrator or administratrix does not agree with the deceased's wishes for estate distribution.

The administrator or administratrix is required to post a fidelity bond, the cost of which comes out of the estate. If the testator of a will so desires, this requirement for a bond may be waived. In most jurisdictions the cost of this bond is 1½ percent of the value of the estate (in some states the cost is more). Even though bonding costs sometimes seem rather moderate, the cost is money that could be needed by the survivors. If the executor or executrix is honest, the bonding cost may be unnecessary. It is also worth noting that the executor or executrix is already liable in tort for any misuse of funds. Often, too, the only heirs are the surviving widow and the deceased's children. If the widow is appointed executrix in the will, there is little real likelihood that she would cheat her own children of their inheritance. Often there are other costs and fees assessed if the estate is settled by an administrator, rather than by an executor.

If the estate includes real property, it may have to be sold. At times a good offer for the sale of such property may expire before court approval can be obtained. This requirement for court supervision of a property sale can be waived under the terms of a will.

Except under unusual circumstances, anyone who has property or an estate of real value should make a will. In addition to the reasons previously noted for will preparation, estate planners point out that a will is one of the most valuable tools available for reducing or avoiding payment of estate taxes, inheritance taxes, or gift tax levies. Properly planned and drafted, a will can offer many advantages in accumulating, using, and leaving money. Almost without exception, a will should be prepared by a lawyer.

Businesses sometimes use wills of the company executives, along with company-paid life insurance, to keep the firm in good financial condition in spite of the death of an executive or partner. This technique is occasionally coupled with a buy-back arrangement to enable surviving members of the firm to purchase a deceased's interest.

Characteristics of a Will

The courts say that the right to make a will is not an inalienable freedom such as those of speech or of worship. The right to leave a will is set by state statutes, and the maker must comply with those statutes in every detail. Requirements for will preparation vary from state to state. All states require the maker of a will to have reached a minimum age—14 years in a few states and either 18 or 21 years in most.

In some states a person convicted and sentenced to life imprisonment is said to be "civilly dead" and cannot leave a valid will. But the right to make a will is not limited to any social class or monetary worth. The courts uniformly require the maker to be a person of sound mind. But in the words of one judge, the person making a will "does not have to be a literarian, a financial genius, an athlete, or an expert cook." All that is required is that the maker understand and appreciate the consequences of his or her act that results in giving away property.

Most states recognize two types of wills: formal and holographic. A *formal will* is typed and must be signed by the testator in the presence of two witnesses, who also sign the will attesting to the fact that the testator did, in fact, sign the will in their presence.

A *holographic (handwritten) will* must be completely dated, written, and signed by the testator. After the testator dies, someone who is familiar with the handwriting must testify that that person did, in fact, write the will. It is usually advisable to prepare a formal will in order to prevent problems later when the will must be probated. One may only recall the controversies inherent in the probate of Howard Hughes's handwritten (holographic) will to understand the benefits of writing a formal will.

It is also important that the wording of each clause of the will be very precise. For instance, many individuals fail to make provision for property left to predeceased children. The courts must then decide whether to give it to that child's surviving children, who are grandchildren of the testator, or to other children as part of their share. However, with proper wording, this problem may be eliminated. It is usually advisable to have an attorney prepare a will, even if there is very little property involved. While an individual may know what is intended when writing a will, the courts must interpret that person's wishes after death. Sometimes the court's interpretation is different from the meaning which the testator intended.

A few states, such as California, have devised a partially holographic will called a *statutory will*. The format is very precise, and forms may be purchased. Basically, a certain format is preprinted, and the blanks are filled in in the individual's own handwriting. There are very strict rules for what may be included in this type will, so it is not for everyone.

It is important to remember the formal requirements for all individuals who are preparing wills:

1. The testator (maker) must have *testamentary intent*. That is, the person must have the intent to dispose of his or her property by will.
2. The testator must be of the proper age in that state, usually the age of majority (18 or 21).
3. The testator must be of sound mind at the time the will is signed. That is, one must know that he or she is making up a document which will dispose of his or her property and must have the mental capacity to know what is being done in this regard.
4. There must be intent by the testator that this be a last will.
5. The testator must sign freely and voluntarily. There must be no fraud, duress, mistake, or undue influence on the testator. (This situation is seen most often when the testator leaves property to a nonrelative and the relatives try to set aside the will because of undue influence or duress.)

Some additional special requirements for formal wills follow:

1. The testator must sign the will in the presence of the required witnesses, who also must sign in conformity with that state's statutory requirements. Usually two witnesses are required, but some attorneys recommend three to be sure there will be at least one available when the testator's will is probated. Most attorneys also recommend that the testator choose younger witnesses to increase the possibility that they will be alive at the time the will is probated and the witnesses have to come forward and state that they signed the will in the presence of the testator. Many states have developed "Proof of Subscribing Witnesses" forms for this purpose.
2. In most states, the will must be typed.

Most attorneys require that the testator initial each page of the will at the bottom at the end of the printing to ensure that pages or other material is not deleted, added, or changed later. While this is not a statutory requirement, it is usually advisable as a precautionary measure.

Disinheritance; Undue Influence

One should consult an attorney before attempting to disinherit a lawful heir by will. For instance, an individual not knowledgeable in the law may feel that by not mentioning one child no property will be inherited by that child. This is usually not the case due to "pretermitted heir statutes," which state that if one of your children's names is left out of the will, it must have been an oversight and that child will inherit his or her statutory share of your estate, which varies by state.

Many states require that you leave a certain portion of your estate to your spouse. If this is not done by will, the spouse may take property "against the will" (which means the share established by statute.) In community property states, half of the marital property belongs to the surviving spouse, and a portion of the other half may be taken by the spouse "against the will" if no provision is made therein.

A will may be set aside by the courts if it can be proved that someone unduly influenced the maker to turn against heirs who would normally be the object of the maker's bounty. Courts are not in exact agreement concerning the definition of *undue influence*, and the term may be difficult to prove to the satisfaction of the courts unless there is a substantial amount of evidentiary proof. Some courts have defined *undue influence* as the abuse of a relationship of trust for one's own gain.

Codicils

Minor changes to a will may be made by using a *codicil*. However, the same formalities are required as were utilized in the original will. A formal codicil must be written with the same enumerated requirements discussed above. A holographic codicil must be in the testator's handwriting, as discussed above.

If many complicated changes are being made to the will, it is preferable to write an entirely new will. Lawyers point out that after a codicil or two have been added, there is always the danger of misinterpretation or lack of clarity.

Cancellation (Revocation)

When more than one will has been prepared by a testator, the probate court accepts the most recent valid will that can be found. Consequently, lawyers recommend that the original and all copies of an old will be destroyed after a new one is prepared. In addition, the new will should state that "this will revokes all other wills written by me." For this reason, it is imperative that the will be dated.

Probate

Not all of a deceased's property goes through probate. The proceeds of life insurance policies are usually paid directly to the beneficiary named in the policy. Under joint tenancy ownership, the surviving tenant automatically takes title to such property.

Most probate courts require that one or more witnesses to the will appear in person before the probate judge to authenticate the will. Some states, however, permit the witness to make this authentication by sworn affidavit. Some jurisdictions also permit the use of a *self-proving will* in which the testator and witnesses swear at the time of the will's execution that the legal formalities were met. Proof of authentication is not thereafter required at the time of probate unless someone comes into court and disputes the authentication.

The executor, executrix, administrator, or administratrix advertises in newspapers for persons owed money by the deceased. The debts and costs of burial are then paid off and estate assets are thereafter distributed according to the terms of the will or, if there is no will, according to state inheritance laws.

Holographic Wills

As noted, about half of the states do permit the use of a *holographic* or *olographic will* as an alternative to a formal will. The holographic will requires no witnesses, but it must be completely dated, written, and signed in the testator's own handwriting. This does not mean handprinting, and a blank sheet with any kind of heading such as a printed date is not allowed to qualify. It is to be emphasized that the document must be entirely handwritten and signed at the end by the maker. Lawyers frequently encounter difficulty in having a will of this kind authenticated, especially where there are few people who can swear that the handwriting is that of the maker.

——— *DISCUSSION* ———————————————

CASE 42   A farmer was trapped under his tractor in an isolated field when the vehicle overturned. Seriously injured and unable to free himself, he apparently realized that he would likely die before help could arrive. Evidently in great pain and without conventional writing materials, the farmer scratched out a short statement on the underside of the tractor's fender with a sharp tool: "In case I die in this mess, I leave it all to the wife. Cecil George Harris." There were, of course, no witnesses to the incident. Harris died before help arrived to free him and the tractor fender was submitted to the probate court as his will. Should it be accepted?

TRUSTS

The Express Private Trust

A *trust* is a fiduciary relationship in which property or money is held by one party (the *trustee*) for the benefit of another (the *beneficiary*). The trustee is under an absolute legal obligation to act solely for the financial benefit of the beneficiary. The *corpus* of the trust (the trust assets) may consist of either real or personal property. The trust can be created for any purpose that is not illegal. The person supplying the money or property that goes into the trust (corpus) is called by any one of a number of legal names: *trustor, settlor, founder, creator,* or *donor.*

From an ownership standpoint, a trust involves a unique legal concept. In a sense, there is double ownership of the trust property. The courts say that the trustee holds legal title to the trust property and has the duty to manage it, but the beneficiary of the trust also has an "equitable interest" or equitable title in it.

The most common type of trust created for the benefit of a private individual is called an *express private trust.* A trust of this kind may be created during the trustor's lifetime or by the trustor's will. The former is an *inter vivos* trust (living trust), the latter is a *testamentary trust.* The trustee who misuses trust assets or funds in any way is liable in a suit for damages. The trust may be set up for the benefit of several individuals (multiple beneficiaries) or for a whole class of persons.

Frequently the trustor is also the beneficiary of the trust. For example, an elderly man in poor health set up a trust and turned his rental property, stocks, and bonds over to the trustee, his son. This permitted the elderly trustor to have a good income without having to manage his property. Upon the death of the trustor, the trust agreement provided that the trustee should distribute the trust funds and assets equally among the trustor's children or their heirs.

A trustee is normally entitled to be paid reasonable fees and expenses for the administration of a trust. In most situations the trustor cannot revoke the trust unless this possibility is provided for in the original trust agreement.

Some trusts are set up to provide regular income for spendthrifts, drunks, or ne'er-do-wells who are unable to handle financial matters. This type of trust is usually called a *spendthrift trust.* A beneficiary of another trust may be a small child who is unable to care for personal needs or a widow who has had no experience in handling money.

In certain instances a trust may be set up with successive beneficiaries. For example, a wealthy grandfather set up a trust for his son with the income to go to the son's children or their heirs upon the son's death. Trusts of this type may be limited in duration, however, to the life of an individual who was living at the time the trust was created.

In some trusts the trustee may be permitted to use his or her judgment in giving more income to a needy beneficiary than to a well-to-do one. This is a so-called *sprinkling trust*. In still other trusts, the beneficiary (usually a widow) may be permitted to sell off trust assets when in financial need.

Using Trusts in Estate Planning

In the hands of an attorney who specializes in estate planning, a trust may be a valuable tool in avoiding the costs and delays of probate. The trust technique may also be very useful in reducing or eliminating burdensome costs of both Federal and state estate and inheritance taxes and in avoiding Federal gift tax liability. This is usually an area of specialization for tax experts and attorneys.

——— *QUESTIONS* ———————————————————————

1. What is a will and how is it used?
2. Why is it almost always advisable to write a will? Explain the benefits of doing so.
3. What are the general requirements of a formal will?
4. When may a codicil be used?
5. Describe a holographic will. What are the objections to the use of this kind of will?
6. Describe the workings of an express private trust.
7. Enumerate the benefits of various kinds of trusts.
8. Advise, in general, how a trust may be used for financial benefit.

——— *ANSWER TO DISCUSSION CASE* ———————————————

CASE 42   The court accepted the scratched message as a holographic will. This is somewhat similar to the old English case in the 1700s when a shipwrecked sailor scribbled his will on a piece of 2-by-4 planking from the breakup of a vessel. The maker of this will died of exposure, but the board was brought back to England by another sailor, where it was accepted as a will. This case served as the basis for our holographic will law.

——— *PROBLEM CASES* ———————————————————————

1   A man murdered his wife. Would he be permitted to receive money as the beneficiary of his wife's will? (*In re Wilkins Estate*, 211 N.W.652.)

2   Suppose that a will prepared in California was written in Italian. Would preparation in a foreign language make the will invalid? What if the maker could read and write only Italian? (*In re Estate of Cuneo*, 384 P.2d 1.)

3   A document offered for probate as a will was written on both the front and reverse of one sheet of paper. Would this fact disqualify it from acceptance? (*Stuck* v. *Howard*, 104 So. 500.)

4   If a court found the maker of a will to be "illiterate, disagreeable, untidy, unsocial, miserly, and with unjust prejudices and religious fanaticism," would such an individual's will be admitted to probate? What if the court found that the maker of the will lacked the keen mind needed to carry on a business; would this person's will be accepted? (*Walsh* v. *Fairhead*, 219 S.W.2d 941.)

5   A codicil was added to a will. The legal formalities in executing the codicil differed somewhat from those used in drawing up the original will. Is "substantial compliance" all that is necessary to make a codicil acceptable as an addition to the original will? (*Paul* v. *Davenport*, 7 S.E.2d 352.)

19

Criminal Law and Business

NATURE AND WORKINGS OF CRIMINAL LAW

The basic legal concerns of commerce are usually handled by the civil, rather than the criminal, courts. Nonetheless, the impact of crime on business and industry may be enormous. Therefore, business properties and rights can often be protected if owners, managers, and rank and file employees all have an understanding of crime and the criminal justice system.

Both a tort and a criminal offense may arise out of the same transaction. Criminal law, of course, is seldom directly involved in the repayment of losses, compensation for business or employee injuries, or the protection of management or property rights. When a matter involves both a tort and a criminal wrong, the tort is handled in a civil lawsuit and the criminal violation is prosecuted in a branch of the court system that handles criminal matters almost exclusively.

In the latter, procedures are quite different from those used in civil litigation. Because of the great importance of protecting the freedom of every individual, the criminal courts must provide detailed hearings when criminal charges are brought. Arrest and search procedures must be conducted according to prescribed legal standards. In some states, a person cannot be convicted of a crime without first being *indicted* by a *grand jury*, a body that hears evidence prior to a criminal trial to make sure there is real substance to the charge. At all stages the accused must be afforded a number of rights that are guaranteed by the Federal and state constitutions and statutory laws, both prior to and at the time of trial and sentencing. Individual rights also remain in effect after conviction.

The United States Constitution and court interpretations give an accused the right to prompt arraignment (the specifying and bringing of charges before a magistrate), the right to an explanation of the charges, the right to bail in most cases, the right to an attorney (except in minor matters), the right to remain in touch with the lawyer, and the right to subpoena witnesses.

The accused may also have the right to have evidence excluded at the time of trial if it had been obtained by improper or illegal search and seizure. The accused also has the right: to be tried only once for the same offense; to remain silent at all times, including the time of trial; to cross-examine and confront witnesses for the prosecution; to obtain witnesses; to have a speedy trial; to be tried by a jury; to have a public trial; and to have the right to *habeas corpus* (forcing the filing of charges or an outright release). While these are the major rights that are available to the accused, this list is not all-inclusive.

Sources of Criminal Law

All criminal law in the United States comes from one or more of four basic sources:

1. The old English common law
2. Federal and state constitutions
3. Laws passed by the Congress and the state legislatures
4. Court interpretations of these laws, following convictions in criminal prosecutions

However, crimes are presently defined by statute in State Penal or Criminal Codes.

The Criminal Justice System

Under the American system, Congress and individual state legislatures originate most criminal laws. In passing on such laws, the courts say that they will be struck down unless they are clear—"sufficiently definite for those affected thereby to know their duty thereunder." But it is extremely difficult for a legislative body to write a law that is always clear to everyone. If there is any serious question concerning clarity, the courts hold the law unconstitutional.

Criminal trials in the United States are usually presided over by a lone judge or magistrate, although the appellate criminal courts are usually composed of three, five, seven, or nine justices. The lone trial judge is in complete charge of the courtroom and the trial proceedings, having absolute authority to enforce orderly proceedings and to place violators in contempt. The judge instructs the jury how the law should be applied by the jury to arrive at a verdict of guilty or innocent. Unless a jury is waived, the jury hears the evidence and decides on the question of guilt or innocence. The judge may act as both judge and jury if the accused consents. Under the *double jeopardy* provisions in United States law, no person may be tried twice for the same offense. In a few instances it is possible to be tried twice from offenses arising out of one continuous series of activities. For example, a person stealing a car and transporting it across a state line may be prosecuted in state court for theft of the car and may also be prosecuted in Federal court for knowingly transporting a stolen vehicle. The theft is the essence of the state charge, while the interstate transportation is the basis of guilt under the Federal charge.

In the United States criminal justice system, the great majority of prosecutions are those in the state courts for violations of state laws. This came about because there are comparatively few Federal criminal laws and because the Tenth Amendment to the United States Constitution provided that "powers not delegated to the United States . . . are reserved to the states respectively, or to the people." In this country an individual may not be prosecuted for violation of an *ex post facto* law nor on a *bill of attainder*. An ex post facto law is one enacted after the prohibited act actually took place; in short, it was not a violation at the time it occurred. A bill of attainder is a prosecution conducted in a state or Federal legislative body, rather than before a properly qualified criminal court in another branch of the government. In essence, a legislative body may not both condemn or prohibit and subsequently convict.

A person arrested in one state must be surrendered to authorities of the state where a criminal charge was brought, according to Article IV of the United States Constitution. On rare occasions the governor in the state of arrest may not follow the Constitution in granting extradition.

At various times in United States history, the criminal courts have seemed to favor different theories of penology for the convicted. On occasion, officials of the criminal justice system have leaned toward "retribution" against the offender, toward "correction," toward "deterrence," toward "rehabilitation," toward "punishment," or toward a combination of these objectives. The objective preferred by authorities has usually varied with whether the system was trying to benefit the individual convict, society as a whole, or both.

Grades of Crime

While there are sometimes differences from state to state, most crimes are classified according to their seriousness as (1) treason, (2) felonies, or (3) misdemeanors. Treason is usually regarded as so serious that it is in a class set apart. The Federal courts and about half the states define a *felony* as any crime punishable by death or imprisonment for a term exceeding one year. In other states, a felony is a crime punishable by death or by imprisonment in a state penitentiary, regardless of the length of the sentence. Technicalities aside, all states regard murder, robbery, rape, kidnapping, burglary, and major theft (sometimes called grand theft) as felonies. All the less serious crimes are usually termed *misdemeanors*. Anyone convicted of a felony is thereafter called a *felon*. Some jurisdictions have a number of minor offenses that are known as "offenses less than misdemeanors," "infractions," or simply "police regulations."

A number of considerations come into play in the criminal justice system, depending on whether an offense is a felony or a misdemeanor. One of the basic differences is that officers may arrest without a warrant in most instances when there is reasonable cause to believe a felony has been committed.

Often several individuals may be involved in the same crime, some being more deeply involved and more blameworthy than others. Consequently, all states classify parties to crimes, usually specifying different punishments for the differing degrees of involvement. For example, the main mover in a crime may be termed the "principal," and others who assist the principal may be called "accessories before the fact," "accessories after the fact," "principals in the second degree," or "abettors." Various states use different names for these participants, usually specifying punishments of differing lengths.

Basic Requirements of a Crime

In most instances the basic requirements of a crime are that

1. A specifically enumerated kind of forbidden act has taken place;
2. No accident was involved; rather, the harm was from a deliberate criminal act; and
3. It can be established that the accused was the person responsible for causing this harm.

In most instances the courts say that the accused must have had a criminal intent. In some major crimes such as murder, this intent must be very specific, such as the intent to kill. In certain other crimes, however, the courts view a general criminal or evil intent as all that is required. This does not mean that the accused necessarily intended to violate the law or to harm the victim, but rather that the accused had the intent to do the prohibited act. This requirement of criminal intent is sometimes different from the necessary mental status for one who may be charged with the commission of a tort. A damage award may be sustained in a tort action without proving either a criminal or an evil intent.

In some crimes, however, the legislatures have done away with the requirement of criminal intent. For example, a motorist who runs down a pedestrian is held to criminal accountability for negligent homicide or manslaughter in many states if the driver is traveling at excessive speed, even though having no objectionable intent of any kind.

In many instances, in addition to the criminal intent, an affirmative act of misconduct is required before criminal responsibility attaches. Nonfeasance is seldom consistent with guilt in the usually understood meaning of criminality. However, the Supreme Court of the United States has consistently affirmed the right of state, county, and city governments to protect the general public by establishing absolute requirements for sanitary conditions in restaurants, for safe working conditions in industry, for regulations of traffic, and for the use and handling of dangerous drugs and chemicals. This is the so-called "police power" authority by which governments may require protection for the general public even though the violator has no criminal intent. Actually, it includes any kind of regulatory provision that promotes health, safety, welfare, and protection of the general public. For example, to avoid contamination, a city ordinance required all bottled milk to be capped twice with both an inner cardboard cap and an outer covering of foil. The conviction of a milkman was upheld, even though he was not aware of the requirement. Here there was neither a positive criminal act nor a criminal intent.

Under Federal criminal laws, incomplete or partly perpetrated crimes are punishable under a classification usually called an *attempt*. In specific instances the crime may be called an *attempt to murder*, an *attempt to rob*, and so on. The courts usually punish such incomplete crimes when it is clear that the perpetrator had actually gotten into the criminal activity but had been brought up short by some intervening act or condition.

Crimes by Corporations

Whether an impersonal organization such as a corporation can commit a crime has caused legal controversy. Of course, a corporation can be required to pay a fine, which is eventually passed on to the stockholders who likely had no criminal intent and no real power to prevent the criminal act.

CRIMES THAT FREQUENTLY AFFECT BUSINESS ⎯⎯⎯⎯⎯⎯⎯⎯⎯

Businesses are frequently victimized by a great many different types of crimes. Some violations, however, trouble businesses more than others and certain industries are more susceptible to losses than others. For example, a few types of retail stores may suffer problems with shoplifting while a brickyard may never have a loss of this kind. Specialists in business crime point out that many organizations are increasingly subjected to employee theft, burglary, armed robbery, embezzlement, and check forgery problems. Loss specialists are convinced that banks, financial institutions, and businesses with extensive computer records can expect a great upsurge in computer embezzlement in the next few years. Computer misappropriation and embezzlement of money will likely be more costly until effective criminal laws can be devised and applied and until better internal controls and auditing systems can be put into use.

Theft

The word *theft* is used interchangeably with *larceny* and *stealing*. In essence, the crime is the taking of money or anything of value from an individual in lawful possession, without right, and with the intention of keeping the property.

Most states have laws that specify grades of larceny or theft, making it a felony or a more serious crime to steal something with a value over a set limit, varying from $50 in some states to $250 in others. The most serious grade of this crime is usually called *grand theft*. This offense may be committed by either an outsider or a company employee.

Embezzlement

Embezzlement is the "fraudulent appropriation of property by a person to whom it has been entrusted, or into whose hands it has lawfully come."[1] Unlike larceny or theft, embezzlement involves money or property that is already in the rightful possession, but not ownership, of the guilty individual. In theft the wrongdoer takes that which is not rightfully in his or her possession, although it is located where the wrongdoer can get at it.

Employee bonding and insurance are frequently used to protect against embezzlement and theft losses in business.

Burglary

A business *burglary* usually involves breaking into a company building or facility to steal money or merchandise. The law of burglary varies from state to state. In practically all jurisdictions, however, a burglary is a breaking into a building, house, or other structure for the purpose of committing any felony inside. A tramp who breaks in only to keep from freezing in a snowstorm may be guilty of a minor offense but not burglary. Criminal responsibility comes into play when the intruder makes the unlawful entry intending to murder the company president, to rape the secretary who is working in the office alone at night, or to commit any other felony. Usually, of course, the criminal makes the entry to steal company money, business machines, or whatever can be found inside.

State laws sometimes divide burglary into classes, imposing more serious penalties for nighttime burglary or for offenses committed with the use of a burning torch (acetylene) on a safe or with the use of explosives.

---

[1] *American Life Insurance Co.* v. *U.S.F. & G.*, 246 N.W. 71.

Robbery

Robbery is the taking of money or property of another from the victim's person or presence against his or her will and by the use of force or fear. Some state laws make robbery a more serious crime when weapons are used or when the robbery is accomplished by torture. Usually the robber must threaten great bodily harm unless a weapon is exhibited. The courts have never required any great exhibition of force where the criminal has actually wrested the property from the victim.

Arson

Legal requirements for the crime of *arson* vary considerably from state to state. Generally, however, the crime consists of the deliberate burning of a business building, home, or some other kind of substantial structure. If a fire fighter or an occupant of the building should be killed in the fire, some state laws specify that the illegal burning is both arson and murder. In other states the resulting death could be prosecuted as manslaughter, rather than as murder. Most jurisdictions regard damage or destruction of a building with explosives as a variation of the crime of arson. Burning of automobiles, ships, railroad bridges, and similar installations is also prohibited by arson statutes in many states.

   In recent years authorities have reported an alarming increase in business attacks by arsonists as a result of labor troubles. Instances of the burning of unsuccessful small businesses in an attempt to collect insurance have also increased.

Shoplifting

The nature of many businesses is such that they never sustain losses due to *shoplifting*. Retail stores, however, may be subjected to this problem on a continuing basis. Shoplifting is a variation of the crime of theft or larceny. Individuals arrested for such violations often file lawsuits against the business, claiming a "false arrest." State laws differ considerably concerning the business's right to arrest or detain shoplifters. In most cases, shoplifters may be detained on the premises for a reasonable period of time until the police arrive. Consequently, managers should be guided by the advice of local prosecutors and police officials in setting up a program to make arrests.

Kidnapping

Kidnapping is the seizing and holding of a person against his or her will. State laws usually classify the offense as kidnapping if the victim's home or automobile is entered and the victim is forced to drive away. The Federal kidnapping statutes (the so-called Lindberg law) apply only when the victim is forced across a state line. Most business kidnappings involve the taking of a store manager, bank official, or some company employee who can open a safe or cash depository.

Forgery

Forgery involves "false making or material altering with intent to defraud, of any writing which, if genuine, . . . might apparently be of legal efficacy or the foundation of legal liability."[2] Most police departments, of course, have forgery, bad check, or bunco squads that specialize in forgeries involving businesses.

Interstate Transportation of Stolen Property

Interstate transportation of stolen property (ITSP) is a Federal crime handled by the FBI. Federal law makes it a felony to transport any kind of money or property worth $5,000 or more in interstate or foreign commerce, knowing the property to be stolen.[3] This law enables the FBI to become involved whenever a sizable amount is taken from one state to another, regardless of the type of theft originally involved. This law has been enforced often, but many businesses are still not familiar with it.

Counterfeiting

Counterfeiting is a Federal felony involving the making or altering of any kind of United States money or securities with the intent of passing it on as genuine.[4] Businesses are often victimized by counterfeiters. The United States Secret Service and local police agencies handle this problem, with the Secret Service having the primary jurisdiction.

Malicious Mischief

Malicious mischief, or vandalism, is the malicious destruction of, or injury to, the property of another person. Laws that cover this problem are handled by the police and vary from state to state.

Nuisances

A *nuisance* may be both a criminal and civil matter (generally a criminal misdemeanor). A nuisance has been variously defined by the courts as:

---

[2] *People* v. *Routson*, 188 N.E. 883.
[3] United States Code, Title 18, Sec. 2314.
[4] United States Code, Title 18, Secs. 485, 486, 490.

. . . that which annoys and disturbs one in the possession of his property, rendering its ordinary use or occupation physically uncomfortable.[5]

Anything which is injurious to health, or is indecent or offensive to the senses, or an obstruction to the free use of property. . . .[6]

The civil courts usually allow damages to adjoining businesses or neighbors who are harmed by a nuisance, in some cases issuing an injunction requiring the offender to control or abate (discontinue) the harm. In addition, public nuisance may generally be punished under misdemeanor statutes. Handling of such matters is usually complicated and often enforcement is assigned to specialists in the local prosecutor's office.

Drugs on the Job

Enforcement of drug laws is usually performed by both state and Federal officers, varying considerably with the circumstances. It is generally advisable for drug problems affecting business to be brought to the attention of local officers. In view of the increased awareness of the use of drugs and alcohol on the job in recent years, many companies have established specific counseling and rehabilitation programs to assist employees in dealing with these problems.

_____ QUESTIONS _____

1. What are some basic differences in businesses' concerns with civil law and criminal law problems?
2. May a tort and a criminal violation both arise out of the same incident? How are they handled differently?
3. List some of the rights given to accused criminals under the Federal and state constitutions.
4. What are the basic sources from which our criminal law is drawn?
5. What is double jeopardy? *Ex post facto*? A bill of attainder? Entrapment?
6. What is a felony? A misdemeanor?
7. What are the basic elements of a crime?
8. May corporations commit crimes?
9. Explain how thefts affect business.
10. How is embezzlement different from theft or larceny?

[5]*Yaffe* v. *City of Ft. Smith*, 10 S.W.2d 886.
[6]Civil Code of California, Sec. 3479.

11. Explain the business problems of robbery.

12. Describe some of the impact of the following crimes on business: arson, shoplifting, kidnapping, forgery, and counterfeiting. What is Interstate Transportation of Stolen Property?

PROBLEM CASES

1   A police officer arrested an individual on an outstanding warrant charging a criminal offense. At the trial the accused was found not guilty. The man who had been tried for the alleged crime then attempted to file a false arrest complaint (a crime) and to recover damages in a tort suit. Which, if either, of these actions would be allowed by the courts? (*Brinkman* v. *Drolesbaugh*, 119 N.E. 451.)

2   Susnjar harbored and concealed illegal aliens in his home in Detroit, Michigan, in violation of Federal law. Klaich, who was employed by Susnjar, assisted the latter and drove a car taking aliens to a place of concealment in Cleveland, Ohio. When arrested, Klaich said he took this action only on orders from his boss, Susnjar. Was this a valid defense? (*Susnjar* v. *United States*, 27 F.2d 223.)

3   A police officer had bored a peephole in the ceiling above a place where illegal gambling was regularly conducted. An operator of this establishment fired a shot at the peephole in the belief that an officer was watching in the ceiling above. Actually, there was no one at the peephole at that time. The shooter was charged with attempted murder. His defense was that he could not be found guilty since murder had actually been a physical impossibility. Decide. (*People* v. *Lee King*, 95 Cal. 666.)

4   The courts generally require a person to have a criminal intent before conviction for most crimes will be upheld. A man fired a shot intending to kill a specific individual. However, the shot missed its mark and killed an innocent bystander. The accused claimed at the time of the trial that he did not have the necessary guilty intent toward the victim who was killed. Could conviction be upheld? In short, does "intent follow the bullet?" (*State* v. *Batson*, 96 S.W.2d 384.)

20

Sales

DEVELOPMENT OF THE LAW OF SALES

Divergence from General Contract Law

The law of *sales* is a body of law that both builds upon and alters settled principles of general contract law when applied to some specific mercantile situations.

As early as the first part of the nineteenth century, many fundamental ideas of general contract law had been reasonably well settled through legislation and court decisions in the United States and England. Application of these basic legal principles still achieves justice in many situations; consequently, they will likely remain as the foundation of legal agreements for a long time to come.

But during the industrial revolution the development of mass production and the factory system led to some new thinking about business law. General contract law principles did not always work well when applied to the problems posed by mass marketing of goods to retailers and consumers. It was apparent that certain aspects of the distribution and sales could be conducted more efficiently and more expeditiously if some alterations were made to established contract law in commercial transactions. Consequently, a whole new body of principles grew up alongside the settled provisions of contract law. These exceptions and alterations became so important to business interests that an entirely new course of study began in United States law schools, known to lawyers and the courts under the title "Sales" or "Law of Sales." It should be emphasized, however, that this new body of law altered contract law in certain commercial and mercantile transactions, which did not nullify or replace *general* contract law.

The Uniform Commercial Code (UCC)

Trade and commerce in the United States, while being conducted under individual laws in each state, go beyond local boundaries. Business executives have always insisted that uniformity in state laws and court remedies is vital to an unimpeded system of trade. Accordingly, as early as 1906 conscientious legal scholars began drawing up a model state code for the law of sales for state-by-state adoption. This first code found quick acceptance in a number of states. After business leaders suggested other changes in the law, the first code was replaced by a more workable body of law called the Uniform Commercial Code (UCC). The purpose of the UCC was "to provide uniformity in the law of sales throughout the different states."[1]

Today, the Uniform Commercial Code has been adopted as the law of sales in all but three states, and these remaining three states have passed individual laws that are generally quite similar to UCC code provisions. In effect, then, the UCC is now recognized as synonymous with the law of sales. UCC provisions are not being set out in this text owing to their considerable length and detail but basic parts of the code are summarized here.

Statute of Frauds

As discussed in Chapter 9, a contract for the sale of goods valued at $500 or more must be written. However, if the parties both perform on an oral contract, the courts will generally not intervene. For example, if the seller delivers goods to the buyer and the buyer accepts the merchandise, the contract will have been performed even if it involves merchandise valued at more than $500 and it is not written. See Chapter 9 for a more detailed explanation of the Statute of Frauds writing requirements.

APPLICATION OF THE LAW OF SALES _____

Sale Defined

It is worth repeating that Article 2 of the UCC applies only to those transactions that are legally termed "sales," a designation that has a well-defined legal significance. Regular contract law applies to agreements where sales law is not in effect. The UCC defines a sale "as a contract by which title to 'goods' passes from a seller to a buyer for a consideration which is called a price."[2]

A distinguishing feature of a sale is always the immediate transfer of ownership of the property in question. While the consideration in every sale is called the price, the price need not be money; services or other property of value can be paid. This immediate ownership separates a sale from a bailment, loan, consignment, lease, pledge, or other legal arrangement.

---

[1] *Porter* v. *Gibson.* 154 P.2d 417.
[2] UCC 2–106(1); *MacCluney* v. *Kelsey-Hayes Wheel Co.*, 87 F. Supp. 58.

Law of Sales Applies Only to "Goods"

The law of sales applies only to the transfer of the ownership of "goods." The purchase of an inventor's patent rights, for example, would not be a sale under the terms of the UCC; regular contract law principles would apply, even though the inventor and the buyer stated that a "sale" of rights had taken place.

The law of sales does not apply to the transfer of real estate or any interest in real estate, since these matters are not "goods." Likewise, the sale of a business or the transfer of stocks, bonds, promissory notes, the right to sue (choses in action), and insurance policies are not covered by the UCC.

Basically, the designation "goods" is the same as the term merchandise and includes all tangible or movable chattels. Most courts have held that "goods" need not be solids but may include fluids such as salad oil or gasoline. In addition, electricity and natural gas are usually regarded as goods. But the courts have gone much further, holding that the unborn offspring of animals are goods belonging to the farmer. But an agreement to sell the offspring of animals not yet conceived would fail to fall under the UCC.

In general contract law, we know that an individual may bind himself or herself to sell anything, so long as the transfer is not illegal or forbidden by law, even though at the moment the seller neither owns nor controls the subject matter that is to be transferred. While the terms of the UCC do not apply to the sale of land, the courts find that growing crops are goods under the UCC provisions, so long as the crops have been severed and sold apart from the land. Standing timber and minerals that are severed by the owner are now regarded as goods and may be sold under UCC provisions.

"Goods" Must Already Exist for UCC Provisions to Govern

The law of sales (UCC) does not apply to the transfer of "goods" that are not in existence at the time of the transfer. Accordingly, an agreement to sell "future goods" falls within the scope of general contract law, being known as an executory contract for the sale of future goods.

Existing fixtures attached to real estate can be severed and sold by the owner under the provisions of the UCC but only if the fixtures can be removed without serious harm to the realty.

Fungible Goods

Normally, goods must be in existence before the UCC rules apply and they must be identified as those which were intended to be sold. However, an exception is made in the case of fungible goods—commodities that are readily replaced one for another. For example, every grain of rice of a certain grade may be practically identical with every other grain in that grade. Barrels of oil and bushels of wheat are similar fungibles. If the fungibles have been identified as those to be transferred, there is no problem with application of the UCC principles. But even if the fungibles have not been identified, the contract may still be considered a sale under the UCC provisions with the buyer being regarded as the owner in common with other owners of the balance of the unidentified mass.

Contracts to Furnish Both Goods and Services

Many contracts call for one party to provide both technical workers and the materials or supplies needed by such workers to produce unusual designs or products. Consequently, an agreement may be construed either as a contract for technical services or as a sale of the finished product. If the supplying of materials is merely incidental to the furnishing of services, the transaction is not a sale. Usually, the courts look at the total of the services and supplies, using an "essence test" in deciding whether the major worth of the contract was made up of skilled services or materials. If the agreement was basically one to furnish materials, then sales law applies under Article 2 of the UCC. If the services of artisans or unusual technicians are involved, however, the matter involves regular contract law.

When a doctor injects a tetanus shot into a patient, the majority of courts regard the transaction as the supplying of medical services with the sale of the tetanus shot being considered incidental. Similarly, most courts consider that hospitals furnish services, even though medicines, drugs, blood transfusions, and other products may be furnished to the patient as a part of the transaction.

———— DISCUSSION ————————————————————

CASE 43   The Crystal Recreation Association intended to remodel an existing building to open a restaurant, card room, and cigar store. Owing to the unusual shape of the property, Crystal ordered a large, specially made counter and fixture installation from Modern Equipment Corporation. Unusual design and work were involved to fabricate the requested counter and fixtures. Modern Equipment Corporation eventually became insolvent, assigning its property and assets to creditors. Thereafter a lawsuit developed centering around whether the matter was essentially a sale of counters and fixtures or whether it involved a contract for work, labor, and incidental materials. On this answer depended whether Modern's creditors or the Crystal Recreation Association was entitled to the fixtures and counters. (*Crystal Recreation Assn. Inc.* v. *Seattle Assn. of Credit Men*, 209 P.2d 358.)

"Merchants" Under the UCC

The UCC was drafted to help merchants in obtaining goods and in selling them more readily. At the same time, the UCC holds merchants to stricter standards than does contract law. Under the UCC definition, a merchant is one who consistently deals in the type of goods sold or who represents himself or herself as having unusual familiarity with that type of goods.

The UCC holds a merchant dealing in a specific line of goods to specific warranties concerning those goods. (Warranties are discussed in detail in Chapter 22.) Nonmerchants are not held to such strict warranties.[3]

Also, the UCC has merchants maintain "fair dealing in the trade" involved. The code does not specify exactly what is required here, but the courts usually rule that a merchant must be held to a spirit of fair dealing. Approximately half of the states determine that a farmer is a "merchant" when dealing in farm produce that he or she normally grows.

The code binds merchants to oral contracts as an exception to the statute of frauds in cases where the merchant has failed to reply to a communication from another party in confirmation of the agreement.[4]

"Offers to Deal"

Under general contract law, an offer may be made irrevocable for a specified period, but only if the promise to keep the offer open is supported by consideration. This arrangement, of course, is usually termed an option.

The UCC, however, recognizes that merchants need "firm offers" in order to obtain suitable merchandise on short notice. Accordingly, the code provides that a firm offer from a merchant is irrevocable, even without consideration, if the following conditions are met:

1. The offer must be made by a merchant as part of an agreement to sell goods.
2. the offer must be from one regularly dealing in such goods.
3. The offer must be in a "signed" writing. The courts usually construe this to mean that a mere printed circular will be considered a signed writing if the printing or duplicating includes a signature or facsimile of the merchant's signature or that of the merchant's representative (agent). A printed sheet of price quotations without a signature is regarded as a mere offer to deal. Under the code, an offer of this kind must be kept open for the time specified in the writing. If no time has been given, the firm offer must be kept open for a reasonable time.[5]

[3]UCC 2–314, Secs. 160–206.
[4]UCC 2–201.
[5]UCC 2–205.

Contract Acceptance Requirements

Under general contract law, an acceptance must be made by the kind of communication (letter, telegram, or whatever) designated in the offer by a communication of the same kind used to make the offer. But unless specifically forbidden by terms of the offer, the UCC permits acceptance "by any medium [of transmission] reasonable under the circumstances.[6]

When an order is placed under general contract law, the seller must advise the buyer of the acceptance of the offer before a binding contract has been consummated. But under UCC provisions, the act of prompt shipment alone is sufficient to constitute acceptance of an order to buy goods, even though there is never a specific promise by the seller to accept.[7]

What about situations where a manufacturer begins work on an order and the buyer decides to change or cancel the order before completion? The code specifies that the beginning of work to fill an order of goods is sufficient to constitute acceptance, provided that the seller (manufacturer or supplier) notifies the party placing the order within a reasonable time that work has begun.[8]

Counteroffers

Under the usually followed principles of general contract law, an acceptance must be in agreement with the offer in all details and terms. Sometimes the courts say that "an acceptance must represent a mirror image of the offer." A variation in the purported acceptance works as a counteroffer (a new offer), rather than as an acceptance that forms a binding contract.

It is also a basic rule of general contract law that the courts will not supply missing terms if the parties fail to work out all the essentials.

But one of the realities of modern business is that goods must be quickly obtainable for purchase and shipment. A business may not be competitive unless binding purchases can be made without delays in waiting for offers, counteroffers, and acceptances being ironed out in all details.

Sales Agreements When Details Differ

Businesses frequently operate through the use of forms. Sales quotation sheets, order blanks, and other documents may be mailed back and forth between suppliers and customers on a regular basis. Of course, a supplier's forms usually contain some terms drafted by the supplier's attorney to favor the seller. Somewhat similarly, a buyer's order forms may contain some

[6] UCC 2–206(1)(a).
[7] UCC 2–206(1)(b).
[8] UCC 2–206(2).

printed terms that give preference to the buyer. UCC rules were designed to help both the seller and buyer work out an acceptable deal in a minimum of time. Accordingly, the general rule of the UCC is that a binding contract can be made through the exchange of these forms and communications that contain slightly different terms, unless the merchant (seller) actually specifies that exact terms must be accepted. In those instances where certain terms have been specified, any deviation in the purported acceptance is regarded as a counteroffer as in general contract law.[9]

Under UCC provisions, a binding sales contract may be made, even though the buyer (offeree) proposes some additional terms to those included in the original offer. The contract is considered binding as to those terms on which there has been mutual agreement. Further terms proposed by the buyer are considered as a proposal for an addendum to the contract. But the new terms do not actually become a part of the contract unless subsequently agreed to by the other party.

But a sales contract is not always recognized merely because a buyer and seller agree on particular conditions or details. If the offeree (buyer) proposes requirements or terms that are outright inconsistencies, the courts ordinarily hold that no sales contract was formed. The test generally used by the courts is to look at the subsequent behavior of the parties to determine if they both acted as if a contract had been formed. If this was the case, the courts say that the agreement is made up of those terms on which both were in acceptance. Clashing terms are not considered part of the agreement and the courts then look to other standards to determine the missing details that must have been intended by the parties.[10]

If, however, some terms set out by the parties differ so greatly that the buyer's response cannot be reasonably regarded as an acceptance, then the courts will probably rule that there is no binding sales agreement.

The courts recognize that hurriedly drafted sales agreements often do not include every term that might eventually come into dispute, but when it seems clear that the parties intended to contract, the courts will "fill in" the missing terms, using one of the following techniques:

1. The courts look to prior business dealings between the two parties, examining those unresolved provisions that were accepted by the subsequent actions of the parties. For example, a roofing firm bought shingles from the same manufacturer for years with shipping costs always being paid by the buyer. When a dispute arose on the eleventh such order, a court stated that the parties must have intended to continue with the existing arrangement.

[9]UCC 2–207(1).
[10]*Construction Aggregates* v. *Hewett Robbins*, 404 F.2d 505.

2. When there is no prior course of dealing between the individual firms involved, the courts look to prior usages and established customs in the particular business or industry involved.

3. The courts follow any provisions in the UCC that would serve to fill in missing terms.

If the courts cannot find guidance from any of these sources, they usually will not supply the missing terms. This means, of course, that there was no valid sales contract.

Unspecified Price Arrangements

Under UCC provisions a valid sales agreement can usually be made out, even though the parties reached no specific agreement on the price of the goods. The courts usually uphold any specific arrangement where the sale price is to be determined by an independent third party, by market quotations, or by specified industry or trade-determined standards. The test of contract validity is usually whether the price can be definitely and precisely determined and whether the parties actually intended to make a binding agreement although the price was not specified.

When a specific price is not included in the sales agreement, the majority of courts hold that a reasonable price was intended.[11] And if the parties cannot subsequently agree on a reasonable price, the courts will usually have the figure determined by a jury, based on the testimony of witnesses familiar with values for that type of goods.

When the agreement specifies that the seller shall set the price at the time of delivery, the code specifies that the agreement is valid and that the price may not exceed a figure that is reasonable at the time and place of delivery.[12]

The courts consistently recognize the validity of so-called "output contracts" in which one party agrees to buy all the output or production of goods from a specific factory or installation during a certain period. However, if production or output becomes unreasonably disproportionate to expected forecasts, the court holds that reasonable compliance is all that is expected of either party.[13]

Changing of Agreement Terms

It is a basic principle of general contract law that an agreement, once reached, is final. Such agreement may not thereafter be altered unless the modification

[11] UCC 2–305(1)(b).
[12] UCC 2–305(1)(c).
[13] UCC 2–306(1).

is supported by the furnishing of new consideration. But UCC provisions state that changes to a sales contract are legally valid if both parties agree, even though not supported by new consideration. Such a change may come about, for example, when a retail store telephonically obtains permission from the supplier to alter the specifications of a factory order that is being processed. The effect of the UCC provision is to make it easier for retailers and distributers to quickly make adjustments in orders to correspond to new market demands.

The seller (supplier or manufacturer), however, must agree to changes that are requested and the seller may not agree unless the amendments are paid for. The point is that no new consideration need be furnished if the seller agrees to the change.

The problem of altering the specifications of a pending order prior to delivery is further complicated by the requirements of the statute of frauds. When the sales agreement involves goods valued at $500 or more, the transaction or any modification of it must be in writing to be enforceable under code provisions.[14]

An oral agreement to change the terms of a sale valued at under $500 is enforceable, even though the original contract was in writing. This exception does not apply, however, if the original written agreement specified that any modification must be in writing.

"Sale and Return" and "Sale on Approval" Privileges

The volume of business may be increased if the buyer is granted "sale and return" or "sale on approval" privileges. For example, a retailer with some doubts as to the suitability of goods may request the manufacturer to ship with the right to return for credit within 60 days. If unsold, the merchandise may be sent back to the manufacturer for credit, but the buyer must return the goods within that time specified in the sales agreement. If no time is set, then the goods must be sent back within a reasonable period, considering the circumstances. In any event, the courts hold that a valid sale took place which becomes void upon the return of the goods. The buyer must pay for any merchandise kept beyond the date agreed upon for return. If the property is damaged or destroyed before coming back into the seller's hands, the loss ordinarily falls on the buyer. When the goods are damaged on the return shipment, the seller is not obligated to take them back.[15] In any event, the UCC specifies that the goods must still be in substantially the original condition as when they were sent.[16]

It is to be emphasized that if the buyer wants the merchandise with the

---

[14]UCC 2–209(3).

[15]UCC 2–327(2)(b); *Scrogin* v. *Wood*, 54 N.W. 437.

[16]UCC 2–327(2)(a); *Buckstaff* v. *Russell*, 79 F. 611.

right-to-return privilege, the arrangement must be in writing as part of the contract of sale.[17]

When goods are obtained "subject to approval," there is no sale until such time as the buyer approves. Conversely, a retention of the goods by the buyer is considered by the courts as an acceptance (a completed purchase). Under this type of transaction, the buyer is always justified in making a sampling or trial use of the goods; but any use beyond a reasonable testing is construed as a completed sale.

The buyer's obligation to pay does not normally arise when goods are shipped subject to approval until the sampling process has taken place. If the goods should be destroyed by fire or accident before the inspection, the loss falls on the seller. However, the buyer must pay if loss occurred through the buyer's fault or negligence. The costs to return unacceptable merchandise fall on the seller if goods of this kind are not accepted by the buyer, but the potential buyer must follow any reasonable instructions given by the seller for return.[18]

Illegal Sales

Individual laws in all states regulate or prohibit the sale of certain substances. For example, milk or meat must usually be sold under conditions imposing criminal penalties if proper inspection and sanitation are not provided.

Federal statues prohibit the interstate transportation of adulterated or misbranded foods, cosmetics, drugs, and therapeutic goods. Usually the courts will not lend their facilities to the enforcement of contracts for the sale of illegal goods or substances unless the plaintiff is an innocent victim of the scheme.

Bulk Sales

In the past, unscrupulous operators sometimes would manage to open a retail store or business, purchase a large inventory of merchandise on credit, then sell off the entire stock at a discount and disappear with the proceeds. If the purchaser of the goods was an innocent buyer who paid considerable value, the suppliers of the merchandise (creditors) would likely never be paid. Adoption of the Uniform Commercial Code has made this type of fraud more difficult to perpetrate. Code provisions require creditors to be advised in advance of any bulk sale of merchandise (sales other than in the ordinary course of business). If this required notice is not furnished, the creditors may go into court and have the bulk sale set aside, stripping the new purchaser

---

[17] UCC 2–326(4).
[18] UCC 2–327(1)(c).

of title. This law, of course, puts a buyer of bulk goods on guard to determine whether creditors have been previously notified or protected.[19]

If the buyer of a stock of bulk goods has mixed them into an existing inventory so that they can no longer be identified, the purchaser (the transferee) is personally liable to the original creditors for the value of goods sold without notice to the creditors. And of course the transferror of the bulk goods (the party perpetrating the swindle) is also personally liable for selling without proper notice to the creditors.

Basically, the bulk sales law applies to retail and wholesale merchants who are engaged in the sale of inventory goods. The law does not apply to manufacturers, shops, restaurants, barber shops, hotels, or other businesses that sell an incidental line of merchandise. For example, the law would not apply to a machine shop that sold some machine tools as a sideline to the basic business.

QUESTIONS

1. Is there conflict between the general law of contracts and the law of sales? Or does the latter supplement the former? Explain.

2. What is the purpose of the Uniform Commercial Code?

3. Define a sale within the meaning of the UCC.

4. Explain how a sale under the UCC applies only to "goods." Describe what is meant by "goods."

5. Does an agreement to sell future goods fall within the scope of general contract law or sales law? Why?

6. When a contract calls for both goods and services to be furnished (with basic value made up mostly of the services of skilled artisans) is the agreement controlled by general contract law or is it a sale?

7. Explain who is a "merchant" under the UCC. In what instances may a merchant be held to an oral contract as an exception to the statute of frauds?

8. Must a merchant keep a "firm offer" open under terms of the UCC? Explain.

9. Does the UCC give any leeway regarding the type of transmission or communication that must be used to accept an offer?

10. Is prompt shipment, alone, ever sufficient to constitute an acceptance under the UCC?

[19]UCC 6–101.

11. May a counteroffer ever be construed as an acceptance under the requirements of sales law? Explain.

12. Detail what happens when a seller and buyer are not quite in agreement on all terms, but when they both believe a bargain was intended.

13. Specify what sources a court may look to for "filling in" the missing terms of a sales contract.

14. May a sales contract be made even though the sale price for the goods has not yet been set? If so, how is a price eventually determined?

15. May the terms of a sales agreement be subsequently changed under UCC provisions? Expand on your statement. Is new consideration necessary? Must the change be in writing?

16. What is meant by "sale and return"?

17. If a buyer takes goods on approval, who stands the loss if they are destroyed by fire before being returned? Does the buyer have any responsibility to follow the seller's instructions on return of merchandise?

18. Explain the workings of the "bulk sales" law.

ANSWER TO DISCUSSION CASE

CASE 43   The court said that an agreement to build customized fixtures, suitable only for a particular location, was a contract for "work, labor, and materials" and was not essentially a sale but rather a contract for artisans' services.

PROBLEM CASES

1   A contract for the sale of goods did not specify terms under which the shipment was to be made. The goods were destroyed after delivery to the carrier. The shipper claimed the right to recover the price of the goods on the basis that the transaction was automatically considered an F.O.B shipment. Could the shipper recover against the consignee? Against the carrier? Or against either? (*Eberhard Mfg. Co. v. Brown*, 232 N.W.2d 378.)

2   A clothing manufacturer shipped merchandise, turning it over to Denver-Chicago Trucking Company on an F.O.B. arrangement. The goods were shipped "collect" since they had not been paid for. Denver-Chicago turned the merchandise over to another carrier, Old Colony Transportation Company. A delivery was not made by Old Colony because of a dispute in shipping charges. Old Colony continued to hold the goods, but these were stolen or lost from the Old Colony warehouse. The manufacturer filed suit against the buyer. What were the rights of the parties? (*Ninth Street East, Ltd. v. Harrison*, 259 A.2d 772.)

3   After an automobile was stolen, an insurance company paid the owner and then took over ownership. Eventually the car was located in possession of

one Moseley, an innocent purchaser who had bought it from Baker Automobile Dealers, a seller of used cars. Apparently the vehicle had been sold several times and the identity of the thief had not been established. The original engine was replaced by the thief or someone claiming under the thief. Moseley had installed a new sun visor, seat covers, and gas tank. Did the sale by the thief divest the owner of title in favor of the innocent purchaser? If allowed to recover the car, would the insurance company be entitled to keep the replacement motor that had been added by the thief or would someone else in the chain of ownership (or possession) prior to Moseley? What about the sun visor, seat covers, and gas tank that had been installed by innocent purchaser Moseley? (*Farm Bureau Mutual Auto Ins. Co. v. Moseley*, 90 A.2d 485.)

4   Jane Zendman bought a diamond ring for $12,500 from a display of Brand, Incorporated in Atlantic City, New Jersey. Zendman had no indication that Brand was not the actual owner of the ring. For a number of years prior to that, Brand Incorporated had maintained an arrangement to sell diamonds on consignment for New York City diamond merchant Harry Winston. On a once-a-week basis one of Winston's agents obtained payment or an accounting from Brand. Shortly after Zendman purchased the ring, Brand was declared bankrupt. In a dispute over property consigned to Brand, Harry Winston claimed ownership of the Zendman ring. Winston's attorneys contended that there is a general principle of sales law that a seller can convey no better title to property than that which the seller possesses and that Brand had no title. Zendman asserted that, as between two innocent victims of fraud, the one who made possible the fraud on the other should suffer. Decide. (*Zendman* v. *Winston*, 111 N.E. 871.)

5   Paloukos went to the sales room of Intermountain Chevrolet (also called Glen's), where he informed sales representative Rowe that he wanted to buy a truck. The truck was not in stock, so Rowe completed a printed form that bore in bold type the heading: "WORK SHEET—This is NOT a Purchase Order." Both Paloukos and Rowe filled out the form setting out Paloukos's name and address, describing the truck as a new yellow or green 1974 ¾-ton four-wheel drive vehicle, with radio, V-8 engine, and automatic transmission. The form also listed the purchase price as $3,650. Rowe thereafter had the head sales manager approve the transaction and accepted a deposit of $120 from Paloukos. Rowe printed his name on the form and Paloukos signed it at Rowe's request, although there was no signature line. Rowe then stated a factory order was being immediately placed. Several months later Intermountain Chevrolet advised Paloukos by letter that it would be unable to sell the truck. Whether this was due to inflated pricing in the meantime was not made clear. Did Paloukos have a contract to buy the truck? (*Paloukos* v. *Intermountain Chev.*, 588 P.2d 939.)

21

Types of Sales Contracts; Risk of Loss

Performance Requirements

Differing types of sales contracts have varying requirements for performance by the parties involved. Unless otherwise agreed in the sales contract, the seller has a responsibility to turn over the goods in a single delivery.[1] This arrangement can be changed, of course, if the parties agree to multiple deliveries. There may be times when the seller is unable to make a single delivery because of a catastrophic storm.

If the place for the delivery of goods is not specified in the sales contract, the goods are to be turned over to the buyer at the seller's place of business. If the seller's business is conducted from a residential location, the delivery is to be made at the seller's residence.[2]

If both parties are aware that the goods in question are stored somewhere other than the seller's place of business or residence, the code specifies that delivery is to be made at the storage location unless otherwise agreed.[3]

The seller has performed when the goods are made available (tendered) to the buyer. However, this tender must be made before the buyer is in default on the contract. At the time of tender, the goods must measure up to the requirements of the contract.

The buyer always has a right to inspect the goods purchased at any time within reason before or at the time of delivery.[4] If the merchandise is to be delivered to the buyer, the latter may postpone inspection until after the goods are made available. And although the buyer is required to make payment at the time of delivery, this does not prevent the buyer from going

[1]UCC 2–307.
[2]UCC 2–308(a).
[3]UCC 2–308(b).
[4]UCC 2–513(1).

250

back on the seller if a subsequent inspection discloses that the goods did not meet contract requirements.[5]

The buyer has the right to reject nonconforming goods, either at the time of delivery or within a reasonable time following inspection.[6] The buyer has several options if the goods do not meet specifications. The entire shipment may be rejected, or the buyer may accept the complete shipment or any part of it so long as commercial units are not broken up into component parts in the acceptance. Commercial units are assemblies of merchandise, goods, machinery, and so on that are salable as a whole and that would be lessened in value if divided or disassembled.[7]

By accepting all or part of a nonconforming shipment, the buyer does not surrender rights that may be pursued against the seller, including the right to damages. However, the buyer must inform the seller of any rejection within a reasonable time. A failure to notify of rejection or a retention of nonconforming goods by the buyer is legally regarded as acceptance of such goods.[8]

If a merchant receives and rejects nonconforming goods that are perishable or likely to decline in value, the buyer must make a reasonable effort to sell them for the seller's account.

Even though the buyer has already indicated acceptance, this acceptance may be revoked if defects are discovered within a reasonable time. The seller should then be notified of the revocation of acceptance and the reason for such an action. When this information has been furnished to the seller, the buyer is in the same legal position as if the goods had been rejected immediately upon delivery.[9]

If no time of delivery is specified, the code provides that the delivery is to be performed within a reasonable time.[10] Payment is owed at the time delivery is made unless the parties agree to different arrangements.[11]

Shipment Contracts

A *shipment contract* is one in which the seller is responsible for delivering the merchandise to a carrier at the place of shipment. The seller thereafter has no further responsibility in loading, hauling, delivering, or insuring the goods. This is perhaps the most commonly used arrangement for moving merchandise. Unless otherwise agreed by the parties, the UCC provides that all such transportation of goods is considered to be shipping contracts.

[5]UCC 2–512.
[6]UCC 2–513(2).
[7]UCC 2–601; 2-105(6).
[8]UCC 2–601(1).
[9]UCC 2–608(3).
[10]UCC 2–309(1).
[11]UCC 2–310.

A *destination contract* is one that requires the seller to make safe delivery of the goods at a particular destination before the seller is regarded as having performed duties owing under the contract. In some instances the seller may agree to pay freight charges to a designated location, but standing alone this fact is not enough to make the agreement a destination contract.[12]

In a destination contract, if the goods are not properly packed, shipped, or protected, the loss falls on the seller. For example, failure to provide adequate refrigeration for a railroad carload of meat would subject the shipper to damages for spoilage in a contract of this kind.

In either a shipment contract or a destination contract, however, the UCC requires prompt notification by the seller to the buyer of all shipments. Likewise, the buyer must be immediately furnished with any documents that will be needed in taking possession of the goods.[13]

Shipping Terms and Abbreviations. The language in sales contracts often makes use of standardized shipping terms or abbreviations. Both seller and buyer are held to understand what these mean. Among those more commonly used are the following:

1. F.O.B. (free on board) designates that the shipper pays for no costs beyond the shipper's dock or factory loading platform. The seller's responsibility ends upon turning the goods over to a carrier. Any costs involved in loading, hauling, delivering, or insuring will fall on the buyer.[14] "F.O.B. car _____, railroad," specifies the mode of shipment but leaves the costs of loading, shipping, and so on with the buyer.[15]

2. "F.O.B. point of destination" designates that shipping costs will be paid by the seller.

3. "C.I.F." and "C.&.F." are abbreviations for "cost, insurance, and freight" and "cost and freight." Under a C.I.F. shipment contract the buyer is obligated to pay all freight and insurance costs in addition to the agreed price for the goods. Under a C.&.F. contract the shipper (seller) pays whatever insurance may be required under the sales agreement, but the buyer still pays other costs and freight.

4. "No arrival—no sale." This specification retains the risk of loss on the seller during the period while the goods are en route to the buyer. However, the seller is not liable for lost or damaged goods if the fault was not that of the seller. In a situation of this kind, the buyer can look to the carrier for damages if the goods were injured in transit or through fault that cannot be attributed to the seller. If goods are lost or damaged upon

[12] UCC 2–504.
[13] UCC 2–504(c) and (b).
[14] UCC 2–319(1)(a).
[15] UCC 2–319(1)(b).

arrival, the buyer may regard the contract as voided, or the buyer may accept them with a proper deduction from the contract price for damage but with no further claim against the seller.[16]

5. "F.A.S." This term (free alongside ship), used in maritime shipping transactions, denotes that the goods will be delivered to the dock alongside the ship on which they are to be loaded. Further costs, loading, freight, and insurance are to be paid by the buyer.[17]

6. "Shipment under reservation" is a situation in which the seller sends the shipment to himself or herself while retaining ownership and control en route. This enables the shipper to obtain a return of the merchandise while the credit of the buyer is being checked. A negotiable bill of lading is held by the shipper and the carrier is obligated to make delivery to whoever is legally in possession of the bill of lading.[18]

In a shipment under reservation the shipper usually furnishes an invoice, a bill of lading, and other shipping papers to a bank representing the seller. In turn, these documents are transmitted to the buyer's bank, which simultaneously pays the shipper's bank and releases the bill of lading to the buyer so that the property may be obtained from the carrier by presentation of the bill of lading.[19]

_____ *DISCUSSION* _____

CASE 44   A Chicago grower (defendant) made a contract with a Boston buyer to have grain "shipped prompt via H.R." The phrases used in this agreement were technical terms that had a well-settled meaning in the eastern grain trade. The expression: "to be shipped prompt" meant shipment in no less than 10 days. "Via H.R." meant by way of the Harlem River with the buyer having the option of diverting the railcar containing the shipment at either of three shipping points, depending on the buyer's marketing needs. The shipper (defendant), who knew nothing about the grain trade, testified that he believed the term "via H.R." meant by way of the Hudson River, which would have made an appreciable difference in freight rates. Was the shipper bound by the technical meaning of the contract terms that he did not understand? Or was this a case of "no meeting of the minds and consequently no contract"? (*Soper* v. *Tyler*, 58 A. 699.)

Tender of the Goods. When goods are shipped, the buyer must be notified so that arrangements can be made for payment and acceptance of the deliv-

[16] UCC 2–613(b) and 2-324(b).
[17] UCC 2–319(2)
[18] UCC 7–403(1).
[19] UCC 2–308(c) and 2-503(5)(b).

ery. An actual tender, or offer, of the goods must be made before the shipper has a claim for breach of the sales contract. In some cases a constructive tender will be recognized by the courts where goods are so bulky that they are not actually placed in the buyer's hands. Tender "must be made at a reasonable hour."[20] If the sales agreement specifies that the goods will be held available to the buyer for a specific period, the seller need not prolong availability beyond this period. If no time is stated, then the goods must be held for a reasonable time. Reasonableness depends on the particular circumstances, especially where perishables are involved.

General contract law principles, as followed in many states, require a tender of merchandise that conforms to contract requirements in every respect. And under the UCC the buyer may reject the entire shipment, accept the whole, or accept part and reject the balance "if the goods or the tender of delivery fail in any respect to conform to the contract."[21] However, the UCC gives the seller some leeway in many instances. If the time of performance has not passed, the seller may immediately notify the buyer of the seller's "intention to cure" the deficiency and tender a conforming delivery prior to the performance date. The improper original delivery is thereupon legally excused.[22]

At times a buyer may accept goods that fail to conform to all details of the agreement. If acceptances of this kind have not been called to the attention of the seller, and the buyer suddenly fails to accept goods with the same defect, the surprised seller must thereafter be given a reasonable time to cure the defect, even after the time for performance has passed. The parties must act in good faith, however, and the buyer must be promptly advised of the seller's intention to cure.[23]

Handling Rejected Goods

The seller must be advised of the rejection of nonstandard goods within a reasonable time. Notice must be given, even if the shipper is aware that nonconforming goods have been shipped. Usually there is no requirement that the buyer specify why the rejection was made. But if both parties are merchants and the seller has requested to be advised of defects, the buyer must furnish information as to any defects on which a refusal will be based.[24]

In rejecting an order of goods, the buyer must hold onto the shipment long enough to enable the seller to reclaim and remove it. And if the goods

[20] UCC 2–503(1)(a)
[21] UCC 2–601.
[22] UCC 2–508(1).
[23] UCC 2–508(2).
[24] UCC 2–605.

are perishables that are sold for the seller's account, the buyer is entitled to claim reasonable expenses and a sales commission.[25]

RISK OF LOSS _____

The Passing of Ownership of Goods

When goods have been set aside or identified for a particular sale, ownership (title) is usually regarded by the courts as passing to the buyer at that time. Even though specific goods have been associated with a sale, the seller may thereafter substitute identical items for those selected, provided that the seller and not the buyer makes this decision. The courts also add that ownership passes at whatever time the parties intended that it should pass. This intent of the parties is regarded by the courts as always depending on the circumstances of the particular case. In any event, the courts say title to goods can never pass until the goods are actually in existence.

In the great majority of sales agreements, the parties neither come to an express understanding as to when title shall pass nor do they specify any definite intent on this matter. In cases where there is no definite understanding about the passage of title, the UCC follows a presumption that ownership is transferred whenever the seller has finished whatever performance was required by the agreement that pertains to the delivery of goods to the buyer.[26]

Responsibility for Loss of Goods Being Sold

As a generalization of property law, it is the owner who must usually stand the loss if property, merchandise, or money is taken by theft or destroyed by storm, fire, or other catastrophe. In business manufacturing and production processes, raw materials are altered or fabricated into finished goods. Then the product is usually shipped from the manufacturer to the wholesaler, to the retailer, and eventually to a consumer. At each stage of this process there may be a question as to who is the owner of the property and who will bear the risk of loss if it should be damaged, destroyed, or minimized in value.

Of course, if the parties to a sales contract agree, they may allocate all risk of loss at specific stages of the production process among themselves.[27] However, seldom do the parties come to such an understanding.

[25] UCC 2–602(2)(b) and 2-603(1 and 2).
[26] UCC 2–401(2).
[27] UCC 2–303.

Legal Consequences of Ownership

There are important legal reasons why both parties to a sales agreement may want to know whether the seller or the buyer actually holds title to the goods at a particular time. In the first place, the owner (title holder) is usually required to file tax returns and pay taxes on such property. Second, ownership may have a bearing on the right to obtain insurance as well as on other legal problems.

Notice, however, that under sales law, as set by the UCC, the risk of loss does not always follow title (ownership).

The basic concept in the structure of the UCC is that the risk of loss should fall on whichever party has failed to perform as specified by the sales contract. In short, the harm should be suffered by the party that has breached.[28] For example, responsibility continues to be that of a seller who tenders nonconforming goods until the defect is corrected or the buyer accepts the goods notwithstanding the defect. And if the buyer who accepts nonconforming goods is subsequently justified in revoking acceptance when a defect is discovered, the loss again falls back on the seller.

If the buyer disavows the contract after the seller has identified and set aside the goods in question, the courts will usually place a loss upon the buyer for a reasonable time. Thereafter, the seller can proceed with legal remedies for breach of contract but cannot continue to hold the buyer for the risk of loss.

If the Contract Has Not Been Breached and a Shipment Is Called For

If the sales agreement between the two parties calls for delivery by carrier, the risk of loss shifts from the seller to the buyer at the time the goods are turned over to the carrier on a *shipment contract*.

If the agreement specifies a *destination contract*, the risk of loss does not pass to the buyer until the goods have arrived at the receiving point and the buyer has had a reasonable opportunity to take delivery.

If Goods Are Held in Bailment

At times, goods are held in storage in a commercial warehouse at the time a sale takes place. Here the intent is usually to sell the goods without actually removing them from the warehouse. If ownership is represented by a negotiable title document, such as a negotiable bearer warehouse receipt, the risk of loss passes when the seller tenders the buyer the document representing title. UCC provisions specify that risk shifts to the buyer whenever the seller

[28]UCC 2–510(1).

personally informs warehouse officials (the bailee) that the buyer is entitled to take the goods.[29] If, however, ownership of the goods is represented by a nonnegotiable document of title, the risk does not shift until the buyer has had a reasonable time to present the document and pick up the goods. For example, a nonnegotiable document of this kind would be a warehouse receipt ordering delivery to a specifically named person only.

Sales Involving Neither Shipment Nor Bailment

If the sales contract involves neither a shipment nor a bailment, the time when risk of loss shifts to the buyer depends on whether the seller is a merchant or a nonmerchant.[30] The rule of the UCC is that the loss does not fall on a buyer until the goods are actually received from the merchant.

For example, a consumer bought a new color TV set from a department store, paying cash. Title to the merchandise passed at the time the cash was received by the sales clerk. The television in question was stolen in the brief interval needed to bring it from a basement warehouse to the department store's customer dock. Under the code, the loss fell on the department store seller.

In a situation like this, the risk immediately falls on the merchant seller until the buyer actually receives the goods. But this is not the case with a nonmerchant seller. If the TV buyer had made the purchase from a neighboring homeowner, the loss would have been sustained by the buyer. This is because the lawyers who framed the UCC provisions realized that a merchant is better able to stand such a loss than other individuals and that a business can obtain insurance to cover such problems. The code states that a nonmerchant seller immediately shifts the risk of loss to the buyer when the seller makes a tender of the goods.[31]

———— *DISCUSSION* ————————————————————

CASE 45   A woman purchased a new tape player and had it placed in her personal automobile on the store parking lot. Somewhat as an afterthought the customer returned to the sales desk to buy two tapes to be used with the recorder. While she was finishing this subsequent transaction, a thief stole the new equipment. Did the risk of loss fall on the customer or the store?

CASE 46   A housewife had an unneeded baby bed, which she offered for sale. A neighbor agreed to buy the bed and paid cash for it. The seller then offered to load the bed into the buyer's car. The buyer declined to take it at that time, stating that it should be left on the seller's back porch to be loaded into

[29] UCC 2–509(2).
[30] UCC 2–509(3).
[31] UCC 2–509(3).

her husband's station wagon when he got off work that same afternoon. The husband forgot to pick up the bed and it was stolen from the porch during the night. The buyer demanded her money back, claiming that there had been no sale. Was this justified?

Risk of Loss on Goods Being Manufactured

If manufactured goods are not yet in existence (future goods), the raw materials normally belong to the manufacturer unless such raw materials were supplied by the buyer.

If the agreement provides, the buyer does not have to physically take the merchandise until the seller has furnished instructions for use; the courts usually say that any loss in this situation is that of the seller until such time as the instructions are delivered. When the agreement calls for the testing of new goods or equipment, the risk of loss usually falls on the seller until a reasonable time for testing has expired.

Title to future goods does not come into existence until the goods are produced. When no document of title (such as a bill of lading or warehouse receipt) is involved, both title and risk of loss pass to the buyer at the time and place the contract is completed.

Insurance Against Loss

In most instances the owner can hedge against loss by obtaining insurance. But an insurance company will not pay for loss unless the individual seeking recovery is the owner or one who has "an insurable interest" in the property. Usually the courts rule that an insurable interest "is such a relation that a contemplated peril might cause injurious financial loss" or "such a right or stake in the property that loss or damage to the property would work monetary harm to that person."[32]

As soon as goods have been identified with a particular sales contract, the UCC provides that the buyer has an insurable interest in the goods whereby a recovery can be obtained against an insurance company in the event of loss. This insurable interest comes into being, even though the buyer may have an option to eventually reject or return the goods. The code also provides that the seller may retain an insurable interest in goods that have been identified with a particular sales contract until such time as the seller's interest in securing payment of the sales price is satisfied.[33]

---

[32] *Black's Law Dictionary*, 4th ed. (St. Paul, MN.: West Publishing Co., 1968).
[33] UCC 2–501(1) and (2).

_____ *QUESTIONS* _____

1. Does the seller have legal responsibility to turn over all the goods to the buyer in a single delivery?

2. Describe what is meant by tender.

3. Does the buyer have the right to reject nonconforming goods? If so, under what circumstances?

4. What responsibility does the buyer have if nonconforming goods are perishables?

5. What is meant by a shipment contract? A destination contract?

6. Explain the meaning in sales law of "F.O.B."; "C.I.F." or "C&F"; "F.A.S."; "shipment under reservation."

7. Must the seller be advised of the rejection of nonstandard goods? If so, when?

8. How may a buyer of goods make certain who bears the risk of loss in case of a fire or some other catastrophe?

9. Who has the risk of loss in manufactured goods that have not yet been produced? That are already in existence?

_____ *ANSWERS TO DISCUSSION CASES* _____

CASE 44 The court held that in a sale the parties are bound by the understandings of technical terms used in a particular kind of trade.

CASE 45 The merchandise had already been turned over to the customer (buyer) at the time the theft occurred. Even though the merchandise was in a car located on the seller's lot, the car was under the control of the buyer. Thus, the risk of loss fell on the buyer.

CASE 46 Unless the parties specify otherwise, ownership passes at the time the agreement is completed and a tender made. Had the bed been stolen before the husband had an opportunity to make the pickup, the loss would have fallen on the seller. But this involved a seller who was a nonmerchant and tender was sufficient to shift the risk of loss to the buyer, who did not take advantage of the tender.

_____ *PROBLEM CASES* _____

1 An electrical wholesaler delivered to a rural construction site three large, heavy reels of cable. Due to a mistake, two were unsuitable. The contractor attempted to return the unusable reels, but there was an extended trucker's strike. The wholesaler (supplier) was immediately notified to pick up the unusable cable, but the reels remained at the rural site for four months until

they were taken by thieves for the copper content of the wire. The wholesaler then sued the construction company for the price of the two reels. Which party had the risk of loss? (*Graybar Electric Co.* v. *Shook*, 195 S.E.2d 514.)

2   An individual bought a motorcycle from a dealer. Since he was soon leaving on vacation, he left the machine with the dealer. While he was away, looters broke into the dealer's facility during a major blackout and stole the motorcycle. The buyer had already paid for the vehicle and had been given ownership papers that would allow him to buy insurance. He had already sent in the registration papers to the state motor vehicle licensing bureau but had not yet attached license plates. Which party had the risk of loss? (*Ramos* v. *Wheel Sports Center*, 409 N.Y.S.2d 505.)

3   Ellis bought a helicopter from Bell Aerospace Company for about $102,000. The understanding between the parties was that Ellis would not take possession until after finishing flight lessons. In the meantime, the helicopter had been taken away from the Bell premises and was stored at an airport with one Spink. A Bell employee took the aircraft from Spink to give a flight lesson to Ellis. The machine crashed during the lesson and was seriously damaged. In a dispute concerning whether Ellis must pay for the machine, Ellis claimed that the risk of loss was still on the company. Decide. (*Ellis* v. *Bell Aerospace Co.*, 315 F. Supp. 221.)

4   B & B Sales sent stereo tapes and other merchandise to the Collier retail store on an invoice reading: "Sold to Collier . . . Terms 30 -60 -90 . . . this equipment will be picked up if not sold in 90 days." Shortly after receipt the merchandise was stolen from Collier in a burglary. B & B Sales maintained the transaction was a "sale and return." Collier claimed the transaction was a mere consignment of goods. Which party had the risk of loss? (*Collier* v. *B & B Sales*, 471 S.W.2d 151.)

22

Sales Warranties

Legal Definitions of Warranty

In legal terminology, a guarantee made by a seller is called a *warranty*. It is a promise that the seller's claims about items purchased will prove true. UCC provisions define a warranty as

> any affirmation of fact or promise made by the seller to the buyer which relates to the goods and becomes part of the basis of the bargain . . . that the goods shall conform to the affirmation or promise.[1]

In slightly different language, the courts frequently define a warranty as

> an assurance by one party to a contract of the existence of a fact upon which the other party may rely . . . and amounts to a promise to indemnify [repay] the promisee for any loss if the fact warranted proves untrue.[2]

Generally when there is a breach of warranty, the buyer can go back on the seller in a lawsuit. The ability to hold the seller to the warranty is a distinct legal right, separate from the right to sue for breach of contract.

Express and Implied Warranties

Warranties are of two kinds, either express or implied. An *express warranty* is a statement made in express, or specific, words by the seller. An express

---

[1]UCC 2–313.
[2]*Metropolitan Coal Co.* v. *Howard*, 155 F.2d 780.

warranty may be either written or oral, so long as the seller writes or orally describes some specific fact, quality, or feature of the thing being sold. A printed newspaper advertisement is, of course, an express warranty.

When an express warranty is given by a salesperson in a store, a subsequent dispute could come down to the word of the consumer (buyer) against the word of the salesperson. To be protected, the buyer may want to obtain a brief written warranty from the sales clerk. This need not be lengthy or greatly detailed. For example, the clerk could be asked to write across the face of the sales ticket: "This sweater is 100% wool."

In some instances a warranty may be implied from the seller's failure to deny certain facts when specifically questioned about the quality or properties of merchandise.

If the seller has made an express warranty of items being offered for sale, almost all courts agree that the buyer is not under the necessity of making an inspection as to hidden or latent defects that may later come to light. The warranty relieves the buyer of the burden of making the inspection and the buyer does not assume the risk of defects that an examination might reveal.

If the buyer knows of defects at the time the purchase is made, the courts differ about whether the buyer must accept known defects.

"Opinion" or "Sales Talk"

Generally, the courts hold that a warranty must relate to or be a statement of fact and not one of opinion. As stated in UCC provisions:

> an affirmation merely of the value of the goods or a statement purporting to be merely the seller's opinion or commendation of the goods does not create a warranty.[3]

The courts usually distinguish mere words of description from a warranty. If a merchant agrees to sell a housewife some green window curtains, the contract would not be met by delivering tan curtains or a green sofa cover. The buyer is under no obligation to take either, since she would not be getting that for which she bargained. Legally, the furnishing of tan curtains would be a breach of contract, permitting the buyer to back out of the purchase. Many courts, however, allow the buyer in a situation of this kind to treat the improper delivery as a breach of an express warranty. Under either interpretation the buyer would be protected.

The courts have always given the seller considerable leeway in "puffing" of goods in an attempt to sell them. Expressions of opinion and words of praise are consistently regarded as mere sales talk. The legal definition of

[3]UCC 2–313.

"mere sales talk" is never easily drawn. Courts often differ in their interpretations among cases.

To illustrate these differences, a statement that "this sweater is cashmere" is a warranty. So, too, is a salesman's claim that "these suits are 100 percent wool."

But the courts usually consider the following claims as mere puffery: "This coat is worth at least twice what we are asking for it!" "This pair of slacks will wear like iron!" "This suit will fit you like the paper on the wall!"

The courts ordinarily make the legal point that sales puffery may include expressions that are somewhat extravagant so long as they do not misrepresent some specific quality or feature of the article being sold.

For example, the seller could inform a lady looking at a fox fur coat that "you will never be in better style than when you wear this cape." However, had the salesman misrepresented the item as a more expensive mink, then the seller could have been held to the higher quality.

A warranty, then, is a legally binding representation by the seller that specifies the quality or condition of the goods offered for sale. There is no magic in the word "warranty" standing alone. In fact the term may be used in a document that is not actually a warranty. Similarly, a statement that does not contain the word "warranty" may still operate as a warranty.

DISCUSSION

CASE 47   The seller of goods made statements about merchandise that proved to be untrue. When sued for damages by the buyer, the seller maintained that he himself sincerely believed in the truthfulness of the claims made concerning the property. Is the honesty of the seller in question here, or does a warranty automatically come into being when statements of fact are made concerning the goods being offered for sale? (*Legler, Barlow & Co.* v. *U. S. Fidelity & Guaranty Co.*, 10 Ohio N.P., N.S., 601.)

Warranty Rights and Liabilities

English and American courts have long recognized warranties, holding that violating a warranty was a breach of contract between the person making the warranty and the individual to whom it was directed. Early court decisions said an individual could not take advantage of a warranty unless that person was "in privity of contract" with the warrantor; therefore a subsequent buyer of the goods could not sue on the warranty of the original seller. These early decisions said in effect that the warranty right was a contract right and applied only to parties to the contract. Under this old view, a baker sold bread to a grocer, who sold a loaf to a consumer. While eating the bread, the eventual buyer suffered serious throat injuries from an open safety pin that had fallen into the bread dough. The injured consumer filed a lawsuit against the baker, claiming that there was a breach of an implied warranty by the baker that the bread was wholesome and fit for human consumption. The court dismissed the case, deciding that there was no immediate contract between the consumer and the baker.[4]

Eventually the courts began to reason that there was no purpose in a warranty unless it was directed to the person who would ultimately make use of the product. In *Mazetti* v. *Armour*[5] the court ruled that it would be pointless to give a warranty to a middleman who would not be injured. Today most courts agree with the decision in *Miller* v. *Preitz*.[6] In that case a vaporizer-humidifier was being used to relieve the breathing of an infant who was temporarily at an aunt's home. The vaporizer-humidifier had been purchased from a local drug chain by the aunt. The device was defective, and without warning it shot boiling water into the child's lungs, causing death in about three days. The infant's parents sued the manufacturer of the vaporizer-humidifier, based on a warranty from the manufacturer. The court ruled that the warranty extended to the purchaser (the aunt), even though the old requirement of privity was lacking. The court also held that the deceased infant was included in the warranty as a family member or as a guest who might reasonable be expected to make use of this piece of equipment.

The UCC states that a seller's warranty, whether express or implied, extends to any natural person who is in the family or household of the buyer or who is a guest in the home if it is reasonable to expect that such may use or consume the goods involved.[7]

In some cases the courts are not completely clear as to whether the right to damages is a contract right under the breach of warranty theory, a tort, an award for negligence, or a situation where absolute tort liability should be imposed. Most courts now permit anyone injured by a harmful or improper product to sue whoever was in any way responsible for making or marketing the product.

In today's industrial society, some manufactured goods may not be made entirely by one factory. The fact that harm was caused by a single defective component from a separate supplier will not excuse the principal manufacturer or seller. If the principal manufacturer had not previously had problems with the defective component, this fact could be admitted in court as evidence tending to prove the major manufacturer was not willfully negligent.

Current court decisions suggest that a business cannot afford to manufacture or sell defective or injurious products, both out of concern for the consumer and from a dollars-and-cents liability standpoint.

[4]*Peletier* v. *DuPont*, 124 Me. 269.
[5]*Mazetti* v. *Armour*, 75 Wash. 622.
[6]*Miller* v. *Preitz*, 221 A.2d 320.
[7]UCC 2–318.

Timing of Warranty Statements

In many instances a sale takes place long after the statements as to quality of the goods were made. These earlier assertions constitute an express warranty only if such claims by the seller were still an essential part of the bargain. However, if the goods are subject to changes in condition, the seller could be held to a statement of the status of the goods for only a reasonable time after such statement was made. An affirmation as to the character of the goods—for example, that it is "100 percent wool"—would be binding indefinitely.

Normally a seller's claim as to the quality of goods would not be binding if made after the sale was transacted. But in a few cases a claim made by the seller after completion of the transaction has been held to be a modification of the contract requiring no consideration, with such claim being binding on the seller.[8]

Conformity to "Trade Terms" or Description

If the seller uses "trade terms" to describe or specify the particular goods that will be furnished, these products or services must conform to that descriptive term as generally understood in the trade. For example, the seller must ship goods that pass in the trade under the term specified, such as # 1 Durham Wheat, Longbranch Potatoes, or # 20 rag content bond paper.

DISCUSSION

CASE 48   A buyer made a purchase of a large quantity of "boneless chicken." When the cans of chicken were used, it was found that the chicken was tasteful and wholesome. However, chicken bones of considerable size were frequently found in the canned meat. The buyer sued for breach of warranty, claiming that the description of the goods was a vital part of the bargain, constituting an express warranty that the canned chicken meat would correspond to the description furnished by the seller. Would the courts recognize this claim? (*American Paper & Pulp* v. *Denenbert*, 233 F.2d 610.)

Sales by Sample

When sales are made by sample, the UCC specifies that "any sample or model which is made part of the basis of the bargain creates an express warranty that the whole of the goods shall conform to the sample or model."[9]

In an actual case, a consumer with a large flower garden asked to see

[8] *Bigelow* v. *Agway, Inc.*, 506 F.2d 551.
[9] UCC 2–313(c).

daffodil bulbs that were on sale. Samples exhibited were all the diameter of an old silver dollar. Opening a sack of 200 bulbs taken home after purchase, the buyer found that many were of the diameter of a silver quarter. A court agreed with the buyer's claim that this created a breach of an express warranty.

IMPLIED WARRANTIES

Implied warranties are of two basic types: a warranty of merchantability and a warranty of fitness.

When the seller does not make any specific claim about the quality of the thing being sold, should the courts hold the seller to any particular grade or quality of merchandise? In other words, should the courts say that the very transaction itself gives rise to an understood, or implied, warranty? A guarantee of this kind is known as a *warranty of merchantability*.

Warranty of Merchantability

The implied warranty of merchantability is often the most practical protection that the law furnishes to a buyer. Most courts say that the requirement that goods shall be merchantable is implied in every offer to sell by a merchant dealing in that kind of goods. Legally, the warranty of merchantability applies only if the seller is a merchant dealing in goods of the kind being sold. A bicycle store would automatically be held to a warranty of merchantability on every child's tricycle sold. But a neighbor selling a tricycle no longer used by her child would not be held to a warranty of merchantability.

The warranty applies even for the sale of second-hand goods, provided the merchant regularly deals in that same class of merchandise. The different legal standards required here come about because a merchant, even a second-hand dealer, should have knowledge of the products handled, offering only such merchandise as will reasonably come up to expectations. A nonmerchant neighbor offering an item for sale cannot be expected to be an expert on every item that may be sold.

The UCC states that there is an implied warranty of merchantability in every mercantile sales contract, unless the agreement specifies otherwise.[10]

In applying this section of the UCC (which applies only to sales by merchants), practically all courts today hold that the seller is under an obligation to furnish an article that substantially fills the functions and description of the material for which the buyer bargained. For example, in the sale of a bathtub, there is an implied warranty that the tub, by its very nature, is capable of holding water without leaking. In similar fashion, a flush toilet

---

[10] UCC 2–314.

must be capable of automatically emptying into a sewer or cesspool line when activated. A motor boat must have a stern on which a motor could be mounted by reasonable work and without major construction changes in the hull.

Judges and legal authorities state that an implied warranty is not based on the affirmative intentions of the parties to the sale. The courts point out that an implied warranty is "a creation of the law," or "a child of the law," which annexes itself to a sales contract because of the very nature of the transaction.

Merchantable Goods Defined

The UCC specifies that to be merchantable, goods must be

a. able to pass without objection in the trade under the contract description;
b. of fairly average quality within their description (in the case of fungible goods);
c. fit for the ordinary purposes for which they were intended;
d. within the variations permitted by the agreement, of even kind, quality and quantity within each unit and among all units involved;
e. adequately contained, packaged, and labeled as the agreement may require; and
f. in conformance with the promises or affirmations of fact made on the container or label if any.[11]

While the courts quite consistently follow these UCC specifications concerning merchantability, at times some courts have pointed out that other qualifications may be added if the UCC provisions would not achieve justice in a particular case. In supplying goods, the merchant is allowed to deviate in both quantity and quality in individual units of the product furnished so long as there is an overall compliance with established grade tolerances in the complete shipment.

"Wholesomeness" of Food

In the sale of food, the courts quite consistently hold that the warranty of merchantability requires that the food be wholesome and fit for human consumption. This means that a customer may recover from a restaurant when a contaminated meal is served, based on an implied warranty.

The courts usually say, however, that a restaurant customer should be required to approach certain types of food with caution. For example, some-

[11] UCC 2–314(2).

one eating an oyster stew should anticipate the possibility that there could be a piece of shell in the stew or that there could be a pit in a cherry pie. Accordingly, most courts do not permit a recovery against a restaurant in a case of this kind where "the foreign object is indigenous to that kind of food product." However, these same courts would generally allow recovery for an injury if a sharp chicken bone caused injury to a customer eating a cheeseburger.[12]

Most courts have determined that a food supplier such as a grocer should be held to a warranty of merchantability for canned or bottled goods, even though the supplier has no opportunity to inspect such products. Decisions of this kind are based on the idea that the merchant can pass on the loss to the wholesaler and can refuse to deal with suppliers who may not meet proper standard of quality.

Implied Warranty of Fitness

Sometimes a buyer informs a seller, by specific words or by implication, of a desire to obtain an item for a particular purpose. Thus, in effect, the seller is asked to furnish goods that would be adequate for the stated purpose. A seller who accepts an order after such a statement is legally bound to furnish an article that will come up to the intended needs. If the article does not meet that purpose, the seller is guilty of a breach of the *warranty of fitness* as specified by the UCC.[13] A breach of the warranty has taken place if an inadequate article is furnished, regardless of how hard the seller has tried to fill the order properly. If the consumer relies on the seller's judgment and skill to furnish suitable merchandise, there is a warranty that the goods will satisfy the consumer's specific purpose. It is not sufficient that the merchandise is of good, average quality for that kind of product, although this may satisfy a warranty of merchantability.

A man who spent considerable time in the mountains specified to his tailor that he wanted a greatcoat that could be worn under all circumstances in the rain and snow. The tailor made a warm, light garment that gave good protection against bitter cold; however, it was not completely impervious to rain. The tailor had given a warranty of fitness, but the garment furnished constituted a breach of the warranty.

In some instances a single transaction may involve both a warranty of merchantability and a warranty of fitness.

DISCLAIMERS

A *disclaimer* is a written statement which puts the buyer on notice of the seller's refusal to accept responsibility for the quality, quantity, or condition

[12] *Hochberg* v. *O'Donnell's, Inc.*, 272 A.2d 846.
[13] UCC 2–315.

of the goods that are being sold. It is a renunciation of legal responsibility otherwise due. In some instances a document furnished by the seller to the buyer may be labeled as a "warranty," but in effect the terms printed in the document serve as a disclaimer.

As known from contract law, courts generally uphold agreements in which one party consents to bargain away rights in return for something wanted from the other party. But usually a disclaimer is not a mere trade-off of values. Too often a disclaimer seeks to nullify those things that a buyer expected to receive as part of the bargain.

It is the stated objective of most courts and of the UCC to prevent the transfer of worthless goods and to furnish a speedy and adequate remedy for any such breach.[14]

In deciding cases, judges often point out that if a seller is allowed to disclaim, modify, or exclude statements that would otherwise be regarded as an express warranty, the buyer is being cheated out of those very inducements that led up to the bargain. Consequently, it has long been a principle of sales law that any disclaimer should be construed very narrowly by the courts, keeping intact express warranties where possible.

In recent years judges have often gone so far as to state that they are looking for ways to strike down all disclaimers of express warranties.

Disclaimer Never Permitted Unless Buyer Made Aware of It

A disclaimer can never be used to deprive a buyer of warranty rights unless the consumer has actual knowledge of the seller's disclaimer.

In *Weisz* v. *Parke-Bernet Galleries, Inc.*,[15] an art gallery was held liable for breach of warranty in the sale of oil paintings that turned out to be forgeries of old masters. The paintings had been advertised through a printed catalogue which contained a statement that the sale in question would be conducted under terms specified in that catalogue. One of the conditions listed in the catalogue was to the effect that the sales gallery disclaimed responsibility for the authenticity of the paintings. The plaintiff in this lawsuit testified that he had never seen the disclaimer in the seller's catalogue. The court said that the buyer (plaintiff) could not be held to the disclaimer as he had never seen it. In addition, the court pointed out that there was an implied warranty that the paintings were what they had been represented to be—genuine old masters. The buyer was therefore awarded damages.

Under the principle of the *Weisz* decision, which is a leading case on this point, a seller of a new car would not be permitted responsibility for either verbal warranties or implied warranties of merchantability if the seller subsequently had the buyer sign a contract containing a disclaimer that was never read by the buyer.

[14]UCC 2–719.
[15]*Weisz* v. *Parke-Bernet Galleries, Inc.*, 135 N.Y.S.2d 576.

"Fine Print" Disclaimers

Some sellers utilize printed forms or sales contracts that make many promises or offer complete satisfaction to the buyer in large type or colored lettering, only to disclaim parts of these rights and benefits in extremely small print in an obscure part of the document. Court decisions have used various approaches in holding such disclaimers invalid.

In *Henningsen* v. *Bloomfield Motors*[16] the plaintiff had signed a purchase order form at the time a new Plymouth automobile was bought. This document was a single sheet with printing on both sides. The print on the form got progressively smaller and less readable and no one paid any attention to the form at the time of sale. On the back of the form in small print was a disclaimer, limiting the responsibility of the manufacturer to the replacement of specified defective parts. No one at Bloomfield Motors had explained to Henningsen (plaintiff) that either a warranty or a disclaimer was involved in the sale.

In deciding for the buyer, the court pointed out the basic legal principle that, in the absence of fraud, one who does not choose to read a contract before signing it cannot later relieve himself or herself of the obligations imposed by the contract. The court ruled, however, that the buyer could recover on the basis of an implied warranty. The court held, in effect, that the disclaimer was sufficiently hidden in small print in such a way that it was unlikely that many people would read it. Because of this likelihood, a purchaser without actual knowledge of the disclaimer should not be limited by it.

Some other courts have struck down disclaimers, holding them to be invalid if they are in fine print and not a significant part of the sales contract.[17]

Still additional courts reach the same result, concluding that express warranties that are part of the bargaining terms of the sale cannot be disregarded as an essential part of the transaction, even though a printed express warranty is included in the written document that purports to be the sales agreement.[18]

The code requires the courts to construe express warranties as follows:

> Words or conduct relative to the creation of an express warranty and words or conduct tending to negate or limit warranty shall be construed whenever reasonable as consistent with each other . . . negation or limitation (of the warranty) is inoperative to the extent that such construction is inoperative.[19]

---

[16] *Henningsen* v. *Bloomfield Motors*, 161 A.2d 69.
[17] *Woodruff* v. *Clark County Farm Bureau*, 286 N.E.2d 188.
[18] *Mobile Housing* v. *Stone*, 490 S.W.2d 611.
[19] UCC 2–316(1).

The result of the UCC provision and judicial thinking on the subject has led most legal observers to feel that in future cases practically all courts will hold the seller to an express warranty, notwithstanding a disclaimer or exclusion in a written agreement that purports to represent the understanding between the parties.

WARRANTY OF HABITABILITY IN SALE OF A NEW HOME

The courts are in agreement that UCC provisions do not apply to the sale of real estate. For many years the courts consistently held that there was no implied warranty by the builder that the home was reasonably fit for human occupancy and use. By analogy to warranty principles in UCC provisions, however, many modern courts now hold that the builder of a new home gives an implied *warranty of habitability* to the buyer.

At one time, the safest way for the buyer to obtain protection against a builder's defects was to have the builder give an express written warranty in the deed of sale. Today, however, courts in most of the states have pointed out that it is the builder and not the buyer who is in a position to know what may be wrong with the construction. The practical effect is that the builder–contractor must make good on a faulty foundation, improper electrical wiring, faulty plumbing, a leaky roof, or a basement that floods.

Today, almost all courts hold a home builder responsible from two standpoints:

1. The builder must complete the house in a "good and workmanlike" fashion.
2. The builder must make sure that the completed house is "reasonably fit for its intended purpose."

In general, modern courts have decided that the builder–contractor's responsibility extends beyond the first purchaser of the house to subsequent buyers. But the implied warranty would apply only to defects or inadequacies for which the builder was clearly responsible when the property was turned over to the first owner. Just how far the courts will go in extending this protection is not known, but obviously the builder–contractor cannot be held responsible indefinitely.

The courts have extended this liability only to those "in the construction or building business." It would not be imposed on a regular homeowner who resold his or her residence.

Of course, a buyer who suffered damage because of improper construction may be awarded a judgment against the builder–contractor of a new home on a breach of contract or negligence basis. But this result is by no means automatic and may require a costly, time-consuming lawsuit. It is therefore preferable for the buyer to insist that the deed of purchase include an express warranty. This warranty should specify that the structure is reasonably fit for habitation and free from defects.

On a negligence basis (tort suit) the courts may also find the builder–contractor responsible for negligence in construction procedures. Under most recent court decisions, if for example workers select and install weak roof beams with large knotholes, so that as a result the roof collapses, the builder–contractor would also be held responsible to the buyer. If, however, the builder–contractor purchased steel bracing from a legitimate manufacturer and hidden defects in the steel subsequently caused damage, the builder–contractor would not be responsible for negligence. Most modern courts, however, would say that the builder–contractor would still be responsible under an implied warranty of fitness or habitability.

CONSUMER PROTECTION WARRANTY LEGISLATION

In 1975 Congress passed the Federal Warranty Act[20] (sometimes known as the Magnuson–Moss Warranty Act). This law makes it optional whether a seller will offer a warranty of any kind on consumer products valued at more than $10. However, if a warranty is given, it must be conspicuously marked as either a "full warranty" or a "limited warranty." The law further specifies that a "full warranty" must offer the buyer reasonable repair and service facilities. In addition, the seller must allow the buyer to receive a refund or replacement if the item proves defective. The law further provides that this refund or replacement must be completed after a reasonable number of attempts to repair the product are made by the seller. The law also requires that there can be no disclaimer or limitation on liability for implied warranties.

This same statute specifies that anything less than a "full warranty" is a "limited warranty." A complete disclaimer of implied warranty responsibility cannot be made under this Magnuson–Moss law; however, it does permit limiting the period of time under warranty to a reasonable duration.

This act was passed into law because of the belief that most warranties are basically written for the protection of manufacturers and suppliers and not for the buying consumer. Like all such laws, the Federal Warranty Act is difficult to enforce, since there is usually dispute among the parties or the courts concerning what constitutes reasonable efforts to service or repair defective products, automobiles, and so on.

This law specifies that the firm giving a warranty must furnish it in simple and readily understood language. All the terms and conditions must be clearly spelled out. If there are exclusions or exceptions, they must be stated. This law also notes that there must be a step-by-step procedure

---

[20]15 U.S. Code 2310.

described for the buyer to follow in order to obtain satisfaction on the warranty. In the event of a breach of warranty, details must also be included to describe what repairs or replacements will be made by the seller and what expenses the buyer must bear.

It was the stated intent of Congress in passing the Federal Warranty Act to encourage buyer inspection of printed warranties as a consumer shopping tool. It was hoped that the law would give manufacturers an economic incentive to provide better warranty protection for the public. But the passage of the law apparently persuaded many manufacturers to offer only a limited warranty or no warranty at all.

Under this Federal law, the Federal Trade Commission (FTC) was given authority to set up rules requiring sellers to make presale disclosures concerning whether written warranty terms were being offered, along with the basic provisions and coverage in those warranties.

In addition to Federal warranty legislation, a number of state legislatures have passed laws to provide additional buyer protection. Typically, these state statutes limit the use of disclaimers and provide that a manufacturer's warranty applies directly to the eventual consumer, even though the consumer was not privy to the manufacturer's sales agreement. These state laws also frequently specify that repair and service facilities must be made available to buyers when an express warranty is involved.

AUTOMOBILE WARRANTIES

Warranties on New Cars

Automobile buyers and users have traditionally experienced problems with new car warranties regarding repairs. In recent years, many automobile manufacturers have extended their new car warranties to include longer periods of time and additional parts of the vehicle. As competition among American and foreign manufactured automobiles increases, sellers will offer more incentives to buyers to purchase their brand of vehicle, which will increase protection to the buyer against defective automobiles by their ability to receive additional protections in the warranties offered by the automobile manufacturers.

Buyers may, for an additional fee, purchase *extended warranties* which cover the automobile for an extended period of time. These policies should be read carefully, however, to ensure that the parts being covered are those that are likely to be repaired during the warranty period.

Consumer warranty disputes can cover a wide range of problems. Typically, these include arguments over whether a particular defect is covered, unusual delays, the expiration of the warranty period with matters still not satisfactorily handled, or discovery that the defect has not really been fixed. Other buyer problems center around the fact that auto dealer employees are frequently unresponsive, indifferent, or outright hostile. And on a limited warranty the car buyer may be out considerable money to obtain temporary transportation. Then, too, occasionally a new car is simply a "lemon."

Car dealers and manufacturers frequently claim that there is no car that cannot be made right. Experience does not seem always to bear out this claim, however. As a practical matter, a consumer who buys a "lemon" may go back to the dealer time after time for repairs. Under a limited warranty, the Federal Warranty Act does not provide protection so long as the dealer maintains that it is being repaired. However, some states have instituted "lemon laws" to protect buyers with this problem.

As written, new automobile warranties will usually be honored only if the defect was not caused by improper action on the part of the driver. If the oil pan falls off because of a defective bolt, the problem will generally be covered by a warranty. If, however, a hole is knocked in the oil pan because the driver did not manage to avoid a large rock, the damage will not be covered.

But even if a car manufacturer's express warranty has expired or has been denied by the manufacturer, more than half the states in the United States have statutes that provide implied warranties. Thus, a buyer may sometimes use an implied warranty to gain legal relief.

Auto Repair Warranty Problems

All customers leaving a car with a garage mechanic for repairs can expect two legal obligations from the mechanic:

1. To perform the work agreed upon. This does not mean, however, the mechanic will always perform quality work. But the customer can always demand that the work come up to reasonable standards. From a practical standpoint this is an area where legal remedies frequently cost more than the money involved, since it is difficult to prove that repairs were not adequate.

2. To provide reasonable care to make sure the customer's car is not stolen, damaged, or destroyed by fire or other means while under the mechanic's control. If a fender is accidentally damaged in the garage while awaiting repairs, the mechanic must repair it. In most states the mechanic may avoid responsibility, however, if the damage was caused by a disaster such as a hurricane, earthquake, or fire, not due to the mechanic's negligence.

After repairs have been made to the mechanic's satisfaction, the latter may claim a mechanic's lien or workman's lien to hold the car for security until payment is made. If repairs are not to the consumer's satisfaction and if the garage is unethical, the consumer has only two choices:

1. To refuse to pay and to seek a court order for return of the car with the help of a lawyer.
2. To pay the mechanic's bill and then file suit for breach of warranty or breach of contract.

State Legislation on Auto Repairs

A number of states have enacted laws setting up a state bureau of automotive repairs. The California law of 1972 served as a model for other states. The stated purpose of such legislation is

> to foster fair dealings between automotive repair facilities and consumers, to eliminate misunderstandings between them, and to promote safety in the repair of motor vehicles.

In general, these laws provide for registration and licensing of automotive repair dealers, lamp and brake adjusting stations, and individuals employed therein. In addition, such laws may regulate motor vehicle pollution-control device installation and inspection.

The California Bureau of Automotive Repair maintains a number of branch offices along with a toll-free telephone number that may be utilized. When a consumer complaint is received, a Bureau representative promptly discusses the facts with the repair facility. An attempt is made to resolve the dispute or to correct customer misunderstandings. If the matter is not settled at that stage, a technical field investigator will meet with the consumer and the repair facility representative. The questioned work is then actually examined by the Bureau of Automotive Repair field technician. If the repair work was not up to reasonable standards, state disciplinary proceedings will be begun. Criminal action can also be taken in case of fraud, and the consumer is free to sue for damages in small claims court or regular civil court.

_____ QUESTIONS _____

1. What is a warranty? Explain the differences between an express warranty and an implied warranty.
2. What is the difference between mere "sales talk" or opinion and a warranty?
3. Who stands legally responsible for a warranty?
4. Is it the manufacturer of a defective product, the wholesale distributor, or the retail store outlet that is responsible on an implied warranty? Does it make any difference here whether the warranty is express or implied?
5. Must the goods offered to the purchaser conform to the trade terms or description of such items?

6. What is meant by a warranty of merchantability?

7. Does a warranty of merchantability require food products to have a basic "wholesomeness"?

8. What is the difference between a warranty of merchantability and a warranty of fitness?

9. What is a disclaimer? Does a disclaimer apply when the buyer is not aware of it?

10. Do the courts tend to hold "fine print" disclaimers invalid when they conflict with promises made by the seller? What reasoning or legal theories do the courts use in rejecting some of these disclaimers?

11. Is there a warranty of habitability in the sale of a new home? Explain.

12. How does the Federal Warranty Act (Magnuson–Moss Warranty Act) apply to consumer sales?

13. What are some typical warranty problems encountered by buyers of new automobiles?

ANSWERS TO DISCUSSION CASES

CASE 47 UCC provisions (Sec. 2-313(2)) state that no intent on the part of the seller is necessary for the creation of an implied warranty. In the case at hand the court said: "A warranty is a statement of the facts that is made by one party . . . and [that party] no matter how honest . . . and no matter whether he may believe in the truth of the statement, takes risk of it being false."

CASE 48 The courts consistently say that the goods must measure up to the description furnished by the seller. See UCC, Sec. 2-313(1)(a).

PROBLEM CASES

1 A buyer using a home training device called a "Golfing Gismo" was injured in the head when struck by a golf ball. The maker's catalogue advised that the device was a fully equipped item that could be used in a back yard. Instructions accompanying the item said that the ball could be driven with full power and that it was "completely safe." The buyer sued for breach of an express warranty. The manufacturer raised the legal question as to whether the purchaser had proved reliance on the manufacturer's statements. Is such reliance a legal necessity for recovery? (*Hauter* v. *Zogarts*, 534 P.2d 377.)

2 A manufacturer represented to a retail store that a ladder was "safe, strong, durable; made of sound, selected, and thoroughly seasoned lumber; of good workmanship; and of sufficient strength to sustain an individual's weight." One of these ladders proved defective and injured a retail customer (Kaiser) who had purchased it. The retailer was found liable in a lawsuit by Kaiser.

In turn, the retailer sued the manufacturer. Decide liability. (*Liberty Mutual Ins. Co.* v. *J. R. Clark Co.*, 59 N.W.2d 899.)

3   A written contract of sale provided that machinery was made of "good materials." The manufacturer also claimed it would perform well under proper care and management. The machinery performed in a defective manner and the buyer sued on the basis that the seller's statements constituted a warranty. The seller contended that the term "good" was a mere statement of opinion, not a warranty of quality or capacity. Which contention was proper? (*Hansen* v. *Gaar, Scott & Co.*, 65 N.W. 254.)

23

Liens; Mortgages; and Deeds of Trust

LIENS

A *lien* is a hold or claim that someone has against the property of another as security for a debt or charge. It is sometimes said that the word lien means a "string," a "tie," a "bind." It implies that one is in possession of property of another that is being detained as security for a demand or obligation in respect to that property.[1]

Liens may come into being against either personal property or real property. For example, an *innkeeper's lien* (*hotelkeeper's lien*) may be placed against luggage (personal property) by an unpaid hotel manager. *Warehouseman's liens, artisan's liens,* and *mechanic's liens* are other examples of liens placed against personal property.

When real estate is sold, the buyer normally takes ownership subject to unpaid liens that are on record. However, these liens must have been recorded in order to give the lienholder protection against an innocent purchaser of the property who has no knowledge of such liens.

Voluntary and Involuntary Liens

Some liens are involuntary, arising automatically by operation of the law. This classification includes *tax liens, judgment liens,* and *mechanic's liens* that are authorized and enforced by statute.

Other liens come into existence against real property because of the voluntary acts of the landowner. Perhaps the most common type of voluntary lien is a *mortgage,* created when the owner puts up real estate as security on a loan.

---

[1]*Evans* v. *Fanelli,* 157 A.2d 36.

Liens That Need Not Be Recorded

Some liens need not be recorded in order to prevail over subsequent claims against property. Included in this category are state and county real estate tax liens, income tax and inheritance tax liens, and franchise tax liens.

Valid, existing liens against the property of an individual going into bankruptcy are not affected by bankruptcy proceedings; existing liens are still in effect. When bankruptcy proceedings begin, title to the bankrupt's property passes to a trustee who holds this property subject to outstanding liens.

Under Federal bankruptcy laws, the trustee can make an issue in court hearings of the validity of claimed liens. If it can be proved that the lien was fraudently obtained or allowed to give one creditor unlawful preference over other creditors, the lien will be set aside. However, a legal, proper lien will have preference over other claims.

Artisan's Liens and Work Authority

An *artisan's lien*, sometimes called a *mechanic's lien*, gives a worker the right to retain property that has been worked on until payment has been made. If the owner refuses to make payment, the artisan or worker may begin legal proceedings to obtain the right to sell the object under regulations set up by state law. If a sale results thereafter, the artisan is entitled to deduct the original price to the nonpayer of the work done, furnishing the rest of the proceeds to the former owner.

A lien of this kind merely gives the artisan the right to hold the property. The artisan's right to sell the item does not come into being until specific legal requirements have been met. Most states require notice to the owner prior to legal sale by the artisan. This notice gives the owner a reasonable time to get the goods back by paying the artisan's charges. Statutes in most states provide that if procedures to enforce the lien are not filed within a specified period, the lien right terminates.

All states have laws permitting a garage mechanic to hold an automobile until the owner pays the repair bill. This type of artisan's lien is sometimes called a *garageman's* or a *mechanic's lien*. Technically, however, the courts usually consider a mechanic's lien to be one resulting from the furnishing of materials or labor for improvements on real estate, rather than for working on personal property such as an automobile.

In a number of states an artisan's lien is superior to other prior liens of record or to the claim of a party retaining a security interest in the goods that have been worked on by the artisan.

Artisan's Contracts

A promise to perform specified work for an agreed price is a binding contract between the artisan and the customer. If, however, the agreement was only for an hourly rate of work, the artisan should obtain authorization before working more than the specified hours. If the customer is advised that the work cannot be done without additional authorization for work, silence on the part of the customer is usually regarded in most courts as authorization to perform the additional work.

When the work done by the craftsman or artisan is not performed satisfactorily, the customer is within his or her rights in refusing payment and demanding return of the property. Usually the courts will authorize a customer to order an artisan to stop work on a project at any time, but the customer must pay for the work actually performed to that point. If the artisan persists in withholding the object being worked on until the job is completed, most courts will not usually require the customer to pay for labor done after a request for return of the item.

A craftsman or artisan has the same responsibilities to customers and the general public as any other business. When property is brought into a shop for repair, the law expects the artisan–bailee to take prudent care of the goods or services in question. The customer is entitled to be compensated if property is lost, stolen, or damaged while awaiting repair. Many shopkeepers, of course, carry bailment insurance to cover the risk of loss of customer property.

By accepting merchandise for repair, a shopkeeper makes an implied contract to repair the article in a satisfactory way. If a television repair shop returns a customer's TV set as repaired, the shop will be held liable if negligence in making the repairs subsequently causes the set to catch on fire. In like manner, the furnishing of replacement parts constitutes a warranty that the parts are safe for the reason intended.

Mechanic's Liens

Construction or repair of real estate usually begins after execution of a contract between the landowner and a building contractor. If the job is of any size, the contractor usually makes use of carpenters, electricians, plumbers, technicians, laborers, and artisans who are subcontractors responsible for a particular phase of the work. In many instances the landowner is not even aware of the identity of these subcontractors and has no contract with them. This indirect relationship often presented problems for subcontractors who were not paid by the contractor and had no direct commitment from the property owner. To correct this problem, all states have passed "mechanic's lien laws."

A *mechanic's lien* is a statutory claim on buildings and other improvements on realty, and on the real estate itself, in favor of a building contractor, a material supplier, or on any class of workman to secure them priority or preference of payment for their work or material.[2]

Legal commentators point out that the term "mechanic's lien" is somewhat misleading and that it is perhaps better known as a "contractor's lien," "subcontractor's lien," "materialman's lien," or "laborer's lien."[3] In most states a lien of this type attaches only to real estate, while an artisan's lien applies to personal property alone. Artisans have always had liens under English and American law, but a mechanic's lien is statutory, varying considerably in legal provisions from jurisdiction to jurisdiction.

"The purpose of a mechanic's lien statute is to permit a lien upon premises where benefit has been received by the owner and where the value or condition of the property has been increased or improved by reason of the furnishing of labor and materials."[4] The courts usually hold that the lien right exists, whether or not the work has actually increased the value of the property.[5]

The statutory right to a lien applies to (1) the contractor, (2) materialmen who actually furnish building supplies and equipment, and (3) laborers or artisans who work on the construction project. With respect to the workers, the courts usually say that the work must be done on or about a building and that it is necessary for a claimant to have actually participated in the work.[6] However, "work need not actually be done 'upon' a building so long as it becomes an integral part of the building upon completion."[7] A number of states have statutes that cover workers on the fringe of a building contract. For example, it has been held that a bookkeeper and a cook's helper of a bridge contractor have the right to a lien against the railroad that had contracted for the construction.[8] Most courts, however, have not gone this far in extending the lien right.

DISCUSSION

CASE 49   A tenant holding a large property signed a contract with a builder to make an addition as well as extensive alterations to the structure. Some carpenters who worked on the addition filed a mechanic's lien claim when they were not paid. Other carpenters who worked at making alterations filed a mechanic's lien when the main contractor was unable to pay them off. Which group of carpenters could expect to recover on the lien claim, or could both do so? (*Masterson* v. *Roberts*, 78 S.W.2d 856.)

[2]*Tommasi* v. *Bolger*, 100 NTS 367.
[3]AMERICAN JURISPRUDENCE (2d), "Mechanic's Liens," Sec. 1.
[4]*3190 Corp.* v. *Gould*, 431 P.2d. 466.
[5]*Mazel* v. *Bain*, 133 So.2d 44; *Frehner* v. *Mortin*, 424 P.2d 446.
[6]*Ward* v. *Town Tavern, et al.*, 228 P.2d 216.
[7]*Caird Engineering Works* v. *Seven-Up Gold Min. Co.*, 111 P.2d 267.
[8]*Bladen* v. *Marietta & N.C.R. Ry.*, 37 S.W. 135.

CASE 50   Laborers who performed work on property filed a mechanic's lien when the owner's contractor did not pay them. The owner of the property pointed out that the purpose of such a lien law is to recompense workers who create a benefit to a property owner. The owner contended that the value of the land was not increased by the work done since the existing lease on the property gave the tenant the right to remove the building at the end of the lease term. Was this contention proper? (*United Pacific Ins. Co.* v. *Martin & Luther*, 455 P.2d 664; *Nolte* v. *Smith*, 189 Cal. App. 2d 140.)

CASE 51   A veterinarian was called to treat the sheep on a large ranch. When the veterinarian was not paid, he claimed a materialman's lien against the ranch property. Was this claim allowed?

"Perfecting" or Filing a Mechanic's Lien

After a statutory lien has become a right, the holder of such right has a statutory period in which to "perfect" or activate it. In most states the procedure is to file the lien in the county recorder's office in which deeds are recorded. A copy of the filing is then sent to the property owner and to the contractor, if the lien is not sent to the contractor himself or herself. This filing must be done within a statutory period set by law.

During this statutory period, the lien will be enforceable against the owner of the property, even though he or she innocently purchased without knowledge of the lienholder's claim. Accordingly, the purchaser of any piece of real estate should make an inspection prior to signing the papers, determining whether improvements have recently been made on the property. If improvements are discovered, the buyer should find whether the contractor and subcontractors have been paid for the work.

Laws in some states permit the contractor to file a lien within two to three years, while the same laws require a materialman or worker to file a lien claim within a year or less. This difference is allowed because the landowner is aware of obligations owing to the contractor but may not even know of lawful claims of subcontractors.

After the lienholder has filed the mandatory notice in the county recorder's office, practically all states require the holder to file a foreclosure suit within a prescribed period. If this is not done, the lien claim is lost forever.

Rights of Subcontractor

There are two basic types of mechanic's lien laws throughout the United States: the "New York system" and the "Pennsylvania system." The major distinction relates to the rights of a subcontractor against the property owner. Under the New York system the subcontractor cannot recover more than is due from the owner to the contractor. Under the Pennsylvania system, payment by the owner to the original contractor is no defense to a claim made by a subcontractor who performed for the contractor. Under the New York system, the laborer's or materialman's rights are derived through the contractor. Under the Pennsylvania system, both the contractor and the subcontractors have a direct lien.

Under the Pennsylvania system, if the contractor is inefficient or inept, the landowner may be confronted with claims from unknown sources that total more than the original agreed-upon price.[9]

Landowner's Protection Against Subcontractors

Under the law in states that follow the so-called Pennsylvania system, allowing a mechanic's lien may actually work a hardship on the property owner. For example, in *Pipkorn* v. *Tratnik*[10] the court allowed a subcontractor to recover for concrete work done even though the construction was of such poor quality that it was rejected by the building inspector, was never accepted by the property owner, and was replaced by the main contractor.

Statutes in most states provide that, if certain procedures outlined by law are followed, a property owner is liable for no more than the contract price. These procedures usually specify that prior to payment to the contractor a sworn statement must be obtained from that contractor; this document must list all suppliers and subcontractors and the specific amounts to be due to each of them. The owner is then justified in relying on this signed statement in paying the contractor. If the contractor has been inept or dishonest, the subcontractors and suppliers must look to the contractor for any additional amounts that may be due.

In a number of states the owner is relieved of any obligation beyond the contract price by obtaining signed *lien waivers* from the contractor and those others that may be entitled to a lien. In some states a signed lien waiver from the contractor relieves the owner of further lien responsibility since the courts in those states regard other claimants as deriving their rights through the contractor.

MORTGAGES ⸻

Nature of a Mortgage

A *mortgage* represents a loan secured by the pledge of land or other property to stand good for a debt. There is no such thing as an oral mortgage. As ordinarily used, the term "mortgage" refers to a *real estate mortgage*, rather

[9]Virginia Law Review, pp. 121–123.
[10]*Pipkorn* v. *Tratnik*, 152 N.W. 141.

than to the loan arrangement on personal property that is called a *chattel mortgage*.

The word mortgage takes its meaning from two old French words: *mort* (dead) and *gage* (pledge). When the debt is paid, the pledge arrangement is null and void—in short, it is dead.

The great majority of all home and business purchases are financed by use of a mortgage or a similar instrument, the deed of trust. But any kind of property, real or personal, may be mortgaged.

A second or even a third mortgage may be put on property, but the holder of the second gets nothing until the security claim of the first mortgage is satisfied.

The word mortgage is used in two ways: (1) in describing the act itself, whereby such a conveyance is made; and (2) in describing the instrument (deed of conveyance) that actually accomplishes this transfer.

It should be emphasized that a mortgage must be recorded in the county recorder's office. Otherwise, an innocent third party may buy the property for its market price, not realizing that there is a lien (mortgage claim) against it.

Full service banks, savings and loan associations, savings banks, life insurance companies, and mortgage firms have traditionally specialized in lending money on real estate. The amount that these organizations will lend will vary with the appraised value of the property and the creditworthiness of the borrower.

The party that puts up the property (the borrower) is called the *mortgagor* and the lender is termed the *mortgagee*.

The majority of contracts for the sale of real estate contain a provision that makes the actual transfer of title (ownership) conditional on the buyer's obtaining the type of mortgage loan that is required. Therefore the lender will customarily forward a *letter of commitment* to the borrower, outlining the terms of the loan that will be made. With this letter of commitment in hand, the borrower (buyer) can proceed to the closing. The buyer is released from the sales contract if he or she cannot find a loan with satisfactory terms. This release takes place, however, only if the real estate sales contract contains a clause with such a provision.

Two Concepts: Conveyance and Lien

The early legal view of a mortgage was that title to the pledged real estate actually passed to the lender, who was the technical and actual owner. In some states a mortgage is still considered a transfer of ownership as security with the provision that the transfer becomes void on payment. That is, as between the two parties it is a conveyance, but as to a third party it is treated as a lien. This situation can become quite involved.

In most of the United States the courts have followed the view that the mortgage arrangement is not actually a conveyance, but merely a method of putting up security. According to this view, the mortgagor (original owner) retains title unless repayment is not made. This is the so-called *lien theory* of a mortgage, as contrasted to the so-called *conveyance theory* or *transfer theory*. Regardless of the theory that is followed, in some states the borrower is also required to give the lender a judgment note in the amount of the obligation. This note may assist the lender in obtaining a court judgment if there should be a default.

Technically, there are usually two parts to a mortgage. Sometimes it is written as a single instrument in two parts, while in some states it is traditionally written as two documents. Regardless, the papers involved in the transaction include:

1. A transfer or conveyance of the mortgaged property to the lender, and
2. A defeasance provision, which is simply an instrument that defeats the force or operation or the transfer of ownership if the debt is paid; it provides that the transfer is undone.

Mortgage agreements (or notes) always include three basic specifications in the loan arrangement: (1) the principal amount of the loan, (2) the rate of interest to be paid, and (3) the terms and conditions for repayment.

In the mortgage papers the borrower promises to pay off the loan plus interest on a specified date or at regular payment intervals. Usually, the borrower agrees to pay for fire insurance on the property as required to protect the lender's security interest. Mortgages also usually provide that the entire debt falls due if a payment is missed or if the borrower violates any terms of the mortgage agreement. In addition, the mortgagor often agrees in this document to make no structural or major changes in buildings or property that could lower the value of the property unless the alterations have written consent of the lender. The borrower is also responsible for the payment of property taxes and assessments on the property.

Mortgages usually specify that the borrower has a *grace period* in which to satisfy a delinquent payment.

Borrower's (Mortgagor's) Rights

Under early legal views of a mortgage, the lender was entitled to immediately take possession of the mortgaged property unless the agreement specified that the lender could stay until default or until the debt was paid off. Under modern ideas of mortgage law, the borrower is left in possession. Mortgages written in states that follow the conveyance theory ordinarily include a statement that the borrower (mortgagor) is to continue the occupancy of the property.

All courts in this country agree that the mortgagor still has all the privileges of an owner. This means that the mortgagor has the uncontested right of possession and can lease, rent, and collect profits and rents that accrue from the property. In addition, the mortgagor can sell the property with the new buyer taking ownership subject to the mortgage.

Lender's (Mortgagee's) Rights

The courts are in agreement that the lender (mortgagee) can freely sell or pledge the mortgage interest. Legally, this is sometimes termed an *assignment of rights*.

In most jurisdictions, the mortgagee can take over the property in the event of default. This is usually permitted without complicated legal maneuvering, generally by notifying the tenants and demanding that rent be paid to the mortgagee.

If a mortgagee takes over the property after default, this party is called the *mortgagee in possession*. When this position has been assumed, the mortgagee in possession has a legal duty to act in a responsible way for the management, preservation, and protection of the property. Failure to act responsibly in handling the property would result in liability to the mortgagor in a civil lawsuit.

A mortgagee in possession is also liable to a third party injured on the premises through negligence. The mortgagee in possession stands in the mortgagor's shoes in this responsibility.

In the event of nonpayment of the debt, the mortgagee has the right to enforce foreclosure.

Foreclosure Procedures

Historically, mortgagees have been depicted as "greedy, heartless shylocks." A few generations ago this description was sometimes justified. Early-day lenders saw no need for adequate security. They simply had the borrower deed the property over in advance with the proviso that payment of the debt would cancel the transfer. The borrower was required to pay off the loan on or before the due date. If there was even a short delay, the pledged real estate automatically became the property of the lender (mortgagee). This transfer of ownership to the lender took place without any legal procedures.

The result was that too often a borrower lost a valuable estate because of inability to pay a very small debt. In those days loans were hard to refinance, and bank credit was frequently not available. Realizing that injustices were taking place, judges hesitated to enforce forfeitures of title. The courts adopted a procedure of examining each case. If the judge found that the property pledged was worth far more than the debt secured, the judge would no longer let the creditor enforce the debt literally and strictly. The reasoning here was that since the property was pledged merely as security, and since the creditor was more than amply protected, there was no reason why the debtor should not be given a reasonable length of time after the maturity of the debt within which to redeem the property. The amount of the debt, plus interest and a court fee, was required for redemption. Thus, the courts worked out a procedure that is still known in legal circles as the *equity of redemption* or the *right of redemption*.

Regulated from state to state by statute, foreclosure actions and the right of redemption have been a part of our mortgage laws in the United States for many years.

Foreclosure procedures differ from state to state. Foreclosure is a process by which all further rights for a mortgagor to redeem the property are wiped out. Foreclosure can begin only after the debtor's estate has been forfeited by nonpayment and the time has expired to make use of the equity of redemption.

A so-called strict foreclosure provision makes a determination of the debt due under the mortgage, orders its payment within a certain limited time, and provides that the debtor will have no further property interest if the debt is not satisfied by that time. It vests the title absolutely in the mortgagee, without giving the debtor the benefit of a sale and without a further equity of redemption. This type of mortgage foreclosure provision is looked on by the courts with considerable disfavor, but it is still the law in a few jurisdictions.

In most states, the common method for collecting the mortgage debt is by a mortgagee's suit for foreclosure and sale. The mortgagee goes into court and asks for the account to be settled with the mortgagor. The court then looks into the validity of the mortgage and ascertains the amount owing. A sale is then ordered under the supervision of the court. Frequently this is known as a sheriff's sale, but in some states it may be handled by another public officer representing the court.

The sale is usually advertised so that interested individuals have an opportunity to be informed. The property is sold to the highest bidder unless that individual cannot satisfy the terms and conditions of the sale. The sale is then reviewed and confirmed by the court.

If the property sells for more than enough to satisfy the debt, the surplus is tuned over to the debtor. If the property sells for less, the proceeds are turned over to the lender. The lender can then go into court and obtain a judgment against the debtor for this deficiency, which in legal terminology is called a *deficiency judgment.*

During the depression years (1929 to 1940) borrowers were often forced into foreclosure sales for relatively small loans on valuable tracts of farm land or homes. With a nationwide scarcity of credit and money, the lender was frequently the only bidder on property at a sheriff's sale. As a result, often the lender was able to obtain the mortgaged property at very nominal cost while getting a deficiency judgment for a large sum. Because of money shortages, many of these deficiency judgments were not collectible at all and some could be recovered only after the debtor's finances were recouped. But in many instances the lender managed to obtain valuable property and eventually collect on a sizable deficiency judgment.

Recognizing the basic unfairness of this situation, the courts worked out some new principles of mortgage law. Since that time, courts have usually made a searching analysis of mortgage defaults on an individual case basis. Usually, the debtor is allowed credit by the court for the fair market value of the property at the time of foreclosure, even though only the mortgagee submitted a bid at the sheriff's sale. This fair market value is then applied as an offset against the amount of the debt. This, of course, has sharply reduced the amounts of deficiency judgments permitted against borrowers. In effect, this is a practical recognition by the court that mortgaged property is only a security pledge for the debt, rather than a way in which a grasping mortgagee can sometimes take advantage of a debtor's inability to pay.

Most mortgages today are written to require a mortgagee's suit for foreclosure and sale. Every borrower should have an attorney verify that the borrower's mortgage is not of the strict foreclosure type if there is an option.

Today, statutes in practically all states permit the mortgagor to redeem the property within a designated period after the court sale, usually a period of from six months to a year.

Additional Provisions in Mortgages

Some mortgages contain an *open-end provision*, allowing the lender to make one or more additional loans to the borrower without going to the expense or trouble of refinancing or writing up a second mortgage. This may be advantageous in a time of rising interest rates if the borrower has the right to obtain additional money at a specified rate.

A *prepayment provision* allows a borrower to pay off all or part of the mortgage before the debt falls due. This can work out to the borrower's advantage when there is a need to resell the property without an outstanding mortgage or when interest rates are declining. Most mortgages, however, require a penalty charge (prepayment penalty) if the borrower makes use of the prepayment provision.

So-called *package provisions* permit the borrower to include the cost of major home appliances in the basic property mortgage.

Mortgage *modification provisions* allow the borrower to miss a specified number of mortgage payments without penalty or default. In using this option the borrower extends the period of the loan. From the borrower's standpoint this may be beneficial in the event of unemployment or extended illness.

Variable-Interest-Rate Mortgages

During the late 1970s, interest rates for home loans rose steadily. By the early 1980s home purchasing had declined, largely because buyers could not make the large down payments or heavy interest payments for a conventional mortgage. Looking for "creative financing," home builders and sellers then offered numerous variations of a straight payment 20- or 30-year mortgage. Some of these plans offered houses for reduced down payments and a mortgage with variable interest rates that were tied to the cost of living or some other financial index. Some mortgage plans offered the buyer an opportunity to make low mortgage rates for a period of time with monthly payments increasing sharply after two or three years. This type of "creative financing" has continued in recent years as housing prices have risen beyond the reach of many individuals. Financial and real estate experts can only guess about future variations in mortgage terms and conditions.

Assumption of Mortgage

When property carries a mortgage it may be sold, but the property is still subject to foreclosure for a default by the new owner. Of course, the first owner may pay off the indebtedness and leave the property clear of the mortgage if the sale is for cash. But if the first mortgage is erased, it is often necessary for the second buyer to pledge the property on a new mortgage. It is sometimes advantageous for the second owner to buy the property *subject to the original mortgage* or to agree to *assume the mortgage*. In either event, the new buyer will have no greater liability, since the property will stand as security for the loan.

However, if the second buyer takes title to an existing mortgage, the lending agency will have double security. That is, the mortgagee (lender) can still seek satisfaction from the original borrower in addition to looking to the property itself as security. Therefore, it is to the advantage of the original mortgagor (borrower) to obtain a release from the mortgagee at the time the property changes hands.

In addition to putting up the property as security, the borrower assumes personal liability for the mortgage and continues to be liable for the balance if foreclosure of the property does not pay off the debt. The original borrower continues to be liable until the mortgage debt is paid, even though the property may change hands a dozen times. Accordingly, it may be advantageous for the seller to have the new buyer "assume the mortgage" as one of the terms of sale. This means that if there ever should be a deficiency judgment in case of foreclosure, the original borrower could sue the subsequent owner to make up the deficiency.

The original borrower can be relieved of further mortgage responsibility when the property is sold by obtaining a written release from the mortgagee. Most mortgagees will decline to sign such a release, however, wanting to retain as much security for their loan as possible.

Chattel Mortgage

A *chattel mortgage* is a mortgage on personal property, giving a lender a security interest in the property involved. A mortgage of this kind may be given by a businessperson or shopkeeper on equipment or a stock of goods. In many jurisdictions a rancher may give a chattel mortgage on a herd of cattle or a farmer may obtain a seed or equipment loan by signing a mortgage of this kind covering a growing crop.

Although mortgage regulations often vary from state to state, there are generally three ways in which mortgages are regarded:

1. The mortgage acts as a transfer (in whole or in part) of the property covered;
2. The mortgage acts as a lien or charge against the property; or
3. The property is regarded as being placed in trust to a third party until the lien is satisfied.

In most states, if the lender's rights are to be considered superior to those of general creditors of the borrower, the chattel mortgage must be recorded with the county recorder. In some jurisdictions the enforcement of a chattel mortgage can be effected only by court foreclosure or other proceedings. In most states chattel mortgages are usually limited to a loan period of no more than three or four years, becoming void automatically unless the mortgage is renewed or the lender takes legal action to enforce rights.

The majority of states have criminal statutes that make the deliberate removal of mortgaged property to another state a felony. Other provisions of such laws usually require criminal penalties for selling or deliberately concealing the property when the borrower is in default on the loan.

DEES OF TRUST (TRUST DEEDS)

A *deed of trust*, also commonly known as a *trust deed* or *power of sale trust deed*, is in effect a form of mortgage. Legal title to the land that serves as security for a loan is placed in one or more trustees to secure the repayment of the loan or the performance of other conditions. The trustees or trustees have the power of sale in case of loan default.

A regular mortgage involves only two parties, the lender and the borrower. In the trust deed arrangement, the borrower conveys the land not to the lender, but to a third-party trustee who has authority to act for the holder of the note or notes that represent the mortgage debt.

From a lender's standpoint, a deed of trust may be preferable to a mortgage. The basic advantage to a deed of trust is that it can usually be foreclosed by trustee's sale without court proceedings under a "power of sale clause." A trust deed of this type is used in some areas.

_____ *QUESTIONS* _____

1. Define a lien. How is it used?

2. What are some commonly encountered types of liens?

3. Why is it important to record certain types of liens?

4. What are the contractual responsibilities between an artisan and a customer?

5. Explain the basics of a mechanic's lien. What are the two main types of mechanic's liens?

6. What may a property owner do to protect against mechanic's liens?

7. Define a mortgage. What is a second mortgage?

8. Explain the difference between the "lien theory" of a mortgage and the "conveyance theory."

9. Describe some of the borrower's rights in mortgaged property. What are the lender's rights?

10. How do foreclosure procedures work?

11. What is meant by the property buyer's "assuming the mortgage"?

12. Describe the use of a chattel mortgage.

13. What is a deed of trust? Is it frequently used in place of a mortgage? Why?

_____ *ANSWERS TO DISCUSSION CASES* _____

CASE 49   A tenant does not have a right to bind a landlord on a mechanic's lien. Neither group of carpenters could look to the landowner for a recovery.

CASE 50   A mechanic's lien will prevail, whether or not the property is actually benefitted by the work.

CASE 51   The veterinarian's services would not qualify as labor in erecting or improving a structure on the property. A veterinarian could not file a materialman's lien.

PROBLEM CASES

1   An attorney performed services for a client who refused to pay. The attorney had a deed, a voucher, and various other legal papers furnished to him by the client for legal action. The attorney retained these after the client declared that he would not pay. May the attorney continue to hold them? (*Roxana Petroleum Co.* v. *Rice*, 235 P.502.)

2   If a mortgage has no statement concerning payment, does the mortgagor have the right to insist on payment before maturity in order to reduce interest charges? What if the mortgagor offers to pay all interest up to maturity? (*Commercial Products Corp.* v. *Briegel*, 242 N.E.2d 317.)

3   A lender (mortgagee) and a borrower (mortgagor) had an agreement that the lender could look only to the land as security for repayment of the loan. In an instance of this kind, could the lender obtain a personal judgment (deficiency judgment) if the forced sale of the mortgaged property proved insufficient to pay the debt? Would it make a difference whether this agreement was oral rather than written? (*Gagne* v. *Hoban*, 159 N.W.2d 896.)

4   A mortgagor had been making payments before they fell due. When subsequently pressed for ready cash, the mortgagor claimed that there could be no default until prepayments had been exhausted by application to current amounts due. Decide. (*Bradford* v. *Thompson*, 470 S.W.2d 633.)

5   A third party advanced money to purchase property with the understanding that the advance would be secured by a mortgage on the property. The mortgage was properly recorded. The borrower had other creditors who already had a judgment against the borrower. These other creditors claimed that the mortgagee (lender) did not have a superior security interest in the mortgaged property. Who would prevail? (*Van Loben Sels* v. *Bunnell*, 120 Cal. 680.)

24

Commercial Paper: Nature; Types and Characteristics; Negotiability; Holder in Due Course

NATURE OF COMMERCIAL PAPER

What the Term Includes

Commercial paper is the name given to a body of law, called the law of *negotiable instruments* or the law of *bills and notes.*

In general, commercial paper deals with *checks* (sometimes called *demand account checks* or *customer checks*), *cashier's checks, certified checks, traveler's checks, drafts, promissory notes* (often known as *notes*), and *certificates of deposit.*

The term commercial paper is sometimes used to include *warehouse receipts, bills of lading, stock certificates,* and *bonds* issued for corporate or business debts. Some of these instruments are classified under the law as "investment securities" and are not subject to the same rules as checks, drafts, and notes, the kinds of commercial paper that are most widely encountered in everyday business. Then, too, the term commercial paper usually means those instruments that call for payment in money, not in goods. A bill of lading or a warehouse receipt is a right to commodities; while transferable in trade and commerce, it is not payable in money.

Negotiable and Nonnegotiable Instruments

Legally, commercial paper is divided into two distinct classes: negotiable and nonnegotiable instruments. It is important to understand the difference. From the standpoint of one who buys or gets title to commercial paper, special protection is given to a negotiable instrument. The same distinction applies when one discounts or lends money on the security of a negotiable instrument. In summary, then, a person who obtains a negotiable instrument through purchase, trade, or another good-faith acquisition is usually given legal advantages for its collection that are not given to the holder of a nonnegotiable instrument. To be negotiable within the meaning of UCC Article 3, an instrument must meet the following requirements:

1. It must be a writing signed by a maker or drawer.
2. It must contain an unconditional promise (i.e., note) or order (i.e., check.)
3. It must contain a sum certain of money.
4. It must be payable on demand or at a definite time.
5. It must be payable to the bearer or to order.

Negotiability is that characteristic of some types of commercial paper that permits it to be transferred to a new holder by indorsement or delivery. This transfer may be made without the consent or knowledge of the person who made the instrument (the debtor).

Certainly, a nonnegotiable instrument is valid and collectable. It represents a contract that is equally enforceable under ordinary circumstances. However, collection of a nonnegotiable instrument may be defeated if the maker has a legal defense (a legal excuse) against paying it. This is not the case if the holder of a negotiable instrument is a "good-faith," "bona fide," or "innocent holder" for value. Such a person is known legally as a *holder in due course*. A transferee of negotiable paper (holder in due course) takes free from all previous agreements, defenses, or understandings between the original parties.

In some instances where commercial paper is payable to "bearer," this holder-in-due-course principle goes so far as to protect one who innocently acquires the commercial paper from a thief. This principle, of course, differs from the basic idea in property law that a thief can convey no better title than the thief possesses.

To further set the stage for discussion, whether or not an instrument (commercial paper) is negotiable depends entirely on the form in which it is written. These differences are examined in more detail in the material that follows.

Origin of Negotiable Instruments

The first traders to use commercial paper found they needed techniques to pass legal ownership (title) to the document itself that was being substituted for money. This meant that the transfer should have "no strings attached" and that a holder should be able to handle the transfer by placing his or her indorsement (signature) on the back and delivering the document to the new owner. Accordingly, the law merchant and all the modern legal systems based on it (in the United States, Europe, and most of South America) have given preference to commercial paper.

But this special treatment of commercial paper for ease of negotiability comes into conflict with a basic principle of contract law—that of the rights arising from an assignment of a contract. Unless a contract provides for the furnishing of distinctive personal services, the rights arising from it may be sold or assigned to a third party. This, of course, is the legal right of assignment. The person who takes rights under a contract assignment normally "stands in the shoes of the assignor."

Suppose, for example, that a rice dealer in Bombay, India, sold a shipment of rice to a wholesale grocer in San Francisco. The wholesale grocer gave a promissory note (a type of commercial paper) to the rice dealer. In turn, the rice dealer sold the promissory note to a bank in San Francisco. It was subsequently found that the rice did not meet the grading standards for #1 rice, as specified in the contract of purchase. Therefore, the wholesale grocer refused to pay the note on which the transaction was based, offering instead to pay for the cost of #2 rice. Instead of refusing to pay, the wholesale grocer could also have filed suit against the Bombay rice dealer for the difference in value of the two grades of rice.

If the contract rights in the rice had been assigned to the San Francisco bank, then the bank would still be subject to any defenses to payment of the promissory note that the wholesale grocer could assert (here, the defense that the rice was not in compliance with contract specifications). But this transaction did not involve an assignment—it involved the negotiation of an item of commercial paper. Under the law of commercial paper the innocent buyer of the instrument usually takes ownership without being responsible for any disputes between the parties from which the paper originated (this is the so-called "holder-in-due-course" principle).

There is a significant legal difference between an assignment of contract rights and the negotiation of commercial paper. In legal terminology it is said that negotiable commercial paper is "negotiated without baggage," while an assignment is transferred with the buyer "standing in the shoes of the assignor."

Ready negotiability could be seriously hampered if traders, shippers, and bankers had to investigate whether the maker of commercial paper could possibly have some kind of defense against payment. An appreciable delay would automatically defeat the purpose of quick negotiability. Trade and commerce benefit greatly if a merchant, shipper, or banker can tell through a brief examination whether a document qualifies as negotiable commercial paper.

Development of Law of Commercial Paper

When early-day civilizations could only barter, individual possession of goods remained minimal. As soon as money came into general circulation, almost everyone had more usable goods. But there simply never has been enough money available for the needs of trade and business. Early peoples, especially the Romans, worked out the use of written instruments (documents) to represent property rights and money and to serve as substitutes for money in banking and credit transactions. Using commercial paper to represent money, traders found they could increase the flow of commercial transactions several times over. Then, too, the use of paper substitutes reduced the risk of robbery that had always been a threat to every business venture. During the middle ages, merchants continued to use commercial paper in place of money, setting up their own courts to enforce business rights. The body of law that developed became known as the "law merchant," discussed in earlier chapters. This formed the basis for the modern law of commercial paper.

United States laws regulating the use of commercial paper were marked by considerable confusion and lack of uniformity until about 1896, when all states adopted a model code designed to bring about uniformity in state laws. Called the Uniform Negotiable Instruments Law (NIL), this became impractical in some respects as business practices changed. Consequently, in 1942 it was revised and incorporated into the Uniform Commercial Code (UCC), parts of which are already familiar from the laws of sales. After a subsequent revision in 1972, all states except Louisiana adopted those parts of the UCC that pertain to commercial paper. Louisiana adopted parts of the UCC relating to commercial paper as well as UCC provisions regarding "Bank Deposits and Collections" (Article 4); consequently there is near-uniformity with UCC provisions. In interpreting and applying the code, the courts have pointed out that the law of commercial paper has been "a creature of growth, representing the combined results of reason and experience, modified over the years by necessities and changes in commercial affairs."[1]

World experts in trade are in general agreement that the entire economy of the globe would suffer if commercial paper could not circulate freely with ready acceptance in banking and credit circles.

Benefits of Commercial Paper

The circulation of commercial paper performs four vital functions:

1. Some forms of commercial paper are used in lieu of money to pay obligations or to obtain goods when it is impractical, slow, or dangerous to transmit money itself. For example, commercial paper may be sent from one firm to another with a considerably reduced risk of robbery or theft.
2. Some forms of commercial paper are used to obtain the credit needed to stay in business.

[1]Corpus Juris Secundum, "Bills and Notes," Sec. 1, commenting on *Holiday State Bank* v. *Hoffman*, 116 P.239.

3. The use of commercial paper enables individual firms to increase the availability of their working capital, permitting more transactions to be conducted simultaneously.

4. Then, too, the use of commercial paper enables both private firms and national governments to retain better control and regulation of economic matters.

TYPES AND DISTINGUISHING CHARACTERISTICS ——————————

Checks

A *check*, sometimes called a *demand account check* or a *customer check*, is a written order by a bank depositor to pay a specified amount of money from the depositor's account (demand account) to a designated third party.

Actually, a check is the simplest form of bank draft. It is payable on demand and names the bank as *drawee*. Sometimes the bank is termed the *payor bank*. A check is usually a three-party paper. A check differs from other kinds of drafts in that it is always drawn on funds on deposit, whereas a draft is not. A typical arrangement for a check is shown in Figure 3.

Cashier's Check. A check drawn by a bank on itself and signed by that institution's cashier is a *cashier's check*. A check drawn by one bank on another bank has all the attributes of a check but is also sometimes called a *bank draft*.

Certified Check. A *certified check* is one that, in effect, is guaranteed by the bank on which drawn, both as to the amount and as to the authenticity of the signature of the maker. Once presented for certification for a set fee by either the maker or a holder, the check becomes a direct obligation of the

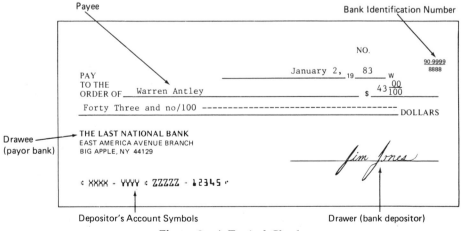

Figure 3 A Typical Check

bank and not an order to pay from the account of the maker. The bank deducts the face amount of the check from the maker's account and marks it "certified" or "accepted." The drawer (maker) (bank depositor) of a certified check cannot stop payment on it as the funds have already been committed.

Traveler's Check. A *traveler's check* is a specialized type of check that is executed or completed by the addition of the owner's signature which must be a duplicate of the owner's signature that was affixed at the time the check was purchased at the bank or issuing agency.

Drafts

A *draft*, known as a *bill of exchange* or simply as a *bill*, is a written order by one person directing a second person to pay a definite amount of money to a third person at a stated time. If desired, the draft may be made payable to the person who draws it. A draft may be payable "at sight" or "on demand" or at a specified date. In one of its most common forms, a draft is addressed to a person who holds money in trust or who acts in the capacity of an agent for the drawer. A typical draft is shown in Figure 4.

Typically, a draft comes into being in a debtor–creditor relationship. Here the drawer-creditor instructs the drawee-debtor to pay all or part of the debt to a third party who is the payee. The payee may be an agent of the drawer or may be someone who is owed money by the drawer. Or, in a different alignment, the drawer may instruct the drawee-debtor to pay the drawer himself or herself.

The mere preparation of the draft does not obligate the drawee on the document, although the drawee may already be obligated by a prior

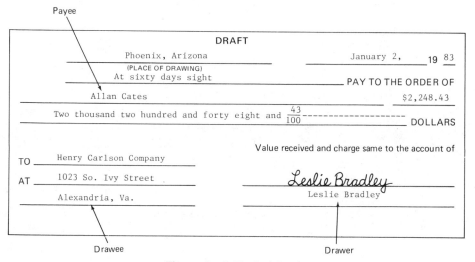

Figure 4 A Typical Draft

transaction. If the drawee does "accept" the draft, this is done by writing the word "accepted" on the face of the draft with the drawee's signature immediately thereunder.

Sellers frequently use a draft to collect money when they feel that a buyer's check may not be good or when the seller does not want to ship merchandise on an open account. For example, a flour mill in California ran short of wheat, needing a full carload. A wheat elevator in Kansas telephonically agreed to ship the grain immediately. While the wheat was being loaded, the grain elevator drew a draft on the flour mill for the agreed price plus the cost of shipping. The draft was attached to the railroad car bill of lading[2] for the shipment and all these papers were taken to the grain elevator's local Kansas bank. This bank mailed the draft (with the bill of lading attached) to a bank in the town where the California flour mill was located. The collection department of the California bank then presented the draft to the flour mill. When payment of the draft was made by the flour mill or credit arrangements worked out, the bill of lading was turned over to the flour mill. The money collected on the draft, except for a collection fee, was sent to the Kansas grain elevator.

A draft for the price of goods or merchandise, drawn on and accepted by a bank in accordance with a previous credit arrangement between the bank and the buyer, is called a *banker's acceptance*.

Promissory Note

A *promissory note*, frequently known as a *note*, is an unconditional written promise to pay a specified sum of money on demand or at a given date to a designated person or "bearer." The individual who signs the note (the debtor) is called the *maker* or *payor* and the one to whom it is made payable is the *payee*. A note is negotiable when it is made payable to "bearer" or "to the order of." A simple form of a negotiable promissory note is shown in Figure 5.

Certificate of Deposit

A *certificate of deposit* is a written acknowledgment or promise of a bank to pay a specified sum of money to a depositor or to the depositor's order on a certain date. In short, it is a type of a promissory note made by a bank. Negotiability depends on the wording of the instrument. The courts in a few states regard a certificate of deposit as an "investment security," along with bonds issued for business or governmental indebtedness. Most courts, how-

---

[2]A *bill of lading* is a written evidence of a contract for the transportation and delivery of a shipment of goods or freight. The holder of the bill of lading is entitled to delivery of the shipment at the point of destination, if freight charges are paid.

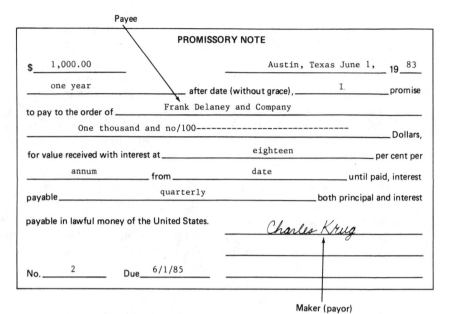

Figure 5   A Simple Negotiable Promissory Note

ever, consider a certificate of deposit as a form of commercial paper. An example of this kind of instrument is given in Figure 6.

NEGOTIABILITY

Requirements for Negotiability

To be negotiable, a piece of commercial paper must comply exactly with five requirements for negotiability specified by the UCC.[3] Nothing else will make the instrument negotiable, even if all parties involved agree that it should be so regarded.

1. The obligation must be in writing.
2. It must be signed by the maker (drawer).
3. It must contain an unconditional promise or order to pay a sum certain in money on demand or at a definite time.
4. It must contain words of negotiability: it must be payable either "to order" or "to bearer."

[3]UCC 3–104(1).

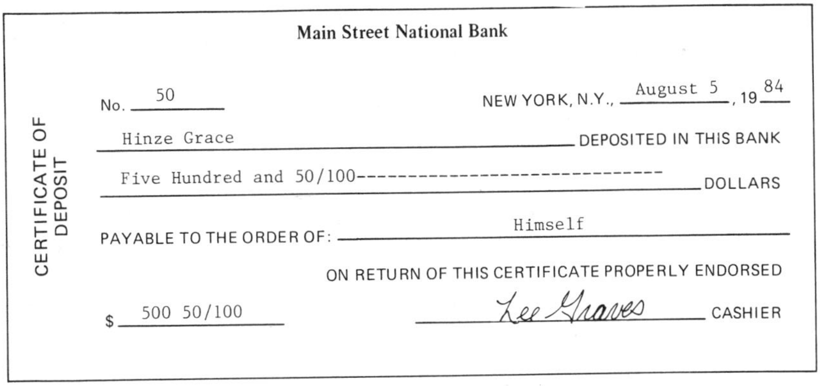

```
                    Main Street National Bank

    No.  50                          NEW YORK, N.Y.,  August 5  , 19 84

    Hinze Grace                                    DEPOSITED IN THIS BANK

    Five Hundred and 50/100-------------------------- DOLLARS

    PAYABLE TO THE ORDER OF:                Himself

                      ON RETURN OF THIS CERTIFICATE PROPERLY ENDORSED

    $   500 50/100              Lee Graves            CASHIER
```

Figure 6   A Certificate of Deposit

5. It must be free from other promises or requirements demanded from the maker.

Requirement of Writing

An oral promise is simply not negotiable. The term "negotiable commercial *paper*" means that it must be a *written* instrument that will pass freely from one trader to another in the commercial field.

_____ *DISCUSSION* _____

CASE 52   A borrower was unusually resentful of the high rate of interest he had to pay to obtain a needed business loan. To dramatize the idea that the lender had "stripped the shirt off his back," the borrower prepared and signed the repayment check on the back of an old, tattered shirt. Would this conform to the UCC requirement that a negotiable instrument must be in writing?

Signature

For negotiability, the obligation must be signed by the maker (drawer). The maker's application of any genuine signature, mark, or symbol on the instrument with the intent to authenticate such instrument constitutes a signature.[4] Placing a trade name, an assumed name, or an alias on the instrument is sufficient to bind the maker if such name is one used by that maker.

As a matter of agency law, a principal is bound on a negotiable instrument when an authorized agent signs for the principal.

[4]UCC 1–201(39).

Unconditional Promise or Order to Pay Sum Certain in Money, on Demand, or at Definite Time

Every negotiable instrument must contain an unconditional promise or unconditional order to pay. A document that purports to be a promissory note is regarded as nonnegotiable if it contains a conditional or limiting statement such as: "I promise to pay $500 per month for rent, but only if the building does not burn down." Similarly, a note was considered nonnegotiable because of a statement that "this promissory note is subject to the terms of a separate lease agreement." However, a statement as to which of the maker's bank accounts should be charged with payment of a note was held not to restrict negotiability.

The courts have decided that payment in any kind of currency, United States or foreign, will satisfy the requirement that payment be made in money.

Negotiability is not affected by a provision in an instrument that in case of default, costs of collection or an attorney's fee shall be added to the face amount due. Recovery of an attorney's fee is limited to a "reasonable amount," but exactly what this means has never been specified by the courts.

An I.O.U. is a mere acknowledgment of debt and is not a promise to pay a sum certain; therefore an I.O.U. is not a promissory note.[5]

The courts hold that the expression "sum certain" does not require absolute certainty at all times. If the amount due can be mathematically calculated as of any given time, this aspect of negotiability has been met. According to UCC provisions:

1. The sum payable is a sum certain even though it is to be paid
   a. with stated interest or by stated installments; or
   b. with stated different rates of interest before and after default or a specified date; or
   c. with a stated discount or addition if paid before or after the date fixed for payment; or
   d. with exchange or less exchange, whether at a fixed rate or at the current rate; or
   e. with costs of collection or an attorney's fee or both upon default.
2. Nothing in this section shall validate any term which is otherwise illegal.[6]

[5]UCC 3–102(1)(c).
[6]UCC 3–106.

Interest Rate

The courts hold that the amount of both principal and interest must be ascertainable and definite from the face of a promissory note. A note specifying that the interest paid shall be "at the bank's prime rate" is not negotiable.[7]

Every state has a so-called *judgment rate of interest*, which is the rate that may legally be added to a judgment. Unless otherwise specified, "a provision for interest means interest at the judgment rate at the place of payment from the date of the instrument, or if it is undated from the date of issue."[8]

Time of Payment

If no time for payment is specified, an otherwise negotiable instrument is held payable "upon presentation" or "at sight."

If an instrument is undated, antedated, or postdated, negotiability is not affected by the date. An undated instrument is regarded as payable on demand. Postdated instruments may be negotiated but are not due until the date stated.

Terms of "Negotiability"

Some key terms must be used if commercial paper is to be negotiable. The instrument must state that it is payable either "to order" or "to bearer." A "bearer instrument" lists no specific individual payee, changing hands without indorsement, in the way that cash may pass from person to person.

An instrument payable "to order" specifies someone as payee, requiring the indorsement of this payee for further negotiation. If the maker intends that an instrument shall be negotiable, it should contain either order or bearer language, since the courts hold that commercial paper "payable to J. Hall" is not negotiable. UCC provisions are to the effect that an instrument is negotiable if payable to "two or more payees together or in the alternative" (jointly or individually).[9]

A check or other instrument payable to "cash" is considered a bearer instrument, being negotiable without indorsement.[10]

If the important phrases of negotiability are left off a document (payable

---

[7] *Alport* v. *Evans*, 317 N.Y.S.2d 937.
[8] UCC 3–118(d).
[9] UCC 3–110(4).
[10] UCC 3–111(c).

to order or bearer), the instrument is nonnegotiable. The consequence is that the holder of such paper can never be a holder in due course. In some cases this may make a considerable difference in the holder's liability.

Freedom from Other Promises

The UCC mandates that:

> Any writing to be a negotiable instrument within this Article must . . . contain an unconditional promise or order to pay a sum certain in money and no other promise, order, obligation or power given by the maker or drawer except as authorized by this Article . . .[11]

In one case the maker of a promissory note stated: "I promise to pay $1,000 or to surrender title to my red Buick convertible automobile, identification # . . . whichever is requested by the bearer." The courts held that this instrument was not "free from other promises" and was therefore nonnegotiable. However, a statement of the transaction that gives rise to the instrument does not affect its negotiability.

In deciding cases of this kind, the courts point out that all obligations of the maker of negotiable commercial paper should be readily ascertainable at the time the instrument was prepared. The courts also say that such negotiable instrument should be "free of clutter or side issues." In short, the courts sometimes add that an instrument of this kind should be "a courier without language."

Court Construction of Ambiguities

As a general rule the courts say that in case of ambiguity in an instrument, the presumption is against negotiability. This is also an underlying theme in some sections of the UCC.[12]

When the sum payable in a negotiable instrument is set out both in words and in figures, the UCC provides that the sum denoted by the written words is to be controlling.[13] Bank sources state that it is relatively common to find examples of this kind of inconsistency on customer checks.

Thus, in case of a discrepancy between handwritten and printed or typewritten provisions of the document, the handwritten provisions are to control.[14]

---

[11]UCC 3–104(b).
[12]UCC 3–104, 3–118.
[13]UCC 3–318(c).
[14]UCC 3–318(b).

THE HOLDER IN DUE COURSE (HDC) ─────────────────

HDC Defined

A *holder* is anyone legally in possession of commercial paper.

A *holder in due course* (HDC) is one who has legal possession of commercial paper (a negotiable instrument), having obtained it in good faith and without any knowledge of fraud or dishonesty involving the instrument. It must be obtained for value and without any awareness that it is overdue or that payment has been refused or that the maker has a legal defense against payment of it.

Qualifying as HDC

UCC requirements specify that:

1. A holder in due course is a holder who takes the instrument
   a. for value; and
   b. in good faith; and
   c. without notice that it is overdue or has been dishonored or has any defense against or claim to it on the part of any person.
2. A payee may be a holder in due course.
3. A holder does not become a holder in due course of an instrument:
   a. by purchase of it at judicial sale or by taking it under legal process; or
   b. by acquiring it in taking over an estate; or
   c. by purchasing it as part of a bulk transaction not in regular course of business of the transferor.
4. A purchaser of a limited interest can be a holder in due course only to the extent of the interest purchased.[15]

The terms *value* and *consideration* do not mean the same thing. Consideration is one of the essentials for a negotiable instrument. Under contract law, an executory promise is sufficient to constitute consideration. But an executory promise does not qualify as value for a holder in due course. A promise to give value in the future is insufficient, then, unless the executory promise is in the form of a *letter of credit* which is an irrevocable commitment of credit by a bank or other financier.[16]

If part of the consideration paid is executory, the person purchasing the

─────────────────

[15]UCC 3–302.
[16]UCC 3–303(c).

instrument can be a holder in due course for that percentage of the price that is not executory.[17]

The courts do not balance or weigh the value given for adequacy, unless the worth of the value paid is so out of proportion that it may be an indication of fraud. A holder also takes "for value" when the instrument is given either as satisfaction for a prior obligation or in payment of such debt.

By crediting a customer's account with the face amount of an instrument, a bank does not become a holder for value until such time as the customer has drawn on the credit created by the instrument.

The requirement of "good faith" means that in obtaining the instrument in question the buyer must have honestly lacked any notice or knowledge of any defense to the instrument or any defect pertaining to it. If the buyer acquires the instrument in good faith, it is immaterial whether the seller's transfer was in good faith. The courts usually say that a mere basis for suspicion does not put the buyer on notice or require an investigation to determine whether defects in the instrument in fact exist. This is sometimes described by the courts as the "doctrine of the white heart and empty head." The courts also say that there is a general policy against imputing notice to an apparently good-faith purchaser, short of actual knowledge.

At the same time, the courts often rule that a purchaser cannot be oblivious to facts that place himself or herself on notice of possible fraud. Neither can the person acquiring the instrument purposefully avoid finding out the truth. The UCC states that:

> A person has "notice" of a fact when . . . from all the facts and circumstances known to him at the time in question he has reason to know that it exists.[18]

DISCUSSION

CASE 53   Partner A was observed by a bank employee to strike through the indorsement on a check reading: "Deposit to A and B Partnership Account" which had been signed by both Partner A and Partner B. In the presence of the bank employee, Partner A then deposited the check in his personal checking account. The bank made no inquiry concerning Partner A's authority to strike out the indorsement to the partnership account. Could the bank thereafter claim to have taken the check in "good faith" as a holder in due course? (*Christian* v. *California Bank*, 30 Cal.2d 421.)

Generally the courts have determined that the fact that a purchaser has acquired an instrument at a discount—that is, at less than the face amount—

[17] UCC 3–302(4).
[18] UCC 1–201(25)(c).

does not in itself constitute "bad faith." But a purchase at a very large discount, coupled with other suspicious circumstances, could justify a court in a finding of a lack of good faith, depriving the buyer of a holder-in-due-course status.[19]

Ignorance of Overdue or Dishonored Status

Commercial paper may still be negotiated, even though it is overdue, has been dishonored (payment refused), or has been outstanding for more than a reasonable time. And the buyer may sometimes still recover against the maker, although the buyer cannot qualify as a holder in due course.

Sometimes it is not apparent from an examination of the instrument that it is overdue or has been dishonored. If a due date appears on the instrument and that date is past, obviously a purchaser cannot be a holder in due course. A check has been held for more than a reasonable time after issue if it is still outstanding after 30 days.[20]

_____ *DISCUSSION* _____

CASE 54   A merchant gave a promissory note to a manufacturer for a shipment of toys. Needing money for raw materials, the manufacturer sold the merchant's note to a bank for a discount. At the time the note was purchased by the bank, the manufacturer commented that the merchant claimed toys in part of the shipment were defective. Was the bank entitled to claim the status of a holder in due course?

Successors to a Holder in Due Course

UCC provisions state that:

> Transfer of an instrument vests in the transferee such rights as the transferor has therein, except that a transferee who has himself been a party to any fraud or illegality affecting the instrument or who as a prior holder had notice of a defense or claim against it cannot improve his position by taking from a later holder in due course.[21]

The courts hold that those acquiring an instrument from a holder in due course are entitled to take the rights of a holder in due course, whether or not the new holder can also qualify as a holder in due course. It is immaterial how far down a chain of transferees an individual may be, pro-

[19] *U.S. Finance Co.* v. *Jones,* 229 So.2d 495.
[20] UCC 3–304(c).
[21] UCC 3–201.

vided that someone in the prior chain qualified as a holder in due course. The only exception to this rule is that a person who once held the instrument with knowledge of illegality or defect cannot eliminate this knowledge by selling to a holder in due course and thereafter repurchasing it.

――――――― *DISCUSSION* ―――――――――――――――――――――――

CASE 55 A farmer gave a promissory note to a merchant to pay for a plow that was later found to be defective. The merchant sold the note for value to another merchant who acquired the instrument as a holder in due course. Thereafter, the second merchant learned that the farmer had a defense to payment of the note. The second merchant then gave the note to his son as a gift. Clearly the son was not a holder in due course, since he had not paid value. In addition, the son was aware of the farmer's defense at the time he acquired the note. In view of these problems, did the son have the same status as a holder in due course?

Limitations on HDC Principle in Consumer Sales

The holder-in-due-course principle in the law of commercial paper was originated as fundamentally a trader's or merchant's law. Its purpose was to insulate lenders from quarrels between the immediate parties to the instrument. Between traders and merchants the principle is still considered as necessary and practical as ever. But in recent years the application of the HDC principle to consumer purchasing transactions has often caused hardships.

Because of the great number of consumer products now available in the marketplace, buyers are often unable to judge the quality of items offered for sale. In addition, goods manufactured from new raw materials and through new processes are not familiar to consumers. When an unscrupulous trader or merchant sells defective or shoddy merchandise on credit, the buyer may be injured if the courts follow the HDC principle. The buyer may be unable to obtain repairs or replacements from a seller who has gone out of business. If in the meantime the seller has sold the buyer's promissory note to an "innocent" finance company, the buyer will be forced to pay, notwithstanding the fact that the buyer had a good defense against the dishonest or "fly-by-night" seller.

The consumer problem in the HDC situation was described by the court in a leading case, as follows:

> The protections offered a holder in due course were evolved by merchants, bankers, and lawyers to facilitate the flow of *true* commercial paper. . . .
>
> It has been assumed they [consumer contracts] were negotiable instruments which, after a quick transfer, were impregnable to most

defenses the consumer would have against the purveyor. Under the umbrella labeled "free flow of commercial paper" have flourished not only legitimate businesses but the most pernicious rackets. . . .[22]

Consumer Legislation and the HDC Principle. To protect consumers, a number of states have enacted laws in recent years that limit or eliminate the application of the HDC principle in consumer purchasing and financing transactions. These statutes take varying approaches to the problem:

1. Some state laws provide that any assignee of a retail buying contract takes the instrument subject to any defenses the retail buyer had against the seller. Enactments of this kind actually eliminate the HDC principle in consumer situations.
2. Some laws simply prohibit the use of *waiver of defense* clauses in sales to consumers.
3. Still other laws require that the consumer shall be advised of the sale of his or her obligation (promissory note, or whatever) and given 10 days in which to advise of claims that the consumer has against the retail seller.
4. Statutes in still other jurisdictions require that the seller's contract obligations be spelled out on the face of the consumer sales obligation, thus destroying negotiability by putting a buyer of the paper on notice. Consequently, the buyer of the instrument cannot be a holder in due course.

As yet, not all states have statutes that protect the consumer from the operation of the holder in due course doctrine. In some of these jurisdictions an increasing number of courts have "imputed" knowledge of the consumer's defenses to the financing company that buys commercial paper where that buyer worked closely and regularly with the company or individual making the retail sale to the consumer.[23]

FTC Regulation of the HDC Principle in Consumer Sales. The Federal Trade Commission (FTC) has authority to issue administrative rules "to prohibit unfair or deceptive acts or practices in or affecting interstate commerce."[24] This authority of the FTC extends only to "interstate commerce," but this phrase has been held to include intrastate transactions completed through use of the telephone or the mails. Consequently, the FTC authority extends to the bulk of all consumer sales. In 1976 the FTC issued a rule that any consumer credit contract must contain a printed notice that any holder or assignee of the consumer's obligation is subject to all claims and defenses that the consumer could raise against the seller. For all practical purposes,

---

[22] *Geiger Finance Co.* v. *Graham*, 182 S.E.2d 521.
[23] *Commercial Credit Co.* v. *Childs*, 137 S.W.2d 260.
[24] Title 15, U.S. Code, Sec. 45.

the FTC ruling has effectively eliminated the application of the holder-in-due-course principle in most retail consumer sales transactions.

———— *QUESTIONS* ————

1. Is the study of commercial paper sometimes called the study of negotiable instruments or the study of bills and notes?
2. What are the advantages to business or trade in utilizing commercial paper?
3. Why is there a need for ready negotiability of commercial paper?
4. Explain how a regular check differs from a cashier's check.
5. Describe how a draft may be used in a debtor–creditor relationship.
6. What are the requirements for negotiability?
7. What is a holder in due course? What is the advantage in being such a holder?
8. If a purchaser buys a negotiable instrument for value, but at a discount, is this fact alone sufficient to deprive the buyer of a holder-in-due-course status?
9. Explain the rights of a successor to a holder in due course in the chain of ownership of a negotiable instrument.
10. Does the holder-in-due-course principle apply in consumer purchases? What is the legal trend in this regard?
11. How has the Federal Trade Commission stepped in to negate the holder-in-due-course principle in most consumer sales?

———— *ANSWERS TO DISCUSSION CASES* ————

Case 52   The writing on the shirt, or on any other material, is sufficient to satisfy the legal requirement that a negotiable instrument must be in writing.

Case 53   The bank did not take as a holder in due course. The bank's employee should have made inquiry to ascertain whether Partner A had authority to strike out the indorsement to the partnership account.

Case 54   The bank was aware that the toys were apparently defective; consequently the bank could not claim to be a holder in due course.

Case 55   The son of the second merchant was not a party to any wrong and was a successor to a holder in due course (merchant number 2). Therefore the son was entitled to be a holder in due course by succession, although he had not paid value.

_____ *PROBLEM CASES* _____

1   Humphrey wrote a check on his account and gave it to the payee. Subse-
    quently, a thief stole the check and passed it after forging the payee's in-
    dorsement on the back. The check continued to be circulated and was
    negotiated to one Miller, an innocent party who had no knowledge of any
    irregularity. Miller indorsed the check and cashed it at the Citizen's Bank.
    When payment was refused, Citizen's Bank sued Miller as a prior indorser.
    Who would prevail? (*Citizen's Bank* v. *Miller*, 11 So.2d 457.)

2   An individual had a checking account at a bank where he also had loans
    outstanding. He wrote checks on this account to pay off his loans, but he
    was accidentally killed before these checks were credited against his loans.
    Creditors of the deceased, other than the bank, claimed that the bank was
    giving preference to its own loans and that the money in the deceased's bank
    account should be available equally to all creditors. Could the bank cash the
    checks within a reasonable time and thus make such payments to itself? (*In
    re Schenk's Estate*, 313 N.Y.S. 277.)

3   A maker executed a promissory note that incorporated a promise to "pay
    interest at bank rates." The holder of this note filed a lawsuit to collect on
    the note as a holder in due course. The maker contended that the note was
    not negotiable since the interest rate was not definite. Decide. (*Alport* v. *Hotel
    Evans*, 317 N.Y.S.2d 937.)

25

Commercial Paper: Negotiation; Claims and Defenses; Liability of the Parties

Requirements for Negotiation

Negotiation is the process by which commercial paper and other instruments are passed along from one person to another, with the latter person being legally termed the *holder*.[1]

An instrument payable to order is negotiated by the payee when he or she writes his or her name on the back and delivers it to the new holder. This affixing of the signature is, of course, called an *indorsement* (sometimes spelled *endorsement*).

If the instrument is payable to the bearer or if the last indorsement consisted merely of the signature of the payee, it may be negotiated by delivery to a new holder, passing as freely as money.[2] No indorsement is needed for a bearer instrument.

The Nature of Indorsement

An indorsement may consist of any writing or printed material placed on the back that has a relationship to the instrument. While an indorsement is typically placed on the reverse side, the courts also recognize a signature placed on the front so long as it was intended as an indorsement. The party writing the indorsement is called the *indorser*, and the one receiving the instrument is called the *indorsee*. A portion of the back of an instrument may be used for indorsements as it passes through a series of negotiations. Federal banking regulations limit the space available for this purpose.

[1]UCC 3–202(1).
[2]UCC 3–111.

At times a payee (transferor) of a bearer instrument may fail to indorse it prior to transfer, through oversight or otherwise. As we shall see, the legal effect of indorsement in most circumstances is to make the indorser responsible to pay the instrument if the maker does not pay it when due. The delivery of such an instrument without an indorsement is treated by the law as a mere assignment of rights and not as a negotiation to a holder in due course. Until the transferee receives the indorsement, the instrument cannot be negotiated. This is because the courts say the transferee has not yet received "title," which is a requirement for negotiation. But the transferee can usually correct the lack of an indorsement, even if the transferor of the instrument refuses to cooperate.

The law gives a transferee who paid value for the instrument the right to go into court and have the judge order an indorsement. When the indorsement is obtained, the transferee automatically becomes a holder with both title and possession.[3] While this legal remedy is effective, it may involve the time and cost of a lawsuit.

The missing indorsement could deprive the transferee of ever becoming a holder in due course. This is because the transferee's knowledge of defenses against the instrument is measured as of the time he or she obtains the missing indorsement so that the transferee who learned of a defense to the instrument during the interval between obtaining possession and securing the indorsement would not be a holder in due course.

In addition, when the indorsement is lacking, the transferee can sue to enforce the instrument if it is due. But to collect in such a suit the transferee would have to prove ownership rights and would be subject to defenses that might be raised by the maker.

If an indorsement is required, therefore, both individuals and businesses should make certain the transfer is not made without an indorsement.

Validity of Indorsement

Before title to an instrument passes, the payee's indorsement must be both valid and authorized. For example, a merchant taking delivery of diamonds gave a check payable to the seller. While the seller was en route back to his office, the check was taken from the seller's billfold in an armed robbery. The robber forged the diamond seller's name as an indorsement on the back of the check and succeeded in cashing the check at a bank some distance away. There was no valid indorsement. The forgery broke the chain of title so no subsequent possessor of the instrument could qualify as a holder, much less as a holder in due course.[4] Consequently, the maker of the check (the merchant) was not required to pay it. The bank that cashed the check

[3] UCC 3–201(3).
[4] UCC 3–404(1).

for the armed robber was the loser. This result in the law of commercial paper is consistent with general principles of property law where it is held that a thief can never transfer better title than he or she possesses.

The UCC provides that a forged or unauthorized indorsement of the payee's signature can be subsequently made valid by ratification if circumstances should ever be such that the payee desired that result.[5]

Usual Forms of Indorsement

Various kinds of indorsements, usually called *blank, special, qualified, restrictive,* or *collection indorsements,* may have an effect on the instrument involved. New banking regulations require individuals to indorse their checks on a specified portion of the back of the instrument to enable their computers to read the signatures. Most banks invalidate indorsements if they are not placed within the marked area on the check.

Blank Indorsement. Perhaps the great majority of all indorsements are so-called *blank indorsements* or *regular indorsements* of the kind usually placed on a check (see Figure 7). The indorser simply writes his or her name on the back of the instrument which then becomes payable to the bearer and may be cashed by whoever is the bearer.

If you receive a check payable to you, you should never indorse it until you are ready to cash it. If you should lose the check after indorsing it, the finder may cash it at any bank without question.

Special Indorsement. An *indorsement in full* or *special indorsement* designates the person to whom the instrument is to be paid or upon whose order it is to be paid. Typically, a special indorsement written by Mary Atwell may read: "Pay to the order of Joe Gates. Mary Atwell." With such an indorsement the instrument is not payable to anyone except Joe Gates. This indorsement is shown in Figure 8.

If a blank indorsement has already been placed on the instrument by Melvin Kaler, it can be converted to a special indorsement by writing above Kaler's blank indorsement the notation: "Pay to Mae Cooper." This conversion is shown in Figure 9. The special indorsement means that Mae Cooper alone, upon gaining possession, has title and consequently is the only possible holder. No one after Cooper can qualify as a holder without Cooper's valid indorsement.

Qualified Indorsement. A indorsement that includes the words "without recourse" above the payee's (indorser's) signature is a *qualified indorsement.* These words serve to limit the legal liability otherwise placed on the indorser. Normally, indorsing one's name on the back of negotiable paper makes the

---

[5]UCC 3–404(2).

Figure 7   Blank Indorsement

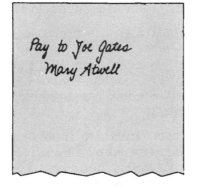

Figure 8   Special Indorsement

Check made payable to Melvin Kaler
has become "bearer paper" by Kaler's
indorsement. Mae Cooper, a holder
after Kaler, may convert it back to
"order paper" by writing: "pay to
Mae Cooper" above Kaler's
signature.

Figure 9   Example of Conversion of Blank Indorsement to Special Indorsement
("Bearer Paper" to "Order Paper")

indorser a kind of surety for both the maker and all parties who indorsed earlier. The qualified indorsement "without recourse" has the effect of passing title without placing liability for nonpayment on the indorser. It avoids any promise of payment. At the same time, the courts usually hold that a qualified indorser warrants that the instrument is genuine. Consequently, a qualified indorser is still held to liability by most courts if the maker's name or that of one of the prior indorsers was forged, or if the maker had been adjudged insane or if the maker was a minor at the time the instrument was made. A qualified indorsement is shown in Figure 10.

Restrictive Indorsement. A *restrictive indorsement* is an indorsement so worded as to restrict the further negotiability of the instrument. Sometimes an indorsement of this kind includes conditions, such as: "Pay to Mary Caton only if she has paid her note to the First National Bank in full." Some indorsements of this kind are used to restrict any further negotiation of a check except for collection such as: "Pay any bank," "For deposit only," or "Pay to the Dime Savings Bank for collection." An indorsement of this kind prevents the misuse or embezzlement of a check by a company messenger or by a finder in the event it blows out a car window en route to the bank. An example of a restrictive indorsement is shown in Figure 11.

Collection Indorsement. A *collection indorsement* or *indorsement for collection* is a type of restrictive indorsement that limits the instrument to being collected upon only with no further negotiation. While such an indorsement may sometimes be used with checks or any kind of commercial paper, it is typically used with promissory notes. An example of a collection indorsement is shown in Figure 12.

Accommodation Indorsements; Irregular Indorsements. In some instances an instrument may be indorsed by a third party before the payee indorses it. Usually the purpose in this third-party signature is to lend the credit of the indorser (third party) to the maker, although at times the purpose may be to lend the indorser's credit to the payee. An indorsement by a

Without Recourse

Clara Nell McDermett

Figure 10   Qualified Indorsement

Figure 11   Restrictive Indorsement

Figure 12   A Collection Indorsement

third party to lend credit to one of the other parties is termed an *accommodation indorsement*. When the accommodation signature appears before that of the person who has been accommodated, this type of indorsement is also called an *irregular indorsement*. The law provides that: "An accommodation party is not liable to the party accommodated. . . ."[6] To all subsequent holders the accommodation indorser is liable just as a regular indorser is.[7] But an accommodation party forced to pay has the right of recourse on the instrument against a defaulting accommodated party.[8]

Conditional Indorsement. A *conditional indorsement* annexes some contingency to the indorser's liability. This technique is usually used to transfer possession of the instrument to another party without transferring title until some condition has been met. For example, a garage mechanic wanted payment in advance for fixing an automobile. The owner wrote a check to himself as payee, indorsing it, "Pay to the order of _____Garage upon

[6]UCC 3–415(5).
[7]UCC 3–415(1).
[8]UCC 3–415(5).

completion of repairs to my pickup truck. Will Bennett." The garageman can transfer the check to another holder, but such a subsequent holder accepts the check subject to having the automobile repaired.

Partial Payment Indorsement. It is accepted procedure for the payee to make a notation of any amount paid on the back of a promissory note, followed by the payee's signature. This is sometimes termed a *partial payment indorsement.*

Order of Indorsers' Liability

When there are a number of indorsers on a negotiable instrument, the law provides:

> Unless they otherwise agree, indorsers are liable to one another in the order in which they indorse, which is presumed to be the order in which their signatures appear on the instrument.[9]

Indorsement of Partial Interest

Sometimes the holder of an instrument adds an indorsement that attempts a negotiation of less than the face amount of the instrument. For example, one indorsement read: "Pay $100 to Henry Haines and $50 to Warren Wilson (signed) Alice Barnard." The courts usually rule that an indorsement of this kind is ineffective for negotiation. Reasoning of the courts here is based on a UCC provision: "An indorsement is effective for negotiation only when it conveys the entire instrument or any unpaid residue. . . ."[10]

However, an indorsement such as "Pay Henry Haines and Warren Wilson (signed) Alice Barnard" would constitute a negotiation. In this instance, both Haines and Wilson would be legally qualified as "holders" with ownership as tenants in common of the whole amount.

Indorsements of Multiple Payees

Sometimes a check or other negotiable instrument will be made payable to multiple payees. If the payees' names are connected by the word "and," then the instrument is payable to both jointly. Further negotiation of the instrument is effective only if all such payees indorse. For example, a dividend check from General Motors Corporation payable to "Charles and Mary King, Joint Tenants" would require the indorsement of both Charles King and Mary King before a bank would cash it. Without both signatures, the bank could not further negotiate the check. But a check payable to Charles

[9]UCC 3–414(2).
[10]UCC 3–202(3).

or Mary King could be negotiated by the indorsement of either. Ownership of the check would be established in either Charles King or Mary King, whoever indorsed the instrument.[11]

Error in Payee's Name

When an instrument is made payable under a misspelled name or under a wrong name, the payee should first indorse by signing with the misspelled or incorrect version listed on the face of the instrument. The payee's correct name should then be indorsed immediately under the erroneous version. A subsequent holder should never accept an indorsement that does not correspond exactly to the name listed for the payee. The UCC specifies that a transferee giving value for the instrument may require the payee to indorse in either or both the incorrect version and the payee's correct name.[12] Banks or businesses cashing checks usually ask that the incorrect indorsement be followed by the correct one.

Ambiguity Concerning a Signature

At times there may be a dispute concerning whether a particular individual signed an instrument as a maker, indorser, or guarantor. UCC provisions state that "unless the instrument clearly indicates that a signature is made in some other capacity, it is an indorsement."[13] The courts ordinarily do not allow oral testimony (parol evidence) of the parties to explain. This, of course, automatically results in indorser liability.

Most courts allow one exception to this presumption that the person signing was an indorser. If the questioned signature was located in the lower right-hand corner of a promissory note, the courts will assume that it was intended to be that of the maker, unless there is some indication to the contrary.[14]

DEFENSES TO PAYMENT OF NEGOTIABLE INSTRUMENTS _____

A "defense" is a legal basis for refusing to pay all or part of the money due on a negotiable instrument. Some defenses can be asserted against anyone holding the paper, but most defenses cannot be raised if the person demanding payment is a holder in due course.

Defenses to payment fall into one of two classes, according to their nature: (1) *personal defenses*, and (2) *real defenses* (sometimes called *absolute*

[11] UCC 3–116.
[12] UCC 3–203.
[13] UCC 3–402.
[14] *Philadelphia Bond and Mortgage* v. *Highland Crest Homes, Inc.*, 288 A.2d 916.

defenses). A personal defense is one that can be claimed only between the original parties to the instrument. A real defense, however, is said by the courts "to attach to the instrument itself," following along wherever the instrument is negotiated. A real defense, then, may be claimed against a holder in due course or against anyone.

Real Defenses

The following real defenses may be raised against either a holder in due course or any other holder: (1) want of execution of the instrument; (2) infancy; (3) incapacity to contract; (4) duress; (5) forgery, fraud, or material alteration; (6) illegality; and (7) discharge by insolvency proceedings, including bankruptcy.

Want of Execution: Fraud in the Factum. If the maker is induced to sign a paper that he or she believes is something other than a negotiable instrument, but that is actually a negotiable instrument, there is a real defense against payment. A fraudulent inducement of this kind is sometimes legally called *want of execution* or *fraud in the factum*. It results from such misrepresentation as has persuaded the maker to sign the instrument with neither knowledge nor reasonable opportunity to learn of the document's essential makeup. For example, a foreign immigrant who could not read English was persuaded to sign a promissory note in the belief that it was an employment contract. This is the type of fraud that provides a real defense.

Most courts say that want of execution or fraud in the factum cannot be raised if the maker of the instrument did not take reasonable steps to determine the real nature of the transaction in question. The maker who fails to use prudence cannot claim to have been victimized by fraud.

_____ *DISCUSSION* _____

CASE 56   The purchaser of an automobile was allowed to read a printed form that appeared to be a bill of sale. After he had read the document very carefully, the person selling the car managed by sleight of hand to substitute another paper that from a distance appeared to be the one the buyer had just read. This new form merely gave the prospective purchaser the right to use the automobile on a yearly lease. Believing that he had read the instrument in question and understood it to be a bill of sale, the prospective customer signed. Could the fraud be raised as a defense?

Infancy. Infancy is a real defense if it would be permitted as a defense under state law in a suit to enforce a contract against a juvenile.

Incapacity. An incompetent signing a negotiable instrument, such as one who is feebleminded or insane, usually cannot be held for payment of the instrument. Such incapacity can be used as a real defense, but only if state law specifies that the contract of an incompetent is void from the outset, rather than merely voidable.[15]

Illegality. Illegality in the basic transaction may be used as a real defense in some instances while constituting only a personal defense in others. If the contract that gave rise to the negotiable instrument is declared illegal by state statute, then the illegality will make the instrument void even in the hands of a holder in due course. But if the contractual obligation is merely voidable under state law, then it can be used only as a personal defense.

For example, an individual who gambled widely, traveling from state to state, gave a check to pay for gambling losses in a state where gambling was illegal by statute. The winner negotiated the check to a bank, which received it as a holder in due course. The maker of the check (the gambler) tried to stop payment on it and was able to assert illegality as a real defense against the bank, a holder in due course. Shortly afterward the traveling gambler gave a check to a Las Vegas, Nevada, casino to pay gambling losses at that place. The casino negotiated the check to a bank. The gambler was forced to pay this check since gambling is legal in Nevada.

Duress. Duress is sometimes a real defense; occasionally it is merely a personal one. The UCC states that duress is a real defense if it is the kind that will render "the obligation of the party a nullity."[16] In applying the law, courts look to the degree of duress. If a negotiable instrument was signed only after someone held a knife to the maker's throat, the courts are in agreement that the maker would have a real defense. However, if the victim of a theft threatened a criminal prosecution unless the thief's father signed a check for repayment of the loss, the duress involved would not constitute a real defense. Some courts would allow such duress to be used as a personal defense, however.

Forgery. A negotiable instrument cannot be enforced by any holder who obtained possession from one who forged the maker's name. The forgery is a real defense against anyone in the chain of possession.

But one who indorses a forged instrument and passes it on to another cannot be relieved of liability since the essence of indorsement is to warrant that the instrument is genuine, that the indorser has good title to it, and that all prior parties had capacity to contract.

Any *material alteration* on the face of an instrument or a change in terms may provide the basis for a partial real defense. For example, a thief stole a check from the cash register of a store, raising the amount of the check from $25 to $250. Thereafter the thief negotiated the check to a holder in due course. In a situation of this kind, the maker of the instrument could use the

[15]UCC 3–305(2)(b).
[16]UCC 3–305(b).

material alteration as a real defense against paying the entire amount of $250. The maker was already liable to pay $25, however, and could therefore claim a real defense only against the amount above $25 ($225).

Discharge by Insolvency Proceedings (Including Bankruptcy) as a Real Defense. The code provides that a discharge from debt under insolvency proceedings is a real defense against payment of a negotiable instrument prior to the insolvency.[17] Insolvency proceedings means any *assignment for the benefit of creditors*, any other liquidation proceeding authorized under state law, or a discharge under the Federal Bankruptcy Act. The latter is the most commonly used kind of discharge in insolvency, excusing the bankrupt from almost all the debts listed in the bankruptcy petition. Consequently, the bankrupt would have a real defense against payment of negotiable instruments and other debts not specifically exempted under the bankruptcy laws.

Personal Defenses

Personal defenses are those that the maker of a negotiable instrument may assert against one to whom the maker transferred it. They include every defense available in ordinary contract lawsuits. Typical personal defenses include prior payment, lack of consideration, failure of consideration, breach of contract, breach of warranty, impossibility of performance, and mutual mistake. Personal defenses will not prevail against a holder in due course.

Prior Payment or Cancellation. When commercial paper is paid before it falls due, the individual paying off the obligation should demand delivery of the instrument. Otherwise there is the possibility that it may be negotiated again. If the previously paid instrument is negotiated to a holder in due course, the prior payment may not be raised as a defense. Of course, it would be a personal defense among the original parties.

Thus when the holder and the party primarily liable on an instrument have agreed to mark it "cancelled," this action should not be overlooked.

As a somewhat similar application of this rule, an order to stop payment of a check cannot be raised as a defense by the drawer (maker) of the check against a holder in due course.

Nondelivery of Completed Instrument. As a general rule, an instrument is not legally effective until it has been delivered by the maker. The reason is that the maker may want to change the instrument before turning it over to another party. If a business executive signs a check and leaves it undelivered inside a desk, the instrument is not legally effective until delivery. Nondelivery may be asserted as a personal defense.

---

[17]UCC 1–201(22).

_____ *DISCUSSION* _____

CASE 57   Jones obtained a loan of $1,000 from Smith, prepared a promissory note in this amount payable to Smith, and left the note in his own desk over the weekend. Jones then discovered that two of the ten $100 bills given to him by Smith were counterfeit. In the meantime Smith found the undelivered promissory note and sold it to the neighborhood bank, a holder in due course. The bank sued Jones for nonpayment of the note and Jones pleaded nondelivery. Would this defense succeed?

Failure of Consideration. Failure of consideration is a typical personal defense that may be used between the parties to a contractual agreement.

_____ *DISCUSSION* _____

CASE 58   A vacuum cleaner repair shop requested a check in advance for repairs. Before the repairs were made the shop burned to the ground with the vacuum cleaner being a total loss. In the meantime the customer's check to the repair shop had been negotiated to the neighborhood bank. As a holder in due course, could the bank collect the check? Could the repair shop collect on the check if it had not been negotiated to the bank?

Fraud as a Personal Defense. Fraud can be claimed as a real defense only when the misrepresentation was such as to induce "the party to sign with neither knowledge nor reasonable opportunity to obtain knowledge of its character or its essential terms."[18] Any other kind of fraud, which includes most examples, may be raised as a personal defense but may not be claimed against a holder in due course.

_____ *DISCUSSION* _____

CASE 59   An individual offering to sell an automobile told a prospective buyer that the vehicle had gone only 10,000 miles, since it had been owned by a little old great-grand-mother in Pasadena who wore a bonnet and tennis shoes. The car actually had 87,000 miles. The odometer had been set back in an effort to hide the fact that the vehicle had been driven for five years by a traveling sales representative. Would this kind of fraud serve as a defense against payment of a negotiable instrument given in payment for the car?

[18]UCC 3–305(2)(c).

RELATIONSHIP BETWEEN BANKS AND DEPOSITORS ————————

The UCC spells out some of the legal relationships between a "payor bank" (drawee bank) and the bank's customer (drawer) who has money on deposit.[19]

Wrongful Dishonor

If a check or another item written by the customer is properly payable from his or her account but the bank refuses to pay it, the customer has grounds for a lawsuit against the bank for "wrongful dishonor." The UCC delineates:

> When the dishonor occurs through mistake, liability is limited to actual damages proved. If so proximately caused and proved, damages may include damages for an arrest or prosecution of the customer or other consequential damages. Whether any consequential damages are proximately caused by the wrongful dishonor is a question of fact to be determined in each case.[20]

The courts have interpreted this UCC provision to mean that actual damage must be proved before a recovery will be permitted against the bank. However, if the bank intentionally refuses to pay a check when funds to cover it are in the customer's account, some courts have awarded damages for mental and emotional stress. Where the bank has gone so far as to refuse to pay in bad faith, punitive damages have been allowed without requiring the plaintiff (bank customer) to prove the actual amount of the injury.

Incompetence or Death of Depositor

Incompetency or death of a bank customer raises questions concerning when the bank should refuse to honor checks or other negotiable instruments payable out of the customer's account.

The law provides that a bank's payment or collection activities taken prior to knowledge of incompetency or death of a customer are valid and proper.[21] The bank has no responsibility to alter bank payment or collection practices until the bank employee responsible for closing down such accounts has actual knowledge of the customer's incompetency or death and "has reasonable opportunity to act on it."[22] In addition, the UCC provides:

---

[19]UCC 4–401 to 4–504.
[20]UCC 4–402.
[21]UCC 4–405(1).
[22]UCC 4–405(1).

Even with knowledge a bank may for ten days after the date of death pay or certify checks drawn on or prior to that date unless ordered to stop payment by a person claiming an interest in the account.[23]

Regardless of the provisions of the UCC, income tax laws in most states require a bank to freeze an account upon hearing of the customer's death.

Payment After Stop Order

If the bank pays a check after a customer has placed a stop payment order, the bank is liable for the loss sustained by the depositor.

A bank is also usually liable to the depositor if the bank pays a check on which the depositor's signature has been forged. Accordingly, the burden of verifying all customer signatures is on the bank. The signature card placed on file at the bank on opening an account is, of course, used to make a comparison of the signature on any questionable checks.

If the bank customer signs his or her checks with a mechanical writer, the customer must exercise reasonable care to prevent unauthorized individuals from using the mechanical writer to forge unauthorized checks.

If the maker's signature is forged and the bank mistakenly assumes that it is genuine, the bank alone will suffer the loss.

——— QUESTIONS ———

1. Why is negotiation of commercial paper desirable?
2. What is an indorsement? Is an indorsement needed for the negotiation of a bearer instrument?
3. Give an illustration of a blank indorsement; a qualified indorsement; a restrictive indorsement.
4. What is meant by an accommodation indorsement?
5. Is a conditional indorsement one that destroys negotiability?
6. When there are several indorsers on a negotiable instrument, what is the order of their liability?
7. May there be an indorsement of a partial interest in the instrument?
8. If there are multiple payees, must each indorse?
9. Describe the proper procedure for indorsement when the check or other instrument is made payable to an incorrect version of the payee's name.
10. What is the difference between a personal defense and a real defense to the payment of a negotiable instrument?

[23]UCC 4–405(2).

11. List some of the personal defenses that are recognized by the courts; some of the real defenses.

12. What is the legal effect of nondelivery of an otherwise negotiable instrument?

13. Is a bank liable for wrongfully refusing to honor a check for which the maker has money on deposit?

14. What kind of damages may be awarded when a bank refuses to honor a check through honest error? Through maliciousness?

15. Is a bank liable for paying a check after payment has been stopped by the bank's depositor?

ANSWERS TO DISCUSSION CASES

CASE 56   This is the type of fraud that most courts will recognize as a real defense to payment.

CASE 57   Jones would be successful in pleading nondelivery. Accordingly, he would not be forced to pay. In the concept of the law, an instrument does not actually come into being until it is delivered. The maker may want to hold the instrument for any one of a number of personal or business reasons.

CASE 58   Most courts would permit the bank to demand payment as a holder in due course if the bank did not know that the customer had a defense to payment. The customer had a defense against the repair shop since there had been a failure of consideration.

CASE 59   The kind of fraud here would give rise to a lawsuit against the car dealer or it would permit the buyer to withdraw from the sale. But fraud of this type is not such as to give a real defense against payment of a check given in payment for the car that had been negotiated to a holder in due course.

PROBLEM CASES

1   A promissory note given by operators of a lumber mill contained a statement that:

> makers of this note are to pay 2% of gross sales to the holder each 30 days . . . makers do not have the privilege of assigning this note, and any time a sale is made of either the mill or standing timber . . . this note becomes immediately due and payable.
>
> Would such a note be negotiable? (*Bradley* v. *Buffington*, 500 S.W.2d 314.)

2   Jean Amoroso and her husband agreed to buy a house from Winter. Amoroso had the Fort Lee Savings and Loan Association write a check to her order for $3,100 as down payment on the house. Amoroso indorsed and delivered

the check to Winter. The next day Amoroso found that Winter had previously sold the house to a third party who had recorded the sale. Amoroso immediately requested the return of the $3,100, which Winter allegedly agreed to do. Proceeding to Winter's office, Amoroso found that Winter had attempted suicide. Winter died shortly thereafter. The Amorosos then advised Fort Lee Savings and Loan of the fraud and issued a stop order on payment of the check given to Winter. Winter, however, had already deposited the check in his account at the Citizen's National Bank of Englewood and had been allowed to draw against this uncollected deposit. Short the sum of $3,100, the Citizen's National Bank sued Amoroso and the Fort Lee Savings and Loan on the basis that Citizen's was a holder in due course. Defendants contended that Citizen's could not be a holder in due course since Citizen's had allowed Winter to draw against the uncollected check when his account was very low or overdrawn. Was Citizen's action permissible? (*Citizen's National Bank of Englewood* v. *Fort Lee Savings and Jean Amoroso*, 213 A.2d 315.)

3   Blackburn Motors gave a check to one Vanella for the purchase of his used automobile. At the time of sale Vanella falsely claimed that there were no liens or debts owed on the car. Vanella succeeded in getting a third party to immediately cash the check from Blackburn Motors but Blackburn Motors stopped payment at the bank where the check was drawn. The bank where Vanella had succeeded in cashing the check then sued Blackburn Motors. At the time of trial Blackburn Motors asserted Vanella's fraud as a defense. Could this defense be used under the circumstances? (*Marine Midland Trust Co.* v. *Blackburn Motors*, 271 N.Y.S.2d 388.)

4   M. Neal was given a promissory note by her husband A. Neal during the course of a divorce proceeding between these parties. The note had been executed and delivered by C. Neal to A. Neal who had delivered the note to M. Neal. Evidence showed that M. Neal was a holder in due course. C. Neal paid the amount due to A. Neal but this money was never passed along to M. Neal. The latter sued to recover the value of the note when it became due. In defense, C. Neal pleaded that the note had been discharged by payment. Is this a satisfactory defense to C. Neal's liability? (*Fogarty* v. *Neal*, 255 S.W. 1049.)

26

Partnership

NATURE AND PURPOSES OF PARTNERSHIP

There is no unvarying rule for selecting the type of organization that should be used to operate a given business. An individual ownership (sole proprietorship), a partnership, or a corporation all have strengths and weaknesses. The nature, size, and peculiar needs of firms vary. Does the firm require a large amount of investment capital? Is it a highly speculative concern in which liability of the owners is undesirable? Will the organization operate more efficiently with only a single top management official? These are just a few of the questions that should be asked in deciding on the legal structure of a new business venture.

What a Partnership Is

A partnership is an association of two or more individuals to engage in a joint operation of a business.[1] More specifically, a partnership is "a contract of two or more competent persons, to place their money, effects, labor and skill, or some or all of them in lawful commerce or business, and to divide the profit and bear the loss in certain proportions."[2] There is no limit on the number of partners who may be involved.

Practically all states in the United States have incorporated the Uniform Partnership Act (UPA) into their laws, and provisions of this model act are usually followed by the courts.

In most instances partnership agreements are formed only on the basis of a carefully drafted understanding, usually termed *articles of partnership*. A document of this kind defines the responsibilities and relationships between

---

[1]As defined by the Uniform Partnership Act (UPA), it is "an association of two or more persons to carry on as co-owners of a business for profit." UPA, Sec. 6.

[2]Joseph Story, *On the Law of Partnership*, Sec. 2, as quoted in 68 Corpus Juris Secundum, Sec. 1.

the parties, but no specific wording is required. A partnership may also be formed by an oral agreement. Experience shows that it is usually preferable to have a written understanding, since rights of the individual partners may be disputed. In addition, without a specific written agreement it may be difficult for the partners to settle tax problems to the satisfaction of Federal authorities.

Formation of a Partnership

The courts hold that a partnership comes into being whenever competent persons agree to go into business together for a profit. In some instances a partnership may be formed even though the individual partners are unaware of it and there is neither a written nor an oral agreement. The courts say that whether there is a partnership depends on the intent of the parties as expressed by their acts. The matter to be determined here is whether the parties set out to form an arrangement that includes the essential elements of a partnership, not whether they intended to become partners. As said in a leading case: ". . . the conduct of the parties will be given greater weight than their language in determining whether or not a business enterprise amounts to a partnership."[3]

The following matters are generally considered by the courts in deciding whether a partnership has been formed:

1. Mutual sharing of profits of a business is almost always considered conclusive evidence of the existence of a partnership unless profits are shared as a bonus or salary arrangement, as an annuity to a widow, or as repayment on a loan, or some other business reason exists for the sharing.[4]
2. Contribution of capital to an enterprise, standing alone, does not prove a partnership. Such a contribution is, however, an indicator unless it is clear that the money furnished is a loan or similar arrangement without participation in the profits of the venture.
3. Joint ownership of property is not conclusive proof; however, an arrangement to share the income or profits from such property is an indicator that a partnership exists.[5]
4. Sharing of gross income is usually regarded by the courts as a strong sign of the partnership relation.[6]

[3] *Preston* v. *State Industrial Accident Commn.*, 149 P.2d 957.
[4] UPA, Sec. 7(4).
[5] UPA, Sec. 7(2).
[6] UPA, Sec. 7(3).

5. Statements by the parties that they are involved in a partnership arrangement are not always conclusive but are usually given great weight by the courts.

In some instances an individual may claim to be a partner or may perform acts indicating that such a relationship exists. An individual who makes these statements or commits such acts is liable to anyone who extends credit to another individual based on a good-faith reliance of these representations. Sometimes the courts refer to such a situation as "partnership by estoppel" which is similar to estoppel principles in the law of contracts.[7]

Partnership Types

Partnerships are generally divided into general and limited partnerships, as well as trading (commercial) and nontrading partnerships.

When the term partnership is used alone, the speaker usually means a general partnership. Each general partner may assist in the management and control of the partnership. A *general partnership* places unlimited personal liability on each of the partners for partnership debts. This, of course, is the reason why individuals exercise considerable caution in entering into a general partnership agreement. In a *limited partnership* a general partner or partners have unlimited personal liability, while other investors are limited partners who stand to lose no more than their investment. However, limited partners may not participate in the management of the partnership.

Partnerships are sometimes classified according to the ability of the partners to bind other partners for debts. A *trading partnership* or *commercial partnership* is the most common type of general partnership and is organized to buy and sell goods and otherwise to engage in trade and commerce. In such an organizational arrangement, each partner has the power to borrow money, buy goods on credit, sign promissory notes, or otherwise commit the credit of the firm.

A *nontrading partnership*, sometimes called a *partnership of employment or occupation*, is usually organized to sell services or professional advice, such as in the practice of medicine or law. Usually such partners do not have authority to buy and sell or to undertake commercial ventures for the partnership. Individual partners have limited power to buy on credit if the item involved is to be used within the scope of the partnership arrangement.

Benefits Sought by Partners

Given their liability for firm debts, sometimes contracted without their knowledge or consent, why do individuals become involved in a partner-

[7]UPA, Sec. 16.

ship? Why not, instead, operate an individual business or form a corporation that cushions individual stockholders from corporate debts? The answer is that often a partnership maximizes the talents and capital investments of the individual participants to an extent not otherwise possible. By pooling their capital, partners may be able to buy more facilities and goods for operational activities. Combined partners may also be able to obtain considerably more credit than would be extended to an individual. Then, too, a partnership may bring together individuals whose experiences and talents greatly enhance and supplement one another. One partner may be an excellent salesman, another may be a specialist in production, while still another may have unusual talent as an artisan. Together they may enhance their individual earnings considerably. Then, too, a partnership enables responsibility to be shared.

Partnership Distinguished from Other Legal Arrangements

It is sometimes difficult to distinguish a partnership from a joint venture, an unincorporated association, or an agency relationship. An *unincorporated association* is usually a nonprofit or charitable operation, while a partnership is always undertaken for profit. An *agent* may sometimes receive a share of the profits as compensation; nevertheless, an agent is not a co-owning partner. The participants in a *joint venture* are co-owners, but their project is undertaken to complete a single transaction or enterprise rather than to continue in business. If such participants decide to continue in business, then they have formed a partnership.

Capacity to Be a Partner

Any individual having the legal ability to contract has the capacity to become a partner. A minor may become a partner, but the contract of partnership is voidable in accordance with the general provisions of contract law. Some courts have permitted corporations to join with individuals or other corporations in forming a partnership, but most courts hold that a corporation has no such authority, at least not unless the corporate charter so provides.

Partnership as a Separate Legal Entity

There is no question that a corporation is a legal entity, separate and apart from the individual stockholders who make up the corporate ownership. This separation frees stockholders from liability for the debts of the corporation. But whether a partnership is an individual legal entity in itself or a mere grouping or association of individual partners has long caused legal problems.

There is no question that individual partners are responsible for all debts of the partnership. But may the partnership own property in its own name? Is a judgment against the partnership collectable against individual partners? Can a partnership sue or be sued in its own right? Does the partnership have the right to buy life insurance on the lives of individual partners with the proceeds payable to the surviving partners?

Early-day courts never regarded a partnership as a separate legal entity. Consequently, when a lawsuit was brought against the partnership in its firm name, each of the partners had to be included as a defendant in the suit.

Under modern law, a partnership is regarded for some purposes as a separate entity but for other purposes is still considered a collection of individual owners. Under current Federal law a partnership can sue or be sued as a separate entity if the suit involves a Federal matter. Among state courts there is a split as to whether a partnership can sue or be sued in the firm name. And in some states a judgment against a partnership can be enforced against partnership assets only.

Under UPA provisions, which are followed in practically all states, a partnership is permitted to own or transfer title to both real property and personal property without all partners signing the deed or document of conveyance.[8] Federal bankruptcy law also provides that bankruptcy of a partner does not bring the partnership itself into bankruptcy.[9]

TERMS OF PARTNERSHIP AGREEMENTS

Usual Contents of Agreement

No specific wording is required in drawing up articles of partnership. Such an agreement is best drawn up by an attorney, however, because of legal entanglements that may result from an improperly prepared document. For example, Federal tax responsibilities of individual partners may vary with the way in which the agreement is worded. Then, too, profits and losses may not be divided in the way partners suppose, unless their arrangement is committed to a definite wording. For situations not reduced to writing, the law has provided rules that may not be in keeping with the partners' intentions.

The partnership agreement usually describes the proposed business in detail. The partnership name, identities of partners, and purposes are usually itemized, along with the location where business will be conducted and the contribution or capital investment of each participant. Typically, a document of this kind provides for the sharing of profits and losses and assigns the powers and responsibilities of each partner. It may specify who has the right

---

[8]UPA, Sec. 8.
[9]Title 11, U.S. Code, Sec. 23.

to handle partnership money and real estate, make purchases, and disburse partnership money, as well as when the partnership may be dissolved, when employees may retire, and when arbitration will be used to resolve partnership disputes. It should also specify the details of any salary to be paid to some or all partners.

Apportionments Between Partners

Unless there is a specific agreement to some other effect, the partners share equally in all profits and losses, even if the individual capital contributions were different. Suppose three partners contributed $50,000, $20,000, and no money, respectively. (The third partner had far more skill and technical knowledge to give.) When the partnership was dissolved, original cash contributions were owing to the contributors. Suppose a profit of $9,000 was made, leaving $3,000 profit for each partner. The three would then receive $53,000, $23,000, and $3,000, respectively.

But suppose a deficit of $72,000 had been incurred before repayment to contributors. In that case there would be a loss of $24,000 for each partner. This means that the $50,000 contributor would receive back $26,000 ($50,000 less $24,000); the $20,000 contributor would owe the partnership's creditors $4,000; and the partner who contributed no capital would owe creditors $24,000. The partners owing deficiencies of $4,000 and $24,000 would be forced to raise these amounts from other sources. When the written articles of agreement do not specifically state the share of losses, they will be shared on the same basis as profits. The partners may, however, agree in writing to any division of profits or losses that they desire.

Right to Manage the Firm

Normally, all partners have equal right to manage the affairs of the firm. This is not affected by the fact that a different share of the profits has been agreed to or that one partner contributed more capital than another. Typically, however, a partnership has a definite understanding that the actual management will be conducted by a specific individual or individuals. Any contract or agreement that significantly alters the partnership must be agreed to by all partners. However, in ordinary affairs of the firm a majority vote will overrule the minority.

Each partner always has the right to inspect books or records of the organization and to obtain copies of such records. A partner may demand an accounting of funds and records when profits have been withheld or other rights violated. Normally, however, this occurs only in case of dissolution of the partnership. All partners have equal rights to use or possess partnership property for the purpose of benefiting or serving the partnership. No partner has the right to hold or use assets or property for any other purpose.

Salary or Compensation of Partners

Unless otherwise provided in the agreement, a partner's compensation is limited to the agreed share of the profits; the partner is not entitled to salary or compensation for services. It is quite common, however, for one or more partners who are closely involved in the business to be paid monthly compensation in addition to their share of the profits or loss.

Usually a partner is not entitled to interest on capital contributions. However, interest is commonly paid if there is a repayment agreement and the repayment is late.

DISCUSSION

CASE 60   Three partners operated a boxcar loading business. All three were active in every phase of management and operation of the firm. On his own, one of the partners devised a mechanical contrivance that enabled the firm to load freight with less labor. This device helped the company cut labor costs and thereby make a better profit. The partner who had made this device sued for a larger share of the partnership profits than the one-third he had formerly received. Was his claim justified?

Fiduciary Relationships Between Partners

All partners owe an obligation of complete frankness to the other partners. Legally, this is called a fiduciary relationship. A partner cannot withhold information of vital interest from other partners, and most courts say that each partner has an affirmative responsibility to come forward with any information that is of interest to the partnership. If a partner owns or operates a business that competes with the partnership, he or she must account to the partnership for all profits obtained therefrom.

In addition, a partner who buys or holds partnership assets in his or her own name does so as trustee for the partnership. The partner who holds such funds or property is fully accountable therefor.

Each partner must present records or books to the other partners when requested, and normally these must be maintained in the partnership's principal office.

Expenses incurred are reimbursable to a partner, even though the partner may not be entitled to a salary.

Notice by an outsider given to one partner is legally considered as notice to the entire partnership. Every partner has a legal duty to communicate important information to other partners.

DISCUSSION

CASE 61   For many years both Holmes and Keets individually dealt in rental properties in Washington, D.C. The plaintiff Holmes was fully aware of these prior real estate holdings by Keets at the time he and Keets formed a real estate partnership. Keets continued to carry on his separate rental ventures in addition to conducting the partnership affairs with Holmes. Subsequently, Holmes maintained that Keets had profited by continuing a business on the side. Holmes sued to have these separate real estate holdings of Keets declared a partnership asset, offering to pay his proportionate share of the cost of such property to Keets. Did Keets's activities constitute competition against the partnership for which Keets was liable? (*Holmes* v. *Keets*, 58 F.Supp. 660.)

CASE 62   Three men became partners in the operation of a grocery store. The partnership agreement provided that any partner could withdraw after giving 90 days written notice to the others. The defendant gave notice of withdrawal and thereafter began to make arrangements to purchase a stock of groceries and open a store of his own after the partnership was dissolved. The other partners sued, claiming that the defendant had violated the partnership agreement in which he promised to "faithfully work to promote the partnership business and not engage in a competing business 'directly or indirectly' during the continuance of the partnership." Should the remaining partners be allowed to collect damages from the departing partner (defendant)? (*Young* v. *Cooper*, 203 S.W. 376.)

Silent Partners

In addition to having active, participating partners, a general partnership may have one or more dormant partners, silent partners, or secret partners. There is some confusion in legal and business circles in distinguishing these terms. Courts sometimes describe a *dormant partner* as one who is merely passive as distinguished from those who are active and conduct the business. Frequently, a dormant partner is unknown to the outside world either by design or otherwise. Sometimes a dormant partner is called a *sleeping partner, silent partner* or *secret partner*. Some courts also describe a silent partner as one who takes no part in management and a secret partner as one who is unknown to third parties. Regardless of the names given to any of these partners, they may all act as agents for the other partners under the basic principles of agency law and all are general partners, personally responsible for partnership debts.

Partnership Property

The agreement of the parties determines what is partnership property. If no express statement was made in this regard, the courts look to the way in which property is used in the operation of the business and the conduct of the partners toward specific items of property. There is a rebuttable presumption that any property obtained with partnership funds is partnership property.[10]

Torts of Partners

The courts usually say that: "The law of partnership is the law of agency: Each partner being the agent of the firm, the firm is liable for torts committed within the scope of this agency, on the principle of *respondeat superior*. . . ."

Withdrawal or Death of a Partner

The death of a top official in a corporation may have serious repercussions for the management and operation of the business. The death of a partner, however, will frequently cause even more serious problems to a partnership, resulting in immediate dissolution. Frequently, the remaining partner or partners may not have the assets to form a new firm by paying off the deceased partner's interest.

To guard against this risk, partnerships commonly obtain life insurance policies on the lives of other partners. Such policies may be individually owned or owned by the firm. In the event of a partner's death, the proceeds of the policy are given to the deceased's executor or administrator to keep the firm in business.

Many partnerships make use of a "buy and sell" agreement, whereby a predetermined price may be paid for the interest of a partner who withdraws or dies. Buy and sell arrangements may require the remaining partners to purchase the interest of the withdrawing partner or may offer an option for such transaction. Some arrangements call for the remaining partners to pay a price based on accounting figures reflecting the real worth of a deceased partner's interest.

Partnership Name

In most states partners have the right to pick a name for their firm, with two legal limitations:

1. If the name chosen is other than that of the partners, the partnership must comply with "assumed name" or "fictitious name" statutes that usually require the filing of a report disclosing the identity of all partners. Failure to file such a report usually constitutes a criminal misdemeanor. When such a report has not been filed, the courts will usually not allow the partnership to bring a civil suit against debtors.

---

[10]*Flynn* v. *Reaves*, 218 N.E.3d 661.

2. Statutes may regulate the use of "& Co." at the end of a firm name. In some instances this designation may be used only if it specifies a partnership.

DISSOLUTION OF A PARTNERSHIP

The termination of a partnership can result from five basic events: (1) mutual consent of the partners, (2) one partner's leaving the relationship, (3) a new individual's joining the existing relationship with the agreement of all existing partners, (4) violation of the partnership agreement, or (5) operation of law.

Death of a partner causes automatic dissolution. In addition, any withdrawal of a partner results in termination. One partner may obtain a court decree of dissolution if another partner commits a fraud. Bankruptcy may also result in dissolution. Frequently, the partners intended that their association would last only through the completion of a particular business project, agreeing specifically to terminate at that time. In addition, a specific date can be set for dissolution, or the agreement may specify that a partner may withdraw after giving a notice, such as one year in advance. In some instances a partnership agreement may specify that withdrawal in violation of the agreement may give the other partners the right to seek damages for harm resulting to the partnership business. Regardless of the terms, dissolution will result when all partners agree to such procedure.

Dissolution also results if the operation of the business becomes illegal—for example, by the loss of an architect's license or the withdrawal of a liquor license.

JOINT VENTURES

A *joint venture* or *joint adventure* is an association of two or more persons or companies to carry out a single business enterprise for profit. Usually a combination of this kind comes about because persons or firms do not possess the individual resources to undertake such a project. The joint relationship ends when the project is completed.

Each joint venture owes a fiduciary relationship to the other, as in a conventional partnership. The participants may withdraw from the project at will, but a joint venture may be liable to other participants if withdrawal causes hardship for the other parties involved. It has been held that the statute of frauds does not apply to a joint venture, even though it may involve a real estate operation.

Many courts have held that the participants in a joint venture are bound by the general principles of contract law.[11] This means that all participants

[11] *Pedersen v. Manitowac*, 27 N.Y.S.2d 412.

would be liable for joint venture debts contracted by any one of the participants.

LIMITED PARTNERSHIPS

A *limited partnership* is a partnership with one or more general partners who participate by providing capital and management skills and one or more limited partners who participate only by providing capital. General partners are responsible for all management and for all partnership debts. Limited partners have no right of management and no financial responsibility for partnership debts. In essence, a limited partner is an investor who risks nothing beyond the original investment.

A limited partnership is a comparatively recent type of business entity, created and wholly controlled by statute. Almost all states have adopted the Uniform Limited Partnership Act (ULPA) which regulates the activities of such organizations.

In a few instances a limited partner has subsequently been permitted by the general partners to participate in management and control of the business. When this happens, the limited partner becomes responsible for partnership debts as any general partner.[12]

Formalities Required

A conventional partnership may be created orally or without formalities. Under ULPA requirements, however, certain formal requirements must be complied with in the formation of a limited partnership:

1. A certificate must be prepared, stating the name of the partnership, the location of the business office, the character of the business, the name and address of each general partner, the name and address of each limited partner, and any specific rights of each general partner in the event rights differ.
2. The certificate must be filed with the county recorder or other county official who handles the recording of deeds.
3. The certificate must be filed with the recorder in the county where the limited partnership maintains its principal office or place of business.

Dissolution of a Limited Partnership

The death, insanity, or retirement of a general partner automatically dissolves a limited partnership. In addition, a limited partnership may be dis-

---

[12]*Holzman* v. *DeEscamilla*, 86 Cal. App. 2d 858 and ULPA, Sec. 7

solved by any of the methods provided for dissolution of a conventional partnership. Death of one of the limited partners, however, does not end the partnership arrangement; all of the rights and privileges of the deceased limited partner pass to the deceased's executor or administrator.[13] A limited partner's interest may be sold or transferred without dissolving the partnership if the agreement so provides.

FRANCHISES

A *franchise* is a contract arrangement by which the owner of a trade name, trademark, copyright, or process grants permission to others to use this property in selling goods or services under specified conditions.

The purchaser of a franchise (*franchisee*) obtains the advantage of offering a well-known or unusual product that may already have wide appeal. The franchisee also receives the benefit of mass buying and advertising. Typically, the buyer of a franchise may pay a flat fee for the franchise as well as an additional percentage based on sales. The franchisee may also be required to pay a fractional share of the franchisor's promotional costs and to purchase certain supplies from the franchisor.

Contract and sales laws pertaining to franchises are comparatively new. If the franchise involves the resale of goods or food, both the franchisor and franchisee will usually be liable under a breach of warranty if the food or other merchandise is not wholesome or proper from the consumer's standpoint. However, tort liability to a third person is usually the responsibility of the franchisee alone. In a case where the franchisee's truck struck and negligently injured a pedestrian, the franchisor would normally have no responsibility.

QUESTIONS

1. Define a partnership. Is there any limit on the number of partners who may be involved?
2. What is meant by *articles of partnership*?
3. Review the factors that determine when a partnership is formed.
4. Distinguish between a *general partnership* and a *nontrading partnership*.
5. How would you distinguish between a partnership and an agency relationship?
6. What legal limitations are there on persons who want to form partnerships?
7. Is a partnership a separate legal entity? Explain your answer referring to the right to sue and be sued and the right to hold property.

[13]ULPA, Sec. 21.

8. List the information that is usually incorporated into a partnership agreement.

9. What rights do partners have to manage the firm? Explain your answer.

10. What are the usual salary arrangements in a partnership when there is no specific understanding in this regard?

11. Comment on the nature of the fiduciary relationship between partners?

12. What is the usual meaning of a *silent partner*?

13. What is the partnership responsibility for torts of other partners?

14. May a partner withdraw from the partnership? How? List the ways in which dissolution may come about.

15. Distinguish a joint venture from a partnership.

16. What are the advantages and disadvantages of a limited partnership?

17. Is a franchise arrangement a type of partnership? Why or why not?

ANSWERS TO DISCUSSION CASES

CASE 60   It is the obligation of each partner to devote his or her skill, time, and energy to partnership affairs. There is no entitlement to extra compensation unless the partnership agreement so provides. Normally, partners are entitled to profits only.

CASE 61   Keets was allowed to retain his separate real estate holdings. The court pointed out that Keets could not take any profit clandestinely for himself or use partnership assets for his own benefit. The court further said that Holmes was fully aware of Keets's holdings and activities at the time the partnership was formed and that Holmes had no claim on such property. It was clear that there was never any intent for the property in question to be partnership assets.

CASE 62   As recovery against the departing partner was not allowed. The court said: "It was in no sense disloyal to his partners for [defendant] to make plans to begin a future business after the partnership . . . would be dissolved."

PROBLEM CASES

1   One of the members of a partnership died. The administrator for the estate took over all the deceased's property, including personal and partnership property. Another member of the partnership sued the administrator, claiming that the remaining partners should be given the partnership property. Who would prevail, the administrator or the surviving partners? (*Fong Sing* v. *Odell*, 194 P. 745.)

2   Leventhal and Epstein bought out all the stock of other stockholders in a corporation. Each then owned 50 percent of the corporate stock. They

worked out an agreement between themselves whereby either one might have the option to dissolve the corporation in specified circumstances. Leventhal and Epstein then began to treat the business arrangement as a partnership between themselves, ignoring corporate procedures and requirements. Leventhal took the approach that the corporation no longer continued to be a distinct legal entity which was separate from the stockholders and that Leventhal and Epstein had created a partnership. Was this view proper? (*Leventhal* v. *Atlantic Finance Co.*, 55 N.E. 2d 20.)

3   The defendant, a building owner, made an agreement with the plaintiff whereby the plaintiff was to prepare and serve meals and handle all details in the operation of a restaurant. The two parties agreed to share profits. Their contract stated that stock and fixtures in the restaurant building remained the property of the defendant, and that their relationship was that of employee–employer. According to the bargain, the building owner retained the right to discharge the plaintiff at will. The plaintiff, however, pointed out that his name was combined with that of the defendant to stimulate business on an electric sign, which held out to the world that they were in a partnership arrangement. Although this public representation made both parties liable to creditors, did it change the relationship between the parties? In short, was there a partnership? (*Heck* v. *Voelke*, 160 N.Y.S. 903.)

27

Corporations

CORPORATE ORGANIZATION

Nature of a Corporation

A *corporation* is an artificial body that operates as a legal unit, separate and apart from its owners (stockholders). It is an embodiment of functions, rights, and duties.

In general, a corporation can hold property, make contracts, file lawsuits, and enter into business activities. Having an individual name in which to do business, its rights and obligations are its own. Taxes must be paid in the name of the corporation.

The courts usually say that a corporation is a legal entity in itself. But when corporate organization is used as a technique to perpetrate fraud, justify wrong, cover crime, or defeat public interests, the courts often hold that a corporation is a mere association of individuals using the corporation as a guise. In cases where it appears that the corporation was used as a cover for wrong, the courts will usually "pierce the veil" and take appropriate action against those individuals trying to hide their illegality behind the corporation.

For example, a property owner authorized a real estate broker to find a buyer who would pay a reasonable price for his property. Thereafter, the real estate broker contracted with a corporation that wanted to purchase. It was subsequently learned that the real estate broker owned 100 percent of the stock of the purchasing corporation and had negotiated the sale at a very low price. In an instance of this kind the courts will allow the realty owner to avoid the contract, treating the facts as if the broker had sold the property directly to himself or herself.

Once established, a corporation may continue indefinitely. Thus, it may be unaffected by the death or disability of its individual stockholders or by the sale or transfer of their interests.

Stockholder's Limited Liability

A corporate stockholder's liability for debt is usually restricted to the invest-ment as represented by the shares of stock owned. For some investors and business operators this is often the corporation's basic attraction. Even if an individual should buy all the stock in a corporation, he or she is usually not responsible for corporate debts unless corporate procedures in conducting business have been disregarded.

Types of Corporations

Corporations may be classified by their functions as follows:

1. Public corporations (governmental units or political subdivisions such as counties, cities, townships, or villages).
2. Quasi-public corporations (public school districts, sewage districts, irriga-tion districts, railroads, public utilities, and so on).
3. Private corporations—those organized to engage in business or to func-tion as clubs or charitable groups.

Corporations may also be classified according to structure as follows:

1. Stock corporations, organized to engage in business for profit with owner-ship represented by shares of stock: (a) banks, insurance companies, and lending firms; (b) business corporations that engage in trade, commerce, or manufacturing of all kinds.
2. Nonstock membership organizations, not organized for profit and in which stock is not issued. These organizations function for purposes related to social, religious, fraternal, or mutual benefit.

Incorporation Procedures

Laws setting out the requirements for incorporation vary from state to state. Those wishing to form such an organization must apply to a designated state official, usually the secretary of state. The application for a corporate charter must set forth the express powers desired by the corporation; these are often stated in broad terms.

Usually residents of one state are permitted to incorporate in another state where registration laws and corporate fees are more favorable. How-ever, statues frequently require that one or more of the incorporators must be a resident of the state where the business is to be incorporated. Most states also require that the corporation do business in the state of incorporation.

The term *tramp corporation* refers to a company chartered in one state without any intention of doing business therein, operating principally or wholly in other states. In some instances an incorporation of this kind may be illegal.

The Corporate Name

In the absence of a statute to the contrary, the incorporators may select any name desired. State laws sometimes require that the word "Corporation" or "Incorporated" or the abbreviation "Corp." or "Inc." follow the name to alert the general public to the fact of incorporation.

Purpose of Incorporation

State laws frequently provide that a general corporation may by formed for any lawful purpose. Exceptions are ordinarily made for public utilities and for firms engaging in banking, lending, brokerage, insurance, or real estate development. Organizations of these types are usually controlled by separate statutes.

Who May Incorporate

All states have some restrictions concerning those individuals who are permitted to incorporate. A number of states allow one or more minors to be among the incorporators. In this connection, the courts regard the charter of incorporation as a contract between the state and the incorporators. Accordingly, the agreement of an under-age incorporator may be voidable at the minor's option, as is any other contract. Most states require three or more adults to be among the incorporators, at least one of whom shall be a resident of the state.

Since the charter is granted by the state, it may be revoked by state officials for good cause. Perhaps the most commonly justifiable cause for revocation is that of fraudulent incorporation.

Typical Statutory Provisions for Incorporation

As noted, statutory requirements for incorporation differ among states. Typically, the following information must be furnished in an application to the secretary of state or other designated state official; this must usually be signed by all prospective incorporators and acknowledged before a notary public and sealed. The application must have:

1. Complete names and addresses of all incorporators.
2. The name to be used by the corporation.

3. A detailed statement of the objects and purposes for which it is being organized.
4. The number of years of duration of the corporation. (This may be indefinitely.)
5. Location of its principal office.
6. The number of shares into which capital stock is to be divided; whether the stock shall have a par value; whether there is more than one class of stock, and if so, a description of the different classes, the number of shares in each class, relative rights of shareholders, and the interests and preferences each class of shares shall present.
7. The total amount of authorized capital stock.
8. Names and addresses of subscribers of capital stock and the amount contributed by each.
9. The amount of capital stock that will be issued at once.
10. The number, names, and addresses of all directors, at least one of whom shall be a resident of this state, and the length of the terms for which elected.
11. Any other provisions, not inconsistent with law, for the regulation of the business and conduct of the affairs of the corporation.

De Jure and De Facto Incorporation

In the assembling and reporting of the detailed information needed for incorporation, errors sometimes creep in. If some of the statutory requirements for the charter have been omitted or improperly recorded, the courts usually do not regard the incorporation as invalid. A corporation that complies with all organizational requirements is called a *de jure* (according to law) corporation. A corporation with some requirements improperly fulfilled is called a *de facto* corporation. The courts interpret that the latter corporation exists in fact but it is defectively incorporated.

A *de jure* corporation is said by the courts to be "impregnable to challenge or question in the courts by any source." But a *de facto* corporation sometimes poses problems. Considerable injustice could result if a *de facto* corporation should be declared nonexistent merely because of a minor error or omission in the incorporating procedure. Many states have statutory limits for valid recognition of a *de facto* corporation if a good-faith attempt apparently was made to comply with legal requirements at the time of incorporation.

As a general rule, only the state itself has authority to question the right of a corporation to exist on the basis that it was never properly organized. If it is clear that a good-faith effort to meet the legal requirements was not made, the courts normally will revoke the charter at the request of the state.

Should this revocation come about, those individuals who assumed to act as a corporation are held to be individually liable on contracts for the supposed corporation.

The Corporate Charter and Bylaws

Corporations are limited by restrictions in the charter and are governed by provisions in it. Normally the corporate charter does not attempt to go into all the technical aspects of management. Accordingly, corporate *bylaws* are used to set up additional rules for guiding corporate affairs. Bylaws typically specify the number of directors and officers who are authorized as well as the method for electing or appointing them. The bylaws may also specify duties and responsibilities of managers and employees as well as the time and place of stockholders' and directors' meetings. Included also may be methods for replacing directors in the event of misconduct.

A corporate director or officer who fails to follow bylaws has committed a breach of a fiduciary relationship with stockholders and may normally be removed and/or sued for damages.

In total, the rules of a corporation come from (1) state statutes that apply to incorporation and the conduct of corporate affairs, (2) charter provisions, and (3) requirements of the bylaws.

Corporate Promoters

A corporation almost never comes into being without the organizational activities of one or more promoters. When a business is originated in the corporate form, contracts must often be negotiated before it is fully operational. Contracts of this kind are negotiated by the promoter. In most instances the courts permit the promoter to enforce preincorporation contracts against an outside party. At the same time, the courts also hold the promoter liable in tort for injuries committed in this phase. The promoter who misrepresents material facts concerning the project will also be held personally liable to the individuals who buy the stock under a misapprehension.

As a general rule, the promoter is not allowed to buy property at a low price and immediately reconvey it to the corporation at an inflated price. It is satisfactory, however, for the promoter to sell to the corporation properties that were already owned if a full disclosure of all pertinent facts is made. This means that the promoter must usually reveal the price paid for the property that was sold to the corporation, the interest that may be applicable, brokerage fees, and other material details.

In some instances the person creating the corporation may be liable to the corporation itself. Cases of this kind usually involve a refusal to turn over all corporate assets after the incorporation has been completed. The courts also point out that a person who sponsors the formation of a corporation is in a fiduciary relationship with both the corporation and the individual stockholders. There are some differences in court decisions, but generally the promoter may be forced to give up any secret profits made at the expense of the corporation or the investors in the organizational process.

The corporation itself is generally held liable to outsiders for its creator's contracts if the corporation accepts the benefits of such transactions.

"Foreign" Corporations

A corporation is termed a *domestic corporation* within the state where it was incorporated. If it does business in an outside state, it is known there as a *foreign corporation*. For example, a firm that was incorporated in New Jersey is a domestic corporation in New Jersey but a foreign corporation in Oklahoma and Oregon.

As a purely state creation, a corporation from an outside state (foreign corporation) has no right to do business except in the jurisdiction where it was chartered. Most states do, however, sanction practically all foreign corporations to operate in their jurisdictions, subject to the restrictions of local statutes.

State laws generally specify that a foreign corporation wanting to do business there must furnish a copy of its corporate charter to the secretary of state, must pay specified license fees, and must furnish the name and address of an agent on whom legal process may be served.

Some foreign corporations are engaged wholly in interstate commerce and therefore are not legally subject to registration laws of other states. Firms that are exempt are those that:

1. Handle mail orders shipped directly to the buyer;
2. Sell through traveling sales personnel with no sales, replacements, or repairs made from a stock of merchandise on hand; or
3. Install equipment or machinery with servicing limited to the time of installation only.

POWERS, MANAGEMENT, AND LIABILITY OF CORPORATIONS ____

Powers Generally Conferred by Statute (Express Powers)

It is generally decreed by the courts that a corporation's powers are those given at the time of creation, and none other. State laws specifically confer certain powers when the corporation is organized in that state. The courts also recognize that corporations must be permitted additional powers that can fairly be implied from those expressly granted—whatever is reasonably necessary to carry out the express grants.

Express powers commonly conferred by state statutes include:

1. The right to buy and sell property, both real and personal, with ownership in the corporate name. Property must be that which is intended for corporate uses or purposes. Ownership of some types of property may be forbidden by state law or by corporate charter.
2. The right to sue and be sued as a corporate entity.
3. The right to borrow funds for corporate purposes.
4. The right to make binding bylaws so long as they are not illegal and do not conflict with the charter or corporation statutes.
5. The right to choose a corporate name and use a corporate seal.
6. The right to purchase stock in another corporation as well as stock of the corporation itself. In some states there are prohibitions against a corporation's purchase of its own stock.
7. The right to make donations for public welfare or civic causes.
8. The right to manage, promote, and handle ventures that are normally carried on in business. Most states do not permit ordinary corporations to engage in banking, insurance, money lending, or the operation of railroads. Such activities are usually restricted to businesses set up under special laws.

Implied Powers of a Corporation

Along with express powers, the courts usually grant a corporation the implied powers to do certain things. In some states a few of the activities usually permitted may be included in express statutory grants. Implied powers may be as follows:

1. The right to use the corporation's credit to obtain needed loans. This should not be construed as implied power to become a borrowing or lending agency as such.
2. The right to issue corporate bonds or to pledge or mortgage corporate property, other than to mortgage or pledge the corporate charter.
3. The right to engage in joint ventures with other businesses. However, this does not include the right to carry on an ordinary partnership.
4. The right to buy and use whatever property or materials are needed to carry on the operation of the business. For example, a shoe manufacturing corporation may buy a tract of land for location of a factory as well as a supply of leather and raw materials for the making of shoes.
5. The right to buy, sell, or handle negotiable paper in the operation of the business. This does not include the right to serve as guarantor for an outside individual or corporation.

6. The right to establish and operate a subsidiary firm that handles part of the corporate business.

7. The right to purchase the firm's own stock unless restricted by statute. A corporation cannot purchase shares of its own stock if the purchase in any way prejudices the security interest of creditors or if it works harm to the interests of individual stockholders. The rights involved here vary from state to state. Under some laws, a corporation can receive shares of its own stock as security for a debt or in payment from a creditor, but it cannot make an outright purchase of its own stock.

Ownership and Transfer of Corporate Property

Ownership of property, both real and personal, is held by the corporation itself as a legal entity. Title to corporate property cannot be transferred to a third party by a stockholder. Normally, a transfer of property is handled by a resolution that is approved by a majority vote of the board of directors. Even though an individual stockholder may own the majority of the corporate stock, the sale of corporate property must come as a result of action by the board.

CORPORATE MANAGEMENT

Authority and Activities of Directors

Except for such limitations that may be imposed by state statutes or company bylaws, the directors manage the business of a corporation. While the stockholders are the owners, the authority to set policy and operate the business rests solely with the directors. From a practical standpoint, stockholders do run the business indirectly since they can be expected to elect directors who will follow their desires. Then, too, a majority of stockholders will usually serve on the board of directors, making certain their control. There is no legal requirement in most jurisdictions that a director must hold stock in the corporation.

Voting by Directors

It is a basic rule of law that the directors' votes are not delegable. Directors may not vote by proxy. (There are exceptions to these rules in the case of close corporations, as will be noted.) Normally, the votes that bind a corporation are those cast at a board meeting. An emergency vote of the directors, taken by telephone, would not be valid. Some states, however, have passed statutes that allow the board of directors to delegate specified duties and responsibilities to an executive committee. In general, directors have the authority to appoint agents, officers, and employees to negotiate contracts and to carry on all those duties and transactions for which the company was formed.

Evidence of the board of directors' exercise of its powers is usually reflected in resolutions passed and copied into the corporate record book.

Computers and Directors' Responsibility

The use of computers has, of course, been of great benefit to management in many corporations. At the same time, computer usage has sometimes complicated the responsibilities of management. The fact that a director or corporate official does not understand computer operations fails to excuse him or her from using proper care in the supervision of computer employees.

Directors' Fiduciary Relationship to Stockholders

To be technical, directors owe no duty to follow the dictates of stockholders in management of corporate business. The directors are agents of the corporation, not of the shareholders, although the directors are elected by those shareholders. At the same time, the courts say that every director owes a fiduciary relationship to the owners. A corporate director will not be permitted to exploit his or her position at the expense of the stockholders. Any interest that a director may have in a contract with the corporation must be fully disclosed.

The courts have usually held directors liable to stockholders when directors have authorized the sale of voting stock to themselves, allowing such directors to change from minority to majority stockholders.

In general, directors are liable for any misconduct that results in loss. But so long as a director is exercising honest judgment, there is no liability to the stockholders, even though the judgment used may have amounted to stupidity.

Corporate officers other than directors are also usually liable to both stockholders and the corporation for losses resulting from dishonesty or misconduct.

Ultra Vires Acts or Contracts

Any act of a corporate director or officer that is in excess of authority granted by the state charter is legally said to be *ultra vires* (Latin for "beyond the scope"). If a corporation engages in a type of business completely different from that authorized in the charter, this activity is *ultra vires*. Or if the directors of a corporation vote to pay themselves a salary of $100,000 a year, although the corporate charter specifies that each director is to serve for $10,000 per annum, the directors' vote is *ultra vires*.

The basic rule of law is that an outside party (third party) has no right to object to *ultra vires* acts committed by a director or employee of the corporation. Since the corporate charter is a contract between the state and the incorporators, the courts usually hold that the state may revoke the corporate charter for the breach of contract arising from an *ultra vires* act. State officials are usually reluctant to take away the corporate charter, however, unless the *ultra vires* acts are substantial and clearly work a serious injury on an innocent party.

There is some conflict in court decisions concerning stockholders' rights when an *ultra vires* act has been committed by a corporate director or other official. Ordinarily a stockholder may obtain a court injunction forbidding further *ultra vires* acts when proof of likely injury can be demonstrated to the court. Frequently a stockholder may also be able to sue a director for *ultra vires* acts when damage has already been sustained.

Under statutory provisions in many states, an *ultra vires* contract made with an outside party may be enforced by either the third party or the offending corporation itself so long as the contract is otherwise proper. The courts reason here that it would be too much of a burden on an outside party to always be informed when an act or a contract is beyond the scope of corporate authority.

Exploitation of Minority Stockholders by Majority

As a general principle of law, the courts will not permit majority stockholders to oppress or take advantage of minority shareholders. A dissolution of the corporation will usually be granted to minority stockholders when it can be proved that majority stockholders are committing fraud or deliberately wasting corporate resources. An action of this kind may also require the wrongdoers to account for the money and assets involved.

Individual stockholders may freely compete for business against the firm in which they hold shares. Shareholders are not agents of the corporation, neither do they have a fiduciary responsibility to the corporation. In addition, individual shareholders are free to make contracts with the corporation.

—————— *DISCUSSION* ————————————————

CASE 63   A corporation purchased a majority of the stock of a competing corporation, obtaining control of its business affairs. The first company refused to accept business for the second, diverting this new business to itself. Thereafter, the first company initiated a court action to force the second to pay off loans which would lead to insolvency and permit all the second firm's assets to be taken over by the dominant firm. Could minority stockholders of the second firm obtain court intervention to prevent this manipulation?

Removal of Directors

State law usually permits the removal of a director by the majority vote of the stockholders. Statutes in some states allow the board of directors to remove one of its own number who is convicted of a felony, who is adjudicated a bankrupt, who is legally found to be insane, who is continuously absent, or who is clearly unable to perform because of illness or disability.

Directors' Criminal Acts for the Corporation

As a matter of criminal law, a director or officer of a corporation is not excused from responsibility for a criminal act because he or she committed the act on behalf of, or on instructions of, the corporation.

SPECIAL TYPES OF CORPORATION

Professional Corporations

A unique type of corporation is authorized in a number of states, allowing a doctor, lawyer, or other professional person to incorporate. In such professional corporations the liability of the shareholders is usually limited. Statutory provisions and court decisions are often to the effect that liability of a professional person for malpractice may not be affected by the fact that he or she had formed a corporation. Tax benefits from incorporation may, however, be of considerable benefit to a professional person.

Close Corporations

Laws in a number of states provide for three classes of incorporation: (1) for regular corporations under the general corporation code; (2) for special service corporations such as banks, insurance companies, and so on; and (3) for so-called *small* or *close corporations*.

A close corporation is sometimes called a *closed* corporation from the fact that its stock is usually closely controlled or held by a family group. Stock of this kind is seldom for sale to the general public. Formation of a close corporation frequently permits special tax advantages.

Close corporations may usually be incorporated with a small number of stockholders. Under state laws, a qualifying organization of this kind is usually permitted a simpler organizational form than regular corporations. Laws vary from state to state, but usually control and centralization of management in a close corporation rests in a single individual (usually the principal stockholder). Directors in close corporations usually have power to replace vacancies in their numbers without taking a general stockholder vote.

STOCK MATTERS AND DIVIDENDS _____

Stock Issuance for Capitalization

A share of common stock is an intangible, contractual right of ownership in corporate assets.

The corporate charter generally specifies the number of shares of corporate stock that may be issued. Usually, additional stock can be issued only by amending the charter. If it were otherwise, unscrupulous directors or officials who owned only a minor part of the stock might gain control of the corporation by issuing additional shares to themselves or their associates.

Courts frequently say that creditors have a right to believe that all stock issued has been fully reimbursed for in cash, in property, or in services already rendered to the corporation. If directors wrongfully issue stock that was not fully paid for, it is said to be "watered stock." Included in stock of this kind is that granted in exchange for work to be done in the future. Directors who authorize or participate in the issuance of watered stock are generally held liable to creditors of the firm for the unpaid balance in the event of insolvency, as well as being liable to company stockholders. Under the law in some states, a director's liability for watered stock can be enforced by a judgment creditor, a trustee in bankruptcy, or directly by the corporation itself.

Par-value stock bears a nominal dollar amount on its face, such as $5 per share. *No-par-value stock* has no statement of value and may be issued fully paid at any price specified by the directors. A notation of value on the face of par-value stock frequently has little relation to its real market value.

Corporations generally issue two kinds of stock, common and preferred. Ownership is represented by the corporate stock certificate which frequently carries the names and signatures of two or more officers of the corporation. In most instances the corporate seal is a necessary addition to each stock certificate. The buyer's name and address are then entered in company books and the buyer becomes a shareholder of record. The owners who are allowed to vote in a corporate election are those shareholders of record.

If new stock is issued by the corporation, the holder of common shares typically has a right to buy a number of the new shares in the same proportion as the percentage of outstanding common stock shares which he or she presently owns.

The ordinary capital stock of a firm is called *common stock*. Some corporations issue other types of stock, the second most frequent type being *preferred stock*. Generally, but not always, the owner of preferred stock is not allowed to vote for directors or in other company elections. There are some differences from corporation to corporation, but usually the owner of preferred stock has a first or preferential right to dividends, if earnings will permit. In some instances the owner of preferred stock will receive a dividend while the holder of common stock receives nothing. Another kind of stock issue, *cumulative preferred stock*, usually entitles the owner to an annual dividend at a fixed rate, if such dividend is earned, and specifies that any arrears in dividends in one or more prior years shall be paid to such holders out of earnings before any dividend is paid on common stock.

Generally, company management solicits proxy votes from owners of common stock who will not be present at a forthcoming meeting. The practical effect of this is that control of the company meeting and corporate management stays in the hands of the directors.

Right to Dividends

The directors of a corporation are not legally obligated to declare a dividend, even though a good profit has been made. Directors are allowed to exercise their own judgment in this regard. Unless it can be proved that honest judgment has been abused by directors, stockholders have no right to demand court intervention. If a dividend is declared, however, every shareholder is entitled to a *pro rata* share.

In most circumstances the courts rule that dividends cannot be declared when such payment would "eat into the capital" or constitute a "waste of assets." The courts do make an exception, however, of the type of corporation that is involved in the production and depletion of mineral resources, mines, or oil and gas wells. Dividends may properly be paid by a corporation of this kind, even though this may represent a return of capital investments (assets) to the shareholders.

Statutory enactments in a number of states specify the conditions under which a corporation may pay dividends. These conditions fall into two basic classes:

1. Dividends may be paid out of current earnings only. With a statutory restriction of this kind, which is followed in some states, a corporation may have a very large surplus but may not have sufficient current income to declare a dividend.
2. Dividends may be paid only if a reasonable surplus exists according to the law in some states. Here, the firm's liabilities must be subtracted from assets to determine whether a surplus exists.

Rights and Liabilities of Stockholders

In general, stockholders are not personally liable for corporate obligations or debts. In some specialized corporations, however, the charter may provide that all stock is assessible, although fully paid for. For example, the charter of some insurance companies provides that assessments may be made to cover all losses. Shareholders in national banks were formerly liable to assessments of twice the face value of the stock they held.

Additional laws in some states place personal liability on corporate shareholders for unpaid wages owing to company employees in the event of insolvency.

Right to Inspect the Books

Most courts grant a stockholder the right to inspect books and records of a firm. A request of this nature must not be made capriciously, but only at a time when there is a logical correlation between the stockholder's interest and the inspection. In addition, the demand for an inspection can be made only at a reasonable time and place.

DISSOLUTION OF A CORPORATION

State officials who granted a corporate charter are usually given the right to dissolve the corporation if illegal acts are committed by certain corporate officers. Dissolution also results automatically upon the expiration of the specified number of years for which a corporate charter was granted. (Of course, many corporations are originally chartered for an indefinite duration.) The courts may also declare the life of a corporation to be terminated by bankruptcy, insolvency, or a reorganization for the benefit of creditors in lieu of bankruptcy. Normally, the courts follow a policy of continuing the life of the corporation where this may legally be done and where such continuance may salvage creditor and stockholder interests.

A number of states have laws that permit dissolution by a competent court when management is hopelessly deadlocked in elections and shareholders will not agree to elect directors who will proceed with the business of the corporation. Some state statutes also provide for court dissolution when management has flagrantly cheated stockholders and the matter cannot be equitably rectified.

Some states allow a corporation to be dissolved upon a vote of the majority of the shareholders (*voluntary dissolution*). *Involuntary dissolution* occurs when the corporation is dissolved by the courts and not at the initiation of the corporation or its shareholders.

Mergers and Consolidations

An indirect dissolving of a corporation occurs when it is merged or consolidated. A *merger* occurs when one corporation is integrated into another and becomes part of that corporation. Both assets and liabilities of the merged corporation become part of the corporation which survives. Although *consolidations* also involve the combining of two or more corporations, in this case the corporations are combined into a new corporation. Neither corporation "takes over" the other in a consolidation; however, in a merger, one corporation becomes part of the other.

QUESTIONS

1. Define a corporation. May it be chartered to remain in business indefinitely?

2. May the courts go behind the corporate entity if it appears that the organization is being used as a technique to perpetrate fraud? Explain.

3. What is the basic difference in owner liability between the owners of a partnership and the owners of a corporation?

4. Classify corporations according to their functions; according to their structure.

5. Describe how a corporation is chartered.

6. What is a *de jure corporation?* A *de facto* corporation? May the charter of a *de facto* corporation be revoked? Who has this right to revoke?

7. How do corporate bylaws add to or expand provisions in the charter for managing or governing a corporation?

8. What are the liabilities of a corporate promoter to third parties? To the corporation?

9. What must a foreign corporation do in order to operate in another state?

10. Describe some of the express powers normally granted to corporations. List some implied powers that may also be used by corporations.

11. Explain how the directors of a corporation are elected. How do they govern the corporation?

12. Do directors have a fiduciary relationship to stockholders?

13. Explain liability for *ultra vires* acts.

14. Describe differences between an ordinary corporation and a close corporation.

15. Are stockholders entitled to a dividend as a matter of right? When may dividends be granted?

16. Explain the differences between common stock and preferred stock.

17. How may directors of a corporation be removed?

ANSWER TO DISCUSSION CASE

Case 63   Court intervention for the minority could be expected in a situation of this kind. The courts have consistently held that a corporation purchasing the stock of a competing firm cannot impose such control as to ruin the second firm. Courts will usually intervene for minority stockholders when the majority is manipulating affairs that ruin the value of minority holdings. Modern courts have usually followed this principle, going all the way back to the old 1896 case of *Farmer's Loan* v. *New York and Northern Railway*, 150 N.Y. 410.

PROBLEM CASES

1   The Kowal and Keywell families each owned half of the shares of the Barlum Hotels. Differences developed and the two families bitterly refused to work together on corporate business. Business suffered when arguments were carried on in front of hotel guests. One dispute actually ended in fistplay. Directors' meetings could not be held for five years and dividends could not be voted even though money was available. Eventually, the hotels began to operate at a loss. Keywell stockholders asked a court for liquidation of the corporation and for the appointment of a receiver to handle the business. Could this be done if the corporation was still solvent? (*Levant* v. *Kowal*, 86 N.W. 2d 336.)

2   Poynter was president of a Ford dealership corporation that was wholly owned by his wife. Poynter himself held all the stock for a corporation that built portable motel units. This latter firm, Economotel, Incorporated, went out of business after about seven months, owing unsecured creditors almost $93,000. Poynter created another corporation, Standard Buildings, with Mrs. Poynter as sole owner and himself as president. This firm similarly went out of business with about $66,000 in debts. Poynter then organized an additional corporation, Modern Structures, which he controlled and owned. Director's meetings were never scheduled or held for any of these corporations. As each corporation succeeded the other, Poynter took over assets and transferred usable equipment without any accounting or sale. Creditors of all Poynter's corporations then joined together and asked the court to hold Poynter personally liable. Would a court "look beyond the corporate veil" to hold Poynter responsible or was he protected behind the corporate arrangement? (*Kilpatrick* v. *Poynter*, 473 P.2d 33.)

3   The administrator of the estate of an individual owning only three-fourths of one share of corporate stock demanded the right to inspect the corporate books. The corporation refused, noting that the interest owned by this stockholder was so small as to be insignificant. If the stockholder's request was made in good faith for an examination at a reasonable time, would it be allowed by the courts? (*Dixon, Administrator* v. *G.S.& M. Co.*, 138 S.E.2d 220.)

4   The charter of the San Antonio, Texas, Public Service Company stated that the corporation was organized for "constructing, acquiring, maintaining, and operating lines of electric motor railway" and for the "manufacture, supplying, and selling of electricity and gas for light, heat, and power to the public and to municipalities." The firm subsequently opened public show

rooms and sold gas and electric stoves and other appliances. Competing appliance merchants complained and the state of Texas sought an injunction to close sales offices of the corporation. Was the sale of appliances an *ultra vires* act? Was such sale an implied right in accomplishing the business objectives of the corporation? (*State* v. *San Antonio Public Service Co.*, 69 S.W.2d 38.)

5   Guerrisi set up the Keystone Macaroni Manufacturing Company, a Pennsylvania corporation, and built it into a profitable business. After he died, the directors of the corporation passed a resolution that the firm should pay his widow the sum of $2,000 per month in recognition of the decedent's long and valuable service. The resolution was never submitted to the stockholders. A stockholder sued to prevent these payments, claiming that they were illegal and *ultra vires*. Judge. (*Moore* v. *Keystone Macaroni Co.*, 87 A.2d 295.)

6   Most Ford Motor Company stock was owned by members of the Henry Ford Family. However, Horace Dodge and a few other acquaintances of the Fords were permitted to buy some stock in a company expansion. For a time both regular and special dividends were paid. Henry Ford, 58 percent stockholder, decided that he wanted to buy some ships and to build a steel plant for eventual use in making cars. The Ford company had a surplus of many millions of dollars at the time. Evidence indicated that Henry Ford felt he "had made his millions" and that it was time to make less profit and share some of his money with the workers. Dodge and his associates were not in the same financial position as Ford and sued to compel the payment of larger dividends to stockholders. Who prevailed? (*Dodge* v. *Ford Motor Co.*, 170 N.W. 668.)

28

Legal Aid
for Creditor or Lender

OBTAINING A MONEY JUDGMENT

Normally, a creditor or a lender has every right to require fulfillment of an obligation or contract. Legal processes and the courts lend themselves to this enforcement.

A creditor with a security interest in the debtor's property, such as a mortgage or lien, may look to the enforcement of that security interest for repayment of the debt. But if no security interest exists, the creditor's usual approach is to reduce the claim to a money judgment. Legally, a *judgment* is an official pronouncement of a court, backed by the state and organized society, fixing the rights and obligations of the parties to an action. In essence, the judgment is awarded by the court as the end result of a lawsuit brought by the creditor. A judgment merges the creditor's claim into a newer and higher obligation—a *debt of record*. Regardless of its character, the original claim no longer exists.

Finality of a Judgment

When a judgment has been rendered by a court (and after the statutory time allowed for appeal has passed), the judgment is binding on all the parties to it and upon those who claim under such parties. Legally, the courts say that a judgment is *res adjudicata* as to all the facts that were in dispute in the suit out of which the judgment arose.

There are times when a judgment may be set aside, but such cases are very infrequent. In rare instances a person may subsequently be able to convince a higher court that the judgment was rendered by a court that had no jurisdiction over the parties or over the subject matter. On some occasions, too, it may be shown that the judgment was handed down because of perjury, fraud, or some kind of collusion between a judge and lawyers or witnesses. But in almost all cases the practical effect of a judgment is to finally dispose of the dispute.

Where a Judgment Is Effective

A state court judgment binds the judgment debtor but only in the jurisdiction in which it is issued. Normally, the creditor cannot automatically compel the enforcement of that judgment in another state. However, the Constitution of the United States provides that "full faith and credit shall be given in each state to the public acts, records and judicial proceedings of every other state."[1] Accordingly, when an individual obtains a judgment in one state, it may be used as the basis to obtain a judgment in another state without further controversy. To accomplish this, the creditor must file a lawsuit in the second state, although it is usually a comparatively simple legal procedure. Once obtained, the judgment in the second state is as effective as any originating in that same state.

Judgments issued by the court of a foreign nation are held to be *prima facie* proof of the merits of the original claim, but most United States courts permit the parties to reopen the controversy on its merits.

What the Judgment Consists of

As a necessary step in the creditor's proceedings against the assets of the debtor, a judgment is a formal crystallization of a cause of action. The judgment empowers the creditor to proceed against the debtor's goods and real estate if the debtor does not promptly pay the obligation. When entered by the court, a money judgment becomes a lien or legal claim against all the debtor's real estate within the jurisdiction of the court. In many states, however, a judgment is not a lien upon real estate in any county other than that in which issued until a copy of the judgment has been filed in the county where the real estate is situated.

The laws in many states require that the judgment or an abstract of it be filed with the recorder of deeds in the county where the debtor's real estate is located. Once filed, the judgment takes priority over the rights of a good-faith purchaser of the property who has no notice of the lien. Thus, anyone thereafter buying the property takes it subject to the judgment lien.

As a general rule, a judgment does not bind the debtor's personal property until a writ of execution has been delivered by a court official to the sheriff or other court officer who is to carry out the order of the court.

Writ of Execution

A *writ of execution* is the legal process to put in force a money judgment or a decree of a court. Depending on state law, a writ of execution is directed to a sheriff, constable, or bailiff instructing such official to seize property of the

---

[1]Article IV, Sec. 1, U.S. Constitution: *Williams* v. *North Carolina*, 325 U.S. 226.

debtor and sell or apply it to the satisfaction of the money judgment. When a judgment is issued, a judgment creditor is entitled to a writ of execution as a matter of right. Often, state statues provide that execution shall not immediately issue against the debtor for a specific period, usually about 10 days. This period gives the debtor the opportunity to keep property intact by immediately paying off the judgment.

State statutes vary concerning the length of time in which the writ of execution may be served. In some states the writ will automatically expire if the sheriff or other officer does not serve it within a year. Most states permit the judgment creditor to receive the writ at any time within a period of seven years by making application to the court.

Levy and Execution

The sheriff or other court official named in the writ of execution must *levy* upon the judgment debtor's property and actually seize it. Money, cars, cattle, and all other forms of personal property may be taken away by the sheriff. Most states have laws that exempt a small amount of personal and household necessities such as toilet articles and kitchen utensils. Most of these exempt items would have little resale value.

Statutes vary from state to state concerning whether the sheriff may seize copyrights, patents, and intangibles such as a lifetime pass to a ball park. Most states do permit the court officer to seize stock certificates, promissory notes, checks, bonds, and similar intangibles.

If the judgment debtor's personal property is being legally held under a bailment, the property may not be seized during the life of the bailment. If the bailment is one that could be terminated at the will of either party, however, such property is subject to seizure.

Responsibility in Levying Execution

The sheriff, constable, bailiff, or other court official charged with making the levy of execution has definite legal responsibilities. Such officer must actually seize personal property of the debtor to make certain that it can be sold for enough to satisfy the judgment. In making this levy, the officer takes personal property and retains it within his or her control. The sheriff or other officer actually goes on real estate, occupying it as necessary and proclaiming official seizure to the public. While it is sometimes impractical to carry away consumer goods, growing crops, or heavy machinery, the officer must inform the general public and those using the property about the levy.

In many states the officer is required to proceed against the debtor's property in a certain order. Sometimes witnesses are required to specific transactions in any forced sale. Usually the officer can use his or her judgment in executing the writ so long as the officer proceeds in an orderly way. It is possible for the debtor to sue the sheriff or other officer making the seizure, but the courts will usually permit a recovery only when it can be proved that the sheriff or other officer clearly abused or destroyed the debtor's property.

Sale and Redemption of Seized Property

After the writ of execution has been served and the property is seized, it is the duty of the appointed officer to dispose of the property by sale. Procedures for this are spelled out by state law. As a general proposition, the sale may be invalidated if its procedures do not comply with state statutes. In addition, the officer handling the sale would be liable for damages in a lawsuit brought by the debtor.

The courts insist that there must be basic honesty in the conduct of judgment sales. As long as the statutory regulations are met, the conduct of the sale is usually left to the discretion of the officer responsible.

When the property has been sold, the officer handling the sale makes a payment in money to satisfy the creditor's judgment claim. If proceeds from the sale were insufficient to pay off the judgment, then the creditor is entitled to sue for a new judgment, which in legal slang is usually called a *deficiency judgment*.

The laws in all states provide that a debtor has a *right of redemption* to reclaim real property sold under an execution sale. As worded in the law in many states:

> Any defendant, his or her heirs, administrators, assigns, or any person interested in the premises through or under the defendant, may within twelve months from said sale, redeem the real estate so sold by paying to the purchaser thereof, his or her executors, administrators, or assigns, or to the sheriff, or other officer who sold the same, or his or her successor in office, the sum of money for which the premises were sold or bid off, with interest thereon at the rate of _____% per annum from the time of such sale, whereupon such sale and court deed to the property shall be null and void.

OBTAINING AN ATTACHMENT OR GARNISHMENT _____

Attachment to Foil an Absconding Debtor

An *attachment* or *writ of attachment* is a legal procedure by which a creditor is permitted to have the debtor's assets brought under court control until the creditor can obtain a money judgment. In effect, the creditor gets the debtor's assets or property tied up first and litigates the claim later.

On first consideration, a procedure of this kind might appear to be an unfair use of a court's powers in favor of a creditor. An attachment proceeding is allowed by the courts only in special circumstances, usually when it is obvious that the debtor is attempting to take unfair advantage of the creditor. Without the availability of a writ of attachment, a creditor could be forced to undergo a long wait for the issuance of a judgment with the debtor meanwhile hiding or deliberately dissipating assets to spite the creditor.

Statutes in most states allow the use of a writ of attachment:

1. When the debtor has made a fraudulent conveyance of real estate or dishonest transfer of personal property;
2. When the debtor intentionally absents himself or herself from the state, or absconds;
3. When the debtor has moved or appears to be in the act of moving property from the state;
4. When the debtor has concealed or is attempting to conceal property within the state;
5. When the debtor owns property within the state but resides within another state and service cannot be obtained on the debtor; or
6. When the debtor hides out to avoid service.

When a writ of attachment is requested, notice of the hearing must be served on the debtor. At the hearing, the creditor must convince an appropriate court that the creditor is making a good-faith attempt to obtain a money judgment against the debtor or has already filed the necessary lawsuit. Then, too, the creditor must show that a judgment is likely to be worthless if a considerable amount of time elapses before it can be obtained. A writ of attachment, then, is incidental to proceedings by which the creditor seeks to recover payment for debt.

Generally, a writ of attachment will not be issued by a court unless the creditor (plaintiff) is willing to post a bond payable into the court registry. This bond is to protect the debtor against loss resulting from a wrongfully issued writ.

Once a writ of attachment has been issued, it will usually apply to any type of property that can be reached under a writ of execution.

If it turns out that the creditor was wrong in obtaining a writ of attachment, the debtor (defendant) is entitled to whatever damages resulted from the wrongful attachment. Some courts allow damages for this even though no property was actually confiscated.

Once a writ of attachment has been issued, the debtor cannot sell, convey, or place property beyond the reach of the creditor.

In instances where the attaching creditor puts up a bond with the court, the debtor is usually allowed to obtain a release of the property by putting up a counterbond. Both the bond and the counterbond usually stay in effect until the matter of the debt is finally settled by issuance of a judgment or by release of the debtor.

Fraudulent Conveyance of Real Property

At times a dishonest debtor may attempt to place real property beyond the reach of creditors by making a fraudulent conveyance or by giving the property away. As a general rule of law, any conveyance made with intent of delaying, hindering, or defrauding a creditor is voidable at the option of the creditor.

In addition, in most states a conveyance by a debtor who will be rendered insolvent thereby is fraud on the creditors without regard to the debtor's (grantor's) real intent if the conveyance was made without a fair consideration. Such a conveyance may be set aside by a creditor in an appropriate court action.

However, the courts are in general agreement that a transfer of property to a person who pays value in good faith and without notice of fraud is a valid transaction, even though the debtor may have made the transfer with an intent to defraud or embarrass creditors. If the courts were to hold otherwise, a buyer might never feel safe in purchasing property. Of course, if the transfer were to a close friend or relative of the debtor, the courts would be inclined to seriously question the sale.

Burden of Proving Fraudulent Conveyance. The burden of proving that a transfer of real property was made in fraud of creditors is on the person making such a claim. Whether a specific conveyance is based on value is a question of fact. The mere fact that the supposed good-faith buyer did not pay full market value is not conclusive, but may be evidence of fraudulent collusion, depending on the percentage of value actually given and the surrounding circumstances. A nominal consideration in such a situation is clearly fraudulent and may be set aside.

If the purchaser is aware of the debtor's intent to defraud or embarrass creditors, the purchaser cannot claim protection against creditors who attack the transaction. Most courts also rule that if the buyer knows of suspicious circumstances that a reasonable person would investigate (anticipating possible fraud), the buyer is not entitled to protection. The courts would set the conveyance aside, terming such gullibility as "constructive notice of fraud."

It is well recognized by most courts, however, that a debtor in failing financial circumstances may prefer some creditors, giving them goods, money, or property to the exclusion of other creditors. If the transfer is made in settlement of legitimate debts, the transaction is usually regarded as legal so long as the value given does not exceed the worth of the existing debt.

Garnishment

Garnishment is a statutory proceeding whereby a debtor's wages, property, money, or credits are taken and applied as payment toward satisfaction of a debt. Under garnishment, an employer can be compelled to pay a worker's wages directly to a creditor of the worker. When this happens, the worker's wages are said to have been "garnished" (legal slang). The employer is known as the *garnishee*—the person against whom process is issued. The person demanding satisfaction of the debt is the *garnishor*. In effect, garnishment is a type of attachment.

Garnishment proceedings must be filed by a creditor before an appropriate court. After a hearing on the facts, the court may order the debtor's employer to pay the debtor's wages directly to the creditor. This, of course, bypasses the worker who has no say as to the disposition of part of the earned wages.

Garnishment can be a particularly brutalizing experience for a worker with low income, especially if the worker has dependents. Accordingly, practically all states have passed laws in recent years placing limits on the percentage of wages that are subject to garnishment.

In addition, a section of the Federal Consumer Protection Act,[2] passed in 1969, provides that the maximum part of the disposable earnings of an individual subject to garnishment in any week may not exceed the lesser of:

1. Twenty-five percent of the disposable earnings for that week; or
2. The amount by which the disposable earnings for that week exceed 30 times the Federal minimum hourly wage prescribed by the Fair Labor Standards Act.

Statutory limitations on garnishment in many states now exempt a larger share of the worker's wages from garnishment than that provided by the Federal law. The effect is that the worker can still obtain whatever is the larger amount since the Federal law does not preempt any state law.

In past years many employers followed a policy of automatically discharging any worker whose wages were garnished, believing that the garnishment process caused extra bookkeeping in addition to indicating serious instability on the part of the employee. The Federal law now prohibits the discharge of any employee because of a single instance of garnishment.

SECURED TRANSACTIONS OF PERSONAL PROPERTY ————————

Position of Secured Creditors

Creditors fall into one of two basic categories: (1) *ordinary creditors*, also termed *general creditors* or *unsecured creditors*, and (2) *secured creditors*. When someone runs a charge account at the corner grocery store, the grocer is an unsecured creditor. A secured creditor is one who holds a claim on property or some special monetary assurance of payment of the debt such as a mortgage or lien.

[2]Title 15, U.S. Code, Sec. 1601.

In the usual conduct of business a creditor extends credit to a debtor, looking to the latter for payment. If the debtor is unwilling or unable to pay, usually the creditor's only recourse is to file a lawsuit and obtain a money judgment. This procedure is invariably costly in time and money. The expenses of a court suit and the forced sale of property may deplete the debtor's available assets. Consequently, sellers often refuse to do business unless the buyer has an excellent credit rating or unless the seller has some protection beyond the right to sue.

Then, too, ordinary creditors are at another disadvantage compared to secured creditors. When a debtor's resources have been depleted so that everyone cannot be paid off, the secured creditor is given a preferred right to payment. This means, of course, that an ordinary creditor may be repaid for only a fraction of the debt or nothing at all.

Nature of Secured Credit

A *secured transaction* is one in which the seller or lender is protected by a pledge, lien, mortgage, property right, or some other special interest in the debtor's property. Some secured transactions apply to real estate and are discussed in Chapter 23. Commercial transactions make frequent use of security devices to aid sellers of goods, merchandise, and all other kinds of personal property.

Perhaps the earliest type of secured transaction was that of the *pledge* or *pawn*. Securities, stock certificates, and bonds are still used today as collateral in pledge transactions. But for most commercial needs the pledge was not a satisfactory arrangement because the buyer or borrower could not gain possession of the property involved.

Consequently, commercial interests and the legal system worked out other types of secured transactions involving personal property that allow the buyer to obtain possession and use of the goods covered under the security arrangement. Some of these new credit devices for personal property are a *conditional sale*, a *chattel mortgage*, a *bailment lease*, a *secured credit sale*, and an *assignment of accounts receivable*.

Beginning in 1962, Article 9 of the Uniform Commercial Code merged all secured transactions relating to personal property into a single legal category, designated by the UCC as the *security interest*. The object of the code is to give the creditor a claim on the debtor's personal property that will be available to ensure payment.

The UCC did not do away with transactions such as the conditional sales contract nor make them illegal. Rather, the UCC set up certain minimum requirements for all kinds of security devices used by credit sellers, regardless of name or how used.

The law concerning secured transactions is still undergoing change in some states. Article 9 of the UCC was revised in 1972. By 1982, some parts of Article 9 had been adopted in most states in this country. However, a number of states have passed amendments to Article 9 with a noticeable lack of uniformity among them. Accordingly, in attempting to ascertain the law in a specific jurisdiction, statutes must be examined on a state-by-state basis.

Creation of the Security Interest

Under the UCC a security interest for the protection of a seller of goods arises as soon as both buyer and seller agree upon the creation of such an interest. The security right attaches whether or not the seller has retained ownership (title) until such time as the purchaser has paid for the goods. In essence, the place where the collateral will be stored or located is immaterial on this point.

UCC requirements specify that the security agreement between the buyer and seller must be written and must sufficiently identify the collateral. This must be signed by the buyer.[3] The seller fails to obtain any security interest in property that is not listed in the security agreement.

This arrangement between the buyer and the seller may be written to extend to goods to be acquired by the buyer at a future date. Security rights to future goods do not attach until the goods are in existence and until the buyer has acquired a right in such goods.[4] An arrangement of this kind permits a manufacturer or wholesaler to retain a security interest in a retailer's current inventory, even though the seller may have lost a security interest in goods previously sold by the retailer to consumers. Typically, security agreements contain other conditions or provisions—terms of repayment—whether the buyer should maintain insurance covering the inventory, and so on.

In most instances the security interest takes effect between the buyer and seller when three conditions have been met[5]:

1. There is an agreement between the parties that the security interest attached;
2. Value must be given; and
3. The buyer has been given rights in the collateral (the goods or services sold).

Under this section of the code, the term "value" has a different meaning than that used in connection with commercial paper. Here value means that the secured party has given the debtor sufficient worth to support a contract. For example, a wholesaler shipped toys to a retailer, taking a security interest

[3]UCC 9–203(1)(b).
[4]UCC 9–204(1)(2).
[5]UCC 9–204(1).

in the retailer's inventory. One of the requirements is that the debtor (buyer) must have rights in the collateral. The courts say that such rights do not exist until the collateral comes into being—there is no right in a farmer's crop until it begins to grow or in timber until it is cut.

Perfecting the Security Interest

In the usual sale of goods from a supplier to a retailer under a secured transaction, there is no requirement that the written security agreement between the parties be filed with the county recorder. The agreement is valid between the secured party and the debtor. But the signing of the security agreement alone is not sufficient to give the secured party (seller) priority over the claims of a third-party creditor of the debtor (buyer). To retain such priority, the seller must take the legal step called *perfecting* the security interest. This involves taking action to give notice to third persons that the seller already has a security interest in the collateral. Others can then extend more credit to the debtor at their own risk. The law recognizes three ways for putting others on notice of the seller's security interest:

1. Taking possession of the debtor's collateral,
2. Filing an attachment, or
3. Filing a financing statement.

A *financing statement* is a separate instrument from a security agreement (however, in a few instances the two documents may be combined into one). The form used for a financing statement is often quite similar to a security agreement. To be effective for filing, a financing statement must be signed by both the debtor and the secured party. It must also indicate that the parties have entered into a security agreement pertaining to certain collateral that can be identified from the information in the financing statement. If the collateral consists of fixtures or farm crops, the instrument must include the legal description of the land where the collateral is located. Business addresses of both parties must be included and repayment terms desired may also be noted.

To be protected against the rights of third parties, the financing statement must usually be filed with the county recorder or other recorder as specified by law on a state-by-state basis. Once filing has taken place, subsequent creditors extending money or goods to the debtor are on notice of the prior secured transaction.

A financing statement that does not specify an expiration or maturity date is deemed to be effective for five years, renewable for an additional five years by filing of a *continuation statement* signed by the creditor.[6]

[6]UCC 9–403(2).

A debtor may sometimes have difficulty in obtaining credit if a financing statement is on file, even though the debt represented by the financing statement has already been repaid in full. Consequently, the code provides that when a security interest no longer exists, the secured party has an obligation to clear the record through filing a *termination statement*. Failure to file the termination statement within 10 days after written request from the debtor will subject the secured party to liability for any damages suffered by the debtor plus a penalty of $100.[7]

One holding a perfected security interest in collateral such as inventory of a retail store does not always have complete protection. If the agreement calls for an ongoing security interest, the secured party will continue to have an interest in whatever inventory has replaced goods that have been sold off. However, a consumer who buys from the retail store takes the purchase free and clear of the security interest of the store's supplier. The rule is different, however, when applied to the purchaser of farm crops. In the farm situation the good-faith purchaser does not take free and clear of a perfected security claim.

Security Interest in Consumer Goods

The code places goods in a special category where they are being sold to a consumer. The code defines consumer goods as those "used or bought for use primarily for personal, family, or household purposes."[8] Goods purchased by a retail outlet for eventual sale to consumers are not considered consumer goods until a sale to an ultimate consumer is actually made. In the meantime such goods in the hands of the retailer are designated by the code as "inventory" rather than as consumer goods.

A security interest in merchandise may be retained by a retailer who sells the item to a consumer. A transaction of this kind is sometimes called a *purchase money security interest in consumer goods*. Under the code it is not necessary for the retailer to file a financing statement or otherwise perfect the security interest. Such a retail seller is protected against purchasers from creditors of the buyer who may acquire the property thereafter,[9] even though the buyer (consumer) is given possession of the goods and the seller does not file a financing statement.

But when no financing statement is filed, a resale by the consumer-purchaser to another consumer-purchaser who is without knowledge of the seller's security interest results in loss of the security interest. There is an additional requirement here that the second consumer-purchaser must have bought the goods in question for personal, family, or household use.[10]

[7]UCC 9–404(1).
[8]UCC 9–109(1).
[9]UCC 9–302(1)(d).
[10]UCC 9–307(2).

Many states have special statues governing installment sales of automobiles to consumers. Provisions in these statutes vary considerably. In addition, UCC provisions also contain variances in the handling of secured transactions for fixtures, agricultural crops, and agricultural equipment. As a result of these and other differences in state laws, both creditors and debtors may be well advised to obtain legal assistance from a local attorney in entering into secured transactions.

SURETYSHIP AND GUARANTY

Credit is almost always extended more readily if the person seeking it can furnish a creditworthy third party who will agree to also stand good for the debt. Then, too, goods are usually easier to obtain if the creditor is able to retain a legal claim, lien, or security interest in the goods themselves. A promise by one person to be legally bound for the debt or default of another is called a *suretyship*. A *secured transaction* is one in which a creditor retains a legal claim on the goods advanced or the property involved until the obligation is satisfied.

Even lawyers and the courts occasionally use the terms suretyship and guaranty interchangeably. This sometimes happens because it is often unnecessary to differentiate between the two. However, differences in them could lead to dissimilar legal consequences. Suretyship is an all-comprehensive term, including all instances in which one person pledges his or her credit for another. A *guarantor* undertakes to pay a debt if the debtor does not, will not, or cannot pay it. The guarantor does not assume the debt, but makes a legally binding promise that it will be paid or can be collected. Thus broadly defined, suretyship includes guaranty as one of its forms.

A *surety* is one who assumes to pay the debt or discharge the obligation of his or her principal. The surety is legally obligated with the principal from the outset—he or she is an original promisor or debtor from the beginning of the transaction. Thus, the guarantor has only contingent liability at the outset, being responsible to pay damages if the debtor defaults.

Contract of Guaranty

A *contract of guaranty* is a written promise to stand good for another's debt or obligation if it is not paid. Three parties are involved in an agreement of this kind: the creditor, the debtor, and the *guarantor* who agrees to be responsible. The contract of guaranty is given to the creditor.

Under the statute of frauds in most states a promise to answer for the debt or default of another party must be in writing and must be signed by the individual who has undertaken it. When a contract of surety is formed at the same time as the debtor's transaction, the consideration for the debt is adequate for the entire agreement. If a contract is entered into subsequently, however, there must be new consideration for the promise to stand good for the debtor's obligation.

Difference in Handling That Creditor Must Take Against Surety and Guarantor

In most surety transactions, the creditor is required to do nothing whatever to fix the liability of the surety as automatically liable. The liability of a guarantor is conditional. To fix liability, the creditor must not only demand payment from the principal debtor but must also notify the guarantor of the debtor's default. Then the creditor must diligently attempt to collect from the principal debtor, taking appropriate legal steps that may involve the filing of a lawsuit against the principal debtor. Only then is the creditor entitled to look to the guarantor for payment. In some states the creditor is not obliged to go into a lawsuit when it is obvious that the debtor has become insolvent.

Except for this difference in the steps a creditor must take, the rights of a surety and guarantor are basically the same. In a few states statutes specify than an undertaking to answer for the debt of another is to be interpreted as a surety agreement unless it is expressly stated otherwise.

Indorser of Negotiable Instrument as Surety

In the study of negotiable instruments it was pointed out than an indorser of such an instrument is a surety. Liability of an indorser is somewhat different from that of other sureties, however. In the first place, the indorser's obligation results from the negotiable instrument and his or her indorsement must appear on the principal obligation. Then, too, the indorser's liability is contingent upon presentment by the holder of the obligation to the party primarily liable and on seasonable notice of dishonor if the party of primary liability refuses to pay it. But in other surety transactions the creditor is required to do nothing to fix the liability of the surety as an automatic and absolute guarantor.

Extent of Guarantor's Continuing Liability

The drafting of a contract of guaranty is governed by the same general principles that apply to the formation of ordinary contracts. The guarantor may draft a letter addressed to a specific creditor or to no one in particular, and a creditor forms a contract by accepting the guarantor's promise and by extending credit to the debtor. Either a surety or a guarantor may revoke an offer at any time prior to acceptance by a creditor.

Many of the legal problems that arise concerning guarantors center around the extent to which the guarantor wants to be bound. For example, a guarantor's contract may read: "I will be financially responsible for all wholesale goods which Ms. _____ may buy from you." Under such an agreement, how far can a creditor safely go in extending credit? Is there any limit on the type or amount of goods that can be furnished? Does the guaranty extend indefinitely? There is general agreement among the courts that a guaranty of this kind is continuing and unlimited.

Another typical guaranty contract may read: "I will be financially responsible for all the merchandise which Mr. _____ may purchase from you to the extent of $25,000." Undoubtedly the guarantor intended to place a limit on the promise. Does this mean that the creditor can continue to extend credit so long as the amount owed at any given time is no more than $25,000? Is the guaranty agreement exhausted by a single purchase or can it be a series of purchases totaling $25,000? Courts are not always consistent on these questions, but most agree that the creditor is not restricted to a single transaction so long as the limit has not been exceeded.

Questions of this kind emphasize the need for the guarantor to draft the contract of guaranty precisely, thereby eliminating any ambiguity.

Defense Available to Sureties and Guarantors

In general, a surety or guarantor can avoid liability by using most of the defenses that are available in any contract situation. The surety or guarantor may void the contract if he or she does not possess legal capacity to contract or is under age. Usually the surety or guarantor may not escape liability because the debtor turns out to be a minor or a feebleminded person. In many instances a minor is unable to make purchases or go into debt unless a surety or guarantor will sign. To allow the guarantor to avoid payment because of the debtor's minority would defeat the whole purpose for which the guarantor signed.

Duress or fraud may be pleaded as a defense in some instances. If the creditor had the guarantor agree to answer for the debt or default using fraud in the inducement, the courts are almost unanimous in allowing the guarantor to avoid his or her promise.

If the debtor used fraud to induce the guarantor to sign, most courts hold the guarantor liable. This is because the creditor was not a party to the fraud and should not be hurt by it.

In case the creditor used fraud to induce the debtor to enter the transaction, the debtor can avoid the obligation. However, if the guarantor knew that fraud was involved, a few courts will not permit the guarantor to get out of the obligation. There is a difference of opinion here and many courts will allow both the debtor and the guarantor to avoid responsibility where there was fraud in such cases.

Creditor's Concealment of Material Information from Guarantor

In ordinary contracts, the parties are under a duty not to actively deceive the other side. But in general the contracting parties are under no obligation to disclose material facts bearing on the negotiations. In suretyship and guaranty contracts, however, the surety or guarantor is seldom acquainted with all the details and negotiations that have transpired between the principals to the credit agreement. Consequently, the courts require the creditor to disclose any unusual information that a surety or guarantor would not anticipate in the transaction.

Changes in Creditor–Debtor Contract

The courts consistently hold that a material alteration of the contract between the creditor and debtor, without the written consent of the guarantor, acts as a discharge of the guarantor's responsibility. The reasoning of the courts here is that the guarantor, undertaking to answer for one debt, could later find himself or herself being responsible for an entirely different one. The courts adhere to this rule, finding that the addition of a party as an original debtor is an alteration, even though this would likely work to the benefit of the guarantor. If there are several principal debtors, the release of one such principal is held to be to be a material alteration, thereby releasing the guarantor from further responsibility.

In some instances, a creditor may release a struggling debtor who makes a partial settlement on the whole debt. Usually a contract or binding promise not to sue the debtor for the balance acts as a discharge for the surety or guarantor. An extension of time to a debtor who is having difficulty in meeting an obligation is also construed as a material alteration. The guarantor's or surety's obligation is strictly limited to his or her contract, and any change that is not consented to discharges liability.

If the debtor has pledged stock or any other kind of collateral, the surety or guarantor is entitled to the benefit of any promised securities. If such collateral is surrendered back to the debtor or the securities are lost through carelessness or negligence of the creditor, the surety or guarantor is still entitled to have the collateral applied to the debt.

Upon adjudication as a bankrupt, a surety or guarantor is discharged by operation of law. If the debtor makes a proper tender of payment which is refused by the creditor, the tender does not always discharge the obligation of the surety or guarantor. There is a split of opinion by the courts, some holding that the surety or guarantor is completely discharged along with the debtor by a valid tender of payment. Some other courts, however, rule that the tender merely stops the running of interest charges and that the surety or guarantor continues to be responsible for the debt.

Subrogation and Contribution

A surety or guarantor who is forced to pay for the debtor is automatically given the creditor's rights and claims against the debtor. This is legal right of *subrogation*.

Even though there may be two or more sureties or guarantors, the creditor is entitled to look to any one of them for full satisfaction. As between themselves, however, the guarantors or sureties are each responsible for a proportionate part of the obligation. A guarantor or surety who has been required to pay more than a proportionate share is entitled to claim a recovery against the other sureties or guarantors. This claim can be enforced by a lawsuit.

Exoneration

Normally a surety or guarantor will not agree to stand responsible for the credit of a debtor who is not both honest and capable of repaying the debt. On occasion, however, trust in the debtor may be misplaced. For example, if the surety or guarantor learns that the debtor is leaving the state and carrying away or fraudulently disposing of assets, the surety or guarantor has the right to call on the creditor to enforce the creditor's claims. If at that time the creditor has the right to proceed against the debtor and does not do so, the surety or guarantor will be *exonerated* to the extent that the creditor's lack of activity caused harm. This is legally known as the *right of exoneration*.

_____ QUESTIONS _____

1. What is a judgment? What does it consist of? How is it obtained?
2. What is a writ of execution?
3. Explain what is meant by the statement that "the sheriff or other court officer must levy upon the judgment debtor's property."
4. Explain how a sale works under a levy of execution.
5. What is meant by the judgment debtor's *right of redemption*?
6. Describe an attachment and the way in which it is used against an absconding debtor.
7. What legal action may be taken by a creditor when a debtor fraudulently conveys real estate to a relative to avoid the creditor's claims?
8. Explain how wages or salary may be subject to garnishment. What are the limitations on garnishment under modern law?
9. What is a *secured transaction*?
10. How is the creditor's security interest usually perfected?

11. Describe the rights of the parties in a typical security interest sale by a retail store to a consumer.

12. Under the statue of frauds, is it usually required that the promise to answer for the debt of another be in writing?

13. Describe some of the defenses typically available to sureties and guarantors.

14. Is a guarantor liable if the creditor and debtor alter the terms of the debt contract?

15. What is meant by subrogation?

PROBLEM CASE

1   The Federal Truth-in-Lending Act provides that a holder's liability on unauthorized use of a credit card is limited to $50. Martin gave his American Express card to a business associate named McBride for McBride's use in a joint business venture. McBride ran up charges of about $5,300 on the card without authorization. Martin refused to stand good for more than $50 on the basis that he had not signed the invoices and that practically all of McBride's expenditures had been unauthorized. Was Martin liable for charges beyond $50? Or does the Truth-in-Lending Act's limit apply only to theft or embezzlement of the credit card? (*Martin* v. *American Express*, 361 So.2d 597.)

29

Debtor's Privileges and Protections; Bankruptcy

DEBTOR'S PROTECTION AGAINST CREDITORS

Exemptions

Practically all states have laws that give debtors some protection against their creditors. Typical are so-called "exemption statutes," granting debtors the right to hold onto a specified amount or certain class of property free from forced sale, judgment, execution, attachment, or any other claim.

Personal property exemptions usually include wearing apparel, toilet articles, family photographs, a specified number of books, a Bible, kitchen utensils, and a limited dollar value of other personal items.

Homestead Exemptions

A real property exemption for debtors is usually called a *homestead exemption*. The homestead right is granted by the state constitution in some states and by statute in others. The basic idea of the homestead exemption is to enable a debtor to keep a roof over the family in times of dire financial straits.

The homestead exemption cannot be used to defeat a mortgage or deed of trust given for the balance of the purchase price of the homestead. For the courts to hold otherwise would make it difficult for a lender to be confident of the security of the loan.

In general the homestead right can be claimed only by the head of the household but in some states the right has been extended to divorced or single debtors. In various states the law operates to allow the debtor to actually withhold from creditors a certain amount of farm or ranch land or a home of less than a set value. Usually, however, laws of this kind provide that upon the forced sale of the family home to satisfy a judgment debt, a specified amount of the sale proceeds shall be paid to the judgment debtor.

The homestead claim is ordinarily made by filing an exemption form with the recorder of deeds in the county where the homestead property is located. Some jurisdictions permit a claimant to transfer the homestead right from one tract of real estate to another by filing a new homestead exemption form along with a form declaring an abandonment of the previous homestead right.

Offer of Legal Tender

Creditors may not assert their powers over debtors without restrictions. Both legislatures and the courts have set up some basic legal safeguards for debtors.

In most instances the debtor's obligation is to pay or deliver money or property to the creditor. In most instances the debtor pays what is owed by furnishing the creditor with the amount of the obligation in "legal tender."

Federal laws[1] define legal tender as those types of United States currency that may be offered to a creditor for the payment of private or public debts. Before the passage of Federal laws on this subject, a debtor who wanted to harrass a creditor sometimes laboriously counted out repayment of a debt in several thousand dollars in pennies. This may no longer be done: today nickels and pennies are legal tender up to only 25 cents. Dimes, quarters, and half dollars are legal tender up to the amount of 10 dollars. United States notes (greenbacks), treasury notes, silver dollars, silver certificates, national bank notes, and Federal bank notes are now accepted as legal tender by the courts. The possession and use of gold was outlawed in 1934, though today one may again legally possess gold. Because of the considerable value of gold coins, today they are merely used as a collector's item.

The Act of Tender

The courts usually consider *tender* to be

> the act by which one produces and offers to a person holding a claim or demand against [the debtor] the amount of money which [the debtor] considers and admits to be due, in satisfaction of such claim or demand, without any stipulation or condition.[2]

or, stated differently

> the actual proffer of money, as distinguished from mere proposal or proposition to proffer it.[3]

[1] Legal Tender Act of Congress, 1980; Act of Congress, June, 1933; Gold Embargo Act of January 30, 1934.
[2] *Kastens v. Ruland,* 120 A. 21.
[3] *Walker v. Houston,* 12 P.2d 952.

Courts often hold that a debtor is not permitted to add any condition or stipulation to the offer that is inconsistent with the debt as it exists. According to the legal maxim, "a conditional tender is invalid." In addition, for a tender to be valid, it must be made at the time or after the debt becomes due. A creditor need not accept payment of an obligation until it is due. Then, too, the debtor must physically exhibit the money to the creditor, stating the amount and making an actual offer to pass it to the latter.

Usually, the courts have decided that the giving of negotiable commercial paper to a creditor for a debt does not constitute payment, whether the negotiable paper was executed by the debtor or by a third party. The courts frequently say that the original debt remains in force until discharged by payment in full. If, however, the parties work out a new contract, there may be a valid agreement that the negotiable paper shall constitute payment in full. This agreement serves to satisfy the original debt, leaving the debt created by negotiation of the instrument. The offer of a check is not a legal tender, neither is a tender part of a debt. In addition to offering the face amount of the debt, the debtor must tender all accrued interest and any costs that may be payable under the terms of the agreement.

Tender of Less Than Full Amount Due

An impoverished debtor sometimes makes a tender of less than the full amount due. As noted in contract law, most courts hold that a promise by a debtor to pay less than the full amount in exchange for a discharge from debt constitutes lack of consideration; such a reduced payment will not act as a discharge unless the new agreement calls for some type of new performance on the part of the debtor.

A creditor may refuse a tender of less than the full amount due without affecting the creditor's rights in any way.

Refusal of the Tender

Most courts regard the debtor as not being relieved of the debt merely because the creditor refused to accept the tender. But if the tender is proper and the creditor refuses, the creditor is not entitled to any further interest or charge based on the debt. Then, if the creditor should subsequently sue for payment of the debt, most courts will require the debtor to pay for the principle of the debt plus interest up until the time of the tender. At the same time the courts will mandate that the creditor pay all costs of the litigation. Consequently, no creditor should ever refuse a proper tender of payment for debt.

Suits on Debt: Statute of Limitations

All jurisdictions have statutes that restrict the time in which certain court actions can be brought. In effect, state statutes of limitations deny the creditor the aid of the courts in the collection of stale debts. The period of time of a lawsuit for enforcement of debt varies from state to state and according to the nature of the monetary obligation. For example, the California Code of Civil Procedure provides:

> Civil Actions, without exception, can only be commenced within the periods prescribed in this title, after the cause of action shall have accrued, unless where, in special cases, a different limitation is prescribed by statute. . . . Any action upon any contract, obligation, or liability founded upon an instrument in writing . . . shall be commenced within four years.[4]

Most courts determine that a statute of limitations does not discharge the debt. However, such a law prevents the creditor from coming into court with a lawsuit after the lapse of the statutory period. The practical effect, of course, is to cancel the debt.

Harassment in Debt Collection

As late as 1830, prisons along the Atlantic seaboard of the United States were filled with persons jailed for failing to pay debts. Laws have changed considerably over the years, but individuals are still held legally responsible for debts that were incurred lawfully. At the same time, a creditor does not have the right to abuse the debtor in making collections. Most courts permit the debtor to sue for damages if the creditor sends fictitious letters that appear to have originated with the courts or if definite threats are made to take legal action that is not permitted.

In one recent case,[5] a finance company set out to harass a man and wife who owed $185 plus interest. The husband had no job but expressed willingness to pay when work was obtained. The debtors' telephone service had been discontinued, and the creditor had the debtor called to the telephone of a neighbor late at night when the weather was bad. The creditor's representative explained to the friend that the debtors were "deadbeats" and made other insulting remarks, also going to the debtors' neighborhood, using loud and abusive language that could be heard throughout the area. Tactics of this kind continued for a considerable period. The debtors then filed a lawsuit and were awarded damages. In holding for the debtors, the court stated:

> Our courts have long since declared and recognized the right to recovery of damages for the infliction of emotional disturbance. . . . [The making of] efforts to coerce payment of debt is actionable under our

[4]Cal. C.P., Secs. 312, 337.
[5]*Boudreaux* v. *Allstate Finance Corp.*, 217 So.2d 439.

laws when the creditor, in an attempt to collect a debt justly due, unreasonably coerces the debtor or seriously abridges the . . . right to privacy . . . in personal affairs.

CONSUMER CREDIT LEGISLATION

Uniform Consumer Credit Code

A number of states have passed the Uniform Consumer Credit Code (UCCC), a model law designed to protect the rights of debtor-consumers. This law requires a written disclosure of the annual percentage rate of interest on the unpaid balance of a consumer purchase.

The Uniform Consumer Credit Code also provides that a creditor who repossesses merchandise worth less than $1,000 from a debtor and sells it cannot thereafter obtain a deficiency judgment against the debtor when proceeds of the forced sale are insufficient to pay the balance due.[6]

Federal Consumer Credit Protection Act (Commonly Known as Truth-in-Lending Act)

In 1969 Congress passed the Consumer Credit Protection Act,[7] more commonly known as the Federal Truth-in-Lending Act. This statute gives protection to debtors both in buying consumer goods and in borrowing money. It does not apply to a sale by one consumer to another, and there are other limits on its application. The basic purpose of the law was to assist consumers who were "remarkably ignorant of the nature of their credit obligations and of the cost of deferring payments."[8]

In essence, Section 121 of the Truth-in-Lending Act provides that any installment contract or sale in foreign or interstate commerce, payable in four or more payments, is subject to the law. As explained by Chief Justice Burger of the United States Supreme Court, this law:

> requires merchants who regularly extend credit, with attendant finance charges, to disclose certain contract information "to each person to whom consumer credit is extended and upon whom a finance charge is or may be imposed. . . ." Among other relevant facts, the merchant must, where applicable, list the cash price of the merchandise or service sold, the amount of finance and other charges, and the

---

[6]UCCC, Sec. 5.103; and see *Central Finance Co.* v. *Stevens*, 558 P.2d 122.

[7]Title 15, U.S. Code, Sec. 1601, adding Title VI.

[8]U.S. Supreme Court Justice Warren Burger, in the opinion in *Mourning* v. *Family Publications Service*, 93 S.Ct. 1652.

rate of the charges. Failure to disclose renders the seller liable to the consumer for a penalty of twice the amount of the finance charge, but in no event less than $100 or more than $1,000. The creditor may also be assessed for the costs of the litigation, including reasonable attorney's fees, and in certain circumstances not relevant here, may be the subject of criminal charges. . . .[9]

When consumer credit is advertised as payable in five or more install-ments and no finance charge is stated, the ad must clearly and conspicuously state that credit costs are included in the price of the goods or services.[10]

The Federal Truth-in-Lending Act also makes it difficult for credit terms to go unnoticed by the buyer of an installment purchase. When the terms of the contract are printed on two sides of a contract, both sides must carry the warning: "NOTICE: See other side for important information." In addition, at the bottom of the reverse side the contract form must be signed by the buyer. The courts have held that signing only on the front is insufficient.[11]

This requirement that such contracts bear "notice" statements on both sides has been defended in the courts. In 1976, an individual paid a down payment of $381.04 on stereo equipment, leaving an unpaid balance of $800. The seller did not finance sales contracts of this kind but rather sold the debt to the Southwestern Investment Company. The buyer signed a sales contract and a finance agreement on a form provided by Southwestern. This contract was printed on two sides of a single sheet of paper. In violation of Regulation Z of the Truth-in-Lending Act, it failed to include all necessary disclosures on the same side of the page as well as above and adjacent to the customer's signature. Because of this failure the buyer sued for damages and attorney's fees. The court pointed out that Regulation Z requires a notice to be printed in large letters on both sides of such a contract; this was missing from the Southwestern form. Accordingly, the court awarded damages and attorney's fees to the purchaser (consumer).[12] Since 1976, this decision has been fol-lowed by other courts.

A consumer may rescind a purchase contract when requirements of the Federal Truth-in-Lending Law are not complied with by the seller. If this happens, the buyer "is not liable for any finance or other charge, and any security interest given . . . becomes void upon such a recission. Within 20 days after receipt of a notice of recission, the creditor shall return . . . any money or property given as earnest money, downpayment, or otherwise."[13]

---

[9]*Ibid*. Under the interpretations placed on interstate goods by the Federal courts, almost 100 percent of all business sales are covered by the law.

[10]See Public Law 93–495.

[11]*McDonald* v. *Savoy*, 501 S.W.2d 400.

[12]*Southwestern Inv. Co.* v. *Mannix*, 540 S.W.2d 747.

[13]Title 15, U.S. Code, Sec. 1635(b).

Federal Fair Credit Billing Act

The Federal Fair Credit Billing Act of 1974 was enacted to help buyers settle credit billing disputes. The law applies if the following kinds of billings are in dispute:

1. Charges incurred by someone not authorized to use the consumer's credit card.
2. Charges made for an item or service that the consumer did not accept or that was delivered in error.
3. Charges that are legitimately questioned by the consumer.
4. Mistakes on the bill that were made by the seller's accounting office.
5. Failure to credit a payment to the consumer's account.
6. Late payment charges imposed when the bill was not forwarded to the consumer's current address, provided the consumer had given notice of this change of address at least 10 days before the end of the billing period.

When a buyer-consumer files a complaint regarding a disputed billing of the kind listed, the law specifies that:

1. The creditor must acknowledge receipt of the complaint within 30 days, thereafter attempting to settle the dispute in less than 90 days.
2. The creditor may not attempt to collect the amount in dispute during the 90-day period.
3. The creditor may not report the consumer as delinquent while the matter is being resolved, if this is the only overdue money.
4. The consumer has the right to withhold payment for defective goods or services. This withholding must be in accordance with the terms agreed to in writing by the creditor when the account was opened.

Since the passage of the Federal Fair Credit Billing Act, a number of states have passed laws that are identical or similar in terms. The great majority of consumer transactions are covered by either the Federal or state legislation.

Federal Fair Credit Reporting Act

The Federal Fair Credit Reporting Act (FCRA) was enacted in 1970 to protect consumers from the possibility of abuses if their credit should be reported improperly. The law applies only to consumer credit for the purchase of items for "personal, family, and household use."

The statute covers two types of credit transactions. First, it covers instances in which a person is refused employment, credit, or insurance because of a poor credit report. After one of these benefits has been refused, the person can demand (1) to be informed of the name of the reporting agency, (2) to be furnished the information given in the credit report, and (3) to have the opportunity to set forth the consumer's version of the information in dispute.

It should be pointed out that a report retained in a file by a business concerning the payment record or credit experience with an individual is not a consumer credit report within the meaning of the law. There is no way that the consumer can force the business to disclose this record.

Second, FRCA covers investigative consumer reports—those produced when a prospective creditor has someone check available reports already on file with a credit bureau or conducts a new investigation concerning creditworthiness. In cases of this kind, the consumer can request the following: (1) the extent and purpose of the investigation, (2) the identity of persons or companies to whom the report has been sent, and (3) the information that has been placed in the credit reporting agency's file.

After examining the material in the file, the consumer can demand that the reporting agency reinvestigate inaccurate information that has been recorded. If facts in dispute cannot be verified by reinvestigation, the consumer has the right to have such facts stricken from the file. In any event, the consumer has the right to insert a 100-word explanation concerning any matter in dispute. The law makes it obligatory that this statement be furnished in future credit reports that contain the disputed material.

In addition, Federal law requires the removal of noncurrent information from consumer's credit files. For example, money judgments issued more than seven years earlier, judgments that are beyond the statute of limitations, or bankruptcies more than 14 years earlier may not be included in credit reports if the consumer objects.

Undoubtedly the Federal Fair Credit Reporting Act has corrected consumer injustices in some instances. On the other hand, the law has sometimes made a mockery of business reliance on credit reports. Neighbors and acquaintances of a questionable security risk are often reluctant to furnish derogatory information when such facts will be made available to the individual in question. Then, too, a poor credit risk may be able to have information deleted from his or her file because it is not readily proved by incontrovertible evidence. Experience with debtors also shows that a poor credit risk in past years is more likely to be a future credit risk.

COMPOSITION OF CREDITORS

All jurisdictions recognize the validity of a debtor's *composition of creditors*. This legal arrangement is sometimes called a *composition*, a *composition of creditors*, or a *composition with creditors*. In essence, a composition is an agreement or settlement between a debtor and creditors to divide the debtor's assets among creditors, or part of them, in satisfaction of the whole debt. Through this arrangement the debtor is released from that which is owed to each creditor individually. The legal problem here is that courts generally hold that a creditor's agreement with a debtor to accept less than the whole sum for the debt is not enforceable, being unsupported by consideration. The courts, however, fairly consistently say that the promise of one creditor to forbear is consideration for the like promise of other creditors to follow suit.

A composition is frequently a device to avoid bankruptcy with each creditor getting a *pro rata* part of the debtor's assets immediately. Creditors usually fare better in this kind of settlement than if the debtor is forced into bankruptcy, since the costs of the administration of the bankruptcy can be avoided.

BANKRUPTCY

Bankruptcy is a financial state or condition of one who is entitled to file for relief of debts or who is liable to be proceeded against by creditors and who wants to take advantage of Federal bankruptcy laws. One may file for bankruptcy if current debts cannot be paid when due or if liabilities exceed assets. The term bankruptcy is often used loosely to mean *insolvency*, an inability to meet financial obligations as they fall due. At times an insolvent may have enough assets to pay off all of his or her debts, but still may have trouble in liquidating them.

Realizing the need for uniformity in business, the framers of the United States Constitution gave Congress the right "to establish . . . uniform laws on the subject of bankruptcies throughout the United States."[14]

Early Theories of Bankruptcy

Bankruptcy laws apparently arose because debtors often did not make an equitable distribution of assets, favoring some creditors over others. It was recognized, too, that many people are simply inexperienced in business, unable to handle credit, or to a limited extent victims of a speculative society. Some early legal minds reasoned that society should meet a debtor halfway, giving a meritorious individual a second opportunity to build a new life.

At the same time courts, legislatures, and the general public historically had a certain skepticism of anyone involved in bankruptcy. Too frequently, the bankruptcy process involved fraudulent conveyances of the bankrupt's real property and concealment of merchandise, money, or other assets, all

---

[14]Article I, Section 8(4), U.S. Constitution.

intended to defraud creditors. A generation or two ago, ethical individuals went into bankruptcy with considerable reluctance, usually only when forced to do so. After being discharged from bankruptcy, a number of these persons devoted a good part of their lives to paying off creditors who had not been reimbursed in full. Typically, people who had gone into bankruptcy were seldom thereafter afforded much credit.

Over the years an increasing number of people in business have come to accept bankruptcy as the only solution for too many debts. Much of the early stigma of bankruptcy has disappeared from the world of commerce, and a bankrupt who appears to be worthy can often obtain credit for a subsequent business. At the same time bankruptcy should never be considered "the easy way out." There is always the possibility that fraud may be involved. And even if the bankrupt is completely honest, creditors often seem to feel a larger part of the obligation could have been repaid by a debtor who was willing "to bend his or her back to the wheel."

Two Basic Types of Proceedings: Voluntary and Involuntary Bankruptcy

Bankruptcy proceedings fall into two classes: voluntary and involuntary. A voluntary petition is filed by the debtor who wants to begin the process; an involuntary petition is filed by creditors if the debtor is unwilling to file. Both are done on special forms available from the U.S. District Court. A filing fee must be paid by all petitioners.

Detailed schedules listing the petitioner's or firm's assets, liabilities, and creditors must be included with the petition. In a voluntary proceeding the debtor files these papers, swearing under oath as to their accuracy. The willful giving of a false oath or concealment of assets is a criminal violation (a felony) under the bankruptcy laws.

When an involuntary petition is filed by creditors, it must allege that the debtor has committed an "act of bankruptcy," specifically set forth by law. These enumerated acts are as follows:

1. By conveying or transferring, while insolvent, any portion of his or her property to one or more creditors, with intent to prefer such creditor or creditors over others;
2. By concealing, removing, or permitting to be concealed or removed any assets or part of his or property with intent to hinder, delay, or defraud a creditor or creditors;
3. By allowing or permitting, while insolvent, the obtaining of a lien by any of his or her creditors through legal proceedings, which lien has not been satisfied or vacated;
4. By giving a general assignment for the benefit of creditors; or

5. By admitting in writing his or her inability to pay debts, along with willingness to be adjudged a bankrupt.

After an involuntary petition in bankruptcy is filed, the debtor is given an opportunity to answer the petition and fill out schedules.

After these have been filed and examined in either voluntary or involuntary proceedings, the court rules on whether the debtor should be declared a bankrupt. If so declared, the court takes jurisdiction over the bankrupt's property and assets. In either type of proceeding, the court notifies creditors of the date by which their claims are to be filed, along with a date for a meeting between creditors and the debtor.

If it appears likely to the court that the debtor's assets may be dissipated or lost, a *receiver* may be appointed by the court to preserve them. Usually a receiver is only a temporary representative of the court, taking charge of property or the bankrupt's business until a *trustee in bankruptcy* can be elected by the creditor. If the creditors fail to designate a trustee, the court will appoint one. Of course, if the debtor no longer has any assets it is not necessary to appoint a trustee.

The debtor (bankrupt) may be questioned by the creditors at a creditors' meeting to determine the location and extent of all assets. Creditors may inquire into whether property may have been concealed or fraudulently transferred. In "no asset" cases, as a practical matter, proceedings are concluded by this meeting. If no fraud has been involved and there actually are no assets left, the bankruptcy court may discharge the debtor within a short time. Bankruptcy may not be filed again for six years.

Discharge of Personal Liability Only

A discharge in bankruptcy does not affect a mortgage, lien, or other secured interest on the bankrupt's property that was valid prior to the bankruptcy; only the debtor's personal liability is discharged.

To receive a *pro rata* share of the bankrupt's assets, a creditor must have a provable claim and must file it with the bankruptcy court. Usually, provable claims are those that result from judgments or from the debtor's liability on commercial paper. To be regarded as provable by the bankruptcy court, a claim must be certain in amount or it must be liquidated. Accordingly, a tort claim or dispute involving a contract may not be considered provable.

The basic belief in bankruptcy is often that the debtor's assets should be converted into cash, the debtor's business wound up, and the cash divided among the creditors. This kind of procedure is usually desirable in settling the affairs of an individual or a small business. But frequently it would be very costly to the creditors to apply this type of procedure to all businesses, particularly those that are large and complicated—especially when the economy may be undergoing a severe shrinkage in property values. Consequently, the bankruptcy court may not wind up the affairs of a business until it is reasonable to do so.

Denial of Discharge

The bankrupt is normally discharged by the court after his or her business affairs have been brought to a conclusion and the bankrupt's assets are distributed to creditors. For most purposes, the bankrupt may then begin a new financial life. But discharge from prior debts may not be granted by the bankruptcy court in all instances. The court may deny a discharge, continuing to hold the bankrupt liable for the unpaid portion of all claims. In the meanwhile, the court goes ahead with the distribution of the bankrupt's assets to the creditors. The Bankruptcy Act specifies that the court will deny discharge if it is found that the bankrupt has committed an act considered a crime, such as destroying, mutilating, concealing, or failing to keep records from which business transactions could be ascertained; concealing and lying about assets; or defrauding creditors in other ways.

—————— QUESTIONS ————————————————————————

1. What is meant by debtor's exemptions?
2. Describe the operation of state homestead laws as a type of real property exemption for debtors.
3. Define tender as used in the payment of a debt.
4. Is there valid consideration for a contract to pay less than the full amount due to a creditor? Explain.
5. What is the legal status between debtor and creditor if the creditor refuses a valid tender?
6. Are creditors sometimes barred from recovery of a debt by the statute of limitations? Explain.
7. What are the debtor's rights when harassed unreasonably by the creditor?
8. Under the Uniform Consumer Credit Code may a creditor who reposesses the property from a debtor thereafter obtain a deficiency judgment? Explain.
9. Describe the basic theory behind the Federal Truth-in-Lending Act as it applies to consumer sales.
10. Outline basic features of the Federal Fair Credit Billing Act and the Federal Fair Credit Reporting Act.
11. What is meant by a composition of creditors?
12. Do the various states have bankruptcy laws?

13. Describe the basic workings of the bankruptcy procedure.

14. Differentiate between voluntary and involuntary bankruptcy.

15. Is a mortgage on the bankrupt's home discharged by bankruptcy?

16. What may be the legal result if the debtor conceals property or assets from the bankruptcy court?

17. Is the bankrupt always discharged at the conclusion of the Federal bankruptcy proceedings? Explain.

_____ *PROBLEM CASES* _____

1 A retail credit bureau erroneously reported that one Bartels was a heavy drinker in a report furnished when Bartels applied for life insurance. The insurance company declined to issue a policy. As a result of this erroneous report, Bartels's automobile insurance was cancelled. Bartels filed suit against the credit bureau. The defense presented was that the credit bureau had been furnished reports in confidence and that they should not be disclosed. Bartels's attorney contended that confidentiality was a side issue and that the credit bureau should be liable if reasonable care was not exercised in obtaining and reporting credit information. Decide the lawsuit. (*Bartels* v. *Retail Credit Bureau*, 175 N.W.2d 292.)

2 The Federal Truth-in-Lending Act requires a full disclosure of financing terms in credit transactions. Jordan bought a stereo set from Montgomery Ward on credit. He relied on a statement in the Montgomery Ward catalogue that stereo sets could be charged with no payment required for several months. Montgomery Ward, however, failed to advise that they charged interest from the outset. Was the seller liable for this unanticipated interest? (*Jordan* v. *Montgomery Ward*, 442 F.2d 78.)

30

Insurance

INSURANCE FUNCTIONS AND PROVIDERS _____

How Insurance Operates

Both individuals and business firms have always faced the likelihood of loss—loss of investments or savings by fire or catastrophe, loss of business property, home, automobile, and other important assets and values. A person, generally speaking, is simply not always able to bear losses as they occur. At times a single loss could overwhelm even those with considerable funds. Insurance serves as a shock absorber, enabling the individual to greatly reduce monetary losses that result from given risks.

Insurance is a binding arrangement by which an insurance company contracts to pay a second party a sum of money if the latter suffers a specified loss. Since the agreement between the two sides is a contract, the general rules of contract law are used to determine obligations and responsibilities between the parties.

Essentially, insurance functions by building up a fund from which the insurance company pays losses by collecting *premiums* or payments from individuals who want to be spared risk. One hundred persons, pooling their risks, can more easily and less disastrously share aggregate losses than an individual can pay for a single loss. One thousand persons can reach the same result with even less cost per individual. By this principle of pooling risks, an insurance company distributes losses over a long period and over a large number of persons.

Reduced to simplest terms, a contract of insurance is called a *policy*. In insurance terminology, the promisor to the contract is the *underwriter* or *insurer* and the individual promised protection is the *insured*.

Types of Insurance Companies

The two basic types of insurance companies are proprietary organizations and cooperatives. The *proprietary* firms include stock companies and syndicates of individual insurers that join together, called underwriters. Stock companies are, of course, owned by individual stockholders. Underwriting syndicates usually issue short-term policies covering unusual property risks, sometimes the types of risks that others do not have the capitalization to cover. Lloyd's of London is probably the best-known syndicate of underwriters in the world.

In *cooperatives* the policyholders are the actual owners of the company and are sometimes known as participating shareholders. Policyholders are entitled to a dividend as a consequence of lower operating costs or favorable loss experience.

Some mutual companies are set up as *assessment mutuals*, levying assessments (or charges) against individual policyholders when money is needed to pay off company losses.

Some major corporations are said to be *self-insured*, meaning that the company has such extensive assets that it carries the risk of loss without purchasing insurance from an outside firm.

Types of Coverage Available

Insurance, as conceived today, existed before the year 1400 among Italian merchants and traders seeking to protect themselves from cargo loss by shipwreck. Marine insurance was introduced to shipping interests in London, where an organization of *underwriters* at Lloyd's began to sell coverage to merchants in 1688. Real growth of fire and life insurance did not come until about 1850.

In today's world, where every individual and every kind of property faces potential loss, insurance is available to cover almost any possible risk. For example, boiler and machinery insurance protects industrial and manufacturing plants from losses due to an exploding boiler or a mechanical breakdown. Coverage provided by a policy of this kind may be limited to the policyholder's plant and property or it may extend to include damage to other property and outside persons.

Some insurance may protect against loss in agricultural crops, plate-glass window breakage, business burglary, or computer damage. Common types of coverage include automobile, fidelity, health, fire, life, casualty, and credit insurance.

Insurable Interest in Property

It is a universal principle of insurance law that the beneficiary, or person seeking to be repaid, must have an "insurable interest" in the property. In general, the courts say a person has an insurable interest in property whenever destruction or loss of the property would cause that party a direct financial loss. The person seeking repayment must be one who has suffered loss and is seeking a return to the same fiscal position. For example, a private citizen could not have an insurable interest in the White House. The private person would suffer no direct personal loss if the White House accidentally burned to the ground.

The titleholder to property, whether real or personal, always has an insurable interest in it. This right is not altered by the fact that the property has been mortgaged or that liens exist against it. In addition, practically all courts hold that the mortgagee who loans money on real estate also has an insurable interest in the property.

When two parties enter into a contract, agreeing to transfer ownership of a tract of real estate, the courts rule that either or both have an insurable interest in the property. In a similar manner, both the lessor and lessee of real property are generally regarded as having an insurable interest, as is the bailor or bailee of property. Some special rules apply in policies covering life insurance.

There is practical logic behind the requirement that the beneficiary must have an insurable interest in the insured property. If this were not so, a stranger could obtain fire insurance on another individual's house and then burn it to the ground without compunction.

Most courts also hold that a stockholder has an insurable interest in corporate property to the extent of the stockholder's investment. Usually, however, courts deny that a creditor has an insurable interest in the debtor's property. In such a situation, again, the creditor might be tempted to put property to the torch in order to recover on a questionable investment.

Insurable Interest in Lives

The courts have always voiced concern about allowing one person to insure the life of another. In some instances the beneficiary of such a policy could be tempted to bring about the death of the insured. The insurable interest here does not necessarily depend on kinship or on any responsibility for support. The courts usually say that "the relationship between the parties must be such that one has a monetary interest in the life of the other." A wife, husband, or child always has an insurable interest. A sister has an insurable interest in the life of a brother, or an aunt in the life of a nephew where it was clear that they had relied on the other in times of need. Between relatives, an insurable interest is based not on the relationship but on the fact that the survivor could suffer financial loss as a result of the death of the other.

The courts are also in agreement that a partner has an insurable interest in one or more partners and that a corporation has an insurable interest in a key company official. The courts have also generally decided that an agent may insure the life of the principal or the principal may insure the life of the agent when an employment relationship exists between them. In addition, a creditor has an insurable interest in the life of a debtor. And, of course, every individual has an interest in his or her own life for insurance purposes.

State Regulation of Insurance Contracts and Coverage

All states now require insurance contracts to be in writing. Practically all activities of insurance companies throughout the United States today are regulated by a state insurance commissioner or other state official. Basic provisions, as well as policy forms and indorsements (sometimes spelled as endorsements), must usually be approved by the state insurance commissioner.

Nineteenth-century fire insurance firms, for example, used individual policy forms, usually drafted to limit company liability. Sometimes containing a great many exceptions, policies often enabled the company to avoid paying for some losses that policyholders supposed were covered. An old saying sometimes heard in this connection was: "the large print (in the policy) giveth, but the fine print taketh away."

Now practically all fire insurance companies use standard policies that are uniform from state to state—policies that have been approved by state insurance commissioners. While there are exceptions and conditions in almost any insurance policy, most of the old "booby traps" have been eliminated. Nonetheless, the buyer of any insurance policy should carefully read the entire document before accepting it. Both the insured and the insurance company are bound only by the coverage set out in the policy. If the coverage is not as expected, the policy can never be construed to cover such losses if they occur.

For example, automobile drivers have sometimes supposed that their automobile insurance was in effect, only to learn after a collision that their policy did not apply when pulling a rented trailer full of household goods. In the same vein, some fire insurance policies have a provision that fire insurance is not in force if the house remains unoccupied for 60 consecutive days.

Liability of Insurance Company for Acts of Its Agents

Fire insurance, automobile insurance, and many other types of coverage are purchased through an insurance *agent* or an insurance *broker*, between which there is a significant legal difference. A broker may represent a number of insurance companies, being the agent of none of them. If a broker fails to obtain insurance for a customer after being instructed to do so, the broker will be personally liable for this failure in the event of loss, but none of the insurance companies that the broker represents will be obligated. If, however, the person who agrees to furnish insurance coverage is an agent of the insurance company, then the insurance company is bound. Here the usual rules of agency apply. If the agent has authority, either actual or ostensible, the insurance company is liable for the loss. The difference in this case is that in the event of loss a broker might not have assets that could be reached through a lawsuit by the customer, whereas almost any solvent insurance company has a great deal in the way of assets.

Insurance agents and brokers almost never have authority to modify a company contract or form. If corrections or alterations must be made, they can usually be handled by an indorsement attached to the original policy. But these are seldom binding until received and approved at the home office of the insurance company.

Concealment of Material Facts from the Insurance Company

Most of the basic rules of contract law apply to every insurance contract. Normally, the parties to a contract need not disclose any confidential information bearing on the agreement, so long as there is an absence of dishonesty and misrepresentation of the facts in reaching agreement. In an insurance contract, however, the courts consistently hold that the person seeking insurance must make a voluntary disclosure of any material that significantly increases the risk of loss to the insurance company. For example, life insurance companies sometimes sell policies in moderate amounts without requiring the applicant to submit to physical examination by a doctor. If an applicant for a policy concealed a heart condition in application questions, the company could refuse to pay when this defect was revealed by the insured's death. Concealment of prior accidents or driving citations by one applying for automobile insurance would also lead to a refusal to pay for claims submitted by the insured.

When an Insurance Policy Becomes Effective

The usual rule is that an insurance policy does not become effective until it is accepted by the company. But there are exceptions. For example, an air travel insurance policy is binding when a passenger pays a clerk at the insurance company booth in the airport or when the payment and application are dropped in the mail box or the insurance company vending machine equipped to receive them.

The Binder

An agent for an insurance company almost never has authority to issue an insurance policy on the spot. Instead, the agent takes an application and forwards it to the company's main office for approval and issuance. Individuals frequently need insurance coverage immediately, however. To effectuate this coverage, the agent issues to the applicant a brief written statement called a *binder*. Thus, this is a temporary policy that covers the applicant until a regular policy takes effect.

The insurance of the binder does not obligate the company to issue a regular policy. In most instances the company does eventually give the applicant a policy, but the insurance of the binder merely gives the right to temporary coverage until the application can be assessed. If a loss occurs after the binder is written but before the policy is issued, the insurance company must stand good for the loss.

Binders often are issued for fire insurance policies, but seldom, if ever, for health or life insurance, for which insurance companies often require medical examination prior to any coverage.

Company's Rights of Subrogation

When someone is injured by negligence or the wrongdoing of another, the injured person has a right to sue for damages. But often an injured person who is insured turns to the insurance company for satisfaction of the loss. It would amount to double recovery if the injured person could also sue the wrongdoer for damages. Consequently, when an insurance company pays for the wrong of a third party, the company is entitled to take over the legal claim of the injured person, asserting this claim in the courts. In legal language this is the right of *subrogation*. In an instance of this kind the insurance company succeeds to all the rights of the injured party.

FIRE INSURANCE _____

Types of Losses Covered

Fire insurance is a contract to indemnify (compensate or reimburse) a policy-holder against property loss caused by fire. Some fire insurance policies will pay off, however, only when damage was caused by so-called "hostile fires." As distinguished from a hostile fire, a "friendly fire" is one that is kept within normal bounds or limits. For example, a fire on a hearth melted a plastic ornament that was located on a coffee table too close to the fireplace. Since the fire that caused the damage had not leaped out of the fireplace, it was a friendly fire, and the loss would not be indemnified. In similar fashion, a fire in a cook stove that stayed within the confines of the stove would be considered a friendly fire. If, however, the stove split open and fire damage resulted when the house burned down, the courts would require that the loss be indemnified. In effect a friendly fire had gotten out of hand and had become a hostile fire.

The courts usually require that loss by fire includes any harm caused by fire itself, as well as damage by water or chemicals used to quench the fire. Loss from intense heat is also included. Fire insurance policies usually specify that there must be an actual fire, however. This means that there must be visible flame with heat and light, rather than a mere smoldering. Often a policy will not pay for damage to furniture or furnishings by smoke from a defective furnace or stove. In like manner, damage by lightning is not considered fire loss unless combustion actually results.

Coverage of loss by a friendly fire is frequently added to fire insurance policies by indorsement. Also, so-called extended coverage fire insurance policies generally protect against loss as a result of internal combustion; smoke; smoldering; exploding furnaces, stoves, and natural gas lines; and other losses. Most fire insurance companies will add almost any desired coverage by an indorsement to their basic fire insurance policy.

The courts usually determine that the policyholder may collect on a fire insurance claim only if the fire is the immediate cause of the loss. The fire is considered the cause if it sets in motion a chain of events that creates damage. But if an earthquake ruptured a natural gas line, thereby starting a building fire, most courts would not find the insurer liable for the loss on the basis of a fire insurance policy.

Coinsurance Provisions

Some fire insurance policies require the insured to provide insurance on property up to a specified amount or to a specified percent of the property value (usually 80 percent). This is called a *coinsurance* provision. The effect is that if the property is insured for less than the set amount, the insurer is legally responsible only for the proportionate part of the insurance required to be carried. For example, the owner of a building valued at $100,000 was insured for $60,000 under a policy with a coinsurance clause specifying that insurance of 80 percent of value be maintained. When a loss of $40,000 was suffered, the insurance company paid only $30,000, since the amount of insurance carried was only three-fourths of the required figure ($60,000 out of a coinsurance specification of $80,000).

Coinsurance clauses sometimes permit less recovery than the policyholder anticipates. Accordingly, coinsurance provisions are not allowed under insurance laws in some states.

_____ *DISCUSSION* _____

CASE 64 A housewife owned an old German cookbook that had been printed in 1727. Worth considerable money as an antique, the cookbook was listed in an inventory of items of unusual value; this inventory was placed on file with the insurance company, in the event it was ever needed to prove loss. The book's owner placed it on top of the kitchen stove while preparing a recipe. Called away to the telephone, the owner forgot to remove the book, and heat from the stove destroyed its value. Could the policyholder collect from the insurance company?

CASE 65   A building in Utah was destroyed by fire, and the insurance companies that had issued policies refused to pay the property owner. When sued, the insurance companies claimed the property owner had made misrepresentations and had concealed pertinent facts concerning the building so that there had been no meeting of the minds to form a valid contract. The facts showed that the building had at one time been a skating rink. The structure was sectional with part of the building in a stored area for collapsed sections.

The bulk of the building was in reasonable condition and was of considerable value. Because of the condition of part of the structure, the insured had the local insurance agent inspect the premises before writing up the policies. The insurance companies maintained they would never have written the insurance had they known of the nature of the property. It is not clear from the court record whether the agent writing the policies actually informed the companies of the condition of the structure. The insurance companies denied responsibility. Should they be forced to pay? (*Farrington v. Granite State Fire Ins. Co. of Portsmouth et al.*, 232 P.2d 754.)

CASUALTY INSURANCE AND SURETYSHIP (BONDING) _____

Casualty insurance (also called *liability insurance*) and *suretyship (bonding)* protect against injury or losses to a third party for which the insured may be responsible or against loss to assets by third-party action. For example, casualty insurance protects against a lawsuit filed by a customer who slips on the slick floor of a business establishment. Similarly, it indemnifies against the outsider who is injured in one's home or as the result of negligence in the operation of an automobile.

Businesses often make use of suretyship insurance by requiring employees, especially those handling money, to be bonded for theft or embezzlement.

AUTOMOBILE INSURANCE _____

Automobile insurance usually combines casualty (liability) protection for the driver or owner of the vehicle with coverage against harm or loss to the vehicle itself.

Under the casualty coverage it is of no consequence that the policyholder himself or herself caused the injury. If the person operating an automobile was not negligent, there is no way that an outsider could have a legal claim against him or her. Consequently, the casualty coverage in an automobile insurance policy is protection against the policyholder's own negligence.

Liability Coverage

Liability insurance may be purchased by either the owner or the operator of an automobile. This type of policy protects against (1) bodily injury or death or (2) property damage arising out of operation of the vehicle.

Most automobile liability insurance protects the owner of the car when it is operated by another person with the owner's permission. Liability insurance may also be extended in some policies to protect the owner and his or her immediate family from tort liability while driving the automobile of someone else. There are differences in liability coverage granted to family members by various insurance companies. There are also nuances in the coverage of commercial vehicles depending on the insurance company and provisions of state workers' compensation laws.

Financial Responsibility Laws

A few jurisdictions require a driver to obtain liability insurance before being issued a motor vehicle operator's license. Many states have statutes specifying that a driver must carry a certain amount of liability insurance in order to be permitted to drive. Usually a law of this kind does not come into play unless a driver has been involved in an accident, at which time the driver must show proof of financial responsibility before being allowed to drive thereafter.

Uninsured Drivers

The operator of a car involved in a collision with an uninsured motorist may suffer considerable financial loss without being at fault in any way, or the owner of a car may suffer loss when a parked vehicle is struck by a hit-and-run driver. Accordingly, many insurance companies include so-called uninsured motorist coverage in liability policies, either by specific wording in the policy or by an attached indorsement. Some states require individuals to carry uninsured motorist coverage.

No-Fault Insurance

Some states have adopted *no-fault insurance*. Such a system compensates those injured while using an automobile, regardless as to which driver was legally at fault. Usually it pays compensation for medical expenses and lost wages but not for pain or suffering, nor does it grant exemplary (punitive) damages. If a third party, such as a pedestrian, is harmed, no-fault insurance usually provides for this person's medical expenses and lost wages. Laws in some jurisdictions allow for disputes under the no-fault system to be settled by arbitration.

No-fault insurance was devised to hold down the continually rising costs of automobile insurance, due in part to large punitive damage awards, and to eliminate the long delays in settlements of tort suits that, in effect, withheld medical payments to the injured.

Most courts that have considered the legal problems of no-fault insurance have held the concept to be valid. A few courts, however, have held that no-fault insurance amounts to a withholding of constitutional rights and is therefore unconstitutional.

Some legal authorities assert that the no-fault system of automobile insurance will eventually spread to additional states while other authorities are not so sure.

Comprehensive Coverage

Some automobile insurance policies cover against loss by fire or theft. Almost all policies include so-called comprehensive coverage which insures the car owner against nearly any type of loss not caused by collision including fire, theft, glass breakage, lightning, and many other possibilities. This insurance typically excludes damage or loss by mechanical failure, lack of antifreeze protection, and normal wear and tear. Often policies of this kind do not cover loss or theft of personal effects from inside the automobile.

LIFE INSURANCE

Life insurance is a contract requiring the payment of the face amount of the policy upon the death of the insured. The *beneficiary* is the person designated to receive these proceeds. Sometimes the beneficiary has the option of receiving a monthly income for life or for a specified number of years. Life insurance may be used to protect the survivors of the family breadwinner or perhaps the surviving partners of a businessperson who might be hard pressed to replace the deceased's skills, or to pay off the estate for the value of the deceased's interest in the business.

Life insurance premiums are based on the age of the insured and on the mortality experience (death rate of those insured) of life insurance companies throughout the United States. Since women live longer on the average then men, life insurance rates for males are higher than for females of the same age. Insurance premiums are increased ("rated up") if the occupation of the policyholder is more dangerous than that of the average person. For example, the premium rate for a police officer may be increased $5 per year per thousand of life insurance. An automobile race driver or a Hollywood stuntman may be able to find few companies willing to provide life insurance coverage, even at a rate up.

Practically all life insurance companies refuse to write more than a minimum of life insurance without giving the applicant a physical examination. Obviously, a person with a bad heart condition would likely be refused.

Ordinary Life Policies

Life insurance policies differ considerably in features, strengths, drawbacks, and costs. The type most frequently issued is an *ordinary life* or *whole life* policy where a specified premium is paid each year during the entire life of the insured. Usually the insured has the option of paying the annual premium on a quarterly or monthly basis at a slight increase over the annual premium. If the insured dies while the policy is in effect, the insured's beneficiary receives the face amount of the policy. The premium payable continues unchanged until the death of the insured.

Most policies provide that a cash surrender value is available to the insured if the policy cannot be continued, although the sum available is usually quite small until the policy has been if effect for a number of years. Policies of this kind also have surrender values in fully paid insurance without further payment of premiums. Frequently this feature does not become effective until premiums have been paid for three years or more. The amount of paid-up insurance credited varies with the number of premiums paid and is never as much as the face amount of the policy.

20- or 30-Year Pay

Other kinds of life insurance policies are written with premium payments for a limited number of years but with the insurance coverage to continue for the life of the insured. A *20-year pay life* policy requires payments for 20 years at which time the policy is fully paid. Coverage continues until the policyholder dies. Premium payments for such a policy are higher than for an ordinary life policy on which the insured will likely make payments for more than 20 years. Annual premiums for a 30 year pay life policy would be less than those for a 20-year arrangement.

Endowment

An *endowment* policy is an insurance contract that pays the full face amount when the insured reaches a set age such as 55. The policy may be paid for in a lump sum or by an annual premium. If the insured does not live to the specified age, the face amount of the policy is paid to a designated beneficiary. Usually the proceeds from an endowment policy may be left with the insurance company at maturity, being used to purchase a greater amount of fully paid up life insurance. Sometimes the holder of a policy of this kind has the option of receiving a guaranteed monthly income for life in lieu of a cash settlement.

Term Insurance

A *term life insurance* policy requires the payment of premiums for a specified period, such as 5 or 10 years. At the end of the policy period, coverage ceases and the insured is required to pay a higher premium to obtain a new term insurance policy. An individual who in the meantime has developed a serious health problem may be unable to buy new term insurance. Some policies of this type do, however, allow the policyholder to buy an ordinary life policy or 20-year pay policy at the end of the term, paying the regular company rate for an insured of that age. The effect, of course, is to guarantee the insurability of the policyholder. In general, rates for term insurance are considerably below those of other types of life insurance, since term life has no cash surrender value or paid-up life insurance provision.

Designating a Beneficiary

Some life insurance policies do not permit the policyholder to change the beneficiary at will. It is usually to the policyholder's advantage to decline a policy that does not grant such an option however. Otherwise, a wife or husband who had been divorced might still be able to receive the proceeds of a life insurance policy, contrary to the wishes of the policyholder.

───────── QUESTIONS ─────────────────────

1. Define insurance. Explain how insurance operates.
2. List a number of the kinds of insurance coverage available and describe how such coverage applies.
3. Is the insurance company entitled to be advised of all material facts concerning the risk? Amplify.
4. What is the right of subrogation?
5. Why must a policyholder have an insurable interest in the subject matter or the human life that is insured?
6. Explain the liability of an insurance company for the acts of its agent.
7. What is a binder? How does it work?
8. When is an insurance policy effective in most instances? Explain.
9. In fire insurance terminology, what is the difference between a friendly fire and a hostile fire? What is the significance?
10. What is the purpose of liability insurance?
11. What is a financial responsibility law?
12. Explain the need for coverage against uninsured drivers.

13. Explain the differences in ordinary life, 20-year pay, and endowment life insurance policies.

14. Why is it important to be able to change the beneficiary of a life insurance policy?

_____ *ANSWERS TO DISCUSSION CASES* _____

CASE 64   The fire was a friendly fire. Damage from such a fire would not be covered by a fire insurance policy unless there was a special indorsement attached, adding such coverage for a higher premium charge.

CASE 65   The court determined that the agent writing the fire insurance policies was unquestionably the agent of the insurance companies so that they were charged with the agent's knowledge of the character of the building and its condition. The court found that both the insurance companies and the agent represented themselves to the world as having a principal–agent relationship and that their true relationship was of no concern. The court also said, "The insurance companies adopted and took the benefits of all his conduct favorable to them. It seems quite inconsistent for them to accept the advantages . . . yet insist they were not responsible for the knowledge he acquired about the building within the necessary and ordinary scope of his duties in handling the transaction." The court held the insurance companies liable.

_____ *PROBLEM CASES* _____

1   A fire insurance company agent solicited a hail insurance policy covering a farmer's crops. When the farmer paid for the policy and eventually suffered damage, the insurance company refused to pay, claiming that its agent had no authority to write such a policy. The firm pointed out that its charter showed it was incorporated to write fire insurance; hail insurance policies were therefore *ultra vires*. The farmer sued on the hail insurance. Decide. (*Denver Fire Insurance Co.* v. *McClelland*, 9 P.771.)

2   Mr. and Mrs. Peck owned a lawn and garden supply store and they purchased a standard fire insurance policy which provided that the insurance company "shall not be liable for loss occurring while the hazard is increased by any means within the control or knowledge of the insured [the Pecks]." Without advising the insurance company, the Pecks added a seasonal sale of fireworks to their usual merchandise. The fireworks in the store were accidentally discharged and the entire inventory was severely damaged. Was the insurance company liable? (*Standard Marine Ins. Co.* v. *Peck*, 342 P.2d 661.)

3   The owner of a valuable ladies' ring left it wadded up inside a handkerchief which was placed on a dresser alongside some tissues. The tissues and handkerchief were brushed into the trash, eventually being discarded into

an incinerator where the ring was damaged to the extent of $900. The ring's owner made a claim for $900 under a residential fire insurance policy. Would such a claim be covered by insurance on the contents of a home? (*Youse* v. *Employer's Fire Ins. Co.*, 238 P.2d 472.)

4   A blaze broke out in a home that was insured against loss by fire, and two of the walls and part of the roof were completely destroyed. All windows were broken and there was water and smoke damage throughout the remaining part of the structure. The insured sued when the insurance company maintained that the loss was only partial and not total. The plaintiff contended that it was a matter for the jury to decide whether the loss was total. Who was correct? (*Home Ins. Co.* v. *Greene*, 229 So.2d 576.)

5   Ruby Brown had a life insurance policy which stated that payment would not be made if death resulted from "mental disorder, alcoholism, or drug addiction." The insured was killed while driving in an intoxicated state. The insurance company refused to pay. The heirs contended that the company must pay unless it could prove alcoholism, which consisted of continued, excessive use of liquor. Decide. (*Physicians Mutual* v. *Savage*, 296 N.E.2d 165.)

31

Legal Research

In order to understand the concept of legal research, one must first know the nature of the law itself. The law is determined by both *statutes* and *cases* in the jurisdiction in which the research is being conducted. For instance, an Arizona statute would not be the law in Nevada.

CODES/STATUTES

In most states, the statutes are compiled into subjects by *codes* which are arranged alphabetically by subject. For instance, the law related to crimes would be found in the Criminal Code or, in California, in the Penal Code. Within each code, the sections are arranged numerically by section number. For instance, if one were to receive a ticket in violation of "VC§2340.5," the law violated would be found in Section 2340.5 of the Vehicle Code.

An alphabetical index is available for the codes if one does not have the appropriate section number. In addition, each separate code will have its own index.

Annotated Codes

Some codes will be "annotated"—that is, footnotes show cases which used that particular code section, along with law review articles and other sources of information about that particular code. If the research being conducted relates to a particular code violation, then the use of the annotated code would enable the researcher to find additional information from other sources.

Pocket Parts

Each year the legislatures of the various states and the Federal government make new laws. However, the publishers of the Codes do not publish new volumes. Instead, they publish "pocket parts" which are inserted in the back of the main volumes. These parts include only the new laws made or changes to the present laws. Therefore, in addition to looking in the main volume, one must flip to the back of the book to determine whether or not that particular code section has been changed or repealed. Any item underlined in the pocket part indicates an addition to the law, while asterisks signify that that portion of the law was deleted.

Federal Law

Codes on the Federal level are arranged in a similar manner in the United States Codes. Included are the Federal Codes and the United States Constitution.

The United States Constitution

The Constitution is the supreme law of the land and takes precedence over all other laws. It may be found as a separate volume in the United States Code. Similarly, each state constitution is contained in the state codes.

CASE LAW

Case law is comprised of the published opinions of the appellate courts on the state and Federal level. State cases may be found in that state's reporter series. Similar reporting services are available on the Federal level. Since the cases are arranged in the order in which they come down from the courts and not by subject, it is necessary to use other sources to find the appropriate cases.

Listed below are the regional reporter series for the states. It should be noted, however, that New York and California have separate reporters for those states.

Reporter Series	States Included
Atlantic Reporter	Connecticut
	Delaware
	Maine
	Maryland
	New Hampshire
	New Jersey
	Pennsylvania
	Rhode Island
	Vermont
	D.C. (Mun.Cts.App.)

Reporter Series	*States Included*
Northeastern Reporter	Illinois
	Indiana
	Massachusetts
	New York*
	Ohio
Northwestern Reporter	Iowa
	Michigan
	Minnesota
	Nebraska
	North Dakota
	South Dakota
	Wisconsin
Pacific Reporter	Alaska
	Arizona
	California*
	Colorado
	Hawaii
	Idaho
	Kansas
	Montana
	Nevada
	New Mexico
	Oklahoma
	Oregon
	Utah
	Washington
	Wyoming
Southeastern Reporter	Georgia
	North Carolina
	South Carolina
	Virginia
	West Virginia
Southern Reporter	Alabama
	Florida
	Louisiana
	Mississippi
Southwestern Reporter	Arkansas
	Indian Terr.
	Kentucky
	Missouri
	Tennessee
	Texas

*Have their own reporters (California Reporter; New York Reporter.)

Citations

All cases are identified by their "citations" which show the name of the case, the volume under which the cases may be found, the reporter series, and the page number. For instance, the case,

Smith v. *Jones*, 49 U.S. 328 would be found in Volume 49 of the United States Reports on page 328.

LOCAL LAWS

In addition to the laws established by the state legislatures, cities have the opportunity to develop their own laws, sometimes called municipal codes or ordinances. For instance, a city may not allow overnight parking on its streets. This law would apply only to the city which enacted it.

PRIMARY AUTHORITY

Primary authority refers to the actual law in the jurisdiction where the case is being tried and must be applied by the court in that particular decision. In a state case, it will be that state's codes, constitution, appellate court cases, and local ordinances if they are the subject of the case. For instance, if Idaho had a law that would not allow buying alcoholic beverages on Sunday, this law would be primary authority in Idaho but would have no bearing on a case in Nevada.

When a judge or justice is making a decision on a case, he or she must apply the law which is primary authority in that jurisdiction. However, only the actual court decision in a case is primary authority. References to other situations or cases (called "dicta") are not primary authority and not binding.

SECONDARY AUTHORITY

Secondary authority may be followed by the court in reaching a decision, but it is not required. It includes a ruling of a lower court, a ruling of a court in another state, law review articles, legal encyclopedias, attorney general opinions, and any other legal material which is not binding. Although these materials may not be binding, they are often excellent sources for finding primary authority or learning about a particular area of law.

Legal Encyclopedias

Legal encyclopedias are written on both the state and Federal level. They are arranged alphabetically by subject and contain general information about a given area of law. They will often contain citations to cases or code sections which may be found and used as primary authority.

Shepard's Case Citations

If a case citation is available, it may be researched in Shepard's to find subsequent cases which cited the main case. One would find the series encompassed in that volume of Shepard's on the spine of the book and go through the volume numbers numerically, and then find the page number for that particular case. When the appropriate case is found, the parallel citation will be given in parentheses and cases which cited it will be listed after it. It is important to note certain identifying symbols, particularly "o" after the citation, which means that the case overruled the main case. The key for symbols may be found in the front of Shepard's.

Since Shepard's is also published chronologically, it is important to research not only the bound volume but also the subsequently published paperback volumes which include later cases.

Digests

Available on both the state and Federal levels, digests are arranged alphabetically by subject and include information on cases on those subjects. A brief paragraph describes each case, followed by its citation.

CASE BRIEFS

After reading a case for research purposes, a case brief should be prepared. While formats will differ among instructors and attorneys, a general format follows:

1. Case name and citation
2. Issue being decided
3. Rule of law utilized
4. Analysis—why the court applied that law to that issue; an analysis of the court's decision (sometimes called "Application")
5. Decision of the court and rationale

Often the most difficult parts of the case brief are the "Issue being decided" and the "Analysis." Sometimes the case itself will indicate the issue statement, but usually one would have to be framed by the writer. It is sometimes necessary to read a case two or three times to determine the true issue. In other cases, there may be more than one issue.

Usually the "Headnotes" given at the beginning of each case indicate the issues being decided. Although they are not actually a part of the court's decision in the case, they may be used to frame the issue.

The Rule of Law is generally written verbatim within the court's decision and is not difficult to find. However, a careful reading of the case is often necessary to find the Rule of Law.

One may usually use the court's analysis of the facts for the "Analysis" section. It is important to keep in mind that the court had this set of facts and had to find a law which applied. How they reached their decision is the "Analysis."

The court's decision will be found at the end of the case report. The rationale for the ruling will be found in the decision, usually near the end.

The "majority opinion" is the actual decision of the court; the "dissenting opinion" is written by a minority of justices who did not agree with the majority. Sometimes a "concurring opinion" will be given, which indicates an opinion which agrees with the majority, but for different reasons.

DISCUSSION PROBLEMS

1. Prepare a Research Plan. Discuss in class.
2. Discuss the use of primary and secondary authority. Under what circumstances would each be used?
3. Prepare a case brief on a criminal case in your state. Use the local law library to find the case.

QUESTIONS

1. What constitutes state law? Federal law?
2. What is the supreme law of the land?
3. What is an annotated code?
4. Why are pocket parts used?
5. What is a citation? Give an example.
6. What is primary authority? Secondary authority?
7. What legal encyclopedias are available in your state?

Employment Law

The employer–employee relationship is based on the law of contracts. The employee agrees to work for the employer, and the employer agrees to pay a certain salary for that work. Although most employees do not have written contracts, in certain instances a written contract or union (collective bargaining) contract exists.

COLLECTIVE BARGAINING

The National Labor Relations Act was passed by Congress to allow employees to bargain collectively with their employers. It guarantees that employees have the right to join labor unions and prohibits employers from interfering with the worker's right to organize.

With the passage of this act, power began to shift in favor of the unions. In order to alleviate this problem, Congress enacted the Labor Management Relations Act in 1947. Under this act, the employers were allowed to campaign against the organizing of their employees by the unions. In addition, individual rights were guaranteed to employees as a protection against unfair practices of the unions. Employees could cross a picket line to work when a business was on strike without restriction by the union. Unions were also required to bargain in good faith with employers. The power of the unions, employers, and individual employees was more fairly equalized by the passage of this act.

EQUAL EMPLOYMENT OPPORTUNITY (THE CIVIL RIGHTS ACT OF 1964)

Many former discriminatory practices were prohibited by the Civil Rights Act of 1964 (Title VII,) which forbids discrimination based on race, color, sex, religion, or national origin. Additional areas covered by the act include sexual harassment and age discrimination. Employers cannot discriminate in hiring or firing of individuals based on these characteristics.

SEXUAL HARASSMENT

Sexual harassment occurs when an individual in a supervisory capacity attempts to gain sexual favors in return for job benefits, such as pay raises and/or promotions. If an employee complains to the proper company officer and the action persists, the employer may be liable for damages. An employer may also be held liable in those situations where the harassment is more subtle—suggestive language, offensive language, offensive sexual advances, and so on. In those cases, if the employee is reasonably offended by such actions, the employer may be held liable.

EQUAL PAY FOR EQUAL WORK

In the past, many positions paid higher salaries for males. Variations based solely on sex are forbidden by the Equal Pay Act. Variances in wages are allowed only for merit raises, seniority, production quantity or quality, or another factor other than sex.

AGE DISCRIMINATION

Employers may not discriminate against employees because of their age. The Age Discrimination in Employment Act protects employees over 40 from discriminatory practices and also from mandatory retirement (except for police officers and firefighters.)

WORKER'S COMPENSATION LAWS

State worker's compensation laws protect employees who are injured during working hours. These laws basically require employers to bear the expense of any injury received while an employee is "on the job." Costs paid include medical bills, lost wages, and therapy or rehabilitation expenses.

OCCUPATIONAL SAFETY AND HEALTH ACT (OSHA)

OSHA protects employees on the job by requiring employers to keep the environment safe. Employees must be protected against toxic substances, unsafe or hazardous conditions, and excessive noise or air pollution.

An employee who feels that a hazardous condition exists may complain to OSHA, who in turn will inspect the workplace. If the hazardous conditions exist upon inspection, the employer will be required to correct them. Employees may not be dismissed by an employer for filing a complaint with OSHA.

_____ *DISCUSSION* _____

CASE 66   An employee truck driver was covered by a collective bargaining agreement which had a clause stating that he should not drive unsafe vehicles. He refused to drive a truck because he felt the brakes were faulty. Subsequently, he was discharged. He sued and lost on the appellate level because he did not mention the collective bargaining agreement in the suit. Was the court correct?

CASE 67   Barbara was a secretary at ABC Corporation. Her supervisor, John, made unwelcome sexual comments and suggestions and asked her to go out with him on several occasions. He told her she would be promoted if she would comply. She refused and complained to his supervisor. The comments and harassment continued, and she quit her job. Was the company liable when she sued for sexual harassment?

_____ *QUESTIONS* _____

1. What is the National Labor Relations Act?
2. Discuss the protections afforded by the Civil Rights Act of 1964. Who is protected?
3. What is OSHA? Whom does it protect?
4. What circumstances must exist for a claim of sexual harassment?

_____ *ANSWERS TO DISCUSSION CASES* _____

CASE 66   On further appeal, the U.S. Supreme Court held that the driver was engaged in an activity which was covered by the agreement and therefore the employer was liable.

CASE 67   Many such cases exist. The company would be liable in this situation as long as she did report the advances to the proper company officer.

Glossary

This glossary includes terms commonly encountered in business law. A few words may have additional legal meanings that will be found in a comprehensive legal dictionary. Of course no word needs to be restricted to the field in which it originated. Consequently, a term may have one meaning in a regular dictionary but a somewhat different connotation from a legal standpoint.

abandonment (1) Giving up property or rights with no intention of reclaiming them and to no particular person; for example, throwing away a book is abandonment but selling or giving it away is not. (2) Failure to take any action on a lawsuit for too long a time; a lawsuit thus abandoned may be thrown out of court.

abate Put a stop to a nuisance; reduce or cancel a legacy because the estate of the testator is insufficient to make payment in full.

absolute liability Liability for an act that causes harm even though the actor was not at fault.

abstract An abridgement; a brief summary.

abstract of judgment A condensation of the essential provisions of a court judgment.

abstract of title A condensed summary, or history, of title to a particular piece of real estate. An abstract begins with a legal description of the land involved and then shows the original government grant. This is followed by a recitation of all subsequent deeds, mortgages, releases, wills, judgments, mechanic's liens, foreclosure proceedings, tax sales, or any other documents that had been recorded about this property. By examining the abstract, one can quickly determine what incumbrances are outstanding against it in the event title is not clear. Abstracts of title are regularly kept current in those states where this system is used. Without the abstract, it might be necessary to search through voluminous county records to sift out the information.

acceleration clause   A clause in a note or trust deed permitting the payee or beneficiary to declare the entire unpaid balance immediately due and payable upon the happening of a stated event such as the failure to pay an installment when due.

acceptance   (1) The agreement to pay a draft (bill of exchange). For proper acceptance the word "accepted" and the signature of the drawee must be written across the face of the instrument. An acceptance is "clean" when unqualified; it is qualified when some modification accompanies the signature. (2) The agreeing to an offer and becoming bound to the terms of a contract. (3) The taking of something offered by another person with the intention of keeping it.

accident   An unforeseen event, a misfortune, or a happening without human will. This word has a variety of meanings in different legal situations. For example, the negligent driver of an automobile may be legally responsible for damages caused by an accident.

accommodation paper   A promissory note, bill, or draft, signed or indorsed by a person as an accommodation, or favor, to help the accommodated party obtain a loan. This practice is used when the accommodated party's credit is insufficient to obtain a loan.

accommodation party   A party who, for the purpose of assisting another person in obtaining credit, signs a note or other negotiable paper without receiving value.

accord and satisfaction   An agreement between two parties, one having a legal right of action against the other, that the former should accept something in discharge of the right of action that is different from (usually less than) that which might be legally enforced. For example, Smith may owe Brown $1,000 on a promissory note and be unable to pay. Brown may take an oil painting in accord and satisfaction of the debt, although the painting might bring only $800 on a forced sale. Brown may not want to expend time or money in court when Smith has little in the way of assets.

account stated   A record submitted by a creditor that has been examined and admitted to be correct by the person owing the debt. The correctness of the account may be admitted (1) expressly or (2) by implication of law when the debtor has had an opportunity to object and has failed to do so.

accounts payable   An obligation or liability of a buyer that usually arises from normal operations of a business. It is not backed up by a negotiable instrument nor is it considered overdue. Contract obligations owed by individuals or corporations on an open account.

accounts receivable   Balances due from debtors on current accounts.

acknowledgment   (1) An admission or declaration that something is genuine. (2) The signing of a formal paper and swearing to it as one's own act before a court official such as a notary public.

act of bankruptcy   Any one of several financial actions (defined by Federal law) that a person may take making him or her liable to be proceeded against as a bankrupt by creditors.

act of God   An event caused entirely by nature alone.

action   (1) A proceeding in a court that is instituted by one party against another. A suit in court for the enforcement of a legal right. A judicial process. Also called a *lawsuit* or *legal action*. (2) Behavior; conduct; something done.

actuary   A person who specializes in the mathematics of insurance—computing, for example, the possibility of a person's dying by a certain age, the money that should be paid for a certain type of insurance, and so on.

add-ons   New purchases made by an installment buyer before the previously purchased merchandise is completely paid for. This usually requires the drafting of a new installment purchase contract.

adhesion   A "contract of adhesion" is one in which all the bargaining power (and all the contract terms) are unfairly on one side.

administrator   A person appointed by a probate court as the representative of a decedent's estate when the decedent left no will.

admissible   (1) That which is legally proper in reaching a decision. (2) Of such a character that the judge must allow it to be presented in the course of the trial (when applied to evidence).

adverse possession   A means of acquiring title to real property after a lapse of time, based on continued possession. Under the decisions and statues in most states, five essentials must be satisfied before title can be acquired by adverse possession: (1) possession of the property must be by actual occupation and must be open and notorious, (2) possession must be hostile to the true owner's title, (3) possession must be under some adverse claim of right such as a defective or duplicate deed, (4) possession must be continuous and uninterrupted, and (5) the claimant must have paid all taxes levied during the statutory period. Statutory periods in some states may vary from 5 to 20 years with other variations in statutes from state to state. Generally, public lands cannot be acquired by adverse possession. In most jurisdictions a mere squatter cannot get title by adverse possession since the squatter has no adverse claim of right.

advisory opinion   An opinion rendered by a judge or an appellate court on a legal matter presented by an executive official of the government or by the legislature. It does not involve an actual court suit between interested parties. In effect, an advisory opinion merely furnishes guidance; it is not binding on anyone and does not really settle any legal dispute. It is an extrajudicial opinion. Court opinions are never binding in hypothetical situations or in any matter that is not squarely before a court in an adversary lawsuit. A trumped-up lawsuit, pursued merely to get an opinion from a court, would not be considered as binding by future judges faced with the same legal question.

after-acquired title In property law, the principle that if an individual attempted to convey ownership in real estate but did not actually have good title, yet subsequently got good title, the ownership would automatically pass to the person to whom the real estate was originally conveyed (transferred).

agency by necessity An agency relationship recognized by the courts which enables a wife or dependent to obtain on her husband's credit whatever is reasonably necessary for her maintenance and support. The courts in following this reasoning state that the situation is an implied agency.

agent One authorized to carry on business for another or for a firm. The general rule of law is that the agent must have authority from the principal before the principal is legally bound or obligated by the agent's acts or contracts. However, this right may be lost by the principal who intentionally, or by carelessness, leads a third party to believe the agent has authority.

aleatory contract A contract that turns on a contingency or uncertain event. For example, the amount of compensation payable to an executive may depend on the amount of profit or loss made by the business.

amicus curiae Friend of the court. A third party (other than the plaintiff and defendant) who, with the consent of the trial judge, is allowed to appear in a lawsuit. This third party sometimes is permitted to present evidence and take an active part but generally is restricted to filing a legal brief. This procedure is followed when the judge feels that broad community interests, going far beyond differences between the plaintiff and the defendant, should be represented.

amortization The process of paying off a debt or reducing a fund by regular payments. It may also apply to paying off bonds, stocks, or other legal indebtedness.

appeal The procedure by which the decision of a lower court is brought to a higher court for review. The system for taking a case to a higher court is set by the rules of the highest state court or in Federal appeals by rules of the United States Supreme Court.

appellant A party to a legal action who makes an appeal to a higher court.

appellate court Any court that has authority to hear appeals from a lower court.

appellate jurisdiction The authority and power of a review or higher court to take over the adjudication and review of a matter that has been tried in a court of original jurisdiction (trial court, lower court, inferior court, or whatever it may be called). Appellate jurisdiction includes the power to correct errors in judgment of the matter under review and to require the case to be sent back to the lower court for additional clarification of the issues.

appellee   One against whom an appeal is taken. This appeal is against the party to the lawsuit who won the decision in the lower court.

assets   (1) From a legal standpoint: money, property, and other valuables that come to the representative of a deceased person and which serve to pay off debts or that belong to the estate. (2) From an accounting view: all money, property, or valuables that are owned by an individual or organization. Assets may be used in whole or in part to pay off liabilities (debts).

assign   (1) To turn over property or a property interest to another—for example, to assign assets for the benefit of creditors. (2) To particularize, point out, or specify. For example, to assign errors in a writ of error (appeal) would be to point out errors to an appellate court as the basis for an appeal.

assumption of mortgage   The taking over of a mortgage when buying real estate.

attorney (or attorney-at-law)   A lawyer, counsel, advocate, or officer employed to furnish legal advice or to prepare and try a cause (case) in the courts.

attorney-in-fact   An individual authorized by law to act for another person either for some specific purpose or to transact business of a general nature. Authority for this is conferred by a written instrument called a *power of attorney* or *letter of attorney*. An attorney-in-fact is actually a kind of agent who handles either a specific transaction or general business for the principal. Any mentally competent adult may serve as an attorney-in-fact and the term does not refer to an attorney or lawyer in the usually understood meaning.

attorney of record   The lawyer or attorney whose name is entered on court records as the lawyer representing a client, although a number of other lawyers may be working on the case for the same client. The attorney of record is the attorney the client has designated as the agent who is authorized to accept service of legal papers. The attorney of record is distinguished from an *attorney of counsel* who is any other lawyer hired by the attorney of record to assist in the case.

attractive nuisance doctrine   The principle in tort law that one maintaining a dangerous machine, instrumentality, or condition on the premises to which young children may be attracted because of their inability to appreciate the peril, owes a legal responsibility to exercise reasonable care to protect children against the dangers of such attraction. The care that must be taken is that which a reasonably prudent person would take to prevent injury. Some courts say that the attraction must be visible from a public place or from a place where the children have a right to be. The person maintaining the attractive nuisance is held liable regardless of the fact that the child may be a trespasser.

authenticate   To make or establish as genuine, official, or final as by signing, countersigning, or doing any other act indicating approval.

bailee's lien   A possessory lien of the bailee on the goods for work done to them. Commonly extended by statute to any bailee's claim for compensation and eliminating the necessity of retention of possession.

bailment   The delivery of goods or personal property to be held in trust. It is a temporary holding; ownership does not change. On the other hand, if return of the same property is not contemplated, the transaction is a sale, rather than a bailment, and ownership does change hands. If the goods delivered, however, are fungible goods, then identical quantities or units of the goods may be returned since individual units of fungible goods are indistinguishable.

bailor   One who delivers goods or money to another in trust. (See *bailment*.)

balloon payment   A large final payment falling due on an installment loan or contract when regular payments are relatively small.

bankruptcy   The procedure, under the Federal Bankruptcy Act, by which a person is relieved of all debts after placing all property and money in the court's care; or by which an organization in financial trouble is either restructured by the court or ended and turned into cash to pay creditors and owners.

bargain and sale deed   A deed in which the seller conveys or transfers real property (real estate) to another party. The seller guarantees that he or she has done nothing to cause a defect in the title while at the same time stating that the seller cannot be responsible should it later turn out that there was some hidden defect caused by a former owner. A bargain and sale deed is roughly the equivalent of a grant deed which is used in some states. A bargain and sale deed is not a complete guarantee of title such as that provided by a warranty deed, but offers more protection than a quitclaim deed.

bearer   The person in physical possession of commercial paper payable to himself or herself.

beneficial interest   The financial advantage, profit, or benefit that results from a contract estate or property, as distinguished from absolute legal ownership itself.

beneficiary   A person or organization benefiting under a will, trust, insurance policy, or agreement.

bequest   A gift of personal property by will.

Best Evidence Rule   The rule followed in all court trials requiring that only the original of written or printed documents be used unless it can be shown that the original cannot be obtained and the copy is an exact one. The object of the rule is to eliminate the possibility of errors in copying or to prevent using a document as evidence that could have been subject to tampering or change. The courts sometimes state the rule as: "a written instrument or document is regarded as the best possible evidence of its existence and contents."

bilateral contract A contract under which both of the parties undertake to fulfill obligations toward each other reciprocally. It is a contract that is executory (yet to be completed) on both sides and where mutual promises are made and accepted. For example, one farmer may promise to harvest the wheat crop of a second who promises to deliver three dressed sides of beef to the first.

bill of lading A document that gives written evidence of a contract between a shipper and carrier for the transportation and safe delivery of goods. A bill of lading has three legal functions: (1) it is a contract that sets out the terms under which the carrier agrees to carry the merchandise, (2) it serves as a receipt for the merchandise, and (3) it is the title document. A *nonnegotiable* or *straight* bill of lading requires delivery to the particular individual named as consignee. A *negotiable* or *order* bill of lading permits delivery at the order of the consignee. Firms often negotiate or transfer bills of lading to individuals buying goods and the purchaser can claim the merchandise from the carrier by presenting the bill of lading obtained.

bill of sale A written instrument evidencing the transfer of title to personal property.

bulk sales law A statute designed to protect creditors of a merchant who sells all or a considerable part of stock to a single buyer, leaving the creditors with no assets that can be attached or reached. Statutes of this kind vary from state to state. In general they provide that a buyer for a major portion of a merchant's stock, other than in the regular course of business, must obtain under oath a list of the seller's creditors. The buyer is then required to give notice of the sale to all creditors to allow them to press their claims before the merchant's stock and other assets are beyond their reach.

bylaws The rules adopted by a corporation or other organization for its own operations and government. Normally a corporation may change its bylaws at any time so long as the bylaw adopted is (1) not in opposition to an existing law, (2) consistent with the objectives for which the corporation was formed, and (3) not in violation of the rights of a company's stockholders. All states have laws that regulate incorporation and set up rules for government of the corporation by passage and implementation of bylaws.

cancellation The termination of a contract because the other side has breached (broken) the agreement.

carrier's lien The right of a railroad, freight line, or other public carrier to retain the consignee's cargo until transportation charges have been paid.

cause of action The subject matter of a lawsuit; a redressable wrong; the right to recover something from another party through court action. The existence of a legitimate cause of action does not always mean that there will be a practical legal remedy.

caveat emptor Latin for "Let the buyer beware." The ancient rule of commercial law, traceable to Roman times and even earlier, that every purchaser must examine, judge, and look for defects in an item before buying it and that the seller will not be held responsible for any such defects after the sale.

cease and desist   An injunction from a court or an order from an administrative agency of the government to immediately refrain from a specific activity that has been declared to be illegal or objectionable. For example, a manufacturer producing dangerous or defective toys may be ordered by a court to cease and desist from making or distributing such items.

certified check   A check guaranteed by the bank on which it was drawn both as to the amount and the authenticity of the maker's signature. Once presented by either the maker or a holder for certification for a set fee, the check becomes a direct obligation of the bank and not an order to pay from the account of the maker. The bank deducts the amount of the check from the maker's account and marks it certified or accepted. The drawer of a certified check cannot stop payment on it.

chattel   Any kind of tangible personal property except real estate. Any type of property except intangible personal property such as stocks and bonds (the paper is not value, it simply represents value) or the freehold on ownership in land. For example, cattle and horses are chattels. In fact, the term chattel derives from an old French word for cattle, an early symbol of wealth.

chattel mortgage   A loan arrangement for borrowing with personal property pledged as security. Laws of the various states take three different viewpoints of such mortgages: (1) a mortgage acts as an actual transfer, in whole or in part, of the property pledged; (2) ownership is not transferred at all, but a mortgage acts as a lien, or charge, against the property; (3) a mortgaged property is regarded as being placed in trust to a third party until the loan is satisfied.

check   A written order to a bank to pay the amount of money specified on the document from funds held by the bank. A check is a type of draft, being distinguished by the fact that the drawer is an individual, whereas the drawer of a draft is a bank. Both are negotiable instruments with a check being generally designated for immediate payment and not for circulation as money.

chose in action   (1) The right to sue for damages; a right of action not yet reduced to possession or judgment but recoverable in a lawsuit; a right to collect a debt, demand, or damages. (2) Sometimes the term includes not only the right of action but also the thing that forms the subject matter of that right such as a written contract, stocks, or bonds.

citation   (1) An order or writ issued by a court directing someone to appear before the court at a specific date and time. (2) A notice of a failure to observe the law. For example, a citation issued by the building inspector to a contractor points out that some phase of construction is not in conformance with the building code and must be corrected under penalty of law. (3) The name and location, usually by volume and page numbers, of legal decisions and references that support legal pleadings or other legal papers.

civil case   A lawsuit or legal action undertaken in civil (not criminal) court. It is usually filed to seek the correction, recovery, or establishment of private wrongs in a civil dispute (not a crime or misdemeanor) and to compel payment of money damages. Some actions may also request an *injunction*, which is usually a court order directing the correction of wrongful acts or restricting the continuance of such action. A civil case is usually presented for trial by a petition called a *complaint*, consisting of written allegations or claims made by the plaintiff. Denials or answers are then filed in written form by the defendant.

closed corporation   A corporation that is effectively owned or controlled by a small number of individuals, often by members of a family. It may or may not be listed on a stock exchange.

cloud on title   Any outstanding incumbrance, claim, or charge against a parcel of real estate. An unpaid tax lien, unsatisfied mortgage, or a previous deed granted for all or part of the property would constitute a cloud on a title.

codicil   An addition to a will that changes or explains the original will.

coinsurance   A division of risk between an insurance company and its customer on all losses less than 100 percent if the amount of insurance is less than the amount of the loss.

collateral   Property that the borrower pledges to the creditor to secure debt payment. If the loan is not repaid, the lender (creditor) can look to the collateral to recover all or part of the debt.

color of title   The appearance of title where for some defect the attempt to establish title falls short.

common carrier   A company or individual in business to transport goods or passengers for anyone desiring such service. The common carrier of goods is legally responsible for any change or loss of merchandise unless it is caused by enemy action in wartime or by an act of God, such as an earthquake or cyclone. The carrier's legal responsibility continues during transportation and for a reasonable time after the goods have arrived at their destination.

community property   The property ownership system applying to husband and wife in many states as well as Puerto Rico. The essential principle is that all property acquired during the marriage belongs equally to both parties regardless of whose name it is in. Generally, if acquired property is to be separate, the property or money used to buy it must be kept separate from the time of marriage.

composition   (sometimes known as **composition with creditors**). A settlement made between a debtor and creditors for a reduced amount from a debtor who cannot pay in full. This is an agreement based on consideration for the sake of prompt payment that is intended to be distributed *pro rata* among the creditors in discharge and satisfaction of the whole debt. A composition is usually an attempt to avoid bankruptcy with the creditors getting their proportionate part of the debtor's payments immediately. Creditors may also receive more in this kind of settlement since the costs for administration of bankruptcy can be avoided.

condemnation   The legal process through which private property is taken by the government for a public use with the award of just payment to the owner.

consideration   (1) Something of value given or promised to induce one of the parties to make a contract. The price, motive, or value inducement for a contract. The courts say no contract was made unless something was done or promised by both sides to the agreement. If a farmer sells a cow to a butcher who promises to pay $100, the promise of payment is the consideration. In some jurisdictions, family love and affection is regarded as sufficient consideration for a transfer of property, even though no actual payment of money took place. (2) The legal assessment of a case and the judicial determination given to it by a court or judicial body.

constructive eviction   Any disturbance by the landlord of a tenant's possession whereby the premises are rendered unfit or the tenant is deprived of their benefit.

contract   A binding agreement that spells out its terms and conditions whereby each party is bound to do or to refrain from doing some act; each party to the contract acquires a right to what the other promises or performs. A one-sided agreement is not a contract as it lacks consideration.

conveyance   (1) A legal instrument by which title to real estate is transferred. (2) The transfer of the title to real estate from one person or class of persons to another.

corporate veil   The legal concept that the acts of a corporation are not to be regarded as acts of the individuals who own the corporation. Stockholders hide behind the corporate veil, so to speak, since they cannot be sued individually for the actions of the corporation. In the contemplation of the law, a corporation is a legal entity.

corporation   An artificial being created under the laws of a state or nation; a body authorized and formed by law to act as a single person. Although composed of several owners, this body has the right to do business according to the charter or franchise under which it was authorized. A corporation is treated as an entity, distinct from its members (stockholders), with rights and liabilities of its own. It may own property in its corporate name.

cosigner   An individual who signs as being responsible for a loan or other credit obligation, thereby being required to repay it in case of default by the primary debtor.

counsel, counselor, counsellor   A lawyer, attorney, legal pleader, legal advocate, or legal advisor. In the United States all these terms are used interchangeably to mean a lawyer. In England and some other English-speaking countries, an attorney may draw up legal papers, prepare testimony, and conduct legal matters out of court; an advocate or barrister may conduct the actual trial of the case in court. In the United States, however, there are no different types or classes of lawyers.

covenant   A written promise or restriction, usually incorporated into the text of a deed, that protects the buyer against defects in the title to the property. A warranty deed, for example, traditionally contains a general sort of covenant by the seller to protect the buyer against all defects. The seller is liable to the buyer if the title should subsequently turn out to be bad.

covenant running with the land   An agreement entered into by writing in a deed whereby one of the parties promises the performance or nonperformance of a specific act or series of acts in connection with the property. This agreement extends to any subsequent purchaser of the land and it may be enforced in the courts even though a subsequent purchaser was not a party to the original covenant. For example, a restriction in the deed to build only one mill on the streams running through a property can be enforced at any future time. Any covenant that is immoral, illegal, or against public policy cannot be enforced. For example, a covenant to sell the property only to a white, Protestant individual of Anglo-Saxon parentage would be struck down by the courts as contrary to public policy.

creditor   The credit grantor; the lender; a firm, financial institution, or person that extends credit.

credit scoring   An internal screening or evaluation of credit applications used by some creditors to determine creditworthiness. The system gives points for the credit applicant's specific characteristics such as income and number of dependents.

damages   Compensation in money imposed by a court for loss or injury caused by the fault of someone else.

debenture   (1) A voucher or certificate acknowledging a debt. (2) An unsecured bond issued by a corporation or agency of the government and which is backed only by the credit issuer. (3) A document issued by a customs collector specifying that an importer is entitled to a refund for import duties paid on some items that are being delivered for exempt uses.

deceit   Trickery; fraudulent misrepresentation; cheating; connivance to defraud.

declaratory judgment   A court decision that merely states the rights of the parties or gives the opinion of the court on a matter of law. A declaratory judgment does not order execution or performance from the defendant. The courts, however, will not accept for adjudication, nor give an opinion in, a theoretical matter; they will deal only with a matter of real fact, although no money award need be involved.

decree The judgment or sentence of a court; an order having the force of law.

deed A legal document by which ownership of land is transferred from an owner or seller (the grantor of a deed) to a new owner. A deed is a conveyance of realty—that is, real estate or land—and not of personal property or intangibles. Normally, a bill of sale or a sales contract transfers ownership of personal items. The essential difference between a deed and a will is that the former transfers a present interest in property, while a will passes no interest until the death of the maker. Old English law required the seller's signature and wax seal on a deed but this has been abolished in most states in the United States. There are different kinds of deeds, some of which will pass only those rights to the new owner (buyer) that the grantor actually possessed at the time the deed was signed. The term deed normally refers to a warranty deed; however, in some states a warranty deed is not used.

deed of trust A document by which an individual transfers the legal ownership of real estate and what is on the land to an independent trustee to be held until a debt on the real estate is paid off. In short, a deed of trust performs the same security function as a mortgage; however, some different legal implications are involved in foreclosure.

defalcation Failure to properly account for money or valuables that have been entrusted to a person. The term "embezzlement" goes beyond defalcation in that embezzlement involves a wrongful taking of money or valuables.

defendant The party against whom a lawsuit is filed; the individual or individuals required to give an answer in a legal action.

default judgment A civil judgment rendered in consequence of the failure of a party to appear in court or the failure to file pleadings within the time set by law.

deficiency judgment A personal judgment for the amount still remaining due the mortgagee after foreclosure which is entered against any person liable on the mortgage bond.

defraud To swindle, cheat, or trick.

demand A formal request or requisition for a right or for the fulfillment of an obligation legally due to the person making the demand. A demand differs from a claim in presupposing there is no defense or doubt on the question of right.

demurrage (1) In maritime or transportation law, the detention of a ship, railroad car, or other cargo conveyance during loading or unloading in excess of a specified period of time. (2) The monetary charge for this detention, usually paid by the day.

descent (1) Succession in the ownership of property or lands through hereditary derivation or lineage. (2) Obtaining of ownership of property or title to lands by inheritance from forebearers rather than by gift or purchase.

devise A gift of land or personal property by will.

devisee One to whom property is left in a will.

devisor One who leaves property to another by will.

de novo New; completely new from the start, for example, a trial *de novo* is a completely new trial.

dictum (Latin; sometimes used as an abbreviated form of *obiter dictum*). Dictum is the singular form of dicta. It means a statement made by a judge in passing. It is generally an opinion or application of law to some question suggested by the case at bar but not necessarily essential to its determination.

directed verdict A verdict ordered by the judge, taking the decision out of the jury's hands. In a criminal prosecution, for example, it is the prosecution's responsibility to prove each of the essential elements of the case. If the prosecution fails to prove one of these essential elements by the introduction of evidence, the accused will be released as a matter of law. At that stage of the case the judge will order the jury to enter a directed verdict without taking a vote on guilt or innocence. This not only saves time, but it averts the possibility that the jury, not understanding what has happened, might vote a guilty verdict on the basis of the evidence presented.

director (1) Head or policymaker of an organization, group, or project. (2) Person elected by the shareholders (owners) of a corporation to make major corporate decisions, such as the hiring of the persons who run the day-to-day operations.

disability The lack of legal capacity to do an act. A legal disqualification or incapacity. A want of legal authority to perform a specific act. For example, an insane person is legally said to be under disability to make a will. A 10-year-old child is under disability to obtain a marriage license. A married person is disabled from remarrying until the marriage ends in divorce or by death.

disaffirm Repudiate; to take back consent once it has been given.

discharge in bankruptcy An order of the bankruptcy court discharging (releasing) the bankrupt debtor from the unpaid balance of most claims.

disclaimer A denial, renunciation, or rejection of liability or legal responsibility in advance in a situation where responsibility would otherwise be due to a wronged party.

discovery A disclosure by the defendant in a civil matter of land title documents, other documents or facts that may be under the defendant's exclusive control and that are necessary to the party seeking the discovery as a part of the action. For example, A made a contract with B, whereby B was to erect a building. B took no action to fulfill the contract. The contract was signed before witnesses and B would have difficulty claiming that it does not exist. A's copy of the contract was destroyed by fire. As part of a lawsuit for breach of contract, A could file a bill of discovery asking that B be ordered to produce the contract for A to use in the lawsuit. Depositions and interrogatories from individuals with knowledge of the facts are techniques frequently used by lawyers as types of discovery.

dishonor To refuse to accept or pay a negotiable instrument that has become due.

dissent The disagreement of one or more judges or justices with the majority opinion in a case being considered. Disagreeing judges may or may not submit a dissenting opinion in writing.

dissolution The termination or breakup of a legal relationship. For example, the dissolution of a contract could arise by mutual consent of the parties. The dissolution of a corporation is the end of its legal existence. Divorce, but not annulment, is the dissolution of a marriage.

domicile An individual's true, fixed, and permanent residence. Any person can have only one domicile, which is the location intended as a permanent home for an unlimited or indefinite period. A domicile is not necessarily the same as a residence.

donee One who is the recipient of a gift.

donor One who makes a gift.

double indemnity A provision for payment of twice the amount specified by the insurance contract if death is caused by an accident and occurs under specified circumstances.

draft (1) An order for the payment of money drawn by one individual on another. A draft is the most common form of a bill of exchange and a check is the most popular kind of draft. Both are negotiable instruments. (2) A tentative writing of a legal document such as a lease, contract, or legislative bill.

draftsman A person who writes a legal document (especially the person who creates an original document) such as a contract.

draw (1) To prepare a legal document. (2) To take money out of a bank account. (3) To write out and sign a draft, check or note.

drawee The person or institution to whom a bill of exchange is addressed and who is expected to pay. For example, a check (which is a bill of exchange) is sent by the bank depositor to the bank (drawee) to be cashed.

drawer The individual who draws or drafts an order for the payment of money. The drawer of a check, for example, is the party who has an account at the bank and issues and signs a check on the account.

duress   The use of force to compel someone to do something. A physical restraint may also constitute duress.

duty   (1) A legal or moral obligation. (2) The requirement to follow all laws or court directives. (3) The obligation to refrain from interfering with rights of others that have been established by law or the court processes. (4) A tax imposed on the import or export of goods or personal items.

earnest money   The payment of part of the purchase price for real estate to bind the sale. Sometimes this payment is called a *binder*. The understanding is usually that the earnest money will be retained by the seller if the buyer backs out before the sale is completed. If the buyer produces the remainder of the purchase price and meets all other terms of the sale, the earnest money is applied as part payment to the purchase price.

easement   An interest in land owned by another permitting the holder to make a specific use of the land. For example, a man may own two lots, one of which does not have access to a public road. He may sell the lot that has no access, granting the buyer an easement across his other lot. This would allow the buyer to use a reasonable part of the second lot as a roadway in order to reach the street. If the owner should eventually sell the second lot, the easement across it would continue. Some easements are granted to public service companies such as for the erection and maintenance of power poles. An easement may be created by an express grant in a deed or contract.

embezzlement   The fraudulent appropriation of entrusted property or money to one's own use or benefit. In other words, the unlawful appropriation or taking of personal property of another by an individual who has gained rightful possession because of employment or by a trust relationship with the owner. The distinction between larceny (theft or stealing) and embezzlement is that in embezzlement the money is in the rightful possession, but not ownership, of the guilty individual. In larceny the wrongdoer takes that which is in the possession or control of somebody else.

encumber   See *incumber*.

endorsement.   See *indorsement*.

entering judgment   The clerical act by which a court's judgment is recorded in the court's official records that are maintained by the clerk of the court. Normally, an appeal or an action on the judgment cannot be taken until the judgment is recorded, even though it has already been rendered.

equity   (1) In a broad sense, equity denotes that which is fair, just, and right. (2) In another sense, equity denotes equal or impartial justice as between two or more individuals whose claims or legal rights are in conflict. (3) In an additional situation, equity is a system of jurisprudence that is collateral to, or existing alongside, the system of jurisprudence based on common law (the established body of civil law). At an early time in England the common law became very strict and narrow. An individual desiring to file a lawsuit could not do so unless it fell within one of the recognized writs or technical forms of action. This frequently left the injured party without any legal remedy in the courts. In addition, common law courts had no provision for preventing a wrong that was about to happen. (They could not issue injunctions restraining someone who was about to commit a wrong.) To correct these injustices, equity courts began to step in and take over cases where it was obvious that justice could not be done by the regular (common law) courts. For a time there were two systems of jurisprudence in England, operating side by side. But since 1875 the law courts and the chancery, or equity, courts have merged. Some of the American colonies brought these separate courts into their own systems. Some states still have distinct courts of law and equity; in other states law and equity are administered by the same judges and courts.

equity in property The monetary value of the owner's interest; the difference between the market value of the property and the amount of liens and encumbrances against it.

equity of redemption The right of an individual (mortgagor) whose property has been foreclosed to obtain a return of the property by paying off the whole mortgage in addition to the costs of foreclosure. Historically, in English courts if the debtor did not make the mortgage payment on or before the day when payment fell due (known as the "law day"), the creditor would become the absolute owner of the land. Because in many cases this worked a great injustice, the equity of redemption principle was eventually worked out by British courts and has been followed in United States law.

escrow A conditional delivery of something to a third party that is to be held until the happening of some event or the performance of some designated act. Perhaps the most common escrow situation involves the delivery of a deed to property to a holder until the person buying the property (the grantee of the deed) makes a specified number of payments on the purchase price. When the payments are made, the holder delivers the deed to the grantee.

estoppel The legal doctrine that one cannot allege or deny a fact when one's previous actions or words have been to the opposite effect. It is a prohibition that does not allow one to speak against one's own act or deed in a business transaction. The elements of estoppel include a change of position of the parties so that the party against whom estoppel is invoked has received a profit or benefit or the party invoking estoppel has changed his or her position to his or her detriment in reliance on words or acts of the other party.

execution (1) A judicial writ empowering the sheriff or some other officer to carry out a judgment. (2) A putting of something into operation and effect.

A taking of a matter or course of conduct to its completion. (3) Signing, and in some cases delivering, a legal instrument or document such as a deed of conveyance. (4) Carrying out a death sentence as a legal penalty for crime.

exemplary damages   Damages awarded to the plaintiff beyond those needed to reimburse for the actual loss. Exemplary damages are granted as punishment or to make an example of the defendant. Compensatory damages cover the actual loss.

face   The language of a document including everything in it (not just the front page).

factor   A person who is given goods to sell and who gets a commission for selling them.

failure of consideration   A term used in contract law to describe a situation in which one party to the contract did not perform in the way promised or the goods delivered were not as they were supposed to be. When there is a failure of consideration, the contract cannot be enforced by the party at fault.

family car doctrine (family purpose doctrine)   The rule that owner of an automobile will usually be liable for damage done by a family member driving the owner's car if the driver is negligent.

fidelity bond   Insurance on a person against that person's dishonesty. It is often required when a person is in a position of trust, handles large sums of money, and is seldom checked on by others.

fiduciary   A person who manages money or property for another person and in whom that other person has a right to place great trust.

financial responsibility laws   Statutes that require a driver involved in an automobile accident to prove his or her financial responsibility in order to retain his or her license; this responsibility may be shown by procuring public liability insurance in a specified minimum amount.

fixture   Anything that is permanently joined to land or a building. The word is sometimes used to mean those things that, once attached, may not be removed by a tenant.

foreign corporation   A corporation created under the laws of another state.

forgery   The fraudulent making or altering of an instrument that apparently brings about a legal liability of another.

fraud   Deceit, trickery, or deliberate perversion of the truth in order to induce someone to part with something of value or to give up a legal right; misrepresentation, concealment, or deliberate nondisclosure of a material fact to induce another party to enter a contract that will work to a disadvantage.

fungibles   Products or substances whose units are indistinguishable; where one unit in the whole is like every other. For example, one bushel of wheat in a carload would be indistinguishable from another in the same carload. A shipment of race horses, however, would not be a shipment of fungibles since each horse has individual characteristics and values.

garnishee   (1) A person who holds money or property owing to another and which is subject to garnishment. (2) To serve with a garnishment to attach a debtor's wages.

garnishment   A statutory proceeding whereby a debtor's wages, property, money, or credits are taken and applied as payment toward satisfaction of a debt.

general assignment for creditors or general assignment for benefit of creditors   A transfer of all a debtor's money, property, rights, or other assets to a trustee, to liquidate the debtor's affairs and pay off the creditors.

general creditor   A person who is owed money but who has no security (such as a mortgage) for the debt.

general partnership   A partnership in which the partners conduct as co-owners a business for profit, where each partner has a right to take part in the management of the business and each has unlimited liability.

grace period   A short time during which an insurance policy stays in effect after the premium payment is due.

grant   (1) A transfer by deed of real property. (2) To make a conveyance or pass title to property.

guardian   One who has the legal right and duty to take care of the person or property of another (for example, a child) who cannot legally take care of himself or herself. The arrangement is called *guardianship*.

holder   One who has legally come into possession of a negotiable instrument, such as a check or promissory note, and who may therefore be legally entitled to payment on it.

holder in due course   One who has legal possession of a negotiable instrument (check, promissory note, installment purchase contract, or the like), having obtained it in good faith and without knowledge of any fraud or dishonesty involving it. In addition, the instrument must be obtained for value and without notice that it is overdue, that payment has been refused, or that the maker has a legal defense against payment.

holding company   A firm that owns so much stock in one or more other companies that it has control over them.

holograph   Any instrument prepared wholly in the handwriting (not hand printing) of the individual making the document and whose signature it bears.

holographic will   A will prepared wholly in the handwriting of the person making it. Wills of this type are not always accepted as valid under some state statutes and in some states are completely unacceptable.

homestead exemption A statute in many states that permits the head of a family (or sometimes a single person) to designate a house and land as the family homestead, exempt from execution for the general debts of the family head. Most states place a limit on the value of the house and land that may be so designated. Usually, the head of the household is required to file a homestead exemption form with the county or state recorder placing the homestead right on notice for those who may lend money to him or her. In most states the designation may be transferred from one piece of property to another if the family moves. Normally a new homestead exemption form must be filed for each move.

immaterial Not pertinent to the issue at hand; not essential or of much serious consequence. Not decisive.

implied warranty A warranty or guarantee that automatically comes into existence when a merchant sells goods, promising that they are fit for the purpose for which they would ordinarily be used. This warranty applies even though it is never expressed verbally or in writing. For example, a store that sells a boat has given an implied warranty that it will float when placed in water. If built in such a way that it consistently capsizes, then obviously the vessel does not meet the standards for which a boat would ordinarily be used.

imputed knowledge Sometimes used interchangeably with *implied notice*. Knowledge that an individual is charged with possessing, since the facts in question were easily available and the person charged had a duty to keep himself or herself advised. For example, the owner of a machine shop has imputed knowledge of unsafe working conditions in the establishment because a state statute requires the owner and management to stay abreast of such conditions at all times.

imputed negligence Those damages or injuries that are chargeable to an individual owner or other owners of a commercial venture owing to the negligence or injuries (torts) caused by employees or agents of the owner (principal). By statute in some jurisdictions, negligence of any family member driving the family car is imputed to the owner.

incompetency Lack of legal qualifications or physical fitness to handle one's own legal problems. Incompetency may include mental disabilities such as insanity, chronic drunkenness that robs a person of reason, or physical illness that debilitates. The courts will usually appoint a guardian to look after the interests of incompetents.

incumbrance A charge or lien against land. Incumbrances include mortgages, judgments against the owner, liens, writs of execution, or any other binding liability against the property. Sometimes spelled *encumbrance*.

indemnity The right of a person secondarily liable to require that a person who is primarily liable pay for loss when the secondary party discharges the obligation that the primary party should have discharged.

indorsement   The signature of the holder of a negotiable instrument such as a check that transfers title to the instrument upon delivery. Each indorsement is a new and substantive contract by which ownership of the instrument is passed. By indorsing, one becomes a party to the instrument and is liable for its payment to the person to whom negotiated. By adding some additional wording to the indorsement signature, however, the indorser can change the legal relationship with subsequent indorsers. Sometimes spelled endorsement.

injunction   An order or writ issued by a judge requiring the individual to whom it is directed to take, or to refrain from taking, some specific action. In a typical case an injunction would direct an individual to cease a wrongful kind of conduct that is harmful to another; the wrongdoer would be restrained from the continuance of this conduct. If the wrongdoer persists after issuance of the *injunction*, the judge will order the arrest of the wrongdoer for contempt. An *injunction* may be issued in cases where substantial justice could not be done by waiting for the wrongdoer to go ahead and commit a threatened wrong that may not be adequately compensated for in a lawsuit.

instrument   A writing made for a legal purpose such as a deed, a contract, a will, or a check. An instrument may record a legal right, transfer money or property, or serve as written evidence of a transaction.

insufficiency   In legal pleading, the inadequacy of an answer that does not specifically and adequately respond to the charges, allegations, or interrogatories set forth in the pleadings of the other party.

insurable interest   Any interest in property or liability in respect thereto of such a kind that a loss or peril might directly cause financial harm. For example, if you own a home, you would be caused serious loss if it burned to the ground; you therefore have such an interest in the home that it is insurable. Somewhat similarly, if you have a reasonable expectation of financial benefit from the continued life of an individual, then you have an insurable interest on which life insurance can be based. Usually, this interest arises from marriage or family relationships. But business partners can likewise insure the lives of the partners to compensate for financial losses that would probably arise if one should die.

insurance   A contract agreement between two parties (the insurer and the insured) whereby, in consideration of a payment or series of payments (premiums) made by the insured, the insurer agrees to compensate the other against loss, damage, or liability from a specified event happening during a given time in the future. An agreement to reimburse for specified types of loss if they should occur.

insured   An individual whose property or life is insured.

invitee   A person coming onto the premises to conduct business for the benefit of the property holder. For example, a consumer invited into a retail store to look at merchandise is an invitee whether or not the consumer makes a purchase. In damage lawsuits, the courts usually say that more care to protect from personal injury is required from the property holder toward invitees than toward others permitted on the property.

ipso facto By the very act or fact in itself without any further action by anyone.

joint and several A characteristic of a debt or liability when the creditor has the legal right to sue any one of the separate parties or to proceed against all jointly at the creditor's option.

joint stock company An association in which the shares of the members are transferable and control is delegated to a group or board.

joint tenancy A form of co-ownership of real property. Joint tenancy is regarded as a single estate held by two or more persons jointly. Legally, such joint tenants own as though they collectively constituted but one person, a fictitious entity. The main characteristic of joint tenancy is the right of survivorship. When a joint tenant dies, that individual's interest in the land is terminated and the ownership continues in the survivor or survivors.

judgment The official decision, or adjudication, of a court in a civil lawsuit. A judgment may be based on a jury's verdict or, in the absence of a jury, on the law and facts as found by a trial judge. When the rights of the parties have been determined, the judgment awarded by the court may consist of monetary damages and/or an injunction forbidding the defendant from continuing a wrongful course of conduct. If the defendant fails to appear or fails to contest the lawsuit, the judge may enter a *default judgment*, or *judgment by default*.

judgment lien A lien on all the land of a debtor against whom a court judgment has been obtained. Purchasers of property and mortgages must undertake a search of judgment records to learn whether there are any judgment liens against property about to be purchased or mortgaged. Otherwise, the purchaser buys subject to the lien and the person loaning money on a mortgage may have only a secondary security interest in the land.

judgment note A promissory note containing a clause authorizing the holder to enter judgment against the maker if it is not paid when due. Also called *cognovit note*.

judgment proof A term describing an individual who will not be financially harmed by a judgment against him or her. Those without property or assets or those sheltered by wage protection laws are sometimes described as judgment proof.

judicial notice The court's action in conducting a trial or in framing a decision to recognize the existence of certain facts without requiring evidence to prove them. This is done on the court's own motion. For example, the court might take judicial notice of the fact that the state of Hawaii is not within the continental limits of the United States, or that Valentine's Day fell on Tuesday, February 14, 1978.

jurisdiction   The right, power, or authority to administer justice by hearing and determining legal controversies and trying cases. The legal capacity or authority of a court. In order to handle a criminal case, the court must have jurisdiction over the subject matter.

last clear chance   A legal principle that a person injured in (or having property harmed by) an accident may win damages even when negligent if the person causing the damage could have avoided it after discovering the danger.

lease   A written agreement for the use and possession of property. A lease is granted for a specified time and for a specified payment. The landlord (lessor or leasor), in effect, rents to the tenant (lessee or leasee) for a set period with payments usually being due on a monthly basis.

legal age   The age of legal responsibility; the age at which an individual becomes old enough to transact business and handle legal matters, such as the capacity to make contracts or transfer property. Legal age varies from 18 to 21, depending on individual state law. For some specific purposes, such as the right to obtain a driver's license, the age may be set below that for handling business responsibilities.

legal tender   Money that would be legally acceptable for the payment of debt. It is that kind of money or coins which the law compels a creditor to accept in payment for debt when the right amount is offered. For example, in some jurisdictions payment of more than $10 in pennies would not be acceptable. It would be absurd to require an individual owed $1,000 to wait while a debtor counted out 100,000 pennies in satisfaction.

licensee   (1) An individual who enters another's property with the owner's toleration or permission but without an invitation. Those who come into a retail store to get out of the rain, persons taking shortcuts across a vacant lot, those touring a manufacturing plant for their own enjoyment, traveling salesmen, and social guests are all classified by most courts as licensees. These are in a different class from invitees such as persons invited into a retail store to do business. Under tort law, the courts say that the property holder has a maximum duty to protect invitees, but less responsibility toward the licensee. Most courts determine that the standard of care required of the property holder is greater to the extent that the presence of people on the property is helpful or profitable to the property holder. (2) A person to whom a license is granted.

lien   The right to take and hold or sell the property of a debtor as security for a debt. A lien is a right established by law rather than by an agreement or contract between the parties involved. Examples include the "landlord's lien," the right to hold property of a tenant for unpaid rent, and the so-called "mechanic's lien," giving, say, an auto mechanic the right to keep an automobile until repairs are paid for. The holder of a lien is usually required to give notice of it by recording it in the office of the public recorder or some other designated public place. In most states a mortgage takes precedence over a mechanic's lein.

life estate   An interest in property, real or personal, that lasts only for the duration of the owner's life. A life estate may also be for the duration of another's life or it may end with the happening of a certain contingency. For example, a man may leave a life estate in a cattle ranch to his wife, with the provision that the estate terminates in the event of her remarriage. Ordinarily, the owner of the life estate cannot sell off, consume, or deliberately ruin any of the property that makes up the life estate, but may enjoy its use and benefits. The legal interest left after the termination of a life estate is a *remainder*.

mandamus   (Latin: "We command you.") A writ or order that is issued by a court of superior jurisdiction. The order commands a lower court, board, corporation, or individual to do an act or not to do an act, the performance or omission of which the law enjoins as a duty. If discretion is left to the lower court, the mandamus only compels it to act and cannot control such discretion.

marketable title   A title to real estate that is clear of incumbrances, such being a title that would be accepted as valid by a reasonable, prudent buyer.

mechanic's lien   A claim created by statute, securing priority of payment of the value of work performed and of materials furnished in constructing or repairing a building or other structure or in maintaining a vehicle. The right of priority of payment attaches to land as well as to buildings and improvements thereon. A vehicle mechanic has the right to hold the vehicle until repairs are paid for.

mistrial   A trial that is held invalid and of no effect because of some material defect in procedure such as improper selection of the jury or allowing the jury to hear prejudicial material that is not evidence. After a mistrial the court proceeds as though no trial had previously taken place. A mistrial, in itself, does not constitute double jeopardy so as to excuse the accused from additional prosecution in a criminal matter.

mortgage   (1) A security arrangement that allows land to be used as a security for debt. It is a transfer or pledge of real property passing conditionally as security. (2) The deed or deed or trust by which this pledge is made. (3) The claim of the lender (mortgagee) on the property.

mortgagee   One who loans money, obtaining a mortgage as security.

mortgagor   One who pledges property in a mortgage as security for a loan.

negotiable   Capable of being transferred by indorsement or delivery so as to pass to the holder the right to sue in his or her name.

negotiable instrument   A bank check, promissory note, bill of exchange, or any other written security document that can be transferred by indorsement and delivery or, in some instances, by delivery only. The effect of the transfer is to vest legal ownership, giving the new owner the right to demand payment of the face amount, along with interest that may be due.

no-fault insurance   An insurance system that seeks to have automobile accident victims compensated for their losses without regard to their degree of negligence or fault. The no-fault system also seeks to minimize the number of lawsuits by limiting recovery to actual economic losses, such as medical expenses, wages and salaries, and other real costs, eliminating payments for pain and suffering. States with no-fault systems have varying laws.

nominal damages   A trifling sum (often $1) awarded to the plaintiff in a lawsuit where there was no substantial loss or injury but where the law recognizes a wrong was done, however technical.

notary public   A public official who attests or certifies certain classes of documents to give them authenticity in foreign jurisdictions, who takes acknowledgments of deeds and other conveyances and who takes affidavits, depositions, and protests for nonpayment of negotiable instruments.

notice   Knowledge or information about the existence of some fact. Legally, there are two types of notice: actual and constructive. Actual notice is information that can be proved to have been communicated to an individual directly. Constructive notice is knowledge of a fact, or information, imputed by law to an individual, although the individual may not actually have it, where the individual involved would have discovered the fact by proper diligence and had a duty of inquiring into it. For example, a divorced husband may place a notice in the legal notice section of the neighborhood newspaper stating that he will no longer be responsible for the debts of his wife. (This is the procedure required by law in some jurisdictions.) Thereafter, a merchant who sells to the wife cannot look to the husband for payment, since the merchant had constructive notice.

notice of dishonor   Notice given to parties secondarily liable that the primary party to the instrument has refused to accept it or to make payment when it was properly presented for that purpose.

oath   A solemn swearing in a formal manner. An attestation. A pledge by which one renounces mercy and asks for the vengeance of heaven if he or she does not tell the truth.

obstruction of justice   Any act of hindrance designed to block or prevent the execution of lawful process. It may consist of interfering with a police officer who is trying to make an arrest, hindering a witness from appearing, or wrongfully influencing and tampering with jurors, witnesses, or judges.

open-end mortgage   A mortgage that provides security for additional advances of money that may be loaned to the debtor (mortgagor) after the mortgage has already gone into operation.

order to show cause   A direction of a court obtained on a motion by one party directing a second party to show any good cause why an injunction should not be issued and forbidding the second party from committing wrongful acts that may be harmful to the first party.

ordinance   A legislative enactment of a city or county.

ordinary creditor   A creditor who has no special preference in the order in which debts are paid by a debtor. Ordinary creditors are generally entitled to be paid only after payment to secured creditors such as holders of a mortgage or a lien.

ostensible agency   An agency relationship recognized by the courts when the principal intentionally, or by want of proper care, causes a third party to believe that someone is actually the principal's agent.

overdraft (or overdraw)   A taking out by check of more money from a bank account than one has in the account.

paper   (1) Any written or printed document, book, account book, instrument, or written evidence that may be pertinent to a case in a law court. (2) Sometimes used to mean any negotiable paper or negotiable instrument. (3) That which is of value in name only. For example, a paper owner of mining stock may possess nothing of real worth.

parol evidence rule   The rule in evidence law that all oral agreements or understandings about a matter merge into any written contract on the same subject matter. In the absence of fraud or mistake in the preparation of the written version, the writing cannot be modified or changed by oral evidence. The reason for this rule is to eliminate fraud. Otherwise, one of the parties could later present a new oral version any time it developed that the contract was not as favorable as expected.

payable   Describes a sum of money that is due when someone is under obligation to pay it. When not qualified, the term payable means payable at once, rather than at a future time.

pledge   To hand over physical possession of a piece of personal property (such as a radio) to another person who holds it until one pays off a debt to that person.

police power   The power to enact laws and regulations necessary for the common welfare.

postdating   The dating of an instrument or document later than the date on which it was actually made. Checks and other instruments of this kind may be invalid if postdated, depending on circumstances and individual state laws.

power of attorney   A formal document by which one person gives legal power to another to perform a specific act or to transact general business for the former. It is, in effect, a contract of agency. The person designated to act for the principal may be any legally and mentally competent adult and not necessarily a lawyer or attorney-at-law. The person who holds this power is sometimes called an *attorney-in-fact* or a *private attorney*.

preference (or creditor's preference) (1) An insolvent debtor's payment to one or more general creditors to the exclusion of others. Under the Federal Bankruptcy Act, if creditors are given preference on payments made within four months prior to bankruptcy, the court may order these payments to be distributed to all general creditors on a *pro rata* basis. So-called *preferred creditors*, however, have the first right to be paid off and first claim on the debtor's assets. Claims of these preferred creditors may arise from a lien, mortgage, or another security arrangement. A general creditor is on notice (at least constructive notice) of the existence of the rights of preferred creditors since these are usually on record at the county clerk's office (or another required location) when credit is extended by the general creditor.

prepayment penalty A charge sometimes made for paying off a loan prior to its due date. The charge is usually a percentage of the balance such as one percent. A prepayment penalty is sometimes called an *acquisition charge*.

prima facie (Latin: "at first sight" or "on its face") Describes material or evidence that is legally sufficient to establish a fact or a case unless disproved.

procedural law That part of the law which applies and handles the substantive law; the legal machinery by which rights and duties of a legal nature are enforced. This is distinguished from substantive law which deals with the rights and duties of persons to each other and to society in general. See *adjective law*.

promissory note A written promise by one person to pay, unconditionally, to another person named therein, to order or to the bearer, a certain sum of money at a specified time or on demand.

proof Anything that serves to convince the mind of the truth or falsity of a fact or proposition including evidence for or against it.

property (1) The legal right to the possession, use, enjoyment, and disposal of a thing; an unrestricted and exclusive right or interest in or to a thing. (2) Anything that may be owned or possessed.

protest A formal notification, usually by a notary public, for the holder of a bill or note stating that the instrument was duly presented for payment at the proper time and place and that payment was refused. This is usually a necessary procedure that must be performed to recover from those secondarily liable (the drawer and indorser).

proxy (1) An authorization to vote at a meeting in place of an absent stockholder. Although statutory provisions vary, the usual provisions are: (a) that the proxy shall be in writing, (b) that the individual giving it can revoke it at any time, (c) that it will expire within a statutory number of months or years from date unless otherwise specified. (2) The name given to the individual holding the authority to vote for another.

public domain (1) Publicly owned land. (2) The public-ownership status of writings, documents, or publications that are not protected by copyrights and may be reprinted or quoted by anyone.

purchase money mortgage   A mortgage given concurrently with a sale of land by the buyer to the seller on the same land to secure all or part of the purchase price.

quiet title   A lawsuit or legal hearing to establish title to real property. It is an action that brings into court an adverse claimant and compels him or her to establish claim to the land or thereafter to stop asserting it.

quitclaim deed   A deed that transfers to the buyer only such rights or property title as the seller (grantor) had at the time the deed was delivered. In most instances a quitclaim deed may transfer ownership or title just as effectively as any other type of deed. But if there should be a defect or cloud on the title, a new purchaser buys subject to that defect. In acquisitions under a quitclaim deed, the burden is on the purchaser to find out whether there are claims or incumbrances against the real estate in question.

real property   Land, that which is affixed to the land, and that which is incidental or appurtenant to the land. Any property that is not real property is personal property. A permanent fixture or counter affixed to the floor of a building is a part of the real property unless it is excepted by statute. A number of states, by statute, specify that store fixtures and appurtenances, intended for use by the merchant in the day-to-day operation of a business, may be torn loose and taken by the merchant on the expiration of a lease. The merchant, however, has a legal duty not to seriously harm the building in removing fixtures, counters, or appurtenances. Generally, the term *real estate* is used interchangeably with *real property*.

realty   Real property.

receiver   (1) An independent, outside individual appointed by a court to manage business, property, or money during a lawsuit. (2) A person who gets stolen property. Knowledge of the stolen character of the goods is necessary to convict a party of the crime of receiving.

reconveyance   The transfer of title of real estate from the owner to the preceding owner. A reconveyance is commonly used when a debt is satisfied under a deed of trust; the trustee conveys the title he has held on condition back to the owner who created the trust (in order to borrow on the property). See *trust deed*.

record, court of   Any court that retains a permanent record of proceedings and actions. Part of the record consists of papers and documents filed with the clerk of the court and part consists of transcripts and materials compiled by the court reporter. The lowest-ranking courts, such as the justice of the peace court, usually are not courts of record.

recording   The process of filing certain real estate agreements and other documents with an official recorder for the purpose of legally placing others on notice as to their existence. For example, the recording of a deed for the sale of land places the whole world on notice that the seller has transferred the ownership in the land. If the seller subsequently gave a second deed to a new buyer, the latter could establish no claim to the land if the first deed had been recorded. The act of recording places the second buyer on constructive notice of the first deed and the law treats the second buyer as being on notice even if the second buyer does not check the records in the recorder's office.

redemption   The buying back of one's real estate after it has been lost in a foreclosure.

reinsurance   The transfer by an insurance company of some or all of the risk assumed to another insurance company.

relevant   Having a demonstrable or significant bearing on the matter at hand. Tending to prove or disprove the issue in a lawsuit or criminal prosecution. Unless testimony or other evidence is relevant, it should be objected to by counsel and the judge will order the jury to disregard it as having no bearing on the trial.

relief   (1) Satisfaction granted by the courts for a past wrong. (2) Support or assistance, especially for indigents or those unable to maintain themselves. (3) Freedom or deliverance from injustice, wrong, or oppression.

remainder   The balance of an estate in land, depending upon the particular prior estate created at the same time and in the same instrument; an estate to take effect and be available for use and enjoyment after another estate is determined. For example, if a life estate in an apartment building is created, the remainder is the title in fee simple that vests after the termination of the life estate. See *life estate*.

replevin   A suit at law to obtain the return of unlawfully removed goods to the person entitled to possession.

respondeat superior   (Latin): "Let the master answer." The legal rule that a principal is liable in damages for wrongful acts of the principal's agent. This is an extension of the old rule that the master is liable for the acts of the servant which is still a valid rule of law. This means, for example, that the owner of a bakery company is liable in civil damages for an automobile wreck caused by the negligence of the bakery truck delivery driver. This doctrine applies, however, only when the agent or servant is acting within the legitimate scope of his or her authority. For example, the owner of the bakery company would not be liable if the driver had come back after hours, gotten the truck without authority, and then caused the wreck.

restraining order   An order by a judge that is a type of injunction, usually a preliminary one issued to keep a situation unchanged until a decision can be reached on whether a permanent injunction should be issued.

restrictive covenant   A limitation put into a deed forbidding future owners of the property from using the land for specific purposes. Subsequent owners have a right of enforcement of the restriction by injunction or by lawsuit for damages against any future owner. For example, the deed could carry a restrictive covenant to the effect that horses may not be kept on the land. Anyone in the chain of title could thereafter enforce this restriction against a future owner.

restrictive indorsement   The signing of a negotiable instrument in a way that ends its negotiability—for example: "Pay to Robert Smith only."

reversal   The making void or undoing of a judgment because of an irregularity or error committed in the court where the judgment was returned. The reversal is ordered by an appellate court reviewing the matter on appeal.

reversion   (1) The return of an estate to the grantor or the grantor's heirs after the expiration of the term of the grant. (2) The name of the estate so returned to the original owner.

reversionary interest   The interest that remains in land or other real property upon the termination of a preceding estate such as a life estate.

review   The judicial reconsideration or reexamination of a cause by an appellate court.

rider   A slip of paper executed by the insurer and intended to be attached to the insurance policy for the purpose of changing it in some respect.

search of title   The examination of official records and registers in connection with a contract for the sale of real estate in order to determine the existence of mortgages, liens, unpaid taxes, or any other cloud on the title of the property.

security interest   Any interest in property, real or personal, that secures payment of a debt or performance of an obligation—for example, a mortgage or a mechanic's lien.

service   (1) The delivery of a writ, summons, or process to the person named. It is only fair, for example, that a person being sued be notified and given a chance to present a defense. This notification is performed by service of legal papers on the defendant. In some matters, the law requires personal service; in others, publication in a newspaper is sufficient; still others require a notice to the last known address of the party to be served. (2) In contract law, employment in the service of another requires the employed person to submit to the direction and control of the employer.

severalty ownership   Sole ownership; ownership by one person.

shop-book rule   An exception to the so-called hearsay evidence rule allowing the introduction in evidence of original bookkeeping records made in the usual course of business after production from proper custody and authentication. For example, the accountant of a business could bring the firm's journals and ledgers into court to show that a customer owed a debt to the business. The accountant would be first required to testify that he or she was the custodian of the records and that they were prepared in the regular course of business. The specific business employee who actually made the bookkeeping entry would not be required to testify.

sight draft   A draft or bill of exchange payable on sight or when presented for payment.

single-name paper   A slang term describing a negotiable instrument signed by only one maker that has no accommodation signer or cosignature by a surety. This means that only the maker can be held responsible for payment of the instrument.

stare decisis   (Latin): "Let the decision stand." The judicial doctrine that a court decision on a set of facts should be binding in the same court, in equal courts or in courts of lesser rank in future cases where the same point is in controversy. The legal policy here is that rights should remain settled as long as injustice was not done so that individuals may have a predictable basis for future decisions and acquisition of rights.

statute of frauds   A statute providing that certain contracts will not be honored by the courts unless there is something in writing to prove that the parties have an oral contract.

statute of limitations   A statute or ordinance that limits the time within which legal action may be brought, either in a civil or criminal trial. The purpose of this is to keep from cluttering the courts with cases that involve stale claims. If a matter goes for many years without reaching the courts, witnesses may have died or lost their recollection and evidence may have been scattered.

stipulation   A formal agreement between the opposing lawyers in a trial where both sides admit to certain facts or waive certain procedures.

stockholder's derivative suit   Either of two types of lawsuits that may be carried out by a stockholder of a corporation: (1) A suit in which the corporation has some cause of action against an outsider and has neglected or refused to take action to protect stockholder or corporate rights. (2) A suit on behalf of some of the stockholders who have been caused damage or loss by the corporation itself in discriminating in favor of other stockholders or outside interests. This suit generally occurs when stockholders with majority control try to benefit themselves or their friends at the general expense of the corporation.

strict foreclosure   A procedure for the foreclosure of a mortgage that vests title to the property in the holder (mortgagee) on default of payment. This foreclosure takes place automatically without any sale of the property or without the debtor being allowed to exercise the right of redemption as is provided for in most mortgages.

sublease   An underlease; a lease by a tenant of all or part of an already leased premises to another individual. The sublease may be for a shorter term than that held by the occupant under the primary lease (lessee). Some primary leases specify that the property may not be sublet under any conditions. It is best to discuss this problem with the landlord before giving a sublease unless such activity is provided for in the primary lease.

subrogate   To substitute one person in the place of another with reference to an obligation.

substituted service   Process service by any means other than by personal service. An example would be service by publication in a newspaper covering the area.

summary proceeding   Any proceeding by which the case can be disposed of, or the dispute settled, or the trial conducted in a simple, prompt manner in comparison with regular proceedings. The term may apply to a criminal prosecution as well as to a civil matter. For example, some states follow a quick dispossess action for nonpayment of rent rather than the more usual lengthy eviction process.

surety   An individual or firm that legally agrees to stand good for another person's debt in the event it is not paid; one who undertakes to pay money or perform some other specified act in the event of failure by the surety's principal. In a contract of suretyship, one party agrees to be answerable for the debt of another. The terms *guarantor* and *surety* are sometimes used interchangeably but there are differences. See *guaranty*.

surplus   (1) Money left over from a fund set up for a particular purpose. (2) Excess of receipts over disbursements. (3) A corporation's net worth over and above the stated value of capital stock.

survivorship   (1) The legal right of a surviving or remaining individual originally having a joint interest with others in an estate to receive the whole estate as the sole survivor. (2) The condition of being the one individual out of two or more who lives longest.

tax deed   A deed given by the government to a new owner following the forced sale of property for nonpayment of taxes.

tax lien   A claim against real property (real estate) that accrues in favor of the taxing agency (county, municipality, or state government) from taxes that are assessed against the property.

tenancy by the entirety   A type of joint ownership by a husband and wife that is utilized in a limited number of states. Title is acquired by the marriage partners jointly after marriage. Upon the death of either spouse, his or her interest automatically passes to the survivor. Ownership of this kind cannot be terminated without the consent of both parties and the property cannot be mortgaged or transferred without the approval of both. Sometimes called *tenancy by the entireties*.

tenancy in common   A form of co-ownership of real property. Cotenants own undivided interests but these interests need not be equal in quantity or duration and may arise from different conveyances at different times. There is no right of survivorship. The interest of each tenant can be devised by a will or can be passed on to the tenant's heirs. See *joint tenancy* from which tenancy in common is distinguished.

tenant at sufferance   An occupier of property who began possession in a legal manner but who has continued to occupy after the termination of a rent or lease agreement. Technically, a tenant at sufferance is not a tenant of anyone. The landlord may elect to treat such an occupier as a trespasser and demand possession of the property; this demand will be enforced by the court.

tenement   Any kind of property that is held by a tenant. The legal meaning is therefore somewhat different from the commonly accepted one. In a legal sense a tenement may be any elegant mansion, slum apartment house, or franchise that is rented to a tenant.

time-price doctrine   The practice followed by some retail stores in charging a higher price for items bought on time payments than for those bought for cash. This is usually upheld by the courts on the theory that the seller runs a greater risk of loss in credit sales and may consequently charge more. Some contend that this doctrine is merely a way to evade usury laws.

title   The joining of all the elements constituting legal ownership. It is the means whereby the owner of lands has just possession of the property. Title is sometimes defined as the outward evidence of ownership as well as the right of full possession, use, and enjoyment of property.

tort   An injury of a private or civil nature other than one arising from a breach of contract. A tort is the actionable wrong usually associated with loss or harm resulting from a defective or dangerous product—in short, it involves product liability. In describing a tort, the courts usually say that there must be a wrongful act or omission coupled with a resulting injury to some person. The injured victim has the right to sue for the damage that results. Corporations are responsible for the torts of their employees committed within the scope of their employment. The more common torts arise out of negligent use of an automobile, assault and battery, negligent maintenance of store premises available to the public, or the selling of adulterated products that cause injury.

trade fixture   Articles of personal property that are annexed to real property and are necessary to the carrying on of a business and are removable by the owner.

trespass   An invasion of an owner's rights in his or her property.

trover   One of the old forms of common law action brought to recover the value of goods wrongfully converted by another to his or her own use. Seldom of any practical use today, this old form of action is of interest in the development of property law.

trust deed   Same as deed of trust.

trustee   The person to whom property is conveyed in trust.

trustor   The person who conveys property in trust.

underwriter   (1) A company or individual who insures another. (2) A firm or individual that undertakes to purchase an entire issue of bonds, stocks, or other securities or subscribes to underwrite a whole block of securities.

unjust enrichment   A legal principle that when one person obtains money or property unfairly, even if legally, it should be returned. (This does not include merely driving a hard bargain or being lucky in a deal.)

usury   The lending of money at greater than the maximum rate allowed by law.

valuable consideration   Something of value given up in good faith in exchange for the receipt or the promise of something of value from the other party. It is the kind of consideration that courts will enforce against another person who does not live up to the other side of the bargain. In short, it is the kind of consideration needed to make a contract.

valuation   The process for determining the worth of a thing. An appraisal. The setting of a price.

variance   (1) Permission or license to do some act that is contrary to rules or laws. For example, a zoning commission may grant a variance to permit construction of a cement block wall eight feet high, although city ordinances specify a seven-foot maximum. (2) A discrepancy in a civil lawsuit between what one party says will be proved and what the evidence actually shows at the time of trial.

venue   The place where, or the territory within which, one or both of the parties has a legal right to have a matter tried in the courts.

vested interest   A presently existing fixed right of future enjoyment or use of property. It is an established property right that is not dependent on anything. For example, an individual may sell you a lot with a garage on it, delivering you a valid deed. You have a vested interest in the lot and garage at that time, even though a condition of sale is that the seller is entitled to garage an antique car there for the next year.

vested right   A legal right that is absolute and subject to no conditions. It is the certainty of enjoyment that distinguishes a vested right in property from a contingent interest.

void   Of no legal effect; without force; without the legal authority it was intended to produce. *Void* is to be distinguished from *voidable* in that a void document or agreement is regarded as never having had any effect and nothing can be done to cure this inadequacy.

voidable   That which is capable of being adjudged void. It is not void in itself but may be considered so at the will of one or more of the parties involved. For example, a contract made by a minor to buy a car may be voidable when the minor comes of legal age. The minor can back out of the contract and return the car but cannot keep a car that has not been paid for. The minor may choose to go ahead with the contract on becoming of age. In that event the buyer will thereafter be bound by the voidable contract.

wage assignment An agreement of a voluntary nature by which a worker permits earnings to be paid directly by the employer to a creditor of the employee. An arrangement of this kind is now illegal in many jurisdictions.

warehouse receipt A piece of paper proving that an individual or corporation owns something stored in a warehouse. It may be a negotiable instrument.

warehouseman A person regularly engaged in the business of storing the goods of others for compensation.

warranty A statement, representation or claim made by a seller to a buyer as part of a sale. It includes the seller's claim that the product is fit for use and is a representation concerning the kind, type, quality, and ownership of the thing being offered for sale. Other warranties arise by implication even though the seller may make no claims whatsoever. These so-called implied warranties entitle the buyer to believe a product will meet the performance or specification standards that are normally expected of an article of its kind.

warranty deed A legal document by which ownership of real estate is transferred from one owner to another. In giving a warranty deed the seller does two things: (1) transfers the seller's ownership of the property and (2) legally agrees to defend the validity of that title forever for the benefit of the purchaser. A warranty deed gives the buyer the right to collect from the seller if anyone ever subsequently establishes a claim or cloud on the title to the property. A warranty deed is sometimes called a *general warranty deed*.

waste The dissipation, destruction, or abuse of property by one in rightful possession; a material alteration or spoilage of real estate by an individual entitled to use it.

watered stock Stock issued by a corporation for which the par value has not been paid in. Stock not backed up by additional assets.

without recourse Without liability. The phrase indorsed on the back of a check, promissory note, or other negotiable to relieve the indorser (other than the original maker) of liability. In short, the intermediate holder is simply passing the instrument on and will not be responsible if the maker fails to honor the obligation.

wrongful death statutes Statutes that allow the dependents of one wrongfully or negligently killed to sue for civil damages. The theory here is that, although the cause of action died with the victim, the dependents have a different cause of action.

zoning The division of a municipality into areas or zones by ordinance, specifying the uses that may be made of property in that area. For example, some areas may be zoned for industry, others for commercial, residential, or other uses.

Index